AFTER THE STORM

Lessons from the Gulf War

The Aspen Strategy Group

The Aspen Strategy Group is a bipartisan committee organized under the auspices of The Aspen Institute. The group's primary goal is to help advance thinking and practice in the areas of international security and East-West relations. It aims to relate the differing perspectives about the long-term direction of American security to current policy debates. As a standing body, the group acts as a source of private policy advice; it contributes to the public debate through reports and other publications; and it encourages the study of broad conceptual issues that shape security but are some times hurried over in the debates regarding immediate policy choices.

AFTER THE STORM

LESSONS FROM THE GULF WAR

Edited by
Joseph S. Nye, Jr.
and Roger K. Smith

The Aspen Institute

MADISON BOOKS
Lanham • New York • London

Co-published by Madison Books and the Aspen Strategy Group of The Aspen Institute.

Published by Madison Books
4720 Boston Way
Lanham, Maryland 20706

3 Henrietta Street
London WC2E 8LU England

Distributed by National Book Network

The paper used in this publication meets the minimum requirements of American National Standard for Information Sciences—Permanence of Paper for Printed Library Materials, ANSI Z39.48–1984. ∞™
Manufactured in the United States of America.

Library of Congress Cataloging-in-Publication Data

After the storm : lessons from the Gulf War.
p. cm.
Includes index.
1. Persian Gulf War, 1991. 2. Middle East—Politics and government—1979– I. Aspen Strategy Group (U.S.)
DS79.72.A35 1992
956.704'42—dc20 92–15611 CIP

ISBN 0–8191–8529–9 (cloth : alk. paper)
ISBN 1–56833–015–4 (pbk. : alk. paper)

British Cataloging in Publication Information Available

CONTENTS

PREFACE

Crises, like flashes of lightening, are usually unexpected, often dangerous, and always illuminating, if only for a brief moment. The crisis which began in the Persian Gulf on August 2, 1990 could not have come at a more turbulent moment in international politics. Throughout 1989 and 1990 the world was treated to a succession of dramatic and farreaching political events. The "velvet" revolutions in Eastern Europe, the crumbling of the Berlin Wall, the steady move toward greater economic and political integration among the countries of the European Community, the slow disintegration of communist authority in the Soviet Union, and the steady progress toward peace in Central America, Southeast Asia, and Southern Africa had led some to conclude that the world might be nearing the "end of history." In the midst of all this change came a throwback to an earlier era. The invasion, occupation, and annexation of a small Persian Gulf city-state by its much larger neighbor to the north suggested that maybe the more things change, the more they stay the same. Iraq's invasion of Kuwait cast into stark relief all the trends which had come to dominate newspaper headlines and public policy.

After The Storm attempts to separate shadow from substance in the light cast by the Gulf War by examining the diplomatic, economic, political and strategic consequences of the conflict for American policy. In order to reach useful judgments on future U.S. policy we need to ask: why the crisis emerged; how it evolved from a diplomatic confrontation into a military clash; what were the tools and tradeoffs that allowed a coalition of thirty states to be assembled and committed to war with Iraq; how American public opinion was mobilized to support a war, which in the fall of 1990 promised casualties in the tens of thousands; what constellation of elements made the allied military victory so swift and decisive; what does the forcible eviction of Iraq from Kuwait mean for the Persian Gulf, the Middle East and the United States as we move further into the last decade of the twentieth century? These questions, all of which are key to understanding the limits and opportunities for U.S. diplomacy in uncertain world, are taken up in successive chapters in this volume.

This study is part of a series of books, reports, and monographs prepared under the auspices of the Aspen Strategy Group, a program of The Aspen Institute. As a bipartisan standing committee, the Group aims to relate differing perspectives about the long-term direction of international security to current policy debates in the United States. Its members are drawn from the American academic, policy, and business communities.

This book was edited and prepared by the Strategy Group's directing staff: Joseph Nye (director) and Roger Smith (executive director). This volume had its origins in two Aspen Strategy Group workshops; the first was held at The Aspen Institute's Wye Center on March 1–2, 1991 and dealt with "Crisis Management After the Cold War: Lessons from the Confrontation with Iraq"; and the second, which looked at "The New World Order?: Lessons from the Gulf War," was held on August 11–16, 1991 in Aspen, Colorado. Participants at the first conference were asked to take stock of the origins and evolution of the crisis with Iraq and to assess the effectiveness of U.S. diplomacy during the crisis; at the second workshop, the participants were asked to examine the crisis from a more distant perspective and consider what lessons were being learned and what lessons should be learned from the Gulf War. Each of the contributors to this volume—Fouad Ajami, Antonia Chayes, Richard Cooper, Richard Gardner, David Gergen, Martin Indyk, Lawrence Korb, William Perry, Strobe Talbott, and Bernard Trainor—made major presentations at the March and August workshops. Later, they updated their work to take account of the proceedings and subsequent political developments in the Middle East and the Soviet Union. Our deepest thanks go to the authors for their excellent contributions.

The concluding chapter, which distills the evolution of the experience in the Gulf into and a handful of critical lessons, draws heavily on the proceedings of both workshops. We wish to thank Les Aspin, Antonia Handler Chayes, Kenneth Dam, John Deutch, Paul Doty, Leslie Gelb, Bryan Hehir, William Hyland, Arnold Horelick, Robert Hormats, Karen House, Bobby Inman, David Jones, Lawrence Korb, Jan Lodal, Richard Lugar, William Perry, Enid Schoettle, Walt Slocombe, John Steinbruner, Strobe Talbott, Albert Wheelon, James Woolsey, and Charles Zraket who, as members of the Aspen Strategy Group participated in one or both August workshops and contributed greatly to the discussion and debate on the ideas presented here.

In addition to the authors noted above, the Group was very fortunate to have in attendance at both workshops a number of distinguished guests: Ruth Adams, Prince Bandar Bin Sultan, Robert Bell, David Broder, Jiri Dienstbier, Thomas Friedman, Leon Fuerth, Francois Heisbourg, Morton Kondracke, Robert Malott, Judith Miller, Clark Murdoch, David Robinson, Henry Rowen, Daniel Schorr, Andy Semmel, Robert Toth, Jane Wales, Louise Walker, Thomas Watson, William Webster, Grayson Winterling, and Mortimer Zuckerman. We are very grateful to these individuals for their participation and contributions to the discussion.

Generous financial support for this project was provided by the Carnegie Corporation of New York and the John D. and Catherine T. MacArthur Foundation. The editors would also like to thank a number of people who provided invaluable assistance in the production of this volume. Ann Callahan tirelessly provided many detailed comments, criticisms, and editorial suggestions; Stephen J. Stillwell, jr. contributed greatly through his research assistance; and Joao Resende-Santos produced a superb chronology of the crisis which helped the discussion at both conferences. Finally, we would like to express our appreciation to W. Daniel Wright and his colleagues at The Aspen Institute for computer services and production support.

Readers should take careful note that the opinions and conclusions expressed in this book are those of the authors alone and should not be ascribed to the membership of the Aspen Strategy Group, The Aspen Institute, or to funding or sponsoring organizations.

PART I

DIPLOMATIC LESSONS

1

STATUS QUO ANTE: THE UNITED STATES AND ITS ALLIES

Strobe Talbott

Every war, it has been said, is either a crime or a crusade. The mobilization of citizens to engage in slaughter requires a political justification nobler than the military objective at hand. Indeed, it requires a justification that transcends politics itself. Particularly in a democracy, a leader asking his compatriots to kill and to die tries to convince them they are doing so for the sake of peace.

Woodrow Wilson sent doughboys across the Atlantic to fight a war to end all wars. "The world must be made safe for democracy," he said in his address to Congress on April 2, 1917. "America is privileged to spend her blood and her might for the principles that gave her birth and happiness and the peace which she has treasured. God helping her, she can do no other."

In that same tradition of idealistic internationalism President George Bush called the United States to arms against the Republic of Iraq. He appealed to a sense of mission that went far beyond the pursuit of mere national interest. "Halfway around the world," proclaimed Bush in his State of the Union address on January 19, 1991, "we are engaged in a great struggle in the skies and on the seas and sands. We know why we're there: We are Americans, part of something larger than ourselves. For two centuries, we've done the hard work of freedom. And tonight, we lead the world in facing down a threat to decency and humanity. What is at stake is more than one small country; it is a big idea: a new world order, where diverse nations are drawn together in common cause to achieve the universal aspirations of mankind—peace and security, freedom, and the rule of law."

Bush fervently believed that a decisive victory over Saddam Hussein would accomplish more than just reversing an act of aggression—more, even, than setting an example that would deter would-be aggressors in the future. On the eve of the Gulf War, the president was among those who predicted that the outcome would prove to be a "defining event"—or, more to the point, a *re*defining event—in the life of the planet.

Part of the reason for optimism was the sheer size and diversity of the thirty-one-member coalition that closed ranks behind U.S. leadership during the fall of 1990.[1] Every continent was represented; participants were drawn from NATO, the nearly defunct Warsaw Pact, and the Nonaligned Movement. Several nations with long histories of neutralism, like Sweden, contributed to the effort. Pairs of states with deep hostility toward each other, like Pakistan and Bangladesh, Turkey and Greece, were, if not together in the same desert encampments, then at least on the same side against Saddam Hussein.

Operation Desert Storm was a monument to multilateralism. Moreover, the outcome—the eviction of Saddam Hussein's army from Kuwait and imposition of punitive international sanctions against his regime—seemed at first to qualify, in Bush's triumphant phrase, as "total victory" both for the coalition and for the ideas, and ideals, that had brought its members together. Surely, if they could join forces in the Gulf, they could make common cause on other issues as well.

However, several months later, Desert Storm seemed a more ambiguous episode in the annals of collective security. Some of the original hopes for collateral benefits from the successful prosecution of the war remained largely unfulfilled. A new round of diplomacy was underway in the Middle East, but the crux of the Arab-Israeli dispute—the Palestinians' demand for a homeland and the Israeli government's refusal to make territorial concessions on the occupied territories—appeared as intractable as ever. But more important, Saddam Hussein was still the president of Iraq. In the summer and fall of 1991, television news programs once again carried footage of him presiding over his cabinet, embracing emissaries, firing an automatic pistol into the air from a balcony while crowds below cheered, and, most ominously, defying the United Nations (UN) as it sought to thwart his ambition to develop weapons of mass destruction.

For all the spectacular changes that had swept the globe during a revolutionary year, the region that had been the focus of Bush's hopes for a "New World Order," the Persian Gulf, evoked a sense of *déjà vu*. That was partly because, despite Bush's rhetoric, the objective that had brought thirty-one nations together was actually, in its essence, the preservation of the *old* order, the restoration of the *status quo ante*, in more respects than just the return of Sheikh Jabir al-Ahmad al-Sabah as the emir of Kuwait.

THE PARADOXES OF DIPLOMACY

The Gulf crisis illustrated three paradoxes in the nature of diplomacy, and of peace itself, in the late twentieth century. Often peace, albeit an uneasy one (the absence of war), prevails between nations that perceive each other to be enemies. That state of affairs, producing anxiety for all concerned but still preferable to at least one alternative, is especially likely to occur if one of the nations in question is a nuclear power. Consider the example of Iraq and Israel. Two more antagonistic states are difficult to imagine, but largely because Iraq presumed Israel to have nuclear weapons, Saddam Hussein has never attacked Israel or even retaliated when Israel committed a textbook act of war by depriving him of his own incipient nuclear program in 1981.

The second paradox is related. During the Cold War, the mutual deterrence operating between the United States and the Soviet Union had a restraining effect on regional conflicts as well. It is often said that the international community would never have been able to close ranks behind the United States over the Gulf crisis in 1990–91 if the Cold War had still been raging. At a minimum, the "old" Soviet Union, protective of its longtime client, Iraq, would surely have vetoed the twelve resolutions in the United Nations Security Council that were necessary to give the operation its multilateral character and hence much of its legitimacy and effectiveness. No doubt that is true. It is, however, also arguable that if the Cold War had still been under way, the Gulf crisis would not have occurred at all. In such a world, Baghdad would surely have been on a much tighter leash from Moscow, and the Soviets would probably have yanked that leash hard rather than let Iraq blunder into a conflict that might have escalated into World War III. In that sense, welcome as it is in so many other respects, the end of the Cold War was among the causes for the outbreak of a hot war in the Gulf.[2]

The third paradox is that sometimes war can all too easily break out between nations that are in the habit of viewing each other as allies, or at least as strategic partners. There are few better examples than the relationship between Iraq and the United States. Starting in the late 1970s, when the Carter administration cultivated Iraq as a counterweight to Iran, some (though not all) policymakers in Washington favored supporting Iraq not just in spite, *but because of*, Saddam Hussein's invasion of a neighboring state. By committing aggression against Iran and starting a war that would last eight years, Iraq was doing the United States, the West, and the conservative Gulf states a great geopolitical favor; he was diverting the attention and resources of the Ayatollah Khomeini from the cause of spreading the Islamic fundamentalist revolution. From September 22, 1980, when Saddam's forces attacked Iran and August 2, 1990, when they poured into Kuwait, U.S. policy remained on autopilot.

Thus one of the more obvious lessons of the Gulf War of 1991 was that as an instrument to affect the behavior of someone like Saddam Hussein, diplomacy can work only if it used in tandem with the plausible threat of force. U.S. policy toward Iraq during the long prelude to the war lacked that vital element. The policy was all smiles, no teeth. The two bywords of the relations of the United States with its long-time rival, the Soviet Union—containment and deterrence—were missing from the dialogue between Washington and Baghdad. However, once Saddam Hussein had invaded Kuwait, U.S. policy was *all* teeth.

U.S. diplomacy was spectacularly successful in two overlapping respects: assembling a coalition and engineering the United

Nations resolutions and sanctions. President Bush fairly quickly came to believe that diplomatic means—sanctions, embargoes, political isolation, and pressure—would not work and that war would be necessary to dislodge Saddam Hussein from Kuwait.

Diplomacy went from being the be-all and end-all of U.S. policy to a cover for the mounting of the military operation. As the United Nations' January 15 deadline for Saddam Hussein to be out of Kuwait drew closer, much of the diplomatic energies of the United States were expended on thwarting bursts of diplomatic unilateralism by various would-be peacemakers to broker a settlement that the United States considered ill-advised. Even the highest ranking diplomat of the United States, Secretary of State James Baker, came under muted criticism from within the administration for being less than totally "on board" the war plan and for being willing to let Saddam Hussein negotiate his way out of Kuwait. With Baker suddenly the odd man out, the Bush administration had passed a point of no return: war-war was better than jaw-jaw.

A GOOD CHOICE OF FOE AND FRIENDS

While Bush was masterly in his role as a war president, he was also incredibly lucky in his draw of an opponent. With an enemy like Saddam Hussein, allies were relatively easy to enlist. The European Community (EC) moved quickly, through instruments available because of the Treaty of Rome, to impose economic sanctions. There was, however, initial reluctance about getting involved militarily, particularly with the dispatch of ground and air forces. Naval forces were, and almost always are, another matter. Warships can be deployed to the area of crisis while remaining in international waters and without coming into harm's way.[3]

Once again, as he coaxed and nudged the allies through Desert Shield toward Desert Storm, Bush's luck mattered as much as his skill. He—and the world—were fortunate in the particular constellation of leaders who happened to be in place at the time of the crisis.

Margaret Thatcher was, in her view of the world and in her preferred method for dealing with aggressors, the arguably most Churchillian prime minister of Britain since Churchill himself. As it happened, she was with Bush at The Aspen Institute on the day that Saddam Hussein invaded Kuwait. She steeled his initial instinct on how to respond, vowed the full backing of her country and promised to do everything she could to see that the rest of the European allies of the United States rose to the challenge.

At the other end of Europe, on the edge of what would soon become known as the Kuwait theater of operations, was another North Atlantic Treaty Organization (NATO) ally whose actions were overwhelmingly the result of personal leadership. Had any prominent politician in Ankara other than Turgut Ozal been president, it is doubtful that Turkey would have been the linchpin of the coalition. Provoking intense criticism from his domestic opponents (as well as from some members of his own government) and incurring considerable financial costs to his nation, Ozal agreed to shut down the pipeline carrying oil from Iraq through Turkey. He also allowed a buildup of U.S. and NATO forces and later permitted U.S. warplanes operating from Turkish bases to conduct operations against Iraq. But, especially in a country that gave the word "Byzantine" to the world, all politics, including geopolitics, is local. By ramming his policy through the Turkish Parliament and overriding the misgivings of several senior military officers, Ozal used the crisis to enhance the powers of his own office. Also, the credit Ozal earned in Washington and Western Europe for his steadfastness was not just a consequence of his policy, it was very much an objective, part of the jackpot he was hoping to win with his gamble.

For decades Turkey had held a position of unmistakable strategic importance in NATO. It had the longest border with the Soviet Union of any member of the alliance. As the Soviet Union turned inward and the Warsaw Pact folded its tents, Ozal worried that his country would slip once again from the appreciation and attention of the West and of the United States.

Early in 1990, the U.S. government had exacerbated Turkish anxieties and therefore resentments by making a series of moves, some symbolic, others more substantive, that made Turks feel as though their country was a pariah, or at least a lesser state neither needed nor respected now that it was no longer on the front line of the U.S.-Soviet confrontation. The Greek lobby in the United States found that it was finally able to strengthen ties between Washington and Athens while whittling away at those between Washington and Ankara without U.S. officials being able to say, "Stop! We need Turkey as a buffer against the Soviet Union!"

The U.S.-Turkish relationship hit something of a low point shortly before the Gulf crisis when Congress and the White House both condemned Turkey for the massacres of Armenians in the final days of the Ottoman empire. The United States also concluded a new military agreement with Greece, allowing the Greeks to infer that there was more to the pact than met the eye while reassuring the Turks that there was less.

Then Saddam Hussein came to the rescue. As the allied buildup progressed, Presidents Bush and Ozal were on the phone to each other repeatedly. There was a feeling in both capitals that the crisis had salvaged a vital relationship that had been in serious trouble largely because the Cold War was over.

Ozal was also concerned about his country's relations with Western Europe. As leaders there struggled with the immense challenge posed by the collapse of communism in the East, they would be even less open to Turkish laborers seeking work permits, not to mention politicians in Ankara seeking membership in the European Community. Ozal saw the Gulf crisis as an opportunity to prove that Turkey still had an important role to play in the new era—not least because it was the only member-state of NATO bordering on the Middle East. Two days before the air war began, Ozal said he fervently hoped that one result of the war would be to improve Turkey's chances of being admitted to the EC after 1992.

If Britain and Turkey were the most stalwart of the allies of the United States, France was the most problematic. In classic fashion ordained by Charles de Gaulle thirty years before, the French balked at putting their forces under U.S. command and complained that they were being dragged into a conflict without being properly consulted. In addition to the impulse to preserve the Gaullist tradition, a relatively new complication in French domestic politics contributed to President François Mitterrand's initial reluctance to fall in line behind the United States: France's large Arab population reflected the pro-Saddam Hussein, anti-American sentiments that swept through North Africa, especially in the early stages of the crisis.

Yet again, however, Saddam Hussein played the indispensable villain. With exquisite timing, he escalated the crisis and committed outrages that helped Bush sustain the cooperation of NATO's most cantankerous member-state.

Early in their occupation of Kuwait, Iraqi troops raided the embassy compounds of Canada, Belgium, the Netherlands, and France. The Iraqis detained five Western consuls and spirited away three French citizens. Immediately afterward, and largely as a consequence, France modified its usual strategic individualism and moved in concert with the rest of the coalition. Mitterrand authorized a degree of coordination between his commanders and those of the other allies that previously would have been hard to imagine. When the fighting began, the French acquitted themselves well. Despite pronouncements from the Ministry of Defense that French forces would not enter Iraq, during the ground war they penetrated deeper into Iraq than units of any other country.

During the Cold War, France had resisted American leadership on principle and managed to appear rather grand for doing so, at least to the French themselves. But in the context of the Gulf War—a real military conflict as opposed to an open-ended and many-sided political competition—the Gaullist posture of refusing to follow Washington's lead seemed simply foolish, even to the French themselves.

The Gulf War generated what at first seemed like ominous strains in Washington's relations with Germany and Japan. The U.S. Congress grumbled that these two important U.S. allies, both economic powerhouses and beneficiaries of the U.S. security umbrella, were "not doing their share."

The Germans were preoccupied with the huge and expensive task of unification. In addition to trying to absorb the former East Germany, the Bonn government was also devoting political attention and financial resources to helping the other countries that were struggling to emerge from the wreckage of the Soviet bloc—a mission of immense and positive importance to the rest of the world, notably including the United States.

Moreover, its post-World War II constitution prevented Germany from dispatching troops abroad. So did Japan's. Despite the constraints under which it was operating, Germany put at the disposal of the coalition much of the federal rail system and barge traffic on the Rhine, enabling the U.S. and British armies to move 150,000 troops to ports of embarkation, and paid six and one-half billion dollars to help underwrite Desert Storm. Japan contributed nearly ten billion, making it the largest donor outside the Gulf. In the wake, and as a consequence, of the crisis, both Germany and Japan began revising their constitutions so that they might be able to play more active roles as part of an international security force, under the auspices of the UN, in the future.

Had the war resulted in significantly higher levels of U.S. casualties, there almost certainly would have been more serious and longer lasting resentment in the United States against Germany and Japan for not having risked the lives of their own troops. At the same time, however, had Germany and Japan sent military units of any sort to the Gulf, there just as certainly would have been a backlash of anxiety among their neighbors, in Europe and Asia respectively, about the possible resurgence of German and Japanese militarism. So not only did Germany and Japan have good excuses for staying on the sidelines and writing checks, but it was just as well that they did so.

THE MOSCOW-BAGHDAD SHUTTLE

Desert Storm also buffeted U.S.-Soviet relations at a critical time in the transition to the post-Cold War era. It had become a truism among kremlinologists during the Gorbachev years that the principal factor in Soviet foreign policy was Soviet domestic politics. No more vivid proof of that proposition was the way in which the Gulf War became one of most contentious issues in the struggle between left and right inside the Soviet Union in late

1990 and early 1991—and therefore a source of strain between the White House and the Kremlin.

For Soviet reformers, Saddam Hussein personified the sort of thug whom the Kremlin had all too often supported in the past. The decision of Mikhail Gorbachev's government to join the West against Saddam Hussein in 1990 was a case study in new thinking.

For their part, reactionary elements saw the votes that their government had cast in favor of the U.S.-backed resolutions in the United Nations as symbols of a willingness to surrender Moscow's influence and to accept subservience in a world run from Washington; Soviet acquiescence in the war against Saddam Hussein was a particularly shameful part of the legacy of Eduard Shevardnadze, who had resigned as foreign minister in December 1990.

However, this debate was limited in a significant way: neither side advocated an active Soviet military role in the Gulf. Delighted as the liberals were to have their government supporting the anti-Saddam Hussein resolutions in the UN, few seriously advocated the contribution of Soviet troops to the coalition. By the same token, angry as the conservatives were at their government's betrayal of Saddam Hussein, few went so far as to favor intervention on his behalf. In that sense, there were no hawks, just happy and unhappy doves—further evidence of how dramatically the Soviet Union had turned inward.

Gorbachev's dismantlement of the Ministry of Fear and the consequent rise of real politics inside the Soviet Union had made possible the end of the Cold War. Now those same internal changes set the stage for a new kind of diplomacy between Washington and Moscow.

During the Cold War, the United States and the Soviet Union had played a zero-sum game on virtually every issue and in every corner of the world.

During the Gulf War, by contrast, U.S.-Soviet diplomacy was, like Soviet internal politics, more "normal." The way in which the two countries interacted during an intense but isolated regional conflict was not, as it had so often been in the past, a manifestation of an overarching perpetual and global enmity. Instead, the

White House and the Kremlin maneuvered in the more subtle and ambiguous way that had characterized relations between states in the nineteenth century. The worldview associated with Vladimir Lenin in Moscow, and with John Foster Dulles in Washington gave way to the precepts of Palmerston and Metternich. The United States and the Soviet Union behaved like two Great Powers that shared some objectives and were at odds on others.

The last days of Desert Shield and the first days of Desert Storm coincided with the crackdown in the Baltic States, which in turn marked the high water mark (until now, at least) of the Soviet military's influence over Gorbachev. Here was the Soviet Union's principal adversary, the United States, pummeling a longtime Soviet ally, Iraq, whose northeastern border was only about 150 miles from the Soviet Union, and decimating a military establishment that was made up largely of Soviet equipment—MiGs, T-72 tanks, and the suddenly famous Scud surface-to-surface missiles.

Many analysts in Moscow predicted that the longer the Gulf War continued, the greater the danger that large numbers of U.S. armed forces would remain in the region indefinitely after it was over. That prospect, too, was acutely unappealing to the Soviet military.

Gorbachev was under pressure from a second constitutency as well. Representatives of the Islamic republics in Transcaucasia and Central Asia were angry at what many of them saw as a *jihad* in reverse: their fellow Muslims were suffering at the hands of infidels. In an era of *glasnost,* democratization, and rampant secessionism, Gorbachev could not ignore the delegations of Soviet Muslims who journeyed to Moscow to protest his policy of support for the coalition.

When Shevardnadze's successor, Alexander Bessmertnykh, came to Washington in late January to meet with Bush and Baker, he was candid in explaining that Gorbachev was under pressure to be seen as making every effort to end the war as quickly as possible and with as little further destruction to Iraq.

Bessmertnykh floated the idea of introducing a new resolution in the United Nations Security Council that would promote "a political solution" to the crisis. The last thing that the Americans wanted to see was a new round of wrangling over the contents of another UN resolution. The twelve passed since August 2 and November 29 had the cumulative effect of demanding much more than Saddam Hussein's withdrawal from Kuwait. In particular, the tenth in the series, Resolution 674, passed on October 29, established the basis for demanding that Iraq pay for the damage that it had caused and for its leaders to be charged with war crimes. All twelve resolutions had been crafted and approved while Shevardnadze was still foreign minister. U.S. officials were worried that a thirteenth might be very unlucky indeed, since it would give the reactionaries in the Kremlin and Soviet foreign ministry an opportunity to bid for support among Arab and Islamic nations opposed to the war.

At a minimum, Saddam Hussein was sure to take comfort from such a development. Worse, a new resolution, showing the effect of the new priorities if not the new direction of Soviet diplomacy, might provide Saddam Hussein with a way of avoiding total defeat and thus surviving in power to fight another day.

While Baker squelched the idea of a thirteenth resolution, he was all the more eager to keep the Soviet Union, now that it had entered the post-Shevardnadze stage of its foreign policy, "on board" the coalition. Largely for that reason he signed with Bessmertnykh a joint statement on January 29. From Baker's standpoint, the communiqué served, in one of his favorite phrases, to "lock in" Soviet support for the allies' determination to drive Saddam Hussein from Kuwait. But the document ended up backfiring on Baker, even wounding him politically, because it appeared to signal a softening of U.S. policy on what would be demanded of Saddam in the way of retribution after withdrawal as well as some degree of linkage between the end of the Gulf War and the resumption of the cooperative diplomacy on the issue of the Arab-Israeli dispute. (Also, much to Baker's embarrassment and the annoyance of the White House, through sloppiness on the part of the State Department, the communiqué was released on the same night as President Bush's State of the Union address.)

The episode created considerable consternation among the Desert Storm partners, who suddenly found new basis for an old worry: the United States seemed, momentarily at least, to have fallen back into the habit of negotiating with the Kremlin over the heads, and behind the backs, of its NATO allies.

In the weeks after the controversial communiqué, it became apparent that the interests and objectives of the superpowers coincided up to, but not much beyond, the point at which Saddam Hussein retreated from Kuwait.

For the United States and most of the others in the coalition, restoring Kuwait to the rule of the House of al-Sabah was only the most immediate task. The next order of business would be the dismantlement of Saddam Hussein's war machine so that Iraq would no longer pose an aggressive threat to the region. Mostly unstated in public, though deeply and widely felt throughout the coalition, was a desire to trigger a *coup d'état* that would, at a minimum, remove Saddam Hussein from power. No one wished this outcome more fervently than George Bush. While he was careful not to voice his hope for Saddam Hussein's demise in public, he often did so in private. On several occasions he voiced the hope that Saddam Hussein would be ousted and killed in "sort of a Ceausescu scenario."

Not only were the Soviets unwilling to endorse the coalition's highly punitive plans for Saddam Hussein, but they did their best to save him from the fate that Bush and the other allies had in mind. Gorbachev's personal envoy, Yevgeny Primakov, and others calculated that if they succeeded in saving not just Saddam Hussein's skin but his face and even his job, the Soviet Union would have unique influence over the Iraqi regime after the war was over, thus reestablishing the special relationship between Moscow and Baghdad that had existed for decades.

Primakov traveled to Iraq and met Saddam Hussein on February 12. The timing was perfect for Primakov to play good cop, since that day the bad cops, the United States and its allies, engaged in the heaviest bombardment and shelling to date. Primakov urged that Iraq "announce its readiness" to leave Kuwait and specify "a period of time" during which the withdrawal would take place; in response, the coalition would accept a cease-fire.

Saddam Hussein saw immediately that the Soviet terms were far more flexible than those coming out of Washington: all he would have to do was utter a few magic words: "I will withdraw," and the bombing would stop. Still, he did not accept the proposal outright. Instead, he asked a series of questions: When would the sanctions be lifted if he agreed to a withdrawal? How could he be sure that his soldiers would not be "shot in the back" as they left Kuwait?

Primakov sent Moscow a message saying that there were "rays of hope" and that the Iraqi foreign minister, Tariq Aziz, was prepared to come to the Soviet capital to continue the negotiations. Meanwhile, Gorbachev was feeling more pressure than ever to distance himself from the Shevardnadze line on the Gulf.[4]

President Bush dismissed the Iraqi moves as a "cruel hoax," while the Soviet government released a statement citing the Iraqi "initiative" as a reason for "satisfaction and hope." This upbeat assessment seemed as much a slap at Bush as a pat on the head for Saddam Hussein.

Primakov and several other Soviet officials took the protests from Washington as evidence that they now had momentum on their side. They believed that the United States was upset because it realized that it might be deprived of the decisive, devastating military victory over Saddam Hussein that it so wanted. Like Saddam Hussein himself, Soviet policymakers and analysts were watching CNN. They knew that the United States and the other coalition partners were fearful that a ground war would be protracted and extremely bloody. Several of Gorbachev's advisers predicted that the United States would accept any settlement that met the minimum condition of removing Iraqi forces from Kuwait.

In the climactic days of the war, Gorbachev gave his personal blessing to a deal that would have given the Iraqis six weeks to withdraw, freed them from all their liabilities under the twelve UN resolutions except their obligation to leave Kuwait, and established linkage to the Arab-Israeli dispute. Bush replied that he appreciated Gorbachev's keeping him informed of what was happening in the negotiations, but that the formula, as it was emerging, "falls well short" of what was needed to end the war.

The Soviets went back to the Baghdad regime with the U.S. objections and requirements. On February 21, Gorbachev telephoned Bush and in a conversation that lasted just over half an hour, outlined the latest refinement of the plan to which Tariq Aziz, now in Moscow, had agreed. In response to the objections earlier in the week from Washington, there was now no linkage between the end of the Gulf War and the resumption of the Arab-Israeli peace process. Iraq's withdrawal from Kuwait would be "full and unconditional."

From Bush's standpoint, the deal that the Soviets were offering Saddam Hussein still left him too much time to get out and, more important, wiped clean the slate of Iraq's other obligations. The central feature of the Iraqi position, which the Kremlin was still attempting to make palatable to the United States, was unchanged: once Saddam's troops were out of Kuwait, all sanctions, reparations, and other demands embodied in the United Nations resolutions would have to be dropped. Some versions of the Soviet plan even suggested that the Soviet Union would guarantee Saddam Hussein's personal safety, which raised in the minds of some U.S. officials the specter of Soviet military intervention *against* the coalition.

In addition to the many flaws in the contents of the Soviet proposal, there was a growing problem of appearances: A full-scale exercise in shuttle diplomacy was now underway between Moscow and Baghdad, with Washington on the sidelines. The Soviet Union was making itself the arbiter of a settlement, leaving the United States in the awkward position of reacting to snippets of an unacceptable deal as the Soviets saw fit to dole them out. Bush's alarm over this development, almost as much as military exigencies, led him to accept the suggestion from General Colin Powell, chairman of the Joint Chiefs of Staff, that the United States impose a twenty-four-hour deadline for Iraqi withdrawal—a condition that was virtually designed to be unacceptable to the Iraqis and thus intended to permit the beginning of the ground war.

Several of Bush's advisers as well as commentators outside the government suspected the worst of Gorbachev's motivations. Many believed that by complicating the coalition's prosecution of the war and trying to cover Saddam Hussein's retreat from Kuwait, the Soviet Union had now abandoned once and for all new thinking and the other benign tenets of the Shevardnadze foreign policy. There were numerous reports of widespread anxiety in Eastern Europe that the resurgent hard-liners in the Soviet Union, particularly in the military, might try first to destabilize, and then to reassert control over, the Kremlin's former satellites.[5]

Other government officials and experts on the Soviet Union had a different view. There was, perhaps, an instructive analogy between Gorbachev's peace offensive and French foreign policy under Charles de Gaulle in the late 1950s and early 1960s. To cloak France's retreat from empire and the swift decline in its influence, de Gaulle struck off noisily on his own, withdrawing France from the military command structure of NATO, proclaiming a special role in the developing world in general and the Arab world in particular, and resisting at every turn the dominance of the United States. This stance bolstered French national pride and made de Gaulle its focal point. Washington did not let its exasperation stand in the way of robust economic and political ties with France.

Similarly, perhaps, as Gorbachev worked feverishly for a settlement to the Gulf War, causing strains in his relationship with Washington, he hoped for U.S. forbearance based on appreciation in the West of his past diplomatic accomplishment as well as on the fear that anyone who replaced him might be worse.

Bush's National Security Adviser, Brent Scowcroft, believed that while hard-liners in the Soviet bureaucracy may have been trying to break the pattern of cooperation that had developed under Shevardnadze, such motives were not necessarily Gorbachev's own.[6] That was basically Bush's own position, too. The president, who valued his personal relationships with so many foreign leaders, attached particular importance to the one he had developed with Gorbachev. Therefore, even in rejecting Gorbachev's effort, Bush took pains to avoid chastising the Soviet leader or rubbing his nose in the failure of his attempt at peacemaking.

In a final blitz of phone calls to a wide variety of allied leaders, Gorbachev tried almost desperately to portray the difference between the Soviet plan and the coalition's conditions as details that could be ironed out in a negotiation that would avert "escalation of combat operations to a new, even more destructive stage." But he seemed to know he was beaten, and with Bush particularly, he played the good loser. He assured the U.S. president that the "ordeal" they had been through would not stand in the way of his determination to continue the larger task of improving relations and realizing the "vision we share of a new world."

Bush thanked Gorbachev for these sentiments, then added pointedly that if the Soviet president was in touch with the Iraqis in the coming hours, he might remind them that they had not taken seriously the January 15 deadline for the beginning of the air war; they should avoid that mistake with regard to the new twenty-four-hour deadline. In fact, Gorbachev's own military advisors had led him to underestimate the seriousness of the American threat to send armor and infantry against the supposedly formidable Saddam Hussein line. Experts from the KGB, the Ministry of Defense, and Gorbachev's own staff had repeatedly predicted that while Bush would keep pounding Saddam Hussein from the air, he would not risk the high allied casualties that so many were predicting in a ground battle.[7]

Thus the coalition's lunge into Kuwait and southern Iraq, when it began right on schedule, just as the deadline expired, came as a shock to the Kremlin. Through its chief spokesman, the Soviet Foreign Ministry expressed official "regret" that "the instinct for a military solution had prevailed" and that "a real chance to solve the conflict peacefully has been missed." The Soviet military, which had been grumbling about the Kremlin's acquiescence in U.S. policy for months, was now fulminating against the ground war.[8]

The total and almost instantaneous collapse of the Iraqi army was not just an extremely unpleasant surprise for the Soviets but a humiliation—another piece of evidence that Gorbachev's opponents on the right could cite in accusing him of having squandered Soviet power.

On February 26, in a speech to factory workers in Minsk, Gorbachev struck a very different tone from the one he had taken on the phone with Bush a few days before. Now he expressed alarm over the "fragility" of U.S.-Soviet relations and hinted broadly that unless the coalition leaders showed "responsible behavior," by which he clearly meant restraint, relations between Washington and Moscow would be in serious jeopardy.

Bush was not about to let Gorbachev dictate to him on Gulf policy. Throughout the episode, he gave priority to the eviction of Saddam Hussein from Kuwait. But the more certain he was of being able to accomplish that objective, the more inclined Bush was to accommodate Gorbachev in what happened afterward. Preoccupied as President Bush was with the war, he knew that larger issues were awaiting him when it was over. Now that the end of the war was in sight, he was beginning to think about the many challenges ahead: other regional conflicts that would require U.S.-Soviet cooperation, the continuing transformation of Europe, and the uncertainties over the future of the Soviet Union itself.

Bush was convinced that for all Gorbachev's miscalculations and missteps, he was still the best available leader of the Soviet Union. Bush did not want to fan the anti-Gorbachev feeling in the Ministry of Defense or in Azerbaijan and Central Asia. Moreover, perhaps by showing restraint in the way he ended the Gulf War, Bush could enhance his leverage on Gorbachev once the United States and the Soviet Union turned to the postwar agenda. With Baker's encouragement, Bush hoped that by consolidating recent improvements in U.S.-Soviet relations, U.S.-Soviet cooperation over the Gulf would establish a model in other regional conflicts as well, from Cambodia to the Arab-Israeli dispute to El Salvador.

These were among the considerations in Bush's mind when, on the morning of February 28, he announced that "Kuwait is liberated" and that the allies would suspend military operations. Without doubt, the president had a variety of reasons for ending the war quickly: The U.S. military, particularly Colin Powell, wanted to quit while it was ahead; rolling to Baghdad would have meant risking much higher casualties and being bogged down in a Vietnam-like quagmire. Nor did anyone in Bush's inner circle want to test the limits of international and domestic political support for Desert Storm. U.S. warplanes had slaughtered Iraqis as they fled Kuwait City at the end of the war, causing a wave of revulsion in the United States and some outrage abroad. Bush did not want to invite more criticism that he was engaging in a "turkey shoot." Moreover, virtually all the important allies in the coalition were pressing him to end the war as promptly as possible.

In addition to these factors, Bush was also eager to end the strain in U.S.-Soviet relations and to do his friend in the Kremlin a favor. In the final analysis, Bush cared more about saving Gorbachev than about finishing off Saddam Hussein.

LINES ON THE MAP

Saddam Hussein was also spared for reasons that went to the heart of Desert Storm itself. The operation had the benefit of the most modern, in some cases almost futuristic instruments of military power. The allies were united behind a concept of collective security that had changed little in seventy years. The coalition was dedicated, above all, to preserving the sanctity of international boundaries that had been established after World War I and the concept of national sovereignty that went back at least 400 years, when the idea of the modern-nation state emerged from the wreckage of the Holy Roman Empire.

What brought down the wrath of the world on Saddam Hussein's head was his proclamation, on August 8, that Kuwait was the nineteenth province of Iraq. It was this act that elicited from Bush his must succinct battle cry: "This will not stand!" That was, and would continue to be, the essence of U.S. policy—the annexation would not stand—and it was also the common denominator in the explanations offered by officials of other countries for their participation in Desert Storm. If Saddam Hussein were allowed to get away with altering by force an internationally accepted boundary, he would be establishing a precedent that could complicate all of their lives.

As Thatcher put it in Aspen: "Iraq has violated and taken over the territory of a country which is a full member of the United Nations. That is totally unacceptable, and if it were allowed to endure, then there would be many other small countries that could never feel safe."

For many Europeans, Saddam Hussein's challenge awakened the worst memories of the 1930s. Here were the Sudetenland and the Anschluss all over again. These historical associations were surely in Bush's mind when he denounced Saddam Hussein as "worse than Hitler."

For the Arabs, it had long been a guiding principle that their leaders could engage in any treachery as long as 1) they were polite about it, calling one another brother, and 2) they left the post–World War I borders intact. Saddam Hussein broke the second rule. That made it possible for Bush to assemble a coalition that included Arab royals, like the kings of Saudi Arabia and Morocco; moderate, pro-Western, if authoritarian, leaders like Hosni Mubarak of Egypt; and radical, anti-Western dictators like Hafiz al-Assad of Syria. Assad's participation was particularly telling. Over the years he had violated in many ways at many times the sovereignty of Syria's own small, weak neighbor, Lebanon. Because he had not attempted to redraw, much less erase, any lines on the map, he was welcomed into the anti-Saddam Hussein coalition.

A spokesman at the United Nations for the three sub-Saharan African nations in the coalition, Niger, Senegal and Sierra Leone, said in December 1990 that those countries sent troops to the Gulf "because our governments realize that we must nip in the bud the idea that post-colonial frontiers are subject to unilateral adjustment by force; this is a potentially explosive issue for Africa even more than for the Middle East."

The reaction of these African nations was characteristic of another change in the world. They were all members of the Nonaligned Movement, a large groups of developing countries that had, for decades, specialized in playing off the superpowers against each other. With one superpower now out of the game, nonalignment no longer had much meaning or benefit. Hence Third World countries quickly aligned themselves with Uncle Sam. So did members of what had been the second, or communist, world itself, and for reasons similar to those of the African states. A Polish diplomat in Washington remarked in December

1990, "As a nation that has been subject to invasion and annexation more than once in its history, we feel it important to have some of our soldiers in the Gulf as a way of underscoring our commitment to the inviolability of our own borders."

Even Argentina was a case in point. In 1982 the ruling junta in Buenos Aires had tried to seize the Falkland/Malvinas Islands from Britain. The British victory in the resulting war precipitated the fall of the military dictators and the return of democracy. Late in 1990 and early in 1991 several Argentine diplomats in Washington and New York said that by joining Desert Shield, their government hoped to underscore that it had disavowed the irredentism of its military predecessors.

There was both logic and irony in the way that the Gulf War ended. The coalition sent its warplanes against Iraqi forces on January 16 to restore the territorial integrity of Kuwait. Then, about six weeks later, the coalition suspended hostilities *in a way intended to preserve the territorial integrity of Iraq.*

The *casus belli* and the essential condition for a cease-fire came down to the same issue: on which side of the Iraq-Kuwait border were Saddam Hussein's forces? Both in the way it began and in the way it ended, Desert Storm was about lines on a map.

Much as they would have been delighted at the demise of Saddam Hussein, few if any of the allies wanted to see the dismemberment of his country. The governments in Ankara, Damascus, and Tehran were concerned that if the Kurds in northern Iraq succeeded in freeing themselves from Baghdad's rule, they would stir up the Kurdish minorities in Turkey, Syria, and Iran. Each of Iraq's neighbors was concerned that one or more of the others might exploit Saddam Hussein's defeat to carve off a piece of his domain—in other words, do to Saddam Hussein what he had done to Kuwait: annex territory. The Saudis, Kuwaitis, and the smaller Gulf states were especially worried that if the Shiites in the south of Iraq succeeded in their own rebellion, their region might in some fashion become an appendage of Iran. Now that Saddam Hussein seemed to have been cut down to size, the Gulf Arabs began to fret anew over the old specter of Iranian hegemony, which had led them to back Saddam Hussein against Iran in the 1980s.

The dissolution of Iraq would have been alarming to other members of the coalition as well, countries that had their own restive ethnic minorities. Secessionism was a particularly troublesome issue in Czechoslovakia, where Slovaks were pulling away from Czechs, and even in Canada, where the Quebecois were threatening to leave the federation. The Soviets would have almost surely exercised their veto to block any UN Security Council resolution that was likely to strengthen centrifugal forces in Iraq and thereby encourage those that were tearing apart the Soviet Union. Another Permanent Member of the Council, the People's Republic of China, which had invaded and annexed Tibet in 1951, was sensitive on this point as well.

Not surprisingly, therefore, the Bush administration came under a barrage of appeals from foreign leaders both inside and outside the coalition not to do anything that would precipitate the breakup (or "Lebanonization") of Iraq. Among other things, it was said, the day might come when the United States, the West, and the Gulf Arabs would need Iraq, once again, as a counterweight to Iran (and to Syria, which had been the principal perpetrator of the Lebanonization of Lebanon).

As it happened, Bush needed little convincing on this score. He took pride in calling himself a conservative, and his favorite word was *prudence*. By instinct and as a result of lessons learned from long experience, Bush believed that it was only prudent to conserve existing structures unless and until changing them seemed absolutely necessary. Iraq was part of the existing structure. Bush and other U.S. policymakers never supported the Kurds in their campaign for "autonomy," which almost everyone understood to be a euphemism for, or at least a first step toward, independence.

On February 15, Bush urged the "Iraqi people" to "take matters into their own hands" and "force Saddam Hussein, the dictator, to step aside." According to what several of his aides said later, the president was addressing anti-Saddam Hussein elements in the ruling Ba'ath Party and military, who he was hoping would take power and maintain a strong central government in Baghdad. But dissident Kurds and Shiites took Bush's message more literally. They could be forgiven for doing so. A radio station in Saudi Arabia, set up with assistance from the CIA and funding from the Saudi government, broadcast messages of support to the rebels. With official U.S. and Egyptian knowledge and approval, Iran, Saudi Arabia, and Syria sent money, arms, and other supplies to the insurgents. However, the objective of these efforts, covert and otherwise, was to put pressure on Saddam Hussein and to increase the incentive of his subordinates to turn against him—*not* to split up Iraq.

For the next month, the twin rebellions gathered force. Meanwhile, Saddam Hussein recovered. Using the forces he had managed to extricate from Kuwait as well as those he had held in reserve, he began systematically to suppress the uprisings, massacring civilians and bringing to the Shiite holy city of Karbala and the Kurdish center of Kirkuk devastation far worse than anything the allies had done in the air war. The U.S. government had anticipated that there would be uprisings but had hoped that they would lead dissidents in the ruling Ba'ath party and the Iraqi military to overthrow Saddam Hussein. Instead, the Sunni Arabs in the Ba'ath and in the military sided with Saddam Hussein against the Kurds and the Shiites, allowing him to crush the opposition.

On March 13, during a visit to Ottawa, Bush made a statement suggesting that the use of Iraqi helicopters in these operations was a violation of the agreement that had led to the suspension of hostilities. Subsequently, officials of the National Security Council staff, State Department, and Pentagon insisted that Bush had never meant to signal that the U.S. was prepared to shoot down the helicopters or actively intervene on the side of the rebels. Quite the contrary, in a series of meetings at the White House, Bush made clear, emphatically and repeatedly, that he saw what was happening in Iraq as a "civil war," in which the United States must not, under any circumstances, become involved. Even from his position on the sidelines, he was not hoping that the Kurds would win if winning meant achieving their aim of independence.

On March 26, the White House Spokesman Marlin Fitzwater announced that the United States would not interfere with the operations of Iraqi helicopters unless they posed a threat to U.S. or coalition forces. Saddam Hussein now had a free hand.

The winners of the war were congratulating themselves for having reestablished the taboo against aggression: invade a neighboring state, and you will be sorry. Now the loser in the war was taking advantage of an awkward corollary: stay on your own territory, wrap yourself in the cloak of sovereignty, and you can do anything you want. Having been punished for violating the sanctity of borders, Saddam Hussein had found protection behind that same principle as he butchered his own citizens. Having withdrawn from Kuwait, Saddam Hussein was now playing by accepted rules; his abominations were once again in the category of internal affairs, therefore—as Bush repeatedly said—no longer subject to the intervention of the United States or the world community.

The Iraqi leader seemed on the brink of transforming himself from an international outlaw into the champion of Iraq's survival as as state, a cause to which Bush and most, if not all, of the allies were also committed. It was the cruelest twist of the whole affair: Saddam Hussein had, in effect, joined the coalition.

If the postwar horror had remained confined by the boundaries of Iraq, the United States and the international community might well have let it simply play itself out. Even though President Bush had railed against Saddam Hussein as a monster, it was only insofar as Saddam Hussein behaved monstrously toward *Kuwait* that Bush and most other coalition leaders felt it was the international community's business and responsibility to do anything about him.

Given Bush's repeated comparisons of Saddam Hussein to Adolf Hitler, a hypothetical question comes to mind: What if Neville Chamberlain had stood up to the German dictator at Munich? What if Hitler had contented himself with the real estate of Weimar Germany for building the Third Reich, complete with concentration camps, gas chambers, and ovens? Would the world have done anything about it?

And half a century later, what if Saddam Hussein had set about mass murder among his own people who had risen up against him? Would the world have done anything about that if hundreds of thousands had *not* fled to the frontier areas of Turkey and Iran? Even when such an exodus occurred, it was only reluctantly, belatedly, and under pressure that the Bush administration responded with military force.

The pressure came primarily from four sources: the media, particularly television, which broadcast, night after night, footage of miserable, starving, masses and dead babies; President Ozal of Turkey, whose own territory and sovereignty were now in jeopardy, at least at the periphery, because of the massive influx of Kurds; the West European allies, especially Prime Minister John Major of Britain and President Mitterrand of France (who, in turn, was considerably influenced by his wife, an activist in humanitarian causes); and from James Baker, who visited a refugee camp on the Turkish-Iraqi border. The secretary of state was only in the camp for twelve minutes, but that was long enough for him to see that half a million people were living in unspeakable conditions at an altitude of 8,000 feet and that the United States and the coalition had a huge problem on their hands. Shortly afterward, at his next stop in Tel Aviv, Baker telephoned Bush and urged a dramatic step-up in the effort to deliver supplies to the refugees.

Bush remained extremely reluctant to take any steps that constituted a reintroduction of U.S. forces to the Gulf region. But in the days that followed Baker's call, a number of allied leaders, especially Ozal and Major, convinced him that two looming horrors—massive starvation among the refugees in the border areas and a full-scale massacre of the Kurds by the Iraqi army—could turn the victory in the war into a debacle for the West.

The result was, first, a major relief operation and then, in another impressive display of coordination and cooperation among allies, the deployment of U.S. and coalition military forces to establish safe havens inside northern Iraq so that the Kurds could, at least, come down from the murderously cold and inhospitable mountains.

Large numbers of Kurdish and Shiite refugees were also in Iran, but their plight was largely overlooked, since their encampments were far less accessible to Western journalists and TV camera crews and since the leaders in Tehran were, to put it mildly, not in the habit of telephoning the White House.

As it happened, there was a thirteenth resolution after all. Resolution 687, which the Security Council passed on April 3, specified that Iraq must, under UN supervision, destroy all its biological and chemical weapons and give up its ballistic missiles with ranges of more than ninety miles; Iraq was forbidden from developing or acquiring any of those instruments of war in the future as well as from developing or acquiring nuclear bombs or weapons-usable material. These provisions were safeguards that limited Iraq's ability to threaten its neighbors. As such, they were welcome additions to international law, but they were also in the spirit of what might be called the old geopolitics, the restoration of the *status quo ante.* As usual, the world community was focusing on the threat of aggression. (It would continue to do so throughout the year, as Saddam Hussein, methodically and in brazen defiance of the UN, set about to reconstitute his military forces and resume his development of nuclear weapons.)

Two days later, on April 5, with the refugee crisis growing worse, the Security Council finally broke new ground. Resolution 688 asserted that international humanitarian organizations had the right of immediate access to Iraqi citizens who were victims of repression inside Iraq itself. That measure set the scene for U.S. and allied forces to carve out sanctuaries on Iraqi territory. Only in the aftermath of war had the international community taken a step—and a very small, uncertain one at that—toward redefining its interests and obligations to take account not just of what happens *between* and *among* nations but what happens *inside* them as well.

Similarly, only as an unplanned and halfhearted afterthought to his conduct as commander in chief of Desert Storm and only under goading from his allies and U.S. public opinion, had George Bush even begun to give meaning to the slogan of a new world order. Still, better an afterthought than no thought at all; better late than never.

Just as Saddam Hussein's seizure of Kuwait had galvanized the coalition into resuscitating the old idea of collective security, his vengeance on the Kurds had, however belatedly and tentatively, stimulated the world toward a genuinely new idea: collective responsibility for the behavior of governments toward their own people.

ENDNOTES

1. The more frequently cited figure of twenty-eight for the membership of the coalition treats as a single member the Gulf Cooperation Council, which includes Bahrain, Oman, Qatar, and the United Arab Emirates.
2. In a speech in Amman, Jordan, in February 1990, Saddam Hussein virtually proclaimed that the strategic retreat—indeed, the capitulation—of the Soviet Union had created the conditions in which he could more actively pursue his own plans for hegemony in the region.
3. Greece, for example, could claim to have made a contribution to the allied effort by having one of its cruisers, originally deployed during the Kuwait reflagging operation during the Iran-Iraq war, remain on station at the mouth of the Red Sea.
4. On the day Yevgeny Primakov was meeting with Saddam Hussein in Baghdad, the newspaper *Sovetskaya Rossiya,* one of the leading voices of reaction, complained that the government's decision in 1990 to back the UN coalition had "ended the U.S.S.R.'s existence as a superpower." The next day, senior political officers from the armed forces and KGB border guards held a press conference to denounce "the U.S.-led attempt to destroy Iraq."
5. It was during this period, just before the ground war, that William Safire, as so often before, provided a catch phrase for a widespread perception: "Cold War II has begun."
6. In an appearance on "Meet the Press" on February 24, Brent Scowcroft said, "I think it's probably fair to say that the Soviets have their own objectives in this that may not be entirely parallel with those of the United States. But I think that one has to say that the Soviets have been stalwart members of the coalition." The notion of Gorbachev's Gaullist motives was most fully developed by Steven Sestanovich, a Soviet affairs expert formerly on the National Security Council staff and now at the Center for Strategic and International Studies in Washington, D.C. See Steven Sestanovich, "Inventing the Soviet National Interest," *National Interest,* No. 20 (Summer 1990).
7. In an interview on ABC's *This Week with David Brinkley* on February 10, Marshal Sergei Akhromeyev, the retired chief of the General Staff, who was serving as Gorbachev's personal military adviser, provided a public summary of what he and his colleagues in uniform were probably telling the Kremlin leader: "I think the warfare will not be completed within a short order of time. The Iraqi ground and air forces have rich experience in the conduct of warfare. They are not the kind of soldiers who will flee the battlefield after the first blow. They will offer stiff resistance. I believe the

upcoming ground battle, if it does take place, will be bitter and will last for a considerable length of time."

8. In an interview in *Pravda,* Defense Minister Dimitri Yazov said that by seizing Iraqi territory, the coalition had now definitely exceeded its mandate from the United Nations. Yazov repeated suspicions that the United States was pursuing some larger, sinister plan in the Middle East, one that might jeopardize the Soviet Union's own security interests. Akhromeyev's successor as chief of the General Staff, General Mikhail Moiseyev, told the military daily *Red Star* that the Gulf had become "a testing ground" for advanced U.S. weaponry that would soon be made available to NATO and thus presumably aimed directly against the Soviet Union.

2

COLLECTIVE SECURITY AND THE "NEW WORLD ORDER": WHAT ROLE FOR THE UNITED NATIONS?

Richard N. Gardner

> Now we can see a new world coming into view. A world in which there is the very real prospect of a new world order. In the words of Winston Churchill, a "world order" in which "the principles of justice and fair play . . . protect the weak against the strong. . . ." A world where the United Nations, freed from cold war stalemate, is poised to fulfill the historic vision of its founders. A world in which freedom and respect for human rights find a home among all nations.
>
> — *President George Bush, address to a joint session of Congress, March 6, 1991.*

The last year has seen an amazing renaissance of the United Nations (UN). Until recently the world organization seemed destined to play only a marginal role in United States foreign policy and in international relations generally. But since Iraq's invasion of Kuwait last August, it has been the centerpiece of U.S. strategy for mobilizing an international coalition to defeat Iraq's aggression and to deal with the consequences of the conflict.

The UN is currently deploying an observer group on the Iraq-Kuwait border, is carrying out on-site inspections to assure the elimination of Iraq's weapons of mass destruction and the means for their delivery, is providing the legal framework for a continued embargo on arms sales to Iraq and on Iraq's exports of oil, and is creating arrangements by which Iraq will pay compensation for the damage it has caused once its oil exports resume. It is also providing humanitarian assistance and guarantees of safety for the Kurds in northern Iraq.

Does all this mean that we have suddenly achieved a "New World Order" in which the United Nations will assure collective security and the rule of law for all nations? Of course not. The security of the United States will continue to require military strength as well as the effective use of the UN and other instruments of international cooperation. It will require a wise blending, if you will, of "balance of power politics" and "world order politics." The North Atlantic Treaty Organization (NATO) will continue to be needed to cope with threats to European security arising from within the European region and from "out-of-area" contingencies in the Middle East and North Africa. The Conference on Security and Cooperation in Europe (CSCE) and other regional organizations will have important roles. At the same time, the experience of the Gulf War does open up the *possibility* that the United Nations can become a more important contributor to collective security if the United States and other key members really wish it to be. A significant commitment in this direction was contained in the political communiqué issued on July 16 by the seven participants in the London Summit:

> We believe the conditions now exist for the United Nations to fulfill completely the promise and vision of its founders. A revitalized United Nations will have a central role in strengthening the international order. We commit ourselves to making the UN stronger, more efficient and more effective in order to protect human rights, to maintain peace and security for all and to deter aggression. We will make preventive diplomacy a top priority to help avert future conflicts by making clear to potential aggressors the consequences of their actions. The UN's role in peacekeeping should be reinforced and we are prepared to do this strongly.

This essay will suggest some of the ways in which the United States, its Group of Seven or G-7 (United States, Canada, Great Britain, France, Italy, Germany, and Japan) Summit partners, the Soviet Union, and other key countries could give practical expression to the aspirations in President Bush's New World Order, contributing at one and the same time to their own security and to the collective security of all UN members.

COLLECTIVE SECURITY AGAINST NONMILITARY THREATS

Although this essay focuses mainly on the role of the United Nations in dealing with military threats to U.S. and collective security, it is obvious that nonmilitary challenges to security are growing in importance and that these will have implications also for the role of the UN. The waning of the Cold War has produced rapid changes in the way Americans think about national security challenges. After years in which Soviet aggression was perceived as the main threat to U.S. national security, Americans responding to an Americans Talk Security (ATS) survey in March of 1990 not only ranked Soviet aggression as the last in fourteen top threats but gave priority to nonmilitary over military challenges (see Table 1).

If a group of experts rather than ordinary citizens were drawing up a list of nonmilitary threats to security, they would probably place at the top of the list not drug trafficking but the central challenge of global habitability due to environmental destruction and explosive population growth. There is a growing consensus that carbon dioxide from the burning of fossil fuels together with tropical deforestation could result in an increase of several degrees centigrade in global mean temperature by the middle of the next century, bringing with it catastrophic effects from a rise in the level of the world's oceans. A related threat is that which the use of chlorofluorocarbons presents to the ozone layer, our global atmospheric shield against the ultraviolet radiation that causes cancer and other damage to life on earth.

Table 1 Threats to U.S. National Security

(percentage citing as an extremely important or very serious threat)

Drug Trafficking	84
Third World Nuclear Weapons	74
Air/Water Pollution	74
Violent Crime	72
Cost of Health Care	69
Federal Budget Deficit	64
International Economic Competition	61
Terrorist Activities	61
Man-made Climate Change	53
Radiation/Nuclear Reactors	52
Mideast Conflicts	51
Central American Conflicts	44
Soviet Nuclear Weapons	43
Soviet Aggression/World	24

Source: Cited in Gregory F. Treverton and Barbara A. Bicksler, "Getting From Here to Where," paper prepared for the American Assembly of Columbia University, May 30 – June 2, 1991.

These and other global environmental threats—air and water pollution, soil erosion, the loss of biodiversity—will clearly require action at the global as well as the national and regional levels. The United States and other developed countries could end up as environmental hostages if Third World countries fail to change their present approach to economic development. For example, the present plans of China and India to triple the burning of coal between now and 2025 could nullify any positive effect the developed countries could manage to achieve in reducing their carbon dioxide emissions.

Present rates of world population growth are not only a contributor to environmental insecurity but pose a related challenge in the form of massive and destabilizing South-North migration. World population, which stood at only 1.5 billion at the beginning of this century and is 5 billion today, is predicted by the UN to reach 6.2 billion in the year 2000 and 8.5 billion in 2025. It will level off at 9 to 14 billion some time in the next century. Whether this planet's population stabilizes at the low or high end of that range will fundamentally determine the prospects for economic welfare and security, not only of developing countries, but of developed countries, including the United States.

To understand the gravity of population trends, it is necessary only to consider that between now and the year 2025 Mexico is expected to grow from 85 to 150 million, Brazil from 144 to 246 million, Egypt from 51 to 94 million, Ethiopia from 45 to 112 million, Nigeria from 105 to 301 million, Bangladesh from 110 to 235 million, and India from 819 to 1,445 million. No government, no academic expert has the faintest idea of how to provide adequate food, housing, health care, education, and gainful employment to such exploding numbers of people, particularly as they crowd into megacities, such as Mexico City, Calcutta, and Cairo.

With such an explosive growth in world numbers, there will be little hope of saving the rain forests, the topsoil, or the climate balance so essential to human life. Moreover, the rate of illegal immigration already troubling the United States and Western Europe could reach tidal wave proportions, disrupting public order and requiring dramatic military responses.

If environment, population, and drug trafficking are destined to be the three main nonmilitary challenges to U.S. and global security in the years ahead, the UN will be called upon to assume even greater responsibilities in these three areas. To mention just the most obvious examples:

- The UN system, which has already played the catalytic role in the negotiation of international agreements to protect the ozone layer, will be seeking to make a similar contribution on global conventions to deal with climate change, deforestation, and the protection of biodiversity. The UN Conference on Environment and Development in Rio de Janeiro in June 1992 will also face difficult decisions on measures to help Third World countries through technical assistance, technology transfer, and financial aid. The modest UN Environment Program will almost certainly have to be strengthened and supplemented by some more authoritative Ministerial-level body to stimulate global action.

- The UN system will need to give increasing attention to the population issue, seeking ways to reach the 50 percent of couples in the childbearing years in the Third World outside of China who lack access to modern methods of family planning. The UN Fund for Population Activities and the population-related work of the United Nations International Children's Emergency Fund (UNICEF), the World Health Organization (WHO), the United Nations Educational, Scientific, and Cultural Organization (UNESCO), the United Nations Development Program (UNDP), and the World Bank in family planning, maternal and child health, and education will all need to be intensified.

- The UN will need to intensify global and regional efforts already under way to deal with the drug problem by helping countries in crop diversification, preventive education, treatment of addicts, and law enforcement against drug traffickers.

The United Nations is not yet perceived by most Americans as a major source of assistance in coping with their concerns about the environment, unwanted immigration, or drug abuse. By the beginning of the next century, if progress is being made on those threats to American and global security, it is very likely that the UN's role will be recognized as a vital supplement to national efforts.

COLLECTIVE SECURITY AGAINST MILITARY THREATS

Broadly conceived, the role of the United Nations in coping with military threats to collective security embraces a wide variety of functions spelled out in Chapters VI and VII of the Charter: the peaceful settlement of disputes, preventive diplomacy, and collective measures against an aggressor ranging from the severance of diplomatic relations and economic sanctions to the employment of armed force. It can also include measures of arms control, including the disarmament of an aggressor and limitations on arms transfers, particularly of nuclear weapons and other weapons of mass destruction and the means for their delivery. In the post–Cold War era, there will be new opportunities for the UN in all of these areas.

Even during the Cold War, the UN made important contributions to peace and security through the deployment of peacekeeping forces in places like Cyprus, Lebanon, and the Golan Heights. It was not able, however, to make much progress in resolving the underlying conflicts that made those forces necessary. In the last two years, however, the UN has been a key actor in resolving conflicts in places like Namibia, Nicaragua, and the western Sahara. Most importantly, it has brokered a settlement in Cambodia, where it will have major responsibilities for truce supervision, election monitoring, and public administration.

Beyond this important peacekeeping function, what new measures might be considered to strengthen the UN's role in dealing with military threats to collective security? Three areas deserve priority attention: preventive diplomacy, arms transfers and nonproliferation, and the creation of a UN Rapid Deployment Force (RDF) under Article 43.

With respect to preventive diplomacy, the UN Secretary-General could be given the means which he presently lacks to carry out his authority under Article 99 of the Charter to "bring to the attention of the Security Council any matter which in his opinion may threaten the maintenance of international peace and security." He could be given four or five high-level representatives responsible for the main regions of the world, who could monitor incipient conflict situations and engage in missions of preventive diplomacy. In addition, the five Permanent Members of the Security Council could be asked to share intelligence information with the Secretary-General on a regular basis, including information from satellites, that would help him identify possible threats to peace. With these two new instruments at their disposal, the Secretary-General and the Security Council could engage in a continuing "global peace watch" that might anticipate and possibly head off conflicts like Iraq's invasion of Kuwait or the Falkland Islands War.

The second area of collective security against military threats where there should be a greater role for the UN is in coping with the proliferation of weapons of mass destruction, of the missiles for their delivery, and of advanced conventional arms. Secretary of Defense Dick Cheney said recently that by the year 2000 "more than two dozen developing nations will have ballistic missiles, 15 of those countries will have the scientific skills to make their own and half of them either have or are near to getting nuclear capability as well." He added that "30 countries will have chemical weapons and 10 will be able to deploy biological weapons." Among the countries that either have or soon will have missiles and mass destruction warheads are North Korea, Libya, Iran, Syria, Saudi Arabia, Egypt, Israel, India, Pakistan, and South Africa.

One of the most important achievements in Security Council Resolution 687 was to require that Iraq be deprived of all chemical, biological and nuclear weapons and all missile capabilities. For much of this last year, a UN Special Commission and the International Atomic Energy Agency (IAEA) have been trying to enforce these requirements on a recalcitrant Iraq, backed up by the threat of renewed military action by the United States.

Paragraph 14 of Resolution 687 states that these measures "represent steps toward the goal of establishing in the Middle East a zone free from weapons of mass destruction and all missiles for their delivery." When we consider the prospect that another war in the Middle East would probably be fought with missiles much more accurate than the Scuds fired randomly by Iraq against population centers in Israel and Saudi Arabia, that those missiles could be fitted with chemical, biological, or even nuclear warheads, and that potential victim states with little warning time would be under enormous political pressure to launch preventive strikes, it becomes obvious that the goal stated in this paragraph should not await a final settlement of Middle East conflicts but should be pursued with extreme urgency.

In their meeting in Paris in July of 1991, the five major suppliers of arms, who also happen to be the five Permanent Members of the Security Council, began the first serious discussion among themselves of ways to achieve a Middle East free of weapons of mass destruction and the means for their delivery. They also examined nonproliferation on a global basis and ways to limit destabilizing exports of conventional arms. Whether this hopeful beginning leads to practical results will depend not only on the political will of the five but on the cooperation of secondary suppliers of arms, who should be associated with these discussions at an early opportunity.

Cooperation from the Third World countries whose arms policies are at issue will also be necessary, and here the UN can be a useful supplement to a policy of denial from the major weapons suppliers. Resolutions by the Security Council could provide legitimacy for efforts at nonproliferation and conventional arms limitation, both in the Middle East and in other areas. A registry of conventional arms transfers could be instituted by the UN, as some permanent members have recently proposed. New efforts could be made to give the IAEA a power that it currently lacks and that is essential if its work in non-proliferation is to be credible—the power to make challenge inspections on short notice and to carry them out anywhere in a country, not just at declared nuclear installations.

THE ARTICLE 43 QUESTION: A UN RAPID DEPLOYMENT FORCE?

A central question for the United States and other UN members is whether the UN's system for deterring and defeating aggression should rely on ad hoc coalitions assembled and led by the United States (or another permanent member) or whether an institutionalized system should now be created as provided for in Article 43 of the Charter.

Article 43 provides that "all UN members undertake to make available to the Security Council, on its call and in accordance with a special agreement or agreements, armed forces, assistance and facilities, including rights of passage, necessary for the purpose of maintaining international peace and security.... Such agreement or agreements shall govern the number and types of forces, their degree of readiness and general location, and the nature of the facilities and assistance to be provided." Although Article 43 declares that these agreements "shall be negotiated as soon as possible," efforts to negotiate them were abandoned in the early postwar years due to U.S.-Soviet disagreements.

Article 47 of the Charter provides for a Military Staff Committee, consisting of the chiefs of staff of the Permanent Members of the Security Council or their representatives, to "advise and assist" the Council on all questions relating to "military requirements" and the "employment and command of forces placed at its disposal." The Military Staff Committee is to be responsible under the Security Council for the "strategic direction" of the armed forces placed at its disposal. Questions relating to the command of these forces are to be "worked out subsequently."

How might these Charter provisions now be implemented in a way that would serve the common interest in deterring or defeating threats to the peace and acts of aggression? Certainly not by asking UN members to assign units of their armed forces to a huge UN standing army, capable of defeating military challenges from the permanent members themselves. For both political and budgetary reasons such an ambitious plan would have scant support.

A more modest proposal, however, would deserve serious consideration. Some 20 to 30 UN members in different parts of the world could enter into Article 43 agreements designating units of brigade strength (2,000–3,000 men) that would be available for use by the Security Council as a Rapid Deployment Force to deal with threats to the peace and acts of aggression. These units would be prepared in advance of a crisis with common training, standardized or interoperable equipment, and joint exercises under a UN commander. When a crisis occurred, those national contingents most suited for the purpose would be called up, which, in most cases, would be far less in number than the total potential force of 50,000 or more.

The five permanent members, like other UN members, would assign units of their ground forces under Article 43 agreements (for example, the Ready Brigade of the 82nd Airborne Division could be the U.S. contribution). The permanent members could also be asked to pledge air and naval units and/or airlift and sealift capability. In many conflict situations, it would be preferable to keep the permanent members, or at least the U.S. and the Soviet Union, in a backup military role, with ground forces of other UN members on the front lines.

A UN Rapid Deployment Force of this kind would be available to perform a variety of purposes: 1) to be stationed preemptively on the border of any UN member that was threatened by aggression, 2) to defeat aggression if it occurred, 3) to put an end to mass repression against civilian populations (e.g., the Kurds in northern Iraq) that constituted a threat to international peace and security, 4) to undertake humanitarian relief in the face of natural disasters (e.g., in Bangladesh), and 5) to combat acts of terrorism and international drug trafficking.

The UN Rapid Deployment Force could only be deployed by the Security Council and therefore could only operate where there were nine affirmative votes of the fifteen Security Council members and where no veto was cast by a permanent member. Such a force would not be powerful enough to deal with all kinds of aggression; action by the United States alone or with its allies would still be necessary in certain circumstances in accordance with Article 51 of the Charter. Nevertheless, a UN Rapid Deployment Force would constitute a meaningful political as well as military deterrent in most situations, particularly where it could be deployed preemptively on the border of a threatened country. It is doubtful if Saddam Hussein would have attacked Kuwait if a UN force composed of units of several dozen members, including the permanent members, had faced him on the other side of the border.

Would the creation of a UN Rapid Deployment Force serve the national security interests of the United States? To answer that question both possible benefits and possible risks need to be evaluated. The first benefit would be a fairer sharing of the burdens of keeping peace in today's world. A poll in *Time* magazine in the aftermath of the Gulf War showed that Americans by a margin of 70 percent to 20 percent reject the idea of the United States as world policeman. There will not be very many situations in which Americans will be willing to supply 80 percent of the fighting forces as they did in the Gulf. Had the Gulf War resulted in 10,000 to 20,000 American casualties, as many experts predicted, there would have been a powerful political outcry from the American people against the disproportionate sacrifices imposed on the United States.

To be sure, the burden-sharing benefit will only be realized to the extent that Permanent Members of the UN and a substantial number of others proved willing to pledge their forces under Article 43 agreements. The Soviet Union announced its readiness to commit units of its armed forces to a UN Rapid Deployment Force in then Foreign Minister Eduard Shevardnadze's speech to the 1990 UN General Assembly. Notwithstanding his subsequent resignation, senior members of the Soviet Foreign Ministry confirmed during a meeting in Moscow of an unofficial U.S.-Soviet Working Group on Multilateral Cooperation in June of 1991 that this was still official Soviet policy. They added that an Article 43 agreement would help overcome political resistance in the Supreme Soviet and in the republic parliaments for the use of Soviet armed forces in multilateral actions against aggression.

If the United States and the Soviet Union were willing to pledge units to a Rapid Deployment Force (RDF) under Article 43, the United Kingdom and France would be likely to follow suit. China might not wish to participate, but its behavior during the Gulf War suggests it would not employ its veto to prevent the establishment of a UN RDF by others.

A more difficult question is presented when it comes to the participation in a UN RDF by nonpermanent members. They do not have the veto privilege, are not members of the Military Staff Committee, and may not even be members of the Security Council when a call is made on units that they would be asked to pledge, under Article 43 agreements. But Article 44 of the Charter provides that when the Council has decided to use armed force, it shall invite UN members not on the Council to participate in its decisions concerning the employment of units of that member's armed forces. Article 47 further provides that UN members other than the permanent members can be invited to participate in the work of the Military Staff Committee when this is required for "the efficient discharge" of the committee's responsibilities. These Charter provisions could be interpreted liberally to provide a seat at the decision-making table for nonpermanent members contributing to a UN RDF. In addition, such members could be permitted to insert an "opting-out" provision in their Article 43 agreements, to the effect that in exceptional cases involving important national interests they could decline to make their armed forces available for a particular operation.

As a further measure to overcome domestic political obstacles to making Article 43 agreements, UN members could be encouraged to compose their military units assigned to the UN of volunteers rather than conscripts. In many countries of the world, the idea of voluntary service under a UN flag would have broad appeal to young people. At the recent meeting in Moscow referred to earlier, Soviet participants indicated that having their Article 43 units composed of volunteers would be particularly helpful in coping with the reluctance manifested recently by republic parliaments to having their young people employed in military operations to which those parliaments had not specifically consented. The use of volunteers for the UN RDF could also be helpful with the U.S. Senate, which otherwise might be reluctant to approve an Article 43 agreement giving a blank check to the president to send American servicemen and women into combat at the call of the UN Security Council. Indeed, the composition of a unit composed of volunteers might be the only way to preserve the freedom of action for the president to implement Security Council decisions with U.S. forces as was provided in 1945 by the UN Participation Act.

It is often forgotten that the negotiation of Article 43 agreements is not merely an option available to UN members, it is a legal obligation of membership in the world organization. In a context in which this dead letter provision was being activated, Article 43 could provide a way of securing contributions from two key countries that resisted making human (as opposed to financial) contributions to the Gulf War for domestic political and constitutional reasons—Japan and Germany. The governments of these two countries could argue that their constitutions should be interpreted to permit fulfillment of Article 43 obligations and, failing such an interpretation, that their constitutions should be amended accordingly. The Japanese Socialists and German Social Democrats would not be able to claim any longer that sending armed forces abroad would be caving in to U.S.

demands or encouraging the revival of militarism. They would very likely support an Article 43 regime in which 20 to 30 UN members in different parts of the world were doing their share to provide armed forces for a global collective security system.

Another advantage of the Article 43 approach is that it would provide a degree of legitimacy for UN peace enforcement actions that is not available when they result from coalitions dominated by one country. In the Gulf War, the military operation became identified with the United States rather than the United Nations and Saddam Hussein was able to argue that his enemy was the United States and not the world community as a whole. In addition to the problem of appearances, there was the practical consequence in the Gulf War that once the Security Council authorized the employment of armed force under Resolution 678, it had no control over how that force was employed. Indeed, because of its veto power the United States was in a position to block any effort by the Council to force the termination of hostilities or force the United States to alter the way it was carrying out the Council's broad mandate. Many UN members—and not only those who claimed the United States had "hijacked" the Security Council—are determined to prevent a repetition of the Gulf experience and assure that future peace enforcement operations are run by a UN commander kept under strict UN control. Their presence in the future as non-permanent members of the Council may mean that the Gulf experience is a non-repeatable proposition.

A final argument for the Article 43 approach is that it is more likely, than the use of ad hoc coalitions led by UN Permanent Members, to provide the genuine collective security system protecting all UN members that is implied in President Bush's New World Order. There will be many threats to the peace or acts of aggression where neither the United States nor any Permanent Member of the Security Council will wish to take on the predominant military and political burdens assumed by the United States in the Gulf War. Yet President Bush has presented his New World Order as one in which aggression will be defeated and international law upheld on behalf of *all* nations, not just the United States. In doing so he articulated the same Wilsonian vision set forth by other American Presidents. Franklin D. Roosevelt, announcing U.S. war aims in his famous "Four Freedoms" speech, called for a postwar order that would assure "freedom from fear . . . everywhere in the world." John F. Kennedy, in his inaugural address, called for "a new world of law, where the strong are just and the weak secure and the peace preserved." Similar language can be found in statements of presidents Truman, Eisenhower, Johnson, Nixon, and Reagan.

If statements like these by American presidents are more than meaningless rhetorical flourishes, it must be because the construction of a global security system that protects all nations is something that serves the interests of the United States. But why should the United States care if Rwanda attacks Burundi, and no immediate vital interest of the United States or an ally is evidently at risk? It must be because 1) the United States feels a moral concern for the rights of the Burundians, 2) the United States believes that unpunished aggression will encourage aggression elsewhere, and 3) the United States will not be politically successful in mobilizing coalitions to defeat aggressions that threaten its vital interests if it shows indifference to aggressions that threaten the vital interests of others.

There are thus compelling arguments for the proposition that activating Article 43 would now serve the national interests of the United States. But arguments on the negative side will also need to be examined before a final conclusion is reached.

The first argument is that a UN RDF resulting from activation of Article 43 could be used against the United States. Had such a system existed during the last decade, the Sandinistas could have appealed for protection by the UN RDF against Contra incursions in Nicaragua. General Manuel Noriega could have done the same in advance of the U.S. invasion of Panama.

The short answer to this objection is that the United States could have blocked such deployments of the UN RDF by its veto. Nevertheless, for the United States to use its veto repeatedly in situations where a UN RDF was being called upon to protect other countries against U.S. violations of their sovereignty would be politically costly and could lead to the collapse of the whole UN RDF system. Perhaps the best answer to this objection is to say that, yes, the constitution of a UN RDF could make it more difficult for the United States and others to use force in violation of international law and that this would be one of its benefits. After all, a UN RDF could also have been used to protect El Salvador against Nicaraguan support of the Salvadoran insurgents. On balance, a UN RDF would inhibit aggression from all quarters; the United States should be able to live with that.

A second argument against a UN RDF is that it would be unable to function in situations where it was blocked by a veto or faced with a *fait accompli* by heavily armed aggression, and yet the fact of its existence might rule out a military response by the United States and its allies outside the UN. But there is no reason why this should be true. The United States and other UN members in setting up the UN RDF could make clear that they reserved all their rights of individual and collective self-defense in accordance with Article 51. The president would need to make clear to Congress and the American people that a UN RDF was not intended to be the answer to all security threats to the United States.

A third objection to a UN RDF would be that of military feasibility. It is true that the UN has demonstrated the workability of multinational peacekeeping forces composed of contingents from many nations, but these contingents were used for observation, border patrols, buffer zones, and the maintenance of order, not war-making. Can a successful military campaign be conducted by a coalition of several dozen different national contingents of brigade strength, each under a national commander but subject to an overall UN commander? How would the vital functions of intelligence, communications, and logistics be handled? Could any amount of preparatory training and joint exercises overcome the difficulties of diverse cultures, military doctrines, and national interests? Would the Pentagon ever consent to have U.S. forces under the overall command of a non-American? Are there military figures of politically appropriate nationality available whom the Permanent Members of the Security Council would trust to conduct a military campaign effectively? If these questions cannot be answered authoritatively at this time, should they not be the subject of study by qualified military and political leaders from interested UN members, either under the auspices of the UN or privately?

Lord Caradon, an eloquent British ambassador to the UN in the 1970s, once said that there was nothing essentially wrong with the world organization, "except, perhaps, its members." In the last year we have seen impressive evidence that the members are, at long last, ready to accept the obligations of membership and take the organization seriously. Whether this new attitude will persist, however, is something that cannot be taken for granted. Nor can we take for granted the ability of the United Nations to muster the financial resources, the organizational efficiency, and the qualified personnel to carry out the growing responsibilities that are being placed upon it.

What remains to be done if the United Nations is to realize its full potential in the 1990s? Here is a suggested agenda for action:

- The new Secretary General, with the support of the United States and other UN members, should promptly reorganize, streamline, and upgrade the UN Secretariat staff;

- UN members should reorganize the presently inadequate intergovernmental machinery for dealing with economic, social humanitarian, and environmental questions;

- The United States should promptly pay the approximately $800 million it currently owes in overdue assessed contributions for the regular UN budget, peacekeeping operations, and the specialized agencies;

- The five Permanent Members of the Security Council should initiate informal consultations among themselves and with other members on ways of enhancing the UN's capacity for preventive diplomacy and on the creation of a UN Rapid Deployment Force.

If we wish to move from rhetoric to action on the president's New World Order, these would all be good places to begin.

3

NONPROLIFERATION REGIMES IN THE AFTERMATH OF THE GULF WAR

Antonia Handler Chayes and Abram Chayes

The Aspen Strategy Group last considered weapons proliferation in the summer of 1989. The momentous events of the intervening two years—the end of the Cold War, the changes in the Soviet Union and its relations with its former allies in Eastern Europe, the unification of Germany, and the Gulf War—combine to create a new urgency as well as a moment of possibility and flexibility in the approach to problems of weapons proliferation. At the same time, the difficulties and complexities implicit in the need for broad coverage of controls remain daunting.

There are existing international nonproliferation arrangements or concrete proposals with respect to all the weapons of concern—nuclear, chemical, biological, ballistic missile, and conventional—but they vary widely in conception, scope, and effectiveness. Although almost continuous attempts have been made to improve each of these regimes, there has been little generic discussion of techniques for making regulatory regimes more effective and for improving prospects for satisfactory compliance. The Project on Treaty Compliance of the Program on Negotiation at Harvard Law School has begun to look at regulatory treaties covering a variety of subject matters, including security, economic affairs and environmental regulation, to see if lessons in one area may be applicable in others.[1] This research provides a point of departure for discussion of current proposals to improve nonproliferation arrangements and, in addition, may offer a useful framework for evaluating present and proposed regimes designed to limit proliferation in each area.

LESSONS FROM OTHER TREATY REGIMES

The Importance of a Formal Treaty

We agree with Robert Malott that unilateral action stands little chance of success in stemming proliferation.[2] Beyond that, it seems clear that an international regulatory regime will stand a better chance of achieving its objectives if it is based on a formal treaty, fully vested and ratified by national political processes, rather than more informal arrangements, such as suppliers' guidelines now applicable for trade in nuclear materials. Although a formal treaty is not a necessary condition for an international regime, "[t]reaties are designed, by long-standing convention, to raise the credibility of promises by staking national reputation on their adherence. Informal agreements have a more ambiguous nature. . . . They are chosen to avoid formal and visible national pledges; to avoid the political obstacles of ratification."[3]

It may seem somewhat hollow to argue that a treaty would be preferable when an informal agreement is all that can be secured. The history of U.S. nuclear policy is not very encouraging about the possibilities for concluding formal arms control treaties. Exacting substantive and procedural requirements have created serious obstacles to negotiation. If the Strategic Arms Reduction Treaty (START) enters into force, twenty years will separate this first treaty to reduce strategic nuclear weapons, from the Strategic Arms Limitation Treaty (SALT I), the first effort to limit them. U.S. officials and Congress have demanded both substantive accomplishments and stringent assurances of compliance before any negotiated agreement would stand a chance of ratification. The assumption has been that unless the United States could have a high degree of confidence in Soviet compliance with the letter and spirit of a treaty, it would be better off without constraints that might prove to be one-sided. While the Cold War has receded, the demand for assurance of compliance is not likely to be smaller in a multinational setting where the United States accepts restraints on producing and supplying, if not deploying, weapons.

The type of assurance that the United States and other countries as well may require in order to make the far-reaching commitments needed to curtail proliferation will be hard to achieve unless the international obligation is formalized and fully debated within signatory nations before going into effect. Although it may be possible and even wise to take some smaller steps beforehand, a formal treaty should be the goal. While there can be no empirical "proof" of Professor Louis Henkin's proposition that almost all nations comply with almost all their international obligations almost all of the time,[4] there is a history of positive experience, particularly in the arms control field, with little evidence of significant noncompliance, much less treaty breakdown.[5] To be sure, nations often honor lesser commitments, but a formal obligation creates a stronger presumption in favor of compliance, in part because of the national ratification process that it passes through. The high visibility makes deviation costly. A nation has staked its reputation by making a formal pledge. Moreover, a treaty establishes the basis for internal mechanisms for assuring adherence that less formal obligations do not. Domestic bureaucratic structures are put into place to help assure implementation. Constituencies for compliance may develop. National performance can be reviewed and critiqued, both at home and abroad, in the light of stated and binding norms.

Informal agreements or "soft law," as they are sometimes called, are often quicker to achieve, more flexible, less visible, simpler, and frequently all that can be negotiated.[6] Although they tend to work well, they have the defects of their virtues.[7] Because of the sensitivity and importance of the arms control area, informal agreements are necessarily suspect there. An agreement in principle, or even a more detailed agreement such as the Missile Technology Control Regime, may sometimes be an essential way station to "harder" legal arrangement. But if informal agreements are conceived as an alternative, rather than a step towards a more formal international nonproliferation regime, the ultimate objectives may remain elusive.

Treaty Evolution and Adaptability

For a regulatory treaty to endure and fulfill its objectives over time, it must be able to adapt to changes in technology and politics and respond effectively to experience under the treaty in action. The wisest treaty drafters cannot foresee the multiplicity of events and experience that may unfold. Treaty adaptation can take place in a variety of ways, but for present purposes it is important to distinguish between changes that require ratification through domestic political procedures and those that do not.[8]

Planning for Treaty Evolution. All treaties contain provisions for amendment, and in any case could be changed by agreement of the parties. The amendment process is generally cumbersome, however. And, of course, any amendment must be ratified in accordance with the formalities provided by domestic law. Like the process for amending the U.S. Constitution, these formal amendatory processes are infrequently invoked. Even when they are, they may end with a different set of states ratifying and thus bound by the amendment than were parties to the original treaty.

One response to these difficulties, which has had some success in the environmental field, is the "framework-protocol" format, in which the initial treaty is drafted in very general terms in anticipation of elaboration in a series of later more detailed agreements. This kind of evolving treaty is one response to the need for adaptation and flexibility in a regulatory regime. Although it does not avoid the burden of repeated negotiation and ratification of the protocols, these processes may be facilitated because continuous refinement and adaptation to changed circumstances, scientific or political, were contemplated when the framework treaty was first adopted.

The framework treaty may be general in nature or represent the lowest common denominator, but it is designed to evolve in its scope and coverage. For example, the Vienna Convention for the Protection of the Ozone Layer, adopted in 1985,[9] contained only general obligations for cooperation, data exchange, coordinated research, and the like. It established an annual Conference of the Parties as a mechanism for negotiating additional protocols containing more concrete obligations. In accordance with this procedure, the 1989 Montreal Protocol was adopted[10] and mandated a 50 percent cut in the consumption of chlorofluorocarbons (CFCs) by the year 2000. A further amendment to that protocol in June 1990,[11] responding to new scientific information about the danger of depletion of the ozone layer, requires a complete phaseout by 2000 and also provides for the regulation of additional ozone-depleting chemicals. The Geneva Convention on Long-Range Transboundary Air Pollution (LRTAP)[12] uses a similar format, as does the Barcelona Convention on the Protection of the Mediterranean Sea.[13] Framework conventions on global climate change and on biodiversity are now under negotiation in anticipation of the UN Conference on Environment and Development in Brazil in 1992.

Scientific uncertainty and the rapid expansion of knowledge that characterize these environmental treaties are not the only reasons for choosing a treaty that builds in an evolutionary process. The International Labor Organization (ILO)[14] was formed under a treaty sponsored by the League of Nations in the early 1920s, before a significant consensus on international labor standards had developed. The organization was a forum for the international discussion of labor standards and had the mission of negotiating specific treaties to that end, as the occasion seemed propitious. In its nearly 70 years, it has spawned over 180 treaties addressed to specific labor problems. The establishment of the organization, with national representation from business and labor organizations as well as government, created expectations that kept the process moving forward as a result of the political pressures and constituencies that were mobilized by the original treaty.

Weapons nonproliferation regimes display the same uncertainties as to the nature and speed of technological development, transfer, and production capability that mark the environmental regimes. There is also a similar difficulty in establishing a consensus for detailed and stringent regulation, coupled with a sense of urgency—particularly now—that *some* action must be taken. The framework-protocol model, while cumbersome, has the advantage of setting in motion an evolutionary process to a more stringent regime. The history of U.S. arms control policy records an insistence on increasing detail and elaborate assurances that has created extreme obstacles to negotiation. A hint of the evolutionary approach may be found in SALT I, which was an interim agreement pending more far-reaching constraints on offensive nuclear weapons, and in the review provisions of the anti-ballistic missile (ABM) and Nuclear Nonproliferation Treaty (NPT). In the nonproliferation field, an evolutionary model may be able to reach the objectives of effective constraints sooner and more assuredly than either informal agreements or fully developed, detailed treaties such as intermediate-range nuclear forces (INF), START, and conventional forces in Europe (CFE).[15]

Adaptation by Internal Regulation and Interpretation. In a number of regulatory treaties, the governing body is empowered to develop detailed regulations and to interpret or elaborate ambiguous treaty provisions without the requirement of formal amendment. Most of the provisions of the 1978 amendments to the International Monetary Fund (IMF) Agreement, including conditionality of drawings and surveillance of members' exchange rate policies, were codifications of decisions reached earlier by executive directors' interpretations of the original articles. The content and procedures of surveillance and the creation of enhanced surveillance in cases of debt rescheduling remain the product of executive directors' decisions.

The Council of the International Civil Aviation Organization (ICAO) has the power by two-thirds vote to make regulations covering the whole range of safety and operational requirements as well as concerning aircraft noise and emissions.[16] Although a member of the organization may opt out of a regulation of which it does not approve, the option is rarely exercised. The International Coffee Council, like the governing authorities of other international commodity agreements, adjusts quotas within specified limits.[17]

A frequently used technique in the environmental field and elsewhere is to place scientific and technical provisions in an annex or appendix that can be altered by vote of the parties without formal amendment of the treaty. The Convention on International Trade in Endangered Species[18] prohibits trade in products of endangered species on the "A list" but imposes less stringent regulation with respect to species on the "B list." The Conference of the Parties, by a special majority, is empowered to move species from one list to the other, subject to an opt-out provision. The exercise of this power in 1990 to move African elephants from the B list to the A list has resulted in a sharp decline in the international ivory trade.

In fact, in most international organizations established by regulatory treaties, the governing body has some area of policy discretion. Even the Standing Consultative Commission (SCC) set up by the ABM Treaty is assigned interpretative and rule-making tasks. In the exercise of this authority, the SCC negotiated an agreed interpretation of the prohibition in Article VI of the ABM Treaty against testing "in an ABM mode,"[19] and successfully elaborated procedures for dismantlement and destruction of prohibited weapons.[20] These techniques have been sparsely used, however, perhaps because of the extreme sensitivity of bilateral nuclear relations, and perhaps because of the provisions of Section 34 of the Arms Control and Disarmament Act, requiring that any agreement limiting U.S. armaments must be submitted for senatorial or congressional approval.

These basic modes of adaptation are not mutually exclusive. An evolving treaty will also benefit from mechanisms for adaptation and interpretation that permit adjustment of the treaty without formal amendment. Indeed, the Vienna Convention for the Protection of the Ozone Layer combines the anticipation of additional protocols with the authority of the Conference of the Parties to change the annexes identifying controlled substances.

Information and Transparency

Regulatory treaties characteristically generate information about the activities of the parties by requiring notifications, reports, disclosures, or submission to observation and inspection. This transparency helps to induce compliance in a variety of ways. It provides reassurance that the parties are complying. It permits coordinated policy planning to achieve treaty objectives. Formal, sometimes public review of such reports provides the basis for a wide-ranging array of negative reactions, political pressures, and shaming and embarrassing processes against a party that deviates from treaty norms, helping to bring the defecting party back into compliance.[21]

Arms control verification is the paradigmatic example of the quest for transparency, although some form of verifiability is an issue in most regulatory regimes. The level of acceptable intrusiveness of verification measures has evolved steadily from the tacit agreement to accept national technical means of verification (NTM) in the Limited Test Ban Treaty of 1963, through the cooperative measures of SALT I and II to the elaborate provisions for on-site inspection (OSI) in the INF Treaty, START, and CFE. The effectiveness of these verification systems depends in considerable part on the interplay of inspection measures and national intelligence activities. The experience in Iraq of the UN Special Commission/International Atomic Energy Agency (IAEA) inspection effort, established under UN Security Council Resolution 687, strikingly illustrates the importance of this interaction.[22]

Reporting and review requirements have been important in facilitating coordination of national planning under multilateral economic and environmental treaties. A prime example is the International Monetary Fund, which imposes elaborate reporting requirements, both for general policy purposes and as a basis for detailed review of members' performance. Based on this experience, the General Agreement on Tariffs and Trade (GATT) has recently instituted a process of periodic and comprehensive reviews of national trade policy.[23] In the environmental area, LRTAP was able to produce sharp reductions in sulphur dioxide emissions, a principal cause of acid rain in Europe, in part through the coordination of national research and monitoring programs provided for in the treaty.[24] Systematic reporting and review of national policies and plans within a treaty framework give each party a better opportunity to develop effective measures to meet the treaty requirements.

Furthermore, the governing organs of the treaty organization are often empowered to call upon reporting parties to explain and justify apparent departures from treaty norms. IMF and GATT have developed elaborate procedures to deal with deviations revealed by required disclosures. Acceptance of treaty norms implies standards that each party may need to apply against others in the future. And even in the absence of prescribed formal sanctions, a potential violator is well aware of the opportunities for more diffuse retaliation available to other members of the regime with a strong interest in preserving its integrity. As in the arms control case, there is no need to rely solely on the admissions of the parties to identify potential violations. Other sources of intelligence and information interacting with voluntary reporting can provide a fairly reliable basis for calling defectors to account.

In addition to initiating various forms of state-to-state retaliation, the transparency of the review process can generate pressure for compliance from national and international citizen groups, non-governmental organizations (NGOs), and technical specialists. A country has laid its reputation on the line by entering into a treaty, and although Saddam Hussein may be an exception, national leaders are susceptible to embarrassment and shaming if the state has demonstrably failed to live up to its obligations. Disclosure tends to provide a basis for mobilization of political constituencies both on the national level and internationally. The resulting shaming process can be surprisingly effective. Human rights treaties may have been signed cynically by totalitarian rulers in Latin America and Eastern Europe, but in both regions the international treaty norms catalyzed internal resistance and external support from monitoring groups that brought about far-reaching changes.[25]

Reporting and voluntary disclosure have been increasingly included in bilateral arms control agreements as well. SALT II, the INF Treaty, START, and CFE all require the parties to declare weapons and facilities in categories covered by the agreement. Each provides for an agreed data base to be updated periodically by the parties. Advance notification of weapons tests and troop movements are a familiar feature of recent arms control agreements. Again, the well-understood fact that these reports will be checked by the other party's national intelligence and NTM gives a strong motivation for accuracy. All nonproliferation regimes will have to rely increasingly on such reporting requirements.

We do not regard formal sanctions or incentives as techniques that are likely to improve treaty compliance. Our research shows that formal sanctions are almost never authorized by regulatory treaties. The UN and Organization of American States (OAS) Charters are the only exceptions of which we are aware. Even then, the sanctions provided have only been imposed in cases of transgression of central treaty norms so flagrant as to render the violator something of a pariah state. Incentives involving the transfer of funds present more practical than theoretical obstacles but may be most useful in the area of technical assistance to increase internal capability for second level enforcement, as discussed above. This is not to say that various forms of retaliatory action *not explicitly provided for in the treaty* are not crucial in securing compliance. Such "diffuse reciprocity" is pervasive in relations among treaty partners, and nations find ways—often exquisitely calibrated—to express pleasure or displeasure at the way other nations have fulfilled their obligations under the treaty. The clear understanding that such diffuse reciprocity or retaliation does occur makes disclosure such a powerful tool.[26]

Second-Level Enforcement

The bilateral arms control agreements with which we are most familiar are direct limitations on governmental behavior. Although there may be some cases of bureaucratic foul-up, the decision to comply or not to comply with such a treaty is necessarily and unambiguously a governmental decision. A nonproliferation regime, however, is designed ultimately to regulate not only the acts of governments but also the conduct of non-state actors—producers, traders, and others who possess enabling technology and know-how. In countries with a significant private sector, the regime can be implemented only if the state enacts and enforces internal legislation regulating the conduct of these private corporations and individuals. Much of the leakage in current nonproliferation efforts occurs as a result of violation by private enterprises and individuals of state laws controlling exports.

In a broadly inclusive nonproliferation regime, states will vary widely in their capacity to draft effective internal legislation and even more widely in their ability to enforce it. Under these circumstances, an explicit mission must be to enhance the internal capacities of participating governments where that proves necessary. These efforts could usefully include technical assistance in the form of model laws, enforcement assistance, and even some financial aid to help build internal enforcement capability.

The ILO again provides a pertinent model. The reporting and review procedure focuses primarily on the party's enactment and enforcement of legislation embodying the agreed labor standards. In addition, the Organization adopts recommendations for national action, follows through to see whether the recommendations are implemented, and provides technical assistance to its members for that purpose. Similarly, recent environmental treaties have stressed technical assistance for compliance with treaty standards. This feature is prominent in the Mediterranean Action Plan under the Barcelona Convention. The Montreal Protocol on the ozone layer establishes a multilateral fund to be used to assist developing nations to comply and to defray the costs of compliance. Even the more sophisticated European members of LRTAP rely on common research and standard-setting to assist in national enforcement of sulphur dioxide emissions limits.

REGULATION OF PROLIFERATION

To the extent that the focus is on keeping peace in the Middle East, a comprehensive approach addressing both political and security concerns seems to make sense since both factors are so intertwined.[27] We do not advocate any specific priorities or "baskets" for what is certainly a highly charged and volatile process of agenda setting. Nevertheless, nonproliferation is a critical aspect of achieving security in the Middle East and must be addressed at some point.

Second, it also seems clear that the full range of weapons that can produce vast destruction are to some extent interrelated. How many times has it been said that chemical weapons are the poor nation's nuclear weapons? A negotiation strategy that fails to address these linkages is unlikely to succeed. Nevertheless, each group of weapons has different characteristics, and each regime is in a different stage of negotiation or realization. Even though linkage issues should not be ignored, the quest for effective implementation of a nonproliferation treaty may require different emphases and different structures for different weapons categories.

Third, in this paper, we address international nonproliferation treaties that apply universally, not to the Middle East alone, although their effectiveness in that region may be the testing case. We recognize that possibilities for less inclusive measures—formal, informal, interim, or permanent among states in the region or among supplier states—if accomplished, would help to defuse tensions and assure that the broader universal treaties will be effective. Such possibilities should not be neglected, and some are noted in the discussion below.

Nuclear Proliferation

The nuclear nonproliferation regime is a complex edifice of formal and informal arrangements. Its centerpiece is the Non-Proliferation Treaty, in force since 1970. It includes as well the IAEA statute, regional instruments like the Treaty of Tlatlelco and the South Pacific Nuclear Free Zone, bilateral treaties between non-NPT parties and their nuclear suppliers, and the informal guidelines drawn up by the London Club of nuclear supplier states. Taken together these instruments comprise an international regulatory regime that even its detractors admit has had a distinct measure of success. The early post–World War II fears of uncontrollable nuclear proliferation have not been realized, and even conservative estimates of the 1950s have turned out to have been pessimistic. Membership in the NPT has grown to 140 parties. South Africa has recently agreed to join, and two of the remaining five threshold nations, Argentina and Brazil, have indicated that they will submit to inspections, although they have not yet agreed to sign the treaty. Iraq, which although an NPT member was thought to be the most serious proliferation threat, has had much if not all of its nuclear capacity destroyed during and after the Gulf War. And the two pre-1968 nuclear weapons states that were nonsigners, China and France, have now indicated that they will adhere to the treaty.

The debate about the effectiveness of IAEA safeguards has intensified in the wake of the difficulties experienced by the UN Special Commission/IAEA efforts in Iraq. It now appears that Iraq had enriched uranium as well as equipment usable for enrichment that it had not declared in accordance with its IAEA obligations and that had not been discovered by intelligence sources.[28] Despite public ideas to the contrary, the IAEA can hardly be blamed for not discovering *clandestine military* nuclear activities when its mission is confined to monitoring *declared peaceful* facilities and materials. The professionalism and expertise of IAEA inspectorate staff constitute a strong base on which to build improvements in the existing regime.

Challenge inspections. What the Iraq experience does reveal is the need to equip the IAEA with the authority to conduct challenge inspections. The problem of doing so requires a comparative analysis of the methods of treaty adaptation discussed above. Essentially, the methods available are amendment of the NPT, changes in the safeguards procedures, or reliance on UN authority, as in the case of Iraq.

Amendment of the NPT involves even more than the normal difficulties of the amendment process. At a Review Conference scheduled for 1995, the parties must decide whether to make the treaty of indefinite duration, to extend it for a certain time or to let it lapse. Previous Review Conferences have been a forum for confrontations between less developed country (LDC) non-nuclear weapons states and the nuclear "haves," including demands for the conclusion of a Comprehensive Test Ban Treaty and healthy increases in technical assistance for the peaceful use of nuclear energy. Whether the challenge inspection amendment was considered at a special diplomatic conference or at the Review Conference itself, it would be held hostage to these issues. If the amendment were adopted, some of the opponents would likely refuse to ratify so that it would be ineffective against them. In any event, it would not apply to nonsigners of the NPT, among which are most of the most worrisome cases.

The present safeguard procedures were developed and adopted by the Board of Governors of the IAEA without legislative ratification. They are disseminated to the members in information circulars (INFCIRCs). Safeguard procedures applying to NPT parties, which have accepted "full-scope" safeguards, are contained in INFCIRC 153 and are more far-reaching than those applicable to nonsigners, where safeguards are applicable only in accordance with agreement between the customer and supplier state. The question is whether challenge inspections can be authorized by a simple revision of INFCIRC 153, which can be accomplished by a vote of the governing board. There is some material on the point. In response to interest expressed at the last Review Conference, the IAEA conducted a study of whether it is authorized under the present procedures to conduct "special inspections" or demand access to additional locations "when it has a bona fide reason for doing so." The preliminary results of the study, as reported by Director General Hans Blix to the governing board, concluded that the IAEA had such authority and that "some special inspections have in fact been undertaken where routine inspections were deemed insufficient."[29] These facts lay a strong predicate for the argument that challenge inspections could be expressly authorized by changing the safeguard procedures. But the case is not open and shut. No doubt countries that would oppose an amendment to the treaty would dispute this interpretation and would oppose any action pursuant to it. On the other hand, such opposition might be more easily overcome in the relative seclusion of a Board of Governors meeting than in a highly visible diplomatic conference for amending the treaty. A change in INFCIRC 153, unlike a treaty amendment, would be applicable to all NPT members, but like an amendment, would not affect nonsigners.

UN Security Council Resolution 687 requested the UN Special Commission and the IAEA "to carry out immediate on-site inspection of Iraq's nuclear capabilities based on Iraq's declaration and the designation of any additional locations by the Special Commission."[30] Apart from the Iraq case, it is arguable that the Security Council might find the existence of an alleged clandestine nuclear capability "a threat to the peace" under

Chapter VII of the Charter and order the offending state to submit to an inspection on pain of economic or military sanctions under Articles 41 and 42. In this connection, the General Assembly, in 1987, requested the secretary general to investigate allegations by a member state of the use of chemical, biological, or toxin weapons and to send an investigator to the territory of the suspected state.[31] This mandate, cloaked in a Security Council resolution, might be extended to clandestine nuclear facilities maintained in violation of international obligations. The political problems associated with such *ad hoc* or advance authorizations, not to mention the veto, to say nothing of the legal issues, would undermine the reliability of this approach.

None of the three modalities is wholly satisfactory. On balance, the best course might be to try first a revision of INFCIRC 153, reserving an attempt at treaty amendment as a second string to the bow. In any case, the Security Council remains a possibility in particularly threatening cases.

Supplier restraints. The Nuclear Suppliers Group (NSG), comprised of the major Western nuclear-capable countries, operates under a set of informal guidelines identifying sensitive items that should be exported, if at all, only under license. Each country is responsible for enforcing the guidelines through its own export control laws. Despite considerable U.S. prodding, the NSG has not agreed to require all nations with which it trades to submit to full-scope safeguards. Nor has it agreed on standards for internal legislation, including criminal sanctions for corporate or individual violators, to ensure effective second-level enforcement.

The NSG is similar in many ways to the Coordinating Committee for Multilateral Export Controls (COCOM), which was also an informal arrangement (among North Atlantic Treaty Organization (NATO) countries—except Iceland—Australia, and Japan) for coordinating national controls on exports of militarily sensitive items to communist countries. In the early days of the Cold War, COCOM achieved considerable success, especially with respect to goods with direct and obvious military significance. In later times, and especially for dual-use technology, its accomplishments have been debatable, and it has often become a bone of contention between the United States and its allies.

If the NSG was indeed built on the COCOM model, the effort may have been ill-advised. COCOM had its greatest success when the Western perception of the Soviet threat was at its most vivid, and U.S. "hegemony" was at its height. The NSG has neither such a menacing target nor such a powerful leader. Moreover, COCOM's informality and secrecy were designed in part to avoid the political problems that some of the European governments would have faced if COCOM's list of non-exportables had become a matter of public debate, a disadvantage that is not present in the case of nuclear export controls. Thus, it may be time to consider a more formal arrangement for the NSG, perhaps as a committee of the IAEA, with which it has cooperated closely in the past.[32] Under such an arrangement, it would be easier to bring in new suppliers, including the Soviet Union, who were not members of the London Club (as the NSG is sometimes called). It would even be possible, if not necessary, to extend the membership to recipient states, thus reducing the sense that the NSG is little more than another device for imposing the will of the nuclear "haves" on the "have nots." Such a course, by increasing the legitimacy of the entire process, might more than make up for any increased friction in day-to-day operations.

A Middle East Nuclear-free Zone. The existing nuclear nonproliferation regime accommodates special regional arrangements. The Treaty of Tlatlelco creates a Latin American nuclear-free zone, and by the Treaty of Rarotonga, the countries of the South Pacific Forum established a nuclear-free zone for their region. The European Atomic Energy Community (Euratom) countries have a joint safeguarding arrangement with the IAEA. A similar regional approach has been suggested for the Middle East. Indeed, Security Council Resolution 687 states that the destruction of the Iraqi nuclear capability will be a first step toward this end,[33] and the director general of the IAEA has offered its services to monitor such an arrangement.[34]

With the elimination of the Iraqi threat, Israel remains the only putatively nuclear-capable state in the region, and it seems unlikely that it would agree to a full-fledged nuclear-free zone except in the context of a general settlement, providing reliable assurances against Arab chemical and biological weapons.

Nevertheless, President Bush has made an initial proposal in that direction. On May 29, 1991, he called upon all states in the region to implement a verifiable ban on the production and acquisition of weapons-usable nuclear materials. He has reiterated the need for all nonsignatories to accede to the NPT and urged the "eventual creation" of a nuclear-free zone. Israel itself has endorsed the concept as an ultimate goal, as have all the Arab states in the region.[35] The UN secretary-general published a report in October 1990, "Establishing a Nuclear Free Zone in the Middle East,"[36] without objection from Israel, which had reviewed drafts of the report. The report reiterates that Israel had endorsed the concept and suggests several significant steps to that goal. One step would be for Israel to place the Dimona reactor (which is, in any case, nearing the end of its useful life) under IAEA safeguards. This would not eliminate weapons-grade material already produced nor weapons already manufactured, but it would begin to work toward transparency in the region on nuclear matters. Among the other confidence-building measures recommended by the report, the most interesting may be the suggestion that each nation in the region should commit not to test a nuclear device. While, in theory, untested nuclear weapons are usable, all existing nuclear weapon states have insisted on testing new weapons before deployment.

The importance of such measures should not be underestimated. Even tangential commitments to IAEA safeguards, by Israel, and any additional transparency that might be achieved, for example, by unilateral declarations about the ways that nuclear materials are processed and stockpiled, will begin to unfreeze a situation that has long defied change.

Chemical Weapons Proliferation

The Geneva Protocol of 1925, negotiated in the aftermath of World War I, prohibits the *use* of chemical weapons in warfare.[37] The prohibition held during World War II, although both superpowers began to manufacture and store chemical weapons during the war and to train their armies to use them and to defend against them. While talks have been under way since the late 1960s, for the past ten years, an *ad hoc* committee of the UN Disarmament Commission, consisting of forty states and additional observers, has been laboring at the daunting task of trying to create a chemical treaty regime that would ban the development, production, possession, transfer, or use of chemical weapons or precursors. The committee is close to a final draft of a comprehensive Chemical Weapons Convention.[38] The draft document, over two hundred pages in length, has been heavily negotiated, and if adopted, will set a standard of transparency not heretofore realized in arms control or any other area of international regulation.

An *Annex on Chemicals*[39] lists the items to be prohibited or controlled and establishes guidelines for adding or deleting items. Additional annexes specify procedures for declaring prohibited weapons and storage and manufacturing facilities.[40] Complete destruction of these items would begin within a year of entry into force and would be completed within ten years. Still other annexes establish "regimes" of varying stringency for substances that are dangerous but not prohibited.[41] A *Protocol on Inspection Procedures* details elaborate reporting and verification requirements, including "any time any place" challenge inspections, to be carried out by a highly professional technical secretariat. But a new proposal submitted by the members of the Australia Group in July 1991 backtracks on the original provisions and waters them down considerably.[42]

The complexity and level of detail of the draft convention raises the issue of adaptability in acute form. Article XIII of the draft sets out the usual cumbersome process for amending the convention, including its annexes and protocols.[43] The article also contains a special procedure by which certain provisions can be changed by a two-thirds vote of the conference of parties. Unfortunately, there is no agreement on the provisions to which the special procedure applies.[44] Apparently it can be used for additions or deletions to the lists in the *Annex on Chemicals*, though not for changes in the guidelines.[45] A note to the *Protocol on Inspection Procedures* states that "the question of amendment procedures to be applied to the provisions contained in the Protocol require[s] further discussion."[46] It is absolutely essential that the special amendment procedures apply to all or at least most of the provisions of the annexes and protocol, or the convention will choke in a jungle of unmanageable regulatory detail.

There has been discussion of the establishment of a "system of incentives for those who joined a chemical weapons ban and penalties for those who did not."[47] As we have noted, formal sanctions and incentives are rarely used in regulatory regimes. The attempt to negotiate them would further delay the completion of the convention. The objective should be left to the processes of "diffuse reciprocity" outside the framework of the convention.

The Gulf War has heightened concerns about the speed of the negotiating process. Again, the Middle East is the major hot spot. It is thought that Iran, Iraq, Israel, Egypt, Syria, and Libya already have chemical capability—indeed, Egypt is believed to have used chemical weapons in Yemen in the 1960s. The only other actual use of chemical weapons occurred in the region in the Iran-Iraq War. That event may have already weakened any self-enforcing moral repugnance against further use of the weapons. Although they may not be very effective on the battlefield, chemical weapons are a terrifying prospect for concentrated urban areas of the Middle East.[48]

The sense of time urgency in preventing proliferation is intensified not only because of the widespread possession of chemical weapons, but also because of the low threshold for acquisition, development, and production. It is extremely difficult to ascertain with precision the existence of a capability to produce chemical warfare agents in view of the overlap with legitimate civilian functions, such as the production and use of pesticides, fertilizers, and pharmaceuticals. The sources of supply of chemical weapons precursors are extraordinarily broad, with control of the trade in precursors, as well as the technology of production, remaining elusive. Many nations have strengthened export controls, but no one believes the tide has been stemmed.[49]

In the meantime, the United States and nineteen other Western states have formed the Australia Group along the lines of COCOM and the NSG. It has created a list of fifty chemical warfare agents and precursors to be subjected to national export controls, as well as guidelines to sensitize industry to transactions that might contribute to weapons activities. Additional guidance for second-level enforcement would be useful, as members develop laws, including criminal sanctions against internal violators. A UN register of arms sales, discussed below, could also include chemical and biological toxin sales, thus increasing transparency and permitting national and transnational mobilization of NGOs and concerned citizens.[50]

There has been good cooperation within the U.S. chemical industry. The Chemical Manufacturers Association has endorsed the Chemical Weapons Convention, provided technical assistance to U.S. negotiators, and created self-policing mechanisms.[51] Business Executives for National Security (BENS) has issued guidelines intended to serve as a further self-policing mechanism and constituted itself as a business NGO in the proliferation area.

Biological Weapons

The Biological Weapons Convention (BWC) entered into force in 1975.[52] It has had several review conferences, and another is scheduled in 1991. At the time the BWC was negotiated, the moral stigma involved in using biological weapons, as well as their questionable military value, seemed sufficient to assure its effectiveness. Moreover, there had been little experience with verification in arms control treaties and little tolerance for the degree of intrusiveness that has become acceptable in the late 1980s. Conditions have changed on both counts. According to U.S. intelligence, at least ten nations are developing or actually producing biological agents or toxins.[53] Previous review conferences have strengthened the treaty regime by instituting annual data reporting requirements. We have already noted the UN General Assembly request to the secretary-general to investigate reports of the use of chemical, biological, or toxin weapons.[54]

Many experts including a Federation of American Scientists Working Group have proposed the draft Chemical Weapons Convention as a model for treaty-based verification of prohibitions on biological and toxin weapons.[55] The procedures would be tailored to the special problems created by production that is almost entirely dual use in nature. These experts would place principal reliance on inspections, including challenge inspections, with due sensitivity to proprietary information and special precautions to prevent the outbreak of disease.

Because of the relative ease and low cost of production of chemical weapons, especially when compared to nuclear weapons, universality of adherence has become increasingly important. Several countries have either not signed, or signed but not ratified, the treaty including, in the Middle East, Egypt, Syria, and Israel. In April, Iraq deposited the instruments of ratification as it had been urged to do under UN Resolution 687. As in other areas, unilateral and cooperative political pressures can be brought to bear on most nations that have thus far failed to join. It is also important to be sure that each signatory has the legal models and technical assistance to make second-level enforcement effective.

Missile Proliferation

Recognition has been growing that in order to curb the proliferation of weapons of mass destruction, limits must be imposed on ballistic missile proliferation. This relationship was visible on the world's TV screens during the Gulf War. Fortunately, the Scud attacks on Israel and Saudi Arabia were militarily ineffective. But awareness of technology ratcheting upward and of the potential for use with nonconventional warheads has drawn international attention even more sharply to this type of delivery system. Although air-breathing platforms may be more capable and longer in range, the ease with which missiles and the technology to make them can be acquired, used, maintained, and concealed has made them increasingly attractive to smaller powers.

Janne Nolan's book, *The Trappings of Power*,[56] first presented to the Aspen Strategy Group in summary form in 1989, strikingly reveals the extent of the spread of these weapons, the political dilemmas it creates, and the need for effective controls. A single chart portrays the complexity and interrelatedness of major industrial and developing country suppliers of ballistic missiles and technology, and the availability of alternative sources of supply.[57]

Even after the Gulf War, it will be difficult to stem the tide. First, ballistic missiles and the technology to produce them are already vastly diffused. William Webster testified in 1990 that at least six Third World countries would have missiles with ranges up to 5,500 km by the end of the century. Eight Middle East nations—Israel, Syria, Saudi Arabia, Libya, Iran, Iraq, Egypt, and Yemen—have tested or deployed several varieties of missiles. Each of these countries has some indigenous production capability or more than one source of supply.[58]

Second, although the United States, the former Soviet Union, Western Europe, and China have been the major suppliers, second-tier suppliers, such as Argentina, Brazil, and North and South Korea, have appeared on the scene. They must be brought into a regime to ensure its effectiveness. Even so, with multiple sources of supply and recipients eager to acquire missiles, a suppliers regime alone is unlikely to be effective, particularly where trade is lucrative, and the need for hard currency remains high.

Third, the taboo or element of moral opprobrium that operates against nuclear, chemical, and biological weapons does not apply to missile proliferation. Ballistic missile technology is important to space activities as well as to high-technology conventional weapons, and it plays a role in nation defense, as evidenced by the actions of Egypt, Israel, Saudi Arabia, and Syria since the Gulf War. It may be easier after the Gulf War to mobilize behind export controls, but as Nolan points out, restrictions by industrial powers may in fact spur regional and Third World collaboration.

The response thus far has been the Missile Technology Control Regime (MTCR), established in 1987, an even more attenuated version of COCOM than the NSG. Like them, it is an informal suppliers agreement that produces agreed guidelines for the application of national export controls. Its membership has doubled to sixteen, but it does not yet include two major missile suppliers, Russia and China. The Soviet Union had agreed to join this suppliers group, but thus far, China has done little more than avow a policy of restraint, while marketing a new generation of missiles. The regime has identified some critical issues, such as accurate guidance systems, which require an advanced technological infrastructure. It has been credited with some success in slowing diffusion and encouraging greater internal controls, for example in West Germany, where private firms were engaged in supplying Iraq and Libya, and in discouraging advanced programs, such as the Condor II missile system, which was being developed by Argentina, Egypt, and Iraq. It has focused attention on the dangers of surface-to-surface missiles, and the advisability of a moratorium. But the MTCR is only a beginning.

An inclusive suppliers' agreement is a logical next step, and it will require diplomatic sensitivity and coordination. It is not clear to what extent the United States and the members of the European Community (EC) members have exerted pressure on China and second tier suppliers thus far. There is undoubtedly some combination of trade, debt rescheduling, financial aid, and military assistance that could bring most of the essential nations into the regime.

Yet if our proposition that nations will tend to take formal treaty obligations more seriously is accepted, an effort to metamorphose the MTCR into a treaty, with a secretariat in place to assure implementation, will be needed. Nolan argues the contrary: "[T]o the extent that the MTCR has been successful . . . its success has derived from its modest and consensual nature, and from the fact that it was negotiated outside the glare of the international spotlight."[59] But modest objectives and insulation from public view have not thus far dispelled the ambivalence about ballistic missiles or the reluctance of states to face up to the dangers of the proliferation of missiles and associated technology. The "international spotlight" (and national visibility) may be beneficial in helping to mobilize public opinion and NGO activity.

A treaty regime will have to include recipients and potential recipients as members. This expansion may occur incrementally or as part of regional peace efforts or as a broader framework treaty on conventional weapons, which is discussed below. It will be very difficult to avoid the confrontation between haves and have nots that has plagued the NPT unless the recipients have a say in the regulatory process and are persuaded that they too may reap benefits from retarding the transfer of the most dangerous missile platforms. A missile nonproliferation treaty could preserve the flexibility and adaptability of the MTCR by listing specific components and technology to be regulated in annexes that could be adjusted by the parties without formal amendment.

Because of the inherent difficulties of accomplishing an effective treaty regime for missiles in a short time, interim efforts to increase transparency are worth consideration so long as they are not seen as the final goal. A number of suggestions with merit have surfaced and are now under discussion. At the recent London Summit, the Group of Seven or G-7 (United States, Canada, Great Britain, France, Italy, Germany, and Japan) endorsed the concept of a UN registry of arms sales, mentioned earlier, which would provide monitoring and serve as a focal point for mobilization of political and technical communities. National export controls, particularly of dual-use technology, should provide for end-use disclosure, although such undertakings could not be verified as reliably as under a treaty. Again cooperation in the creation and dissemination of model national laws would enhance national capability and improve second-level enforcement since a large number of business entities are involved in missile proliferation worldwide.

An even more politically sensitive alternative has been suggested—a special missile suppliers club for the Middle East. In our view, this might be useful if it is conceived as part of an arrangement that would ultimately cover the transfer of all dangerous and provocative weapons, including conventional. This seems to be the general direction of recent US policy. Such an arrangement could hardly be seriously considered unless its obligations were embodied in the "hard law" of a binding treaty.

Conventional Weapons Proliferation

There is little consensus about the control of conventional arms transfers, either within the United States or among its allies. Arms transfers have been conceived by both the United States and NATO as an instrument of foreign policy, but the Iran-Iraq and Gulf wars have shown that the weapons transferred can outlast the policies that they were designed to promote and wind up in unfriendly hands. Europeans had to face their own weapons in the Gulf.

U.S. policies have been contradictory, confusing, often mischaracterized and only recently the subject of public scrutiny. Again the Middle East is the principal arena, accounting for two-thirds of all international arms sales from 1983–88.[60] In the wake of the Gulf War, the United States has promised more than $20 billion in military sales and assistance to its Arab allies and Israel. The Gulf states have refused to accept a U.S. ground presence in the region. Instead, they have chosen to attend to their own security, state by state. The Gulf states can pay for their weapons with oil revenues. Israel, unsurprisingly, has demanded more assistance in the form of both weapons and support for its sophisticated defense industry. Leslie Gelb has pointed out the consequences in his pithy article, "Arms Sales Heaven."[61]

While no threat of the proportions of the prewar Saddam Hussein is now looming, circumstances could change in short order. Historic rivalries have not diminished. An arms buildup now justified as defensive may be perceived as a heightened threat by neighboring states or may turn into one with a shift in the political winds. The result will be another turn in the spiral of the regional arms race.

Another possibility is that the Gulf states might be encouraged to move gradually into some sort of security coalition, perhaps under a revived Gulf Cooperation Council or some other organization. However, while enhanced security cooperation in the Gulf, and indeed among all Arab states in the Middle East, might work to diminish historic rivalries and provide greater political stability, it would create a severe policy dilemma for the United States. For the regional forces to be effective, they would need modern weapons in substantial numbers and years of joint training and command and control integration, which the United States would be called upon to supply. Yet the resulting military capability would represent a nightmarish threat to Israel under the present political circumstances. The United States, of course, does not want to see Israel forced to become more of a militarized fortress than it already is, moving to protect itself further with arms and settlements in the occupied territories. But in the face of an effective Arab coalition force, there may be no other way to provide Israel with adequate military reassurance. Unless there is simultaneous progress in political negotiations between Arabs and Israelis, such a development would be highly destabilizing to the Middle East as a whole.

Yet U.S. policy remains schizophrenic, with the administration asking for cooperation and guidelines to control the proliferation of sophisticated conventional arms, while at the same time providing the matériel that increases proliferation in the Middle East. It is a measure of this confusion that the administration's attempt to repeal the restrictions on Export-Import Bank loans in support of arms sales was opposed in Congress precisely because Israel was included among the nations to whom loan guarantees would be provided, thus fueling the Middle East arms race.

The Middle East is only one of the policy dilemmas facing the United States. Reduced military budgets have increased the pressure to defray costs by foreign military sales. An international sales program would seem to be necessary to support a robust domestic industrial base and technological progress while maintaining cutbacks in the defense budgets.

It is becoming increasingly clear that the United States does not have control over the level of arms sales in the Middle East or anywhere else. With the winding down of the Cold War, there is large military overcapacity worldwide. The United States is in competition, not only with friendly nations, but also with the Soviet Union and Eastern Europe whose need for hard currency may now override any foreign policy objectives held heretofore. And new suppliers, some of them from developing countries, are continuously entering the market.

Despite the new competition, the United States, NATO, Europe, and the Soviet Union accounted for just over 80 percent of arms transfers in 1988. The United States exported $14.3 billion in arms, while NATO Europe accounted for another $4.1 billion.[62] Cooperation with allies in an effort to increase their defense industrial base has been a cornerstone of U.S. defense policy, but it has also undermined any possibility for control over international transfers. In 1988, the United States transferred production technology of approximately seventy major weapons systems. NATO, Europe, and the Soviet Union matched that.[63] Ironically, this policy—sensible enough during the Cold War—was to a certain extent in conflict with the policy of exporting weapon systems to allies to help keep unit costs down.

These policy issues and dilemmas have not been sorted out domestically yet. Clearly, there will have to be some internal reconciliation before any serious moves to international cooperation can be made. The United States cannot ask restraint of its allies, much less other nations, if it will not abide by the same restraints.

Clearly, a policy of unilateral restraint would be both ineffective and harmful to the U.S. defense industry. Any effort to limit transfers of conventional arms must be multilateral. And for the reasons repeatedly noted above, this policy must include buyers as well as sellers. No agreement or regime can hold unless it is acknowledged as legitimate by those who have the responsibility for the defense of their nations.

It goes without saying that there is no consensus on an all-embracing treaty to regulate international arms transfers. At the same time, there is a general recognition that all these sophisticated weapons, if generally available, can create mischief abroad as well as harm at home. In these circumstances, we think the subject is a prime candidate for the framework-protocol approach described earlier in this paper. We cannot, of course, provide anything more than a sketch of such an approach and how it might evolve, but we hope we can say enough to suggest its potential.

The parties to the framework convention would undertake generally to cooperate in efforts to limit excessive arms transfers. As a first concrete step, the convention could establish the registry of international arms sales called for by the G-7 in its recent London meeting. Beyond that, it would provide for periodic high-level meetings to review the situation and suggest necessary actions.

Although the framework convention should be envisioned as universal, the subsequent protocols need not be. As already suggested, the MTCR might well be brought under this umbrella and gradually enlarge its membership. Regional limitation arrangements or confidence and security building measures (CSBM) could be negotiated as protocols to the framework agreement, drawing on the experience and capability of an established international secretariat. States that agreed among themselves to higher standards of restraint than those generally applicable could do so, with others adhering to the protocol when they were ready. Particularly dangerous weapons systems or technologies could be addressed in separate protocols when a workable consensus became available.

The framework agreement would at least be a recognition of the seriousness of the problem. Yet the evolutionary approach would afford time to sort out domestic political problems in the United States and elsewhere. It would put both eager recipients and unruly suppliers on notice. Meanwhile the organization would provide a serious forum for discussion of arms transfer issues and would continue its efforts to promote transparency and public understanding in the field. In this way, the foundation of experience, political acceptability, and public support necessary for a more comprehensive attack might gradually evolve.

CONCLUSION

Manipulation of treaty techniques and approaches will not solve all the problems of proliferation. The security issues in the Middle East are substantive and require substantive political, economic and military solutions. The problem of weapons proliferation in all its dimensions is inextricably intertwined with these other issues.

However, proliferation questions cannot necessarily await the slow maturing of these political solutions. Proliferation is part of the problem and needs to be addressed promptly, if need be, in different forums and with differing casts of characters. If technique will not solve everything in those forums, an understanding of the approaches that have worked in other international regulatory regimes may provide guidance to get over some of the rough spots.

ENDNOTES

1. For a fuller discussion of this research, see Abram Chayes and Antonia Handler Chayes, "Adjustment and Compliance Processes in International Regulatory Regimes," in Jessica Matthews, ed., *Preserving the Global Environment: The Challenge of Shared Leadership* (1991), pp. 280–308; and Chayes and Chayes, "Compliance Without Enforcement: State Behavior under Regulatory Treaties," *Negotiation Journal*, July 1991, pp. 311–330.
2. Robert H. Malott, "New Approaches to Arms Export Policy," address to the Center for the Study of the Presidency, *Fortune* Symposium on the Presidency, Washington, DC, June 26, 1991.
3. Charles Lipson, "Why Are Some International Agreements Informal?" *International Organization* Vol. 45, No. 4 (Autumn 1991), pp. 501–511.
4. Louis Henkin, *International Law: Politics, Values and Functions* (1990), p. 69, citing his earlier work *How Nations Behave: Law and Foreign Policy*, 2nd ed. (New York, NY: Columbia University Press, 1979), p. 47.
5. See Chayes and Chayes, "Living Under a Treaty Regime: Compliance, Interpretation, and Adoption," Antonia Handler Chayes and Paul Doty, eds., *Defending Deterrence: Managing the ABM Regime into the 21st Century* (Washington, DC: Pergamon-Brassey, 1989), pp. 197–216. See also Gloria Duffy, *Compliance and the Future of Arms Control: Report of a Project Sponsored by the Center for International Security and Arms Control, Stanford University, and Global Outlook* (1988), especially pp. 17–29.
6. Lipson, "Why Are Some International Agreements Informal?" p. 518.
7. Ibid., p. 534.
8. Chayes and Chayes, "Adjustment and Compliance Processes in International Regulatory Regimes," p. 282.
9. See the Convention for the Protection of the Ozone Layer, Done at Vienna on March 22, 1985, *International Legal Materials*, Vol. 26 (1987), p. 1516.
10. See the Protocol on Substances that Deplete the Ozone Layer, Done at Montreal on September 16, 1987, *International Legal Materials*, Vol. 26 (1987), p. 1541.
11. See the Report of the Second Meeting of the Parties to the Montreal Protocol, United Nations Environment Program, UNEP/OzL.Pro.2/3, June 29, 1990.
12. See the Convention on Long-Range Transboundary Air Pollution, Done at Geneva on November 13, 1979, *International Legal Materials*, Vol. 18 (1979), p. 1442.
13. See the Convention for the Protection of the Mediterranean Sea Against Pollution, Signed at Barcelona on February 16, 1976, in M.J. Bowman and D.J. Harris, *Multilateral Treaties: Index and Current Status* (London: Butterworths, 1984), p. 406.
14. *Constitution of the International Labour Organization and Standing Orders of the International Labour Conference* (Geneva, ILO, 1982).
15. See the Interim Agreement Between the United States of America and the Union of Soviet Socialist Republics on Certain Measures With Respect to

the Limitation of Strategic Offensive Arms, Signed at Moscow on May 26, 1972, Article VIII, paragraph 2; the Treaty Between the United States of America and the Union of Soviet Socialist Republics on the Limitation of Anti-Ballistic Missile Systems, Signed at Moscow on May 26, 1972, Article XIV, paragraph 2; and the Treaty on the Non-Proliferation of Nuclear Weapons, Signed at Washington, London, Moscow on July 1, 1968, Article VIII, paragraph 3, United States Arms Control and Disarmament Agency (U.S. ACDA), *Arms Control and Disarmament Agreements* (Washington, DC: United States Government Printing Office, 1975).

16. See the Convention on International Civil Aviation, Signed at Chicago on December 7, 1944, Chapter XX, *Treaty Series/United Nations* Vol. 15 (1948), p. 296.
17. See the International Coffee Agreement, September 16, 1982, Misc. 4(1983), Article 45, Cmnd 8810.
18. See the International Convention on International Trade in Endangered Species of Wild Fauna and Flora, Signed on March 3, 1973, in Bowman and Harris, *Multilateral Treaties: Index and Current Status*, p. 370.
19. See the Treaty Between the United States of America and the Union of Soviet Socialist Republics on the Limitation of Anti-Ballistic Missile Systems, Article XIII, in U.S. ACDA, *Arms Control and Disarmament Agreements*.
20. Chayes and Chayes, "Living Under a Treaty Regime," pp. 205–208. See also *Balancing National Security Objects In An Uncertain World* (Lanham, MD: University Press of America, 1989).
21. Chayes and Chayes, "Compliance Without Enforcement," p. 321. See also Oran R. Young, *Compliance and Public Authority: A Theory with International Applications* (Published for Resources For The Future by the Johns Hopkins University Press, Baltimore, MD, 1979).
22. See United Nations Security Council Resolution 687 (1991), Adopted by the Security Council at its 2981st Meeting on April 3, 1991, Section C, UN Doc. S/RES/687.
23. Bureau of National Affairs, *International Trade Reporter*, December 14, 1988, p. 1619.
24. See the Convention on Long-Range Transboundary Air Pollution, Article 9; this account relies on the unpublished research of Marc Levy at the Department of Government, Harvard University.
25. Chayes and Chayes, "Adjustment and Compliance Processes in International Regulatory Regimes," pp. 295–298. See also Oran R. Young, "The Effectiveness of International Institutions: Hard Cases and Critical Variables," in James N. Rasenau and Ernst-Otto Czempiel, eds., *Governance Without Government: Order and Change in World Politics* (Cambridge, U.K.: Cambridge University Press, forthcoming), pp. 28–31.
26. Robert Keohane, "Reciprocity in International Relations," *International Organization*, Vol. 40, No. 1 (Winter 1986), pp. 1–28.
27. Roy Mottahadeh and Antonia Handler Chayes, "Security Diplomacy for the Middle East," unpublished paper, June 1991.

28. See "Consolidated Report on the First Two IAEA Inspections Under Security Council Resolution 687 (1991) of Iraq's Nuclear Capabilities," in UN Doc. S/22788, July 15, 1991; "Report of the Third IAEA On-Site Inspection in Iraq Under Security Council Resolution 687 (1991)," in UN Doc. S/22837, July 25, 1991; and "Report of the Fourth IAEA On-Site Inspection in Iraq Under Security Council Resolution 687 (1991)," in UN Doc. S/22986, August 28, 1991. See also William J. Broad, "Iraqi Atom Effort Exposes Weakness in World Controls," *New York Times*, July 15, 1991, p. 1.
29. Statement of the Director General of the IAEA to the Board of Governors, February 26, 1991.
30. United Nations Security Council Resolution 687 (1991), Section C, paragraph 13.
31. Matthew Meselson, et al., "Verification of Biological and Toxin Weapons Disarmament," in Francesco Calogero, Marvin L. Goldberger, and Sergei P. Kapitza, eds., *Verification: Monitoring Disarmament* (Boulder, CO: Westview Press, 1990).
32. A similar committee known as the Zangger Committee prepared the IAEA "trigger list", which identifies the items that require safeguards when sold to non-NPT countries. See Ronald F. Lehman, "The Nonproliferation Policy of the United States of America," speech to the World Affairs Council, Riverside, CA, March 1, 1991, p. 6.
33. United Nations Security Council Resolution 687 (1991), Section C, paragraph 14.
34. See Statement of the Director General of the IAEA.
35. "Establishment of a Nuclear-Weapon-Free Zone in the Region of the Middle East," Report of the Secretary-General, UN Doc. A/45/435, p. 8, citing diplomatic correspondence of the Secretary-General with the relevant states at note 6.
36. Ibid.
37. See the Protocol for the Prohibition of the Use in War of Asphyxiating, Poisonous or Other Gases, and of Bacteriological Methods of Warfare, Signed at Geneva on June 17, 1925, in *Arms Control and Disarmament Agreements*.
38. See the Report of the *Ad Hoc* Committee on Chemical Weapons to the Conference on Disarmament, CD 1033, United Nations, August 10, 1990.
39. Ibid., p. 59.
40. Ibid., annexes to Articles III, IV, and V, pp. 83, 85, and 104. A separate annex deals with Protection of Confidential Information, Ibid., p. 77.
41. Ibid., annexes 1, 2, and 3 to Article VI, pp. 122, 130, and 138.
42. Ibid., p. 145. But see the Working Paper of the Ad Hoc Committee on Chemical Weapons to the Conference on Disarmament, CD/CW/WP.352, July 15, 1991. This has been criticized by Colby and Harris in an op.ed. piece "Look Who's Barring Access to Weapons Sales"; *Washington Post*, July 28, 1991, p. C-7
43. Ibid., Article XIII(1), p. 49.

44. Ibid., Article XIII (5), (6), pp. 50–51.
45. Ibid., p. 69–71. See also ibid., Article VI(2), p. 35.
46. Ibid., p. 145, note 1.
47. Trevor Taylor, "The Arms Trade, Including the Proliferation of Nuclear, Biological and Chemical Weapons and Missile Technology, With Special Reference to the Middle East," Ditchley Conference Report No. D91/3, United Kingdom, p. 4.
48. Thomas L. McNaugher, "Ballistic Missiles and Chemical Weapons: The Legacy of the Iran-Iraq War," *International Security*, Vol. 15 (Fall 1990).
49. Elisa Harris, "Current Capability and Prospects for Control," Aspen Strategy Group, *New Threats: Responding to the Proliferation of Nuclear, Chemical, and Delivery Capabilities in the Third World*, (Lanham, MD: University Press of America, 1990), pp. 67–88.
50. Lehman, "The Nonproliferation Policy."
51. Ibid., p. 8.
52. See the Convention on the Prohibition of the Development, Production and Stockpiling of Bacteriological (Biological) and Toxin Weapons and on Their Destruction, Signed at Washington, London and Moscow, April 10, 1972, in U.S. ACDA, *Arms Control and Disarmament Agreements.*
53. Lehman, "The Nonproliferation Policy," p.4.
54. Meselson, et al., "Verification of Biological and Toxin Weapons Disarmament."
55. "Implementation of the Proposals for a Verification Protocol to the Biological Weapons Convention," Report of the Federation of American Scientists (FAS) Working Group on Biological and Toxin Weapons Verification, Washington, DC, February 1991. See also Meselson, "Verification of Biological and Toxin Weapons Disarmament."
56. Janne E. Nolan, *Trappings of Power: Ballistic Missiles in the Third World*, (Washington, DC: Brookings, 1991).
57. Ibid., Figure 2-1, p. 18.
58. Ibid., Table 4-2, pp. 68–69.
59. Ibid., p. 163. See also Lipson, "Why Are Some International Agreements Informal?"
60. U.S. Congress, Office of Technology Assessment (OTA), *Global Arms Trade: Commerce in Advanced Military Technology and Weapons* (Washington, DC: OTA, 1991), p. 6, Figure 1-6.
67. Leslie H. Gelb, "Arms Sales Heaven," *New York Times*, March 24, 1991, p. 17.
62. U.S. Congress, OTA, *Global Arms Trade*, pp. 5 and 16.
63. Ibid., pp. 13–15.

Part II

REGIONAL LESSONS

4

THE POSTWAR BALANCE OF POWER IN THE MIDDLE EAST

Martin Indyk

The Middle East is the one region of the world that most closely replicates a Hobbesian state of nature in which the law of the jungle prevails over any alternative concept of order between states. It has therefore been the place where a realpolitik approach to U.S. policy has proved the most effective way of preserving U.S. interests. When the United States pursued a policy that sought to maintain the balance of power in the region in favor of states that shared its interests, it was best able to ensure stability and order in an otherwise lawless, conflict-ridden area. When Washington neglected the balance of power, it found its interests most threatened.

However, while maintaining a favorable balance of power is a necessary requirement for promoting U.S. interests in Middle East stability, it has not proved a sufficient condition. It has also been necessary for the United States to engage in efforts to resolve some of the region's conflicts and attempt to correct some of its manifold injustices. This has only been possible when a favorable balance of power had already been established.[1] In this sense, the maintenance of order through the promotion of a favorable balance of power needs to be a prior goal of U.S. policy in the Middle East. But it will tend to be inadequate to the task of protecting U.S. interests if it is not supported by efforts to resolve long-standing conflicts and thereby create a more stable order.

These are the primary lessons of the Gulf War for U.S. policy in the Middle East. The war became necessary because the United States had neglected the balance of power and had allowed it—even encouraged it—to tip in favor of Iraqi-led radical forces. In the war's aftermath, a favorable regional balance of power has been restored, which leaves the United States with its strategic objectives achieved: the free flow of oil at reasonable prices from the Persian Gulf has been assured, and the security of U.S. allies and friends in the region has been reinforced. Beyond that, the United States has emerged as the dominant power in the region. Subsequently reinforced by the collapse of the Soviet Union, the status of the United States as the only superpower has provided a unique opportunity to create a new order in the Middle East by laying the foundations for a new security structure based on the resolution of conflict, the control of the Middle East arms race, and the forswearing of threats and use of force as instruments for dealing with disputes.

The fact that Israel and all its Arab neighbors are now prepared to engage in direct negotiations for the first time in forty-two years is evidence of the potential for this kind of collective security ideal in the aftermath of the Cold War and the Gulf War. It also demonstrates the influence that the United States can now bring to bear as the dominant power in a region where radical forces have been dealt a double blow: the destruction of Iraq's offensive capabilities and the loss of Soviet patronage.

The promotion of direct Arab-Israeli negotiations, however, stands in stark contrast to the U.S. failure to remove Saddam Hussein from power in Iraq. The Bush administration's willingness to allow him to reconsolidate his brutal regime indicates a profound ambivalence about using the dominant position of the United States in the region to intervene in a way that would produce structural changes in the balance of power. A similar ambivalence is evident in the arms control arena where the priority has remained one of supplying advanced weapons to regional allies and friends of the United States rather than promoting an alternative method for meeting their security needs through serious efforts to control the regional arms race.

Some would argue that the restoration of the old order has served to protect U.S. interests well for the foreseeable future and that the United States should accept it and do what can be done to maintain it. In effect, the United States should contain Saddam Hussein, protect its friends, and leave the Arab-Israeli peace process well enough alone because pushing ahead will only reward those who sided with Saddam Hussein (Jordan and the Palestinians) and those who seek regional preponderance in the vacuum left by him (Syria). However, Iraq's invasion of Kuwait demonstrated the difficulties in maintaining a balance of power in the complex Middle East security environment. The results of the ensuing war, combined with the end of Cold War rivalry, have provided the opportunity to adopt a more ambitious approach.

In the short term, the restoration of the old order can serve to protect U.S. interests. Over time, however, the United States will find them threatened again unless it is able to complement the maintenance of a favorable balance of power with the promotion of settlements to long-standing conflicts, a more equitable distribution of wealth, greater political participation, and, of course, the demise of Saddam Hussein's regime.

THE COMPLEXITIES OF THE MIDDLE EAST BALANCE OF POWER

Because of the conflict-ridden nature of the Middle East and its strategic importance for the central balance between the superpowers, the regional balance of power is actually a complex amalgam of four separate balances of power. First, there is the balance between Israel and the Arab states, which the United States is committed to maintain in Israel's favor. This is an inherently doubtful proposition because of Israel's small size and resources relative to the Arab world. But it is the only way in which Israel can hope to deter an Arab attack and persuade its neighbors that it will not be destroyed and must therefore be accepted and accommodated in the region.

A favorable Arab-Israeli balance has traditionally been achieved by ensuring that Israel's qualitative military advantages outweighed the permanent quantitative superiority of the Arabs. The maintenance of Israel's qualitative edge on its own has proven inadequate to the task, unless it is supported by a favorable inter-Arab balance.

Second, there is the inter-Arab balance of power, which, viewed from Washington, is seen as a balance between friendly, conservative regimes (Egypt, Jordan, Morocco, Saudi Arabia, and the Gulf Cooperation Council [GCC]) and hostile, radical regimes (Iraq, Syria, Libya, and the Palestine Liberation Organization [PLO]). However, in the Arab world, the balance is determined less by ideological predisposition and more by calculations of a temporary convergence of interests between Arab states engaged in a struggle for primacy (referred to as "leadership of the Arab world") in the case of the strong, and for survival (referred to as "Arab unity") in the case of the weak. This gives rise to the phenomenon of seemingly perpetual and rapid realignments—Arab leaders at each other's throat on one day, embracing each other on the next.

Historically, in the case of the stronger Arab powers, the balance was determined by the triangular struggle for power between Egypt, Iraq, and Syria[2]: at any particular time, the two weaker powers would tend to align against the stronger. The emergence of Saudi Arabia in the 1970s as an oil power made Riyadh a player in this game of Arab power politics, too, but its lack of military strength and political weight tended to make it less influential and more prone to blackmail. It preferred to maintain relations with all sides and attempt to mediate the differences. The weaker Arab states and the PLO tried to play the stronger powers off against each other, but when the balance tipped in favor of one side, they manifested a tendency to "bandwagon," i.e., to side with the stronger Arab power. In the 1950s and 1960s, hostility towards Israel and fidelity to the Palestinian cause became useful devices for playing the game of Arab power politics. The Six-Day War of 1967 was in large part the product of such an outbidding contest. The disastrous defeat suffered by the Arabs in that war tended to produce a more cautious approach, with Arab leaders being careful to distinguish between rhetorical hostility and actual behavior.

The idiosyncratic nature of the inter-Arab struggle for power created three difficulties for Washington's efforts to maintain a favorable inter-Arab balance. First, the United States had to manage the problems generated by the fact that its friends would often take positions on opposite sides of the balance (thus Saudi Arabia and Jordan sided with the Syrian and Iraqi "rejectionists" against Egypt after Anwar a-Sadat made peace with Israel). Second, the United States had to cope with persistent efforts by its Arab partners to bring hostile Arab powers into the camp that it was supporting (thus Egypt and Saudi Arabia tried to persuade the United States of Iraq's moderation before the invasion of Kuwait just as they are assuring it of Syria's moderation now). Finally, the United States often failed to distinguish between rhetoric and reality on the issue of Israel and the Palestinians, thinking that Arab states would restrict their relations with the United States because of its support for Israel when they really cared about whether the United States would support them in their inter-Arab rivalry.

The third regional balance of power is between the Arab states and Iran. The balance is manifested in the Persian Gulf where Iraq and Iran have for centuries vied for hegemony. The smaller Arab states of the Gulf, organized in the 1980s in the GCC, traditionally played the role of the balancer of these two powers. In the days of the pro-U.S. Shah, it was possible to use this balance to complement the inter-Arab balance between radicals and conservatives because of the cooperative relations between Iran and Egypt, Saudi Arabia, and the GCC. But the rise of a radical, fundamentalist regime under Ayatollah Ruhollah Khomeini created a new threat to the Arab neighborhood and a realignment of Arab states (only Syria sided with Iran), requiring the United States to support an anti-Iranian balance of power, spearheaded by a radical Arab state—Iraq.

The fourth balance of power derives from the central balance between the superpowers. Because of the Middle East's strategic importance to both superpowers—it provides the West's oil and it was the soft underbelly of the Soviet empire—the rivalry between the United States and the Soviet Union found intense expression here with Moscow offering military and economic support to radical regional powers that opposed U.S. interests. This superpower rivalry added another deadly challenge to the task of maintaining a favorable regional balance by fueling a regional arms race and by threatening to tip the balance in favor of the hostile local powers. It also added another layer of complexity for Washington, since the United States often found itself driven by this rivalry to support both sides of a local balance of power (by supplying arms to both Israel and the Arabs for example).

THE BALANCE OF POWER IN THE 1980s

Given these inherent difficulties in tending to the task of maintaining the balance of power in favor of pro-Western regional powers, the pre–Gulf War decade of the 1980s seemed to bring some unusual and welcome relief. Overall, it was a period of relative stability for U.S. interests in the Middle East compared to the turbulence of the previous decade when the region had become known as "the arc of crisis."[3]

In the Arab-Israeli arena, the balance of power had been secured by the successful implementation of the Egypt-Israel peace treaty. This removed Egypt—then the largest and militarily most powerful Arab state—from a potential Arab war coalition against Israel and therefore made it impractical for any other Arab state to contemplate war with Israel. This was particularly the case because Iraq, having launched an invasion of Iran in 1979, was preoccupied throughout the decade with a war for survival on that front. This removed the possibility of an eastern front Arab coalition confronting Israel (involving a military alliance between Syria, Iraq, and Jordan). Syria thus raised the banner of "strategic parity" in an attempt to build an indigenous military capability that could alone match Israel's power. By the end of the decade, the Syrians had all but bankrupted their economy and were publicly admitting that this objective was unachievable in the short term.[4]

Israel's 1982 war in Lebanon demonstrated the stability of these key elements in the Arab-Israeli balance of power. Although Sadat had been assassinated less than a year before, and the war severely strained relations between Israel and the new Mubarak government in Cairo, the Egypt-Israel peace treaty held. The Syrian Air Force and air defense system received a thorough drubbing at the hands of the Israeli Air Force without precipitating Soviet intervention. This quick and effective demonstration of Israeli superiority neutralized the potential for a full-scale war between Syria and Israel.

Meanwhile, the Arab world stood by and watched while the PLO was defeated on the battlefield and then forced to withdraw from Beirut. This marked the beginning of Arab state disengagement from the conflict with Israel, underscored by the Arab League Summit in Amman in November 1987, when the Palestinian issue did not make it into the final communiqué. Although the Palestinians in the West Bank and Gaza launched their *intifada* (uprising) soon after, the Arab states gave little political and no financial backing to their cause. Jordan disengaged from the West Bank, the Gulf Arabs cut their financial support of the "confrontation" states, and it was left to the PLO to try to convert the uprising into some political gain.

The inter-Arab balance of power was also stabilized in the 1980s. The intense rivalry that had marked earlier decades disappeared as each power became preoccupied with more pressing concerns than Arab leadership and Arab unity. Because of its peace treaty with Israel, Egypt had been expelled from Arab institutions and treated as a pariah in inter-Arab politics. Over the decade it was able steadily to regain entry first on the PLO's coattails because of Yasser Arafat's need for Egyptian backing in his conflict with Syria's Hafiz al-Assad and his rivalry with Jordan's King Hussein. Subsequently, Iraq and the Saudi Arabia turned to Egypt for support in their increasingly desperate struggle to prevent Iran from consolidating its beachhead on the Arab side of the Gulf.

Nevertheless, Egypt's effective absence from the game left a power vacuum that neither Syria nor Iraq were able to fill: Saddam Hussein was preoccupied with his war with the Ayatollah and needed all the Arab support he could muster; Hafiz al-Assad was bogged down in Lebanon and had succeeded in isolating himself in the Arab world by siding with Iran against his archrival in Baghdad. Instead, inter-Arab politics became focused on the Arab-Iranian balance, which threatened to tip dangerously in Iran's favor. Here, too, however, the balance was eventually corrected with massive financial and logistical backing provided to Iraq by its fellow Arab states. Despite moments of considerable concern—when Iran seized the Fao Peninsula, threatened Kuwaiti shipping, and attempted to penetrate Saudi air space—the Iraq-Iran war waned through much of the decade with both sides inflicting significant damage on each other but with neither being able to prevail. As long as that continued to be the case, the other powers in the region felt relatively secure with the general attitude reflected in the common belief that both sides deserved each other and in the common hope that they should enjoy a long war.

The superpower balance in the Middle East had also become stabilized after the tense confrontations of the 1970s. The Soviet invasion of Afghanistan had provided the Reagan administration with the superpower incentive and the regional justification to bolster its strategic capabilities in the region. The Rapid Deployment Force was developed along with new strategic relationships with the Gulf Arabs, Oman, Egypt, Morocco, and Israel. Although the Reagan administration's initial notion of an anti-Soviet Arab-Israeli "strategic consensus" was mocked by its U.S. critics and rejected by the Arabs, the fact remains that by the end of Reagan's second term, the United States had managed to establish arrangements in some form for access to facilities, prepositioning of military equipment, joint exercises, and joint military planning with all the friendly powers in the region and all the geostrategically located smaller states. To be sure, the Gulf Arabs still insisted on an "over the horizon" U.S. presence (with the exception of Oman and Bahrain) with no guarantee that in a crisis they would agree to grant access. But the Saudis, as we now know, had used the U.S. Corps of Engineers to overbuild their facilities, and the Kuwaitis had gone to considerable lengths to have the United States protect their shipping.

Beyond securing these arrangements for military intervention in a crisis, the United States was able to contribute to the consolidation of a favorable regional balance of power on all four levels. Strategic cooperation with Israel, as well as continued military assistance, defense procurement from Israeli industries, and joint research and development (R&D) projects (most notably the Arrow anti-tactical ballistic missile [ATBM] program) served as a force-multiplier, significantly enhancing Israel's ability to deter an Arab attack. Diplomatic efforts by Secretary of State George Shultz failed to bring Jordan and the Palestinians into negotiations with Israel, but painstaking U.S. diplomacy did resolve the outstanding issues in the Egypt-Israel peace treaty. The Palestinian uprising did generate a final effort by Shultz and a further initiative by Secretary of State James Baker to launch Israeli-Palestinian negotiations. However, the question of who ruled in Nablus was of human rather than strategic interest to the United States. Accordingly, the collapse of both efforts had no recognizable impact on the Arab-Israeli balance of power. Given that reality, the failure to "solve the Palestinian problem" was unlikely to generate another Arab-Israeli war.

On the inter-Arab level, the Reagan administration's failure to stand up to the Syrians in Lebanon might have weakened the Arab states aligned with Washington and strengthened the radicals in the Arab world. However, as already noted, the radicals were in no position to take advantage of the apparent lack of resolve of the United States. And when the United States subsequently retaliated for a terrorist raid with bombing strikes on Libya in April 1986, there was a notable deterrent impact on the behavior of those Arab states sponsoring terrorism (Syria and Libya especially).

On the Arab-Iranian level, the United States intervened to ensure that the balance did not tip in favor of Iran. The "Iraqi tilt" as it was known, began in the mid-1980s out of concern that Iran might succeed in spreading its revolution to the oil-rich Arabian side of the Gulf. Intelligence sharing, removal of Baghdad from the terrorism list, the extension of agricultural credits, and the shipping of military-related equipment to Iraq while attempting to embargo arms supplies to Iran were all designed to bolster Saddam Hussein as the Arab bulwark against Iranian fundamentalism.[5] When Iran began to threaten Kuwait and the Gulf Arab states, the U.S. naval presence in the Persian Gulf was bolstered in a successful effort to deter Iran and confine the war to Iraq.

Soviet inability to counter increasing U.S. influence in the region, already evident in the 1970s, was dealt a further setback by its invasion of Afghanistan, which increased the incentives for cooperation with the United States among the regional powers. By the time of Gorbachev's rise to power in the Soviet Union in 1985, the Soviet Union had been well and truly relegated to the periphery in the region. Its only allies were Syria and Libya, although it was able to exploit Iran's needs during the war to build a new relationship with Tehran, which nevertheless remained constrained by ideological and strategic differences. (Tehran supported the *mujahidin* in Afghanistan, and Moscow maintained a military relationship with Iraq.) Gorbachev's "new thinking" reinforced this trend of declining Soviet influence at the same time as it reinforced the existing balance of power by beginning the shift of Soviet support from the forces of extremism to the forces of regional moderation and stability.[6]

In short, by the time George Bush entered the Oval Office, the Middle East posed few threats to U.S. interests. The Iran-Iraq war was coming to an end; the Soviet Union was turning inward and withdrawing from Afghanistan; and the Arab states were disengaging from their conflict with Israel, leaving the Palestinians to negotiate the best deal they could get. The United States, it was commonly assumed in Washington, could now afford to reduce its naval presence in the Gulf and concentrate on a low profile effort to "cultivate the environment" for Arab-Israeli negotiations. With dramatic events unfolding in Europe, the Middle East was given a lower priority on the Bush administration's foreign policy agenda. And correctly so, for the balance of power was such that a careful tending of the Middle East garden was all that appeared necessary.

THE EMERGENCE OF THE IRAQI CHALLENGE TO THE BALANCE OF POWER

In the Middle East, calm should never be mistaken for peacefulness; it is usually only the interlude before the next storm. Thus it happened that while the president was preoccupied elsewhere and the secretary of state was worrying about whether a Palestinian from East Jerusalem and a deportee could be included in a Palestinian delegation that would negotiate the modalities of an election in the West Bank, an Iraqi threat to the Middle East balance of power emerged virtually unnoticed by Washington.

How could such a benign balance become destabilized so quickly? The answer lies paradoxically in the very elements that looked so positive to the balance of power: the end of the Iraq-Iran war and the end of the Cold War. Although a few analysts recognized the shift in the regional balance of power at the time, the import of Iraq's massive battlefield victory over Iran was not generally understood in Washington.[7] Militarily and economically, revolutionary Iran was left prostrate, with its foreign policy paralyzed by a dispute among its clerical rulers about the appropriate means for recovery. Iraq was not in great economic shape either, but the war had left Saddam Hussein in control of the largest army in the Middle East by several orders of magnitude—fifty-five well-equipped divisions and a strategic weapons production capability unmatched by any power in the region other than Israel.[8] It was generally assumed that after such a prolonged, costly, and brutal war, Saddam Hussein would demobilize at least part of his army and concentrate on reconstruction at home. But instead, he wasted no time in throwing his new weight around. First he settled scores with his own Kurdish population by dropping chemical bombs on the village of Halabja. Then he got even with Assad for Syria's support of Iran during the war by providing arms to General Michel Aoun in Lebanon, thereby stiffening the Lebanese Army's resolve to resist the Syrian takeover there.[9] And in April 1990, he began to focus on Israel, boasting of his binary chemical weapons and threatening to "make fire eat up half of Israel, if it tried [to do anything] against Iraq."[10] As early as February 1990, the Bush administration had been made aware of Saddam Hussein's demand that Kuwait cede the strategic island of Bubiyan; by July he was demanding that Kuwait and the United Arab Emirates (UAE) change their oil production policies. Iraq had emerged from the war as the dominant Arab power in all three regional balances, and Saddam Hussein wasted little time making it clear that he intended to exact his dues.

These regional developments happened to coincide with the end of the Cold War, which in other circumstances would have helped to stabilize the regional balance by reducing superpower competition for influence in the Middle East. However, in a situation where one regional power had decided to exert its dominance and had in its possession the means to do so, the impact of the end of the Cold War actually served to assist the process.

The end of the Cold War removed the Soviet threat from Washington's calculus. This had been the organizing principle for U.S. foreign policy since the end of World War II and, especially after the Soviet invasion of Afghanistan, had provided the strategic rationale for U.S. engagement in the Persian Gulf. With this danger gone, and developments in Europe demanding Washington's attention, there was little apparent reason, let alone sufficient time, to focus on Saddam Hussein's threatening behavior.[11]

On the regional level, the end of the Cold War advantaged Iraq by weakening its potential competitors. Syria, in particular, had lost its superpower patron, its arms supplier, and its ultimate guarantee against the consequences of defeat should it become engaged in another war with Israel. Similarly, Iran had been building its relations with the Soviet Union as the road back from defeat but could no longer rely on this strategy. Saddam Hussein faced no such difficulties. During the war he had been able to secure Western arms as well as build an indigenous missile production capability and had therefore significantly reduced Iraq's dependence on the Soviet Union.

In combination then, the impact of the end of these two wars was immediately to destabilize all three local balances. On the Arab-Israeli front, Iraq's strategic capabilities and Saddam Hussein's threats to burn Israel and return Palestine to the Arabs had two effects. First, it heightened Israel's concerns about the potential for an eastern front coalition between Iraq, Syria, and Jordan. Israel had been surprised by Iraq's use of ballistic missiles against Tehran and now became disturbed by the rapid construction of missile sites in western Iraq and the stepping up of military coordination with the Jordanian armed forces.[12] Syria's Assad remained a bitter enemy of Saddam Hussein but Israel's military planners had seen Arab leaders bury their differences overnight to take on Israel, and they began to plan for the eventuality that Israel might have to confront a vast Arab coalition on its eastern borders. Jerusalem issued stern demarches to Jordan about the dangers of Saddam Hussein's embrace while signaling King Hussein that they wished him no harm. Yitzhak Shamir also sent reassurances to Saddam Hussein via Egypt and the United States that Israel had no intention of attacking, and he called for Syria to enter negotiations with Israel.

Israel also became alarmed at indications of new efforts by Saddam Hussein to acquire nuclear weapons. In April 1989, they had first sounded the alarm about Iraq's renewed nuclear weapons program. The concern increased with the revelation in spring 1990 that Iraq had been circumventing international restrictions to acquire nuclear weapons technology. By July, Israel's defense minister was providing new intelligence to the Pentagon about Iraq's efforts to acquire gas centrifuge technology to produce fissile material.

The second impact on the Arab-Israeli balance was on the Arab side. Since the heyday of Gamal Abdel Nasser, no Arab leader had dared to threaten Israel with destruction. But now an Arab leader, fresh from victory over "the enemies of God on the eastern front" was raising the banner of pan-Arabism again and promising to liberate Jerusalem. His grandiose threats resonated in the Palestinian street and produced a "bandwagoning" effect on Jordan and the PLO.

Wedged between more powerful Israeli, Syrian, and Iraqi neighbors, King Hussein chose to side with the stronger Arab power. Beyond the increasingly intimate military ties with Iraq, Jordan's economy became dependent on the Iraqi market and, on the political level, the king fashioned a new role for himself as the interpreter to the West of Saddam Hussein's actions and the supposed civilizer of the Baghdad peasant.

Arafat pursued a similar course, transferring the PLO's military headquarters to Baghdad in April 1990 and taking an increasingly belligerent tone towards Israel and the United States.

When the Baghdad-backed, Palestine Liberation Front of Abul Abbas launched a terrorist raid on Israeli beaches in May 1990, Arafat was unwilling to do anything to condemn the raid and thereby salvage his dialogue and nascent relationship with the United States. He had, by this time, decided on a different course—to hitch his wagon to Saddam Hussein's war machine.

These developments began to ratchet up Arab-Israeli tensions. At the same time, the collapse of U.S. efforts to promote an Israeli-Palestinian dialogue in Cairo and the suspension of the U.S.-PLO dialogue following the Abul Abbas raid left no avenue for diverting attention from Saddam Hussein's renewed focus on confrontation.

Nevertheless, a favorable Arab-Israeli balance could still be maintained as long as no major Arab power sided with Saddam Hussein. Here the inter-Arab balance became a critical determinant of the Arab-Israeli balance. Saddam Hussein had begun to press for new pan-Arab security arrangements in Arab forums. In February 1990, he tried to turn the Arab Cooperation Council (ACC), which grouped Iraq, Jordan, and Egypt, into a security alliance; in May he hosted an Arab League Summit in Baghdad whose purpose, he declared, was to deal with "pan-Arab security and threats to it."[13] Through these efforts and his public pronouncements, Saddam Hussein's intentions to dominate the Arab order became clear. He argued that the end of the Cold War had produced a dangerous situation for the Arab nation because the United States had been left as the only superpower. In five years, he claimed, Europe and Japan would emerge as balancing powers, but, in the meantime, he asserted that the United States would seek to dominate the region, dictate the price of oil, and support Israel's usurpation of Palestinian rights. Saddam Hussein's answer was for the Arab world to unite behind his leadership in order to balance the power of the United States. The Arab oil producers were to provide financial support for the confrontation with Israel and the United States; the Arab powers were to coordinate their military activities; and his contribution would be to put Iraq's force at the disposal of any Arab state threatened by Israel.[14]

Since the days of Anwar a-Sadat, Egypt had offered an alternative vision of the Arab future, one based on the peaceful resolution of the conflict with Israel, the control of the Middle East arms race, and economic and political development at home. With Egypt back in the Arab fold, it fell to Hosni Mubarak to counter Iraq's challenge by promoting negotiations instead of confrontation with Israel and friendship with, rather than, antagonism towards the United States. While he preferred to try to moderate Saddam Hussein rather than challenge him, Mubarak nevertheless articulated this alternative approach, arguing that the revolutionary changes in Europe required the Arab world to join the movement toward detente, democratization, and "new thinking."[15] Egypt also successfully resisted Saddam Hussein's efforts to convert the ACC and the Arab League into instruments for his paranoid vision.

In terms of the balance of power, what really mattered was which camp Syria would join. If Damascus sided with Baghdad, then the Arab world was bound for war with Israel; if it sided with Cairo, then Saddam Hussein's power would be countered. For Assad, always a careful and shrewd calculator of the balance of power, it was not much of a choice. He was not about to be dragged by his archrival into a premature war with Israel in which Syria would suffer most; for the moment, Saddam Hussein presented more of a threat to his interests in Lebanon than Israel; and Iraq's power needed to be countered, not supplemented. Thus in July 1990, Assad traveled to Cairo in a journey that symbolized his realignment with Egypt, the country he had once traveled to Baghdad to ostracize. To underline his point, at the end of that month Assad boycotted Saddam Hussein's summit.

If Saddam Hussein had been outmaneuvered in inter-Arab politics for the time being, there was one arena in which he could more easily have his way. The defeat of Iran had left Iraq dominant in the Gulf; no regional power was capable of countering Saddam Hussein there. He could only be balanced by the power and presence of the United States. Saddam Hussein understood this instinctively. It was the reason he now adopted a strident anti-Americanism, demanding that the U.S. Navy be withdrawn from the Gulf and accusing the United States of manipulating oil prices in a conspiracy to weaken Iraq and the Arab nation. When he discovered, however, that the United States preferred to appease than counter him, he took advantage of what he perceived as weakness.[16] The invasion of Kuwait may have been generated by Saddam Hussein's need for revenue and his desire to convert Iraq's dominance in the Gulf into hegemony in the Middle East, but it was also the logical consequence of the Bush administration's failure to balance Saddam Hussein's power.

In retrospect, it is easy to see that Washington's failure to appreciate the impact of Iraq's victory on the regional balance of power was a major cause of the war. If the mistake is to be avoided again, it is therefore important to establish the reasons for this failure. As already suggested, part of the explanation lies in the preoccupation with other issues at a tumultuous time in world affairs. With its global horizons, it is difficult for a superpower to pay equal attention to all regions, whereas regional powers with their horizons restricted to their immediate neighborhood have a more intense interest in calculating the regional balance of power correctly. Kuwait is the exception that proves this rule: its inexplicable failure to make the correct calculation led to its occupation. However, as we have noted, the other regional powers did not make the same mistake.

A second factor was the animus felt in Washington towards the Ayatollah's Iran. Its fundamental anti-Americanism combined with the accumulated ill will caused by Iran's behavior (the embassy hostage crisis, the continued hostage-holding by the Iranian-influenced Hezbollah, the humiliation of Desert One, the terrorist bombing of Pan Am flight 103) made a policy based on the rational calculation of the balance of power simply impossible. Moreover, the fact that a previous attempt to restore relations with Iran had resulted in the Iran-Contra scandal discredited any new approach to Tehran. Thus while the dictates of balance of power politics required a tilt back towards Iran after Iraq's victory, the dictates of domestic politics made such a move impossible. Indeed this shift in policy was recommended to Secretary of State Shultz in the last year of the Reagan administration, but it was leaked to the press and quickly rejected.[17]

A third factor in the Bush administration's miscalculation was the role of the Arab friends of the United States. They should have been the most attuned to the Iraqi threat, and yet they repeatedly urged Washington to avoid confrontation and leave Saddam Hussein to their mediation and influence. Given its weakness and alignment with Saddam Hussein, Jordan's behavior is explicable and should have been interpreted in Washington as a sign that something was seriously wrong with the balance of power rather than accepted as sage advice. The behavior of Egypt and Saudi Arabia was a different matter. They appear to have assumed that they could handle Saddam Hussein on their own and preferred to try to domesticate him rather than confront him—such was the way of Arab politics. Given their approach and the paranoia of Saddam Hussein, a shift in U.S. policy would make their task more difficult. Both Mubarak and King Fahd now insist with vehemence that they were deceived by a Jordanian-Iraqi conspiracy—which only means that Washington should not have been listening to them.

Their entreaties fell on very receptive ears because the willingness to accommodate Saddam Hussein had become deeply entrenched in U.S. policy. It was probably the single most important factor in the failure to react to the shift in the balance of power. Developed in response to the overthrow of the shah, the Iraqi tilt in U.S. policy took on a life and logic of its own. Support for Iraq required aid, but aid could only be forthcoming if Iraq were removed from the list of states that supported terrorism and if it were portrayed to Congress as a "moderate" country ready to come to terms with Israel. As Iran became more threatening, the rationale became more entrenched until it began to replace reality. Thus Washington was prepared quickly to forgive the Iraqi attack on the USS *Stark*, turn a blind eye to Iraqi infringements of technology-export controls and misuse of agricultural credits, resist congressional efforts to impose sanctions, raise only the slightest concern about Saddam Hussein's use of chemical weapons against his own people, and treat with skepticism Israeli warnings about his nuclear weapons program. By the time of Iran's defeat, the conception had been so firmly established and reinforced by the other three factors that nothing short of

Saddam Hussein's outright aggression against Kuwait could shake it. As the signs of Saddam Hussein's destabilizing dominance of the balance of power accumulated, Bush administration reassessments simply concluded that to confront Saddam Hussein would be counterproductive, only driving him to more reckless behavior. Here was a man with the ability to hurt U.S. interests. As National Security Adviser General Brent Scowcroft explained, it was judged wiser to try to "make this guy a reasonably responsible member of the international community."[18] Accordingly, a week before Saddam Hussein invaded Kuwait, Ambassador April Glaspie was simply following her unchanged instructions when she reassured Saddam Hussein that President Bush sought "better relations with Iraq."[19]

In the wake of the war, much attention has been focused on the failure of Glaspie and the Bush administration to warn Saddam Hussein of the consequences of his aggression. Even if such warnings had been issued at the last moment, it is doubtful that the United States could have deterred him. By that time, his mind-set mirrored that of the United States: he had become so accustomed to U.S. willingness to appease him that he probably would not have taken such warnings seriously. Indeed, he did not take the United States seriously even when it deployed 500,000 troops and 1,000 combat aircraft to the Gulf. So it was that the strongest power in the world, controlled by an administration that prided itself on its realist approach to power politics and that placed the preservation of international order above any other foreign policy concern, came to ignore the most fundamental principle of its own approach to world affairs—the maintenance of the balance of power.

THE EMERGING POSTWAR BALANCE

At war's end, with U.S. forces occupying southern Iraq and Saddam Hussein's war machine lying in pieces on the ground, the United States was suddenly catapulted into a position of dominance in the Persian Gulf. At that moment, the United States could lay down the law to Saddam Hussein, the emir of Kuwait, and the king of Saudi Arabia alike. At that moment, the United States was in a position to reshape the Middle East order in ways that could have had a lasting impact.

Instead, the advance of U.S. forces and the destruction of Saddam Hussein's army were halted, and the president announced that the troops would be coming home forthwith. The events that followed—Saddam Hussein's survival, the regrouping of the Iraqi army, the brutal suppression of the Shia and Kurdish rebellions, the restoration of authoritarian rule in Kuwait, and the Saudi retreat from engagement in peace negotiations with Israel—all flowed naturally from those initial decisions by the Bush administration.

The president may have spoken about bringing the Middle East into a "New World Order," but his actions ensured that the old order was simply reinforced and made more stable and comfortable for all the regional powers. They chose to go back to business as usual and the United States let them.

There are many reasons for this less than satisfactory outcome: the fear of the Middle East quagmire, the historical impulse to bring the troops home, the absence of an imperialist urge to establish a Pax Americana. The most important is surely that the national interest, as defined by the president and his advisers, did not require a more ambitious approach. They sought to restore the balance of power, not restructure it. In the short term, from a strategic perspective, it is difficult to argue with this approach. The interests of the United States in the free flow of oil at reasonable prices and in the security of its regional allies and friends have all been secured by the significant diminishment of Saddam Hussein's power.

In the Persian Gulf, the destruction of much of Iraq's offensive capabilities now matches the destruction of Iran's offensive capabilities in the Iran-Iraq war. Thus, for the time being, the balance of power has been reestablished in the Gulf at a much lower level of military capability. Moreover, the United States is now in a much better position to hold the balance and counter any adverse development. Having demonstrated the awesome capabilities of its air power and the willingness to use all means necessary to protect its interests, the United States now has a much enhanced ability to deter adverse activity by Iraq or Iran.

Coercive diplomacy may have failed to influence Saddam Hussein's behavior during the post-invasion period, but it has certainly worked more effectively since the war to enforce Iraq's compliance with the terms of the United Nations cease-fire. Put simply, a squadron of stealth bombers has become the 1990s equivalent of a British gunboat during the heyday of imperialism. Moreover, if the United States is assiduous in negotiating new access arrangements with Saudi Arabia and the GCC, its deterrent capability will be further enhanced by removing the doubt from the calculus of the regional powers about whether the weaker states could be intimidated into denying the United States access in a new crisis.

The inter-Arab balance has also been stabilized by the radical reduction in Iraq's power. For the time being, Iraq is incapable of playing a role in inter-Arab politics. It is likely to be ostracized and preoccupied with trying to rebuild its power. This leaves the arena to Egypt and Syria, with Saudi Arabia in the role of balancer. These three Arab powers—the most populous, the most nationalist, and the richest—were allied in the effort to defeat Saddam Hussein, and, in the immediate aftermath, there was some expectation that they would form the dominant axis, capable of bolstering regional security arrangements in the Gulf and moving together into peace negotiations with Israel.

However, despite an early agreement in principle for the maintenance of an Egyptian and Syrian troop presence in Kuwait and Saudi Arabia, the Gulf Arabs soon developed second thoughts. In particular, the bargain that would have cemented Saudi-Egyptian relations never materialized. Egypt expected to play a new strategic role in the Gulf as protector—with U.S. backing—of the Gulf Arabs, for which it would receive its due in terms of Saudi aid for the ever-ailing Egyptian economy. With Saddam Hussein's threat receding, however, the Saudis did not fancy depending on Egyptian protection. They remembered the proxy war fought in Yemen in the 1960s to prevent Nasser from gaining a foothold on the Arabian peninsula and were not about to invite the Egyptian Army now to take up residence in Saudi

Arabia. Moreover, the high cost of the war had forced the Saudis to borrow on the international capital markets for the first time; they were not about to look favorably at the idea of taking on responsibility for the Egyptian economy. They clearly preferred to make low-profile security arrangements with the United States. But what the Saudis regarded as a bad deal—second-rate protection at too high an economic and political price—the Egyptians viewed as ingratitude.

This tension in Saudi-Egyptian relations ensured that Cairo would not be able to extend its influence to the Gulf. Nevertheless, in the wake of Saddam Hussein's defeat, Egypt was still left with considerable room to maneuver. The return of the Arab League headquarters to Cairo in the wake of the war and the election of Egypt's foreign minister as its secretary-general put Egypt back in the formal position of leadership of the Arab world.

The key to the stability of the postwar inter-Arab balance, however, depended on Syria. If Syria remained part of the Egyptian-Saudi axis that had been forged to counter Iraq's power, the destructive aspects of inter-Arab rivalry might be kept in check. Conversely, if Syria tried to rally the Arab radicals behind its leadership, eventually a new radical pole would emerge to challenge the status quo again. In theory, a Syrian-led alliance comprising a post–Saddam Hussein Iraq whose leadership was influenced by Damascus and a post–Khomeini Iran could provide an alternative to Egypt's leadership, especially if it received backing from a Soviet Union that had become dominated by the military. However, in practice the chances for such an alliance were slim in the short term. Saddam Hussein's continued survival not only made a Syrian-Iraqi rapprochement impossible, it also ensured the further weakening of Iraq's military capabilities as the allies persisted in gaining control of his remaining offensive capabilities. Nor could Assad depend on a change of course in the Soviet Union, which had both put him on notice that it would not support his effort to achieve "strategic parity" with Israel and was now insisting that Syria repay all its military debts promptly. In these circumstances, there was little alternative for the time being to remaining in the Saudi-Egyptian camp: it had paid handsome dividends during the war,[20] it held greater prospect of gain in a postwar era of U.S. dominance.

For Assad, however, the most compelling reason for remaining in the pro-Western camp in inter-Arab politics stemmed from the impact of the war on the Arab-Israeli balance of power. Here, the destruction of Iraq's offensive capabilities coming hard on the heels of the collapse of the Soviet empire and the enhancement of U.S. credibility in the region had reinforced the balance in Israel's favor. Assad had now lost both his superpower patron and the potential to form an eastern front coalition with Iraq against Israel. In this context, as he told an American visitor, the destruction of Iraq's strategic capabilities "represents a defeat for the whole Arab nation."[21] This new reality has not prevented Assad from spending every penny he gained from Syria's involvement in the coalition against Saddam Hussein to acquire more offensive weapons (M9 missiles from China, improved Scuds from North Korea, tanks and aircraft from Czechoslovakia and the Soviet Union), but it has produced the sober calculation that the only way to balance Israel's strength in the short term is to improve relations with its superpower patron.

If Assad can succeed in building a U.S. stake in Syria, at a minimum he might be able to replace what he lost with the demise of his own patron—a guarantee of superpower intervention to restrain Israel. Beyond that, he might be able to secure the continued acquiescence of the United States in his takeover of Lebanon, turn Damascus into the focus of U.S. diplomatic activity, and gain access to Western aid and technology. At best, he might succeed in weakening Israel by driving a wedge between Yitzhak Shamir's right-wing government and a Bush administration that is no longer prepared to give Israel the benefit of the doubt. However, Assad knows that he can only begin to achieve these advantages if he agrees to engage in the Arab-Israeli peace process. His apparent willingness to do so, evident in his belated acceptance on July 13, 1991 of President Bush's proposals for the convening of Arab-Israeli negotiations, should be seen for what it is—a tactical shift brought about by the impact of the defeat of Saddam Hussein on the Arab-Israeli balance of power. Assad has hardly decided that his interests require a change of heart towards the idea of peace with Israel, but he appears to understand that they do require Syria's participation in the peace process. Because Syrian engagement also opens the door for Palestinian and Jordanian involvement in the peace process, it may yet provide the impetus to a breakthrough in Arab-Israeli negotiations. And, over time, it is possible to envisage a further stabilization of the Arab-Israeli balance through a U.S.-brokered disengagement in southern Lebanon and the implementation of an interim agreement for Palestinian autonomy in the West Bank and Gaza. This, in turn, would do much to reinforce the inter-Arab balance of power by ensconcing Syria in the Egyptian-led, pro-Western camp.

U.S. efforts to maintain and promote these favorable developments in all three regional arenas will also be boosted by the shift in Soviet regional behavior. For the moment, the Soviet Union's competitive instincts have been converted into an urge to cooperate in regional arrangements that will help to stabilize the Middle East balance of power. Moscow's willingness to follow the lead of the United States in the peace process is hardly likely to be decisive in generating the breakthrough that is sought, but it can help to convince recalcitrant Arabs that the alternatives to peace negotiations are unpromising because they will no longer attract the support of the Soviet Union. More importantly, if Moscow continues to cooperate in the promotion of arms control arrangements for the region, it may just be possible to head off the next round of the arms race with its inevitable emphasis on weapons of mass destruction and their delivery systems.

Finally, the war has produced two other positive elements in the regional balance, which can help to bolster the favorable trends. First, is the renewed role of Turkey as a factor in the strategic equation. Situated on the borders of Syria, Iraq, and Iran—the region's three radical states—Turkey had previously been reluctant to bring its power to bear in the regional equation. President Turgut Ozal's decision to side with the coalition was highly controversial among Turkey's political-military elite and is yet to be vindicated. But Ozal seems determined that Turkey will play a more active and positive role in the region. Enhanced strategic cooperation with Ankara can therefore help to contain Iraq in the short term and may prove useful in countering Iran or Syria should that become necessary. Turkey's long-standing, if low profile, relations with Israel can also bolster efforts to normalize Jerusalem's relations with its neighbors.

Similarly, more constructive behavior from Europe and Japan in support of U.S.-led efforts to promote Arab-Israeli negotiations, regional economic development and arms control arrangements is also evident in the wake of the coalition's success in the war against Saddam Hussein. These external powers had previously complicated Washington's strategy by offering competitive sources of arms, aid, and political support: Iraq's strategic weapons systems were built with vital assistance from European and Japanese companies; the PLO gained much of its international credibility from European responsiveness. For the time being, Europe and Japan seem more willing to follow Washington's lead in the peace process and lend their support to arms control efforts.

In these circumstances, it is therefore difficult to argue that U.S. strategic interests require the pursuit of more ambitious objectives that run the risk of prolonged engagement and ultimate failure. The presence of Saddam Hussein, the absence of political change in the Arab world, and the rearming of the regional powers do not appear to present a sufficient threat to the reestablished Middle Eastern order to justify a more interventionist approach.

However, the favorable postwar balance described above is a snapshot of an ever-changing scene. Saddam Hussein is down but not yet out and is clearly prepared to go to any lengths to retain his nuclear capabilities. He will try to conserve and rebuild his power as quickly as he is able. If he succeeds, he will exact his revenge on all those whom he considers responsible for his setbacks. Although his behavior has managed to consolidate international support for strict enforcement of controls on Iraq's strategic facilities, the United States can no longer have complete confidence in the ability of inspectors to ferret out all his programs.[22] And if the resolve of the international community wanes, Saddam Hussein will immediately exploit the opening.

Thus the price of allowing him to survive is one of eternal vigilance. If the attention of the United States is diverted over time, the balance of power could well be detrimentally affected.

While keeping Iraq weak, the United States will also have to be watchful of Iran, which could exploit the obsessive focus on Saddam Hussein to rebuild its own position of influence in the Gulf. At the moment, Iran is still in poor shape and recognizes U.S. dominance in the region. Its primary concerns now are to rebuild its strength and ensure the departure of the United States from the Gulf. It will probably try to achieve these objectives through accommodation, first with the Gulf Arabs, then with Europe, and eventually with the United States. Through this process, the United States may be able to defuse the radical impulses of the clerical regime in Tehran, but there is an equal prospect that it will fail. The United States would then need to be very wary of an Iran-Iraq rapprochement on the basis of their common concern to remove the United States from the Gulf. Just as the Reagan and Bush administrations allowed their antagonism toward Iran to blind them to the rising danger of a powerful Iraq, so too should the United States not make the mistake of allowing its obsession with Saddam Hussein blind it to the dangers of the balance in the Gulf tipping too much in favor of a radical Iran.

A similar lesson needs to be remembered in dealing with Syria. Assad's desire for better relations with the United States is a direct product of his inferior position in the postwar regional balance of power—just as Iraq turned to the United States when it found itself threatened in its war with Iran. If, in the service of Syrian involvement in the peace process, the United States allows Assad to build his power and drive a wedge between itself and Israel, it will have undermined Israel's deterrent capability and allowed the Arab-Israeli balance of power to become destabilized. On the other hand, if the United States exploit Syria's current weakness adroitly to negotiate arrangements that will secure Israel's northern border with Lebanon and promote an interim agreement for the Palestinians in the territories, it will have helped to bolster the Arab-Israeli balance by defusing some of the tensions. In short, the United States should base its policy toward Syria on the recognition that Assad needs to be contained rather than embraced, and use his current weakness to enable negotiations to proceed rather than hand him the veto over the negotiating positions of the other Arab parties.

The problem with this approach is that for the United States to remain merely the custodian of the recreated status quo, the constant countering of the rise of radical regional powers will be required. The history of U.S. policy toward the region suggests that the success of such an approach is short-lived if it is not bolstered by a more ambitious effort to encourage the restructuring of the Middle East order. The removal of Saddam Hussein, support for greater political participation in Arab states, encouragement of Arab governments to deal with the basic needs of their constituents more effectively, and a more radical approach to regional arms control are all essential components of such an alternative U.S.-led order in the Middle East. A settlement of the Palestinian problem is also essential to that new order, but it should not take precedence in U.S. policy over these other issues on the mistaken assumption that a Palestinian solution alone would remove the instability from a volatile region.

The United States is now in the fortunate position of being able to use its dominance to reshape the regional order on all these fronts. All the regional powers now recognize the United States as the preponderant power and seek its good graces. All of the friends of the United States in the region have been strengthened by the war's outcome; all of the enemies have been weakened. The United States now faces a choice. It can preserve its strategic interests by attempting to quarantine the region, or it can undertake a more ambitious effort to bring the Middle East into the New World Order that is busily being created elsewhere. The latter approach would require the removal of Saddam Hussein from power in Baghdad, the promotion of democracy in Kuwait, the control of weapons of mass destruction in the Middle East, and a settlement of the Arab-Israeli conflict. It is unlikely, given the record of the Bush administration, that this more ambitious approach will be adopted. But the United States should at least be aware of the road not taken so that some five years from now, if the balance of power in the Middle East is disrupted again, the United States will remember that there was a moment when it was in a position to lay down the law and chose not to do so.

ENDNOTES

1. The 1973 Arab-Israeli war is a case in point. The United States was taken by surprise when Egypt and Syria attacked Israel because it had been assiduously and successfully, the United States thought, promoting a balance of power in Israel's favor. That particular Middle Eastern order had failed to take sufficient account of Egypt's grievances. The United States intervened in the war to ensure that the balance of power was retained in Israel's favor (through a massive military resupply effort) and then intervened in its aftermath to negotiate a settlement that took account of Egypt's grievances. This resulted eventually in the Egypt-Israel peace treaty, which has since provided the cornerstone of a new Middle Eastern order, which has prevented any major conflict between the Arab states and Israel for the past eighteen years. (Arab-Israeli wars used to occur once a decade.) The resolution of the Egyptian-Israeli conflict has therefore done much to contribute to Middle Eastern stability, but it was only achievable by the maintenance of a favorable balance of power.
2. The classic text on this subject is Malcolm Kerr, *The Arab Cold War 1958–1967* (New York, NY: Oxford University Press, 1967).
3. The term was coined by Zbigniew Brzezinski. In the 1970s, the United States faced a major Arab-Israeli war leading to a superpower confrontation, an oil embargo, a revolution in Iran, and the Soviet invasion of Afghanistan.
4. See, for example, Hafiz al-Assad's speech on the anniversary of the March revolution, *Foreign Broadcast Information Service (FBIS)*, Near East and South Asia, March 9, 1989, pp. 35–36.
5. For a detailed analysis of U.S. policy toward Iraq, see Paul Gigot, "A Great American Screw-Up," *National Interest*, No. 22 (Winter 1990/91), pp.3–10.
6. See John Hannah, *At Arms Length: Soviet-Syrian Relations in the Gorbachev Era*, The Washington Institute for Near East Policy Paper, No. 18 (Washington, DC: The Washington Institute for Near East Policy, 1989).
7. For the only prescient analysis of the shift in the balance of power at the time see the remarks by Zalmay Khalilzad in "U.S. Policy in the Middle East: Toward the Next Administration," *Proceedings of The Washington Institute*, The Washington Institute for Near East Policy, Washington, DC, September 1988, pp.12–13; and "The Middle East in an Era of Changing Superpower Relations," *Proceedings of the Washington Institute*, The Washington Institute for Near East Policy, Washington, DC, April 1990, pp. 34–37.

8. Saddam Hussein had demonstrated his ability during the war to enhance the range of Scud missiles to enable him to hit targets throughout the Middle East. He also demonstrated his ability to manufacture chemical weapons and his willingness to use them. His nuclear program was believed to be ambitious, but most predictions put him at least five years away from producing a nuclear bomb. Some did suggest that he had the means to produce a crude device, but no one had any idea of the clandestine enrichment program that has now been discovered. See Mike Eisenstadt, *"The Sword of the Arabs": Iraq's Strategic Weapons*, The Washington Institute for Near East Policy Paper, No. 21, (Washington, DC: The Washington Institute for Near East Policy, 1990).
9. The arms included T-55 tanks, armored personnel carriers, multiple rocket launchers, artillery, and heavy machine guns. See Eisenstadt, *Sword of the Arabs*, p. 42.
10. See speech by President Saddam Hussein to Armed Forces General Command, April 1, 1990 in *FBIS*, April 3, 1990, p. 35.
11. As Paul Gigot reports, Saddam Hussein's April speech occasioned a policy review in the State Department that "died aborning." See Gigot, "The Great American Screw-Up," p. 7.
12. Since June 1989, Israel had observed Iraqi planes flying reconnaissance missions along the Jordan River, the integration of the Jordanian and Iraqi air defense systems, increased intelligence cooperation, the formation of a joint air force squadron, and visits by Iraqi division commanders to the Israel-Jordan border. See Eisenstadt, *Sword of the Arabs*, pp. 42–44.
13. See the speech by Saddam Hussein at the opening of the extraordinary Arab League Summit, May 28, 1990, in *FBIS*, May 29, 1990, p. 2.
14. See Saddam Hussein's speeches to the Arab Cooperation Council (ACC) in *FBIS*, Near East and South Asia, February 27, 1990, and the Arab League Summit in *FBIS*, Near East and South Asia, May 29, 1990.
15. See Hosni Mubarak's speech to the Arab League Summit, in *FBIS*, Near East and South Asia, May 29, 1990.
16. As Saddam Hussein analyzed it: ". . . the weakness of a big body lies in its bulkiness. . . . We saw that the United States as a superpower departed Lebanon immediately when some Marines were killed, the very men who are considered to be the most prominent symbol of its arrogance. . . . The United States has been defeated in some combat arenas for all the forces it possesses and it has displayed signs of fatigue, frustration and hesitation." ACC speech, in *FBIS*, Near East and South Asia, February 27, 1990, p. 5.
17. See Elaine Sciolino, *The Outlaw State* (New York: John Wiley and Sons, 1991), pp. 170–171; and Gigot, "The Great American Screw-Up," p. 6.
18. CNN interview with General Brent Scowcroft, July 14, 1991, cited in John Goshko, "State Department Sees No Problem in Glaspie's Cables on Saddam Meeting," *Washington Post*, July 16, 1991, p. A-14.
19. Transcript of the meeting between April Glaspie and Saddam Hussein, July 25, 1991, released by the Iraqi Foreign Ministry and published in *New York Times*, September 23, 1991.

20. These include $2 billion in aid from Saudi Arabia, U.S. acquiescence in Syria's takeover of Lebanon, and meetings with President Bush and Secretary of State Baker.
21. Assad said this in a meeting with Congressman Les Aspin, chairman of the House Armed Services Committee, March 1991, at which the author was present.
22. In fact we still know very little about his nuclear weapons production capability, biological weapons, or plutonium production.

5

SHOOTING AN ELEPHANT: THE EXPEDITION AND ITS AFTERMATH

Fouad Ajami

I

For those who love irony in history, the outline of the story has it in ample supply.

A great liberal power is concerned over its vocation. It had stood sentry against an ideological rival for nearly half a century. It held the line and kept the peace of a divided continent, but in an amazing year, an *annus mirabilis,* which put the pundits and the forecasters to shame, the enemy of the great liberal power collapses; the wards of the liberal power are no longer "between the grindstones," and the liberal power itself is at loose ends. With the unexpected victory came confusion about what looms over the horizon. No sooner had this happened than a certain kind of answer was supplied by a local despot on the periphery of power. He, too, had seen the great drama. Lamenting that the liberal power's rival had pulled off a "disappearing act," the despot pulls off a grand heist. His heist was both a challenge to the liberal power and an invitation to become its local enforcer and partner in a troubled zone of its traditional influence. But the liberal power does not play; instead it dispatches a vast expeditionary force against the local claimant. The despot's bid is thwarted. The great liberal power gets an imperium (of sorts) in a region that it had approached in alternate cycles of passionate interest and exasperation.

We know Saddam Hussein's heist of Kuwait, his *fait accompli*, as a challenge to American power. And so it was. But the claimant from Baghdad meant his deed as a fair division of the spoils in the Arabian peninsula. Kuwait would be his, but the privileged American position in Saudi Arabia staked out half a century ago would be honored. He had no claim against the realm of Al Saud. Riyadh had never reported to the *Wali* (the provincial governor) of Basra during Ottoman times, Kuwait had. Moreover, Saudi Arabia had willingly slipped within the American orbit; Kuwait had played the game of inter-Arab politics and lost.

More than a division of the spoils was even possible, the claimant suggested. He could order the peace of the Gulf; he was on the scene; America was far away. There were no other contenders. The Persian state was to be quarantined; the Saudi realm was a cautious realm that possessed no great power, no vast standing army. The "job application" made sense. The Iraqi state would wield enormous leverage over the world's oil markets, but America, Saddam Hussein said on one occasion, had her bountiful agricultural output and the power that came with its exports of food. Since Iraq imported some seventy-five percent of its foodstuffs, a balance was obtained. Food for oil: the deal was easy to see. They had done business, the Iraqis and the Americans. Together they had aborted the Iranian revolution, and contained the hordes from the East. The distant power had supplied military intelligence, agricultural credit, "dual use" technology, and the Iraqis had done the fighting on the ground.

George Bush (to paraphrase Winston Churchill) had not taken office, though, to preside over the liquidation of America's global position. He was not ready to accept the pension that Saddam Hussein offered. More fundamentally, the Iraqi contender had misjudged the temper of the Great Power. There was that anxiety that came with the great changes of that *annus mirabilis* of 1989. As Robert Tucker and David Hendrickson put it in a recent work on "the ideological origins of the New Word Order," that brief period between the fall of the Berlin Wall and the outbreak of the crisis in the Persian Gulf was a period of great confusion over America's world role. "The event of 1989 put an end to containment. . . . The result was to leave the United States without a military or ideological challenge. A long period in the nation's history had apparently come to an end. But if this was indeed the case, what then was the justification for persisting in the global role America had played since World War II? And if this role no longer seemed appropriate, given the recession of threats to the nation's security what is America's new role to be?"[1]

The expedition to check Saddam Hussein's bid rolled together long-standing American commitments in the Gulf and a new definition of America's role in the aftermath of the Cold War. A local despot had risen, but there was no local deterrent worth the name, and the deterrent had to be supplied by American power. Doubts there were aplenty about the lands that had to be rescued and the regimes that had to be shored up. There were worries (we owe this to Bob Woodward's first draft of the historical material, with all its problems[2]) that the Saudis might, as Bush put it "bug out" and accept a puppet regime in Kuwait, and that the ground would crack. There was a risk of rushing to distant shores—with a load of moral arguments—only to find a neighborhood squabble: the foreign power arriving with a great, big arsenal and a whole structure of rhetoric and judgment, the "locals" heading into the bazaar to cut their own deals. It would be quite a spectacle—a true tale of "innocence abroad," with the imperial power as the straight man at a rigged game. The gear would be unloaded, the "honor" and some treasure committed, but the affair would end with a deal over a couple of barren islands and a contested oil well.

It was "invariably the case in the east," George Orwell once wrote, that a "story always sounds clear at a distance, but the nearer you get to the scene of event the vaguer it becomes." The thing could end badly for the outsider. It had been only three or four years earlier that America had been taken to the cleaners by the Iranians over its hostages in Beirut and that the American straight man had walked out of the twisted alley ways of the local bazaar with his pockets picked and his pride battered. A foreign savior assembling a vast expedition had a lot to worry about. From Woodward's "Deep Throat" again, the mood of an August 4 meeting at Camp David: the Rubicon had not been crossed yet. The meeting brought together the president and all his principal lieutenants. "Among those gathered, there was a pessimism about the Arabs in general. Everyone heaped blame on them. They could not be relied on; they could pay off the thief at their throat . . . the United States, after all, had limited power and could not help those who didn't want to help themselves."[3]

But the Rubicon was crossed in a hurry: from deterrence at the Saudi-Kuwaiti border to rollback in Kuwait. If anything, the doubts about the ways of the Arabs steeled the American will that that matter had to be concluded in a decisive fashion. The Great Power could not afford to be snookered or conned: instinctively knowing that they were not good at haggling at the bazaar, the American decision-makers' strategy was to overwhelm the local contender, cut off his routes of escape, and make it as hard as possible for him to walk away with any gains from his adventure. He had thrown down a gauntlet in full daylight; he would not be granted a way out. There would be no French exit, no last-minute Soviet guide taking him past trouble, and no fraternal "Arab solution" that would save the Iraqi from the folly of his ways.

Because this was "the east," it became doubly important for America to be clear. The ambiguity was set aside. The structure of rhetoric was to be American through and through. It was not a "small country" that was at stake—Kuwait's record could not bear the weight of a major war; this was a country whose Minister of Foreign Affairs had dismissed the Carter Doctrine a decade ago on the grounds that "the people of this region are perfectly capable of preserving their own security and stability"—but a "big idea" of a "New World Order" and a world free of aggression. Restoration of the *status quo ante* would not suffice in the early phase of the effort. The endeavor was to be a moral crusade. The language and its symbolism may be lost on the people at the receiving end of the expedition—as indeed most of the symbolism was. It was impossible to convince the majority of Arabs outside the Gulf that America had come into their midst to repel aggression; there was no use trying. The symbolism was for the audience that mattered most: the American public that was being invited to sustain a vast, new expedition. The American public's taste for empire with its costs in blood and treasure—let alone the taste for an imperium in the Arab-Muslim world—was not a sure thing. The support had to be assumed, and then built along the way. The promise of the expedition was that it would be cheap in blood and treasure, and that the sacrifices would be commensurate with the interests and the values being secured.

The memory of the 1980s had to be shaken off if the new American push into the region was to be sustained at home and relied on by those whose interests were to be upheld in the Gulf. A bitter and frustrating decade of American involvement in the Arab-Muslim realms lay behind the Americans and their local interlocutors. The record of that decade hovered over this new endeavor.The trail of trouble had of course begun in Tehran. The "friendly royals" had seen the collapse of America's principal ally in the region, his flight from home with a handful of soil, and his search for a place of exile. The custodians of the Saudi state remembered the Carter administration dispatching a squadron of F-15s to Saudi Arabia in January 1979, as the final act was playing itself out in Iran. The dispatch of the American fighter planes was meant to reassure the Saudis, but President Carter had chosen to announce, while the planes were still in mid-air, that they had been sent unarmed. The key players in the House of Saud would remind the Bush administration of that episode. Then there was the fiasco in Lebanon—the hasty commitment by the Reagan administration in 1982–83 to a narrowly based Maronite regime, the pledges that the "forces of radicalism" would not be allowed to carry the day, and then the sudden abdication. The new commitment had to be made of more serious stuff. The states that opted for American protection had to be assured that America would not "bug out" on them as well. If it was to be dependence, it had to be dependence on a power that saw its commitments through.

A whole edifice was pushed out of the way of Desert Storm: that of Arab nationalism, and the assumption that a foreign power had to pay homage to it, that a war with Iraq would become an "American-Arab war," and that the "Arab street" would rise in rebellion against the outside power and threaten its regional interests. George Bush paid these cluster of unexamined ideas very little attention. These ideas figured prominently in the course of the American debate between August and the onset of the air war in January. They were made by Jimmy Carter, Zbigniew Brzezinski, George Ball, the National Council of Churches, and two former chairmen of the Joint Chiefs of Staff. The American effort would falter, it was said: America was not loved in those impenetrable Arab realms. It was a stranger in the midst of a region with raw nerves and bitter memories of waves of strangers who had come and conquered, only to pack up and leave, or be forced to leave. America was certain to become the "object of widespread Arab hostility," as Brzezinski put it.[4]

Bush was to break with the wisdom he received about the Arab world. It was the course of battle that was going to determine this conflict. That fabled "Arab street" (we should give that street a decent burial) could field no divisions on behalf of Saddam Hussein or cushion him in defeat. The Arab world was divided, it was easy to see. No undue homage was paid by the Bush administration to the protesters in Amman and Nablus and Tunis. The direct beneficiaries of the American expedition were a minority of Arabs—the Gulf and peninsula Arabs. They were less than 8 to 10 percent of that large Arab world. But what of it? The lands of the Gulf were the Arab lands that mattered the most; these were the oil-bearing lands. The flanks of the Gulf states could be covered by pressing Egypt and accepting Syria into the anti-Saddam Hussein coalition. The distinction between Arab "haves" and "have-nots" could thus be blurred. Those who hitched a ride with the Iraqi claimant were to be written off. Back doors were left open to some of them (to the Jordanian monarch, in particular). After the dust settled, the penitents could be rehabilitated. Beyond that, the Bush administration would not go.

Order was at stake. This was not a battle for Arab "hearts and minds." Two great commodities were in plentiful supply in that large Arab world: oil and envy. The lands of the Gulf were to be sheltered against the claims and the passions of the covetous world around them. Revisionist Arab nationalism—an ideology of the cities of the Arab world, Beirut, Damascus, Baghdad, and Cairo—would be kept at bay. No pan-Arab Bismarck would obliterate borders in the name of a phantom Arab nation, nor would a pan-Islamic millennium serve as a cover for Persian hegemony. The natural weight of the larger states—Iran, Iraq, and Saudi Arabia—would be respected. But revisionist bids by the two states given to such temptations (Iraq and Iran) were sure to put them on a collision course with American power.

A circle was closed in the Gulf with Desert Storm and the American victory over Iraq: Where the peace of the Persian Gulf had been a Pax Britannica, Saddam Hussein's audacious bid for mastery in the Gulf legitimized a Pax Americana as no distant Soviet threat could have. A decade earlier the Americans had tried to enlist the states of the Gulf in an anti-Soviet effort, but these states had kept their distance. There were no takers for Alexander Haig's "strategic consensus": the scheme looked like a mere replica of the security pacts of the 1950s. The local predator's bid in the summer of 1990 was made of deadly material. The failed lands of the Arab north had spilled southward into the worlds of the Gulf Arabs. In these vulnerable lands of the Gulf Arabs there would now be a greater appreciation of the work and the presence of a foreign protector.

We shall look back on the time between Britain's withdrawal from "east of Suez" in 1971 and the new American role in the Gulf as an interlude between two orders of power, an interregnum. There was, to be sure, a long-standing American commitment to the freedom of navigation of the Gulf. That commitment had been given expression by the Carter Doctrine in 1980. But the commitment of the Carter Doctrine was designed to combat any "outside force" that threatened vital interests in the Gulf. The Soviets represented that "outside force"; even the re-flagging of Kuwaiti ships in 1987–88, which had committed American power against Iran in the waters of the Gulf, had grown out of that concern. The Kuwaitis, it should be recalled, had succeeded in snaring the United States into that operation in March 1987 only after reports had reached Washington that Kuwait had struck a similar deal with the Soviet Union. In the new order of things, there would be a return to the work that Pax Britannica did. The peace would have to be kept against local predators as well.

British power had protected the smaller realms in the Gulf: Left to their own devices, the Wahhabi zealots of the second Saudi state (1824–1891) would have overrun Oman and Bahrain in the 1850s and 1860s. From the 1860s onwards, the small sheikhdom in Bahrain was sheltered by the British against the claims of the Persian state as well. Ibn Saud, too, had to be checked, early in this century; the temptation of that great desert warrior to claim the "land of his ancestors"—in Qatar and Oman and the states of the Trucial Coast—was discarded in favor of a live-and-let-live strategy with British imperial power. Ibn Saud knew the balance of forces and the might available to the British. He checked the unbridled enthusiasm of his followers, the *Ikhwan*, who wanted to claim their "rightful heritage in Bahrain, Oman, and Qatar and other places." And of course as late as 1961 the British had defended the independence of Kuwait in the face of Iraqi claims. This task now falls to the Gulf's American protectors.

II

America's is not quite an imperium with abandon. It is way too late in the evolution of nations for that. There will be no American political resident in the Persian Gulf. Ground troops will not be needed: The focus will be on air power and naval presence. The juridical equality of sovereign states will be honored. It will be, and appropriately so, a circumscribed imperial role. Order will be its principal concern. No messianic impulse will be unleashed on the lands of the Gulf and the Arabian peninsula. No great theories of reform will be let loose on alien societies. The shape of things to come—the power and then the limits to be drawn on the exercise of that power—was foreshadowed in the prosecution of the campaign against Iraq. After the swift victory, the moral crusade was brought to a halt.

Iraq's American conquerors were to be the most reticent of conquerors. America had no taste for an imperial role that would take it deep into the thicket of Iraqi politics. Old-fashioned imperialism (and the responsibility that went with it) has been banished from today's order of states. Even when the tide had gone out on empire, the British who "marched into Mesopotamia," earlier in this century, in the course of the First World

War, exhibited no reticence. Out of the wilderness of Mesopotamia they fashioned a new Iraqi polity. In a land of divided minorities they set up an Arab national state with Sunni rulers at the helm. Under the cover of a "native government" the British were to stay in Iraq for some four decades.

This new march into Mesopotamia was modest in the prerogatives (and responsibilities) it claimed for itself. General H. Norman Schwarzkopf would not be Schwarzkopf pasha, it was said. There would be no American high commissioner in Iraq. The Shia and Kurdish rebellions inspired by the American victory became the victor's embarrassment. Matters were of course quite different in the age of empire. In one of the memorable essays on the imperial age, "A Few Words on Non-Intervention," John Stuart Mill expressed the consensus of his contemporaries on the kinds of responsibilities that came with a Great Power's intervention. "A despotic government only exists by its military power," he wrote. If an outsider destroys that military power, he is forced "by the necessity of the case" to offer the vanquished society a new order in place of the old despotism. The Kurdish and Shia rebellions (to borrow John Stuart Mill's words again) demonstrated that there were people in Iraq "willing to brave labor and danger for their liberation."[5] A strong case could have been made for restructuring the Iraqi state. The great majority of the people of Iraq would surely have been grateful for the chance to be rid of the despot and the chance for something approximating normalcy after years of living on their nerves. But from that kind of responsibility the Bush administration drew back. The victory had been swift, the American and allied casualties surprisingly light. There was a desire to let well enough alone. The "turkey shoot" into which the campaign had degenerated after the collapse of the Iraqis was a further source of restraint. The British had wanted the military campaign to continue; they wanted to "close the loop" on the fleeing Iraqis. But they were overruled by Washington and told that it was not in the American military tradition to "shoot a fleeing enemy in the back."[6] The Iraqi claimant was pushed back behind an international frontier, the "regional balance" was reestablished: the work of order was done. In new and old world orders alike, a distinction was still maintained between the limits to be drawn for despots when they cross international frontiers and the liberties that they are permitted at home. "America came all this way to liberate Kuwait," an unnamed Iraqi student complained to a visiting American reporter, "but did nothing to liberate us."[7]

History and analogy are used and misused. The "Lebanonization of Iraq" stayed America's hand. The Bush administration did not trust its knowledge of Iraq and its distant ways and sects. America was haunted by the specter of Lebanon: the warring sects, the deadly fault lines. Nor did it trust the rebels and their intentions. The Shia were the country's majority. But it was hard to summon sympathy for them and for their vision of Iraq. In their eyes the Bush administration saw the gleam of theocracy—the distinct possibility of a realm ruled by mullahs. America had seen the terrible harvest of aggrieved Shiism in Tehran and Beirut. No one wanted a replay of the past. The Shia exiles sought to assure all those who cared to listen that they had no "sister republic" of the Iranian theocracy in mind, but it was hard to see them prevailing against the turbaned leaders and just as difficult to see them keeping their distance from the Iranian state.

The American policy that emerged after the defeat of the Iraqi state deferred to the Sunni-Arab states of the Gulf and to Turkey. The Arab states wanted no Shia victory in southern Iraq, and the Turks were sure not to countenance a daring Kurdish experiment in the north that might serve as a magnet for their own disgruntled Kurds. These Arab and Turkish concerns were to be grafted onto American policy. There were uses for that Iraqi state after all. Better the cruel state you know than a multitude of statelets and republics playing havoc with the region's borders and tribal loyalties. Freedom *of* nations was upheld in the new order. Freedom *in* nations was not.[8]

The imperium's legitimacy derived from the turmoil that preceded it. The local order of power—successive bids for dominion by the Shah, by the Iranian revolutionary state, and then by Saddam Hussein—had not produced a workable balance. The two decades of drift thus serve as the basis for the new American writ in the Gulf. And the new order will have, as it were, the consent of the governed. In truth, it must be recalled, the rulers of the small Gulf states had looked with dread on Britain's withdrawal a generation earlier. Wily men, they knew their world. Radical nationalist ideas were blowing their way. The rulers saw these ideological assertions for what they were—a threat to their autonomy and rule and riches. Pax Britannica's wards even offered to pay the costs of an imperial presence, but the British were determined to "untie the knot" and release themselves. The new dependence on America is simply a return to that older sensibility.

This need for American protection is not evenly spread in the Arab lands of the Gulf and the peninsula. It is strongest in Kuwait, no small irony; it is more tempered in the Saudi state. Kuwait, traditionally the most "pan-Arab" of the states of the Gulf, has been betrayed by the very gods that it had tried to propitiate. This was the state that had the cause of Palestine as its banner in international forums. From the early 1960s, the Palestinians had a favored niche in the political life of Kuwait. There was a workable bargain, or so it seemed for quite some time, between the privileged indigenous elite and their tutors, the more politically evolved Palestinians. The merchant principality led a schizophrenic existence: commerce and order mixed with radical pretensions to nonalignment and Pan-Arabism. The Palestinian vocation of Kuwait is now clearly of the past. In its place the Kuwaitis have conceived a deep attachment to American power. A stranger venturing into Kuwait (as I did in late May three months after the expulsion of the Iraqis) walked into a place where the shadow of a great power has fallen.

Virtually everything is projected onto America in Kuwait—the hopes of the "bourgeois" opposition for an American push in favor of political reform, and the hopes of the custodians of order that the American security guarantee will last. Few Kuwaitis believe that the Iraqi designs on their land and treasure have been abandoned. "We will need American protection for a good decade," a noted figure of the foreign policy elite observed. The man had a certain political history; he had been an Arab nationalist; he acknowledged the change in his politics and his new belief in American benevolence. He held out the promise of a deterrent force at some point "in the future." That force, manned by all the six dynastic states in the Gulf could have 200,000 men, he said; it could provide some protection against the threat from "Saddam or future Saddams." But the guarantor of last resort, he conceded, had to be none other than the power that restored Kuwait's national independence.[9]

The disillusionment with Arabism runs deep in Kuwait. The life span of this disillusionment is hard to forecast with any precision. There had been an accord, concluded in Damascus in March of 1991, to bring Syria and Egypt into an Arab force that would be stationed in Kuwait. The Egyptians and Syrians were to join a contingent drawn from the six dynastic states of the Gulf Cooperation Council. All kinds of extravagant hopes were read into these "six plus two talks": security for the dynastic states of the Gulf, subsidies for the Egyptians and the Syrians. But the Kuwaitis (and Saudis) had no great enthusiasm for the project. Egypt's financial needs are virtually limitless, her sheer weight unbearable to the Gulf states. Beyond the costs of the Egyptian and Syrian forces to be borne by Kuwait, the Egyptians made no secret that they wanted large numbers of their citizens admitted to Kuwait to claim the jobs forfeited by the Palestinians who quit the country. The Egyptians may have pushed for the admission of 300,000 of their own countrymen. The Kuwaitis had no intention of accommodating these kinds of numbers. The Kuwaitis have been burned. The Palestinian chapter in their experience—a large and resentful expatriate Arab community—has not been a happy one. In their view of things American protection holds out the promise of an escape from their difficult security dilemma. In early May, a mere two months after the Damascus Declaration, had been concluded the Kuwaitis and the Saudis walked away from it. They had never wanted to cede to a role in their security to begin with the Syrians and the Egyptians They had barely escaped calamity at the hands of a former ally (Saddam Hussein); they were in no mood to flirt with trouble once again. The Iranian state, too, lobbied against the Damascus Declaration, holding out the promise of an accommodation with the Gulf state if the Egyptians and the Syrians were kept out of the affairs of the Gulf.

The Egyptians were quick to shout betrayal: the "ink was not yet dry" on the Damascus Declaration, they noted. One of Egypt's most prominent pundits, Mostapha Amin, wrote that the Gulf States prefer to depend on American power rather than "on the turban and the fez." The Egyptians would not be the gendarmes of the Gulf. That role was assigned to the Great Power from afar. A young Kuwaiti put it with unusual candor in a letter to one of the editors of Egypt's leading daily, *Al Ahram*: The Americans, he said, were "more competent and less oppressive."[10]

Nearly a century ago, Mubarak al-Sabah, the crafty emir at the time, secured the independence of his city-state by making it part of Pax Britannica's burden and turf. A skilled player, Mubarak al Sabah was a beneficiary of the Great Game. As the British put it, they did not really want Kuwait then, but they didn't want "anyone else to have it."[11] Mubarak al-Sabah's inheritors are driven back now to his brand of statecraft.

The "Saudi way" is more steady than that of Kuwait. No sudden conversion to the benefits of an "American connection" was needed in the Saudi realm. That was always the House of Saud's principal line of defense. The Saudis had cast their lot with the Americans: they had borne the brunt of that American connection during the high tide of Arab nationalism; they had also garnered the benefits of that relationship. The defeat of Saddam Hussein was a vindication of the Saudi way. The "special relationship" with Washington had been nurtured for a perilous moment such as this. The realm that Ibn Saud had built lay at the mercy of the claimant from Baghdad. Bedouin society instinctively understood this kind of threat. It went beyond the incantations of nationalism and the worries about "infidels" coming into the peninsula and defiling the "holy land" of the Prophet. (The Saudis wryly noted that not all of Saudi Arabia is holy, that the oil bearing regions in the eastern province are outside that sacred geography of Mecca and Medina.) The whole society was implicated in the decision to invite the American protectors. It was a prosperous society; it lived well; it had no mass conscription and no way of resisting the raider across their border had he chosen to sack the kingdom. The clerical class sanctioned the decision, and looked the other way as those

Arab and Islamic and other "friendly forces" came to the defense of their land.

The Iraqi predator checked, his vaunted military machine demolished, and his economy in ruins, the Saudis could afford to return to the ways of the past. No visible threat loomed over the horizon. The Iranians had given up trying to export "revolutionary happiness"; Arab nationalism, too, was a busted flush. There was thus no corresponding need for a visible American presence. Because theirs was a state possessed of some size and wealth and burden (those holy places do matter after all), the Saudis had to keep sufficient distance from the Americans. American "facilities," and "command centers" could be provided by the smaller Gulf states—coastal lands like Kuwait and Bahrain with a history of free traffic with the outsider. Kuwait's own violation and ordeal could serve it well in that regard. It had not been spared when it observed the "red lines" of the culture; it could thus be forgiven its embrace of American power. Matters were stark in Kuwait. No one there could quarrel with whatever level of American protection and presence its rulers could secure. The Kuwaitis were glad to have the ten-year defense agreement concluded in September of 1991 between Kuwait and the United States, which would allow the United States to preposition equipment and to conduct joint exercises. Saudi Arabia's rulers, though, were bound to be held to a more demanding notion of sovereignty.

Although the monopoly of the House of Saud over matters of "high policy"—the security of the state, defense, foreign affairs—is virtually assured, its Kingdom remains a society where the foreigner treads lightly. (It was so for the interior of the peninsula even at the height of British power; there were British subsidies for Ibn Saud, but the Saudi state was always viewed as a realm apart.) No sooner had the dust of battle settled than a group of clerics, religious jurists, and imams of mosques (prayer leaders)—some fifty men in all—circulated a petition in May (the fax greasing the wheels of desert democratic yearnings) and then submitted it to the monarch. The signatories called for the convening of a *majlis shura*, a consultative assembly, for weeding out of the service of the state those accused of corruption, regardless of their rank, and for an independent judiciary. Though deferential, the petition ventured into those realms of high policy that Al Saud had always monopolized. The petitioners called for the building of a "powerful army, equipped from a variety of sources," for a foreign policy that guarantees "the interests of the nation and keeps it away from alliances which contradict Islamic law." That the American connection of the state and the dependence on American weapons are at the heart of the petition is hard to miss. In a silent polity there are still pockets of discontent, some cultural limits that the rulers of the state try not to cross.

The strength of the kind of sentiment expressed in this petition should not be exaggerated. It does not frighten the custodians of the state or dictate their policies. So thorough is the control of the dynasty and so domesticated is the religious class that the petition was denounced a few days after it was published by the highest clerics of the kingdom, *Hay'at Kibar al Ulama*, the Council of Higher *Ulama*. Advice, said the more senior *ulama* of the realm, should be rendered to the rulers in a "sincere manner" and should not lose its way on "rugged roads and turn into sedition." The dissenting clerics were reminded by their senior colleagues of the troubles that the kingdom was spared, and of "the bounty of security, stability and consensus" that has been its lot. The Saudi state is both *imara* (political authority, a prince's domain) and *ilm* (religious authority and knowledge). But the holder of political power, the man with the *imara* is supreme. The *ulama*, the men of religion, are given their due. But the custodians of political power, the vast royal household who was bequeathed its power and all that came with it by their father and grandfather Ibn Saud, are ascendant. When it truly matters, the dynasty is sure to prevail. Short of that, the cultural limits are observed. There is among the custodians of the realm an intuitive sense of what their land—its heartland in Najd still a very insular one, touchy about the outside world—will bear.

A pledge was made by the Saudi monarch when the American forces were invited into the Kingdom: These forces were there for containing Saddam Hussein's bid; they would leave as soon as the deed was done. The King had been second-guessed at the time. The case for appeasement of Saddam. It was garbed as prudence—fear of what he would do to the fortune of the Kingdom and to its oil installations in the eastern province were war to break out. A few among the ranks of the educated and the zealous also harbored doubts of their own about America's long-term intentions. Perhaps the whole thing (Saddam Hussein's heist of Kuwait) was a conspiracy, they cautioned. America might have lured the Iraqi predator into a trap: he would cross into Kuwait, America would come into the Arabian peninsula to stay. Many subscribed to the conspirarcy, *al mu'amara*. Shortly before the onset of the military campaign against Iraq, forty-three of the Kingdom's best and brightest—journalists, academics, technocrats, and a former minister of information—were to write to their monarch in that vein. "The Saudi people," they said, "wants the foreign armadas to depart from the Gulf as soon as the conflict is settled . . . we hope, Your Majesty, that we can confide in you our fears and the fears of our people that these navies remind us of those navies that colonized the Arabian Gulf under the pretext of protecting it, navies that enjoyed their powers here for tens of years. We fear that these new forces might end up with permanent bases in our region and that we may become pawns in their hands."[13]

The dire predictions had not materialized. The Kingdom's infrastructure had not been laid to waste by Saddam Hussein. In the aftermath, the King's decision, *AlQarar*, had become proof of his wisdom and judgment. His legendary father, Ibn Saud, had been the great chieftain who had unified the anarchic peninsula; his older brother, Faisal, having ruled from 1964 to 1975, had seen the state through a particularly hazardous era. Now it was Fahd's time, and *AlQarar* had been his gift to his people. He was dared by Saddam Hussein who did not think that Fahd would be decisive enough to invite the Americans. King Fahd made the decision. Saudi Arabia was spared the night of terror that descended on Kuwait. But together with the decision to bring the Americans came the added pledge that this would not inaugurate a new age of dependence. Appearances would still be kept; a larger army was promised—a less acute form of dependence on outside protection. Although Saddam Hussein's bid had been thwarted, sufficient questions were raised in the Saudi realm about the military preparedness of the state. "The Saudi citizens," the "liberal" petitioners had written to their monarch, "expected that the strength of the Kingdom in men and modern equipment was on par with the best of this region and that our armed forces were capable of coping with the armies of this region for we had devoted hundreds of billions of dollars to our armed forces. They were surprised before the rest of the world that we were incapable of checking the tyrannical Iraqi regime on our own. Your Majesty . . . we ask for mass military conscription for all Saudis, men and women. We feel great sorrow and bitterness that we stood in such weakness before the Iraqi regime, a regime with a smaller national income than ours, and a population base that is not much larger than ours."

Possessed of supreme confidence that those security pledges made by Presidents Franklin Roosevelt and Harry Truman nearly half a century ago would always be redeemed, the Saudis can balance the sort of deal to be struck with their protector. There was no need, the Saudis let it be known in the aftermath of Desert Storm, for a fundamental change in the their basic security policy. Above all, the Saudis wanted easy access to American weaponry. The American military presence was tied, the Saudis said, to the weapons the Americans were willing to sell. "In the future, we will take just the number needed to train on new equipment. It depends on how much new equipment we take," was the way Prince Khalid Bin Sultan, the Defense Minister's son, put it in an interview two months after the conclusion of the war.[14] With this came a quick trip to the arms bazaar and a message to the U.S. Congress. A few years back, in the mid-1980s, the Saudis had tired of the congressional battles that attended their requests for weapons. They had bought Tornado fighters from Britain, surface-to-surface missiles from China. They sought (within limits) to diversify the sources of their weapons purchases. This was part of their search for cover during that difficult decade that had begun with the revolutionary turmoil in Iran, but they never ventured so far as to damage that relationship that remains the cornerstone of the Kingdom's security. As they ducked for cover, the Saudis quietly prepared for the kind of threat that materialized in the summer of 1990: they built military facilities throughout the Kingdom, support facilities for F-15 and F-16 fighter planes, and airfields with redundant runways; they bought equipment "with an eye to their compatibility with possible American intervention forces."[15] If this was their way during a decade of American angst and rumors about America's decline, the Saudis would surely have no change of heart during a time of American preeminence.

III

An imperium dominated by a great liberal power will always be held to standards and expectations that go beyond the provision of order. More will be asked of it—by its custodians at times, certainly by others. Then, too, it is the "American national style" in foreign affairs that campaigns waged on behalf of stability and a "balance of power" rarely elicit great enthusiasm. It would not have been in the nature of things had this triumph in the Gulf been billed as a policing operation, and little else. The Kurds may not have gotten their "self-determination," the Shia rebels may have been stranded in the marshlands of the south, but Desert Storm still claimed a high moral purpose. The very language in which the endeavor was justified, the symbolism in which it was garbed, the understandable exuberance of the president who made a huge political bet and was vindicated, the mood of a nation anxious to forget previous military expeditions that ended in stalemate and frustration: This precluded a cold-blooded audit of the war and a return to "civilian life," as it were. The great discrepancy in fire power and casualties recalled the battle of Omdurman between Lord Kitchener's army of the Nile and the Mahdist forces in the Sudan in 1898; it was an embarrassment of riches. The runaway victory would beget expectations that went beyond the containment of Iraq. A sober man George Bush was, but he was human. The call of power (affordable power, at that) beckoned. Arabs and Israelis could be brought together; Greeks and Turks, too, could be made to see that in the light of reason, Cyprus could be shared.

This is not the first period of American primacy in the Middle East. There was another, a generation ago, in the aftermath of the October War of 1973. Then, too, there was a sense of American omnipotence. For a brief moment Pax Americana looked imposing: secure in Riyadh and Tehran and Jerusalem, Pax Americana had just incorporated Cairo. Even Damascus gave every indication that it was willing to play, and that the leader at the helm of the Syrian state knew that the balance in the region had tipped America's way. The poor in the region wanted American aid; the rich wanted American weapons and advanced technology and political protection; the Arabs, both rich and poor, wanted a Palestinian settlement, which they were sure lay within Washington's grasp.

As we know with hindsight, the moment of American hegemony was all too brief. Several years later, the Americanization of the region bred its nemesis: anti-Americanization, an aggrieved nativism in Tehran, and a determined campaign to banish American influence from the Arab-Muslim domains. The rejection of American power was only the other side of the dependence and the attraction. By 1979–80 the American structure had come apart.

The new gains made in Egypt still remained from the period of primacy. The Egyptians were determined to break out of the failed policies of the past; their leader, Anwar as-Sadat, had cast his own fate and that of his country with the glamorous power from afar. In America he saw a power that would get occupied Egyptian land back from Israel. In his eyes the distant power was to become something of a magician disposing of Egypt's political and economic troubles with its wand. But elsewhere in the Arab-Muslim world, America was to become a scapegoat for the region's troubles. A decade of promise and economic plenty that had begun in 1973 had closed with disillusionment. The dominant foreign power made an ideal target for all the disgruntled. This could come to pass again. In a region that has repeatedly invited foreign protection and patronage and then rejected it with equal zeal, a foreign power cannot be sure that its primacy is there to stay or that the promises of the local interlocutors will be kept or that the deference shown is for real. The "other superpower," the Soviet Union, has more or less bowed out of the game; it has little to offer. This leaves America with the riches—and the burden—of primacy. That commitment made to the "deradicalization" of Egypt in the mid-1970s required vast American treasure. A similar commitment to the Syrian state is not in the nature of things.

Three large ambitions were to be attached to the victory in the Gulf: arms control in the region, a resolution of the Israeli/Palestinian question, and the promotion of democratic politics and reforms in Arab societies. The first two were proclaimed by George Bush himself. The third goal came with the territory. It is no small irony that the cause of democracy in the Arabian peninsula was proclaimed by many who had opposed the military commitment in the Gulf to begin with. Since America had gone to the defense of these societies, went the argument, they had to be made worth the effort; in their politics Americans had to recognize fragments of their own politics.

There are grounds for profound skepticism about whether Pax Americana can truly deliver on any of these added ambitions. These matters do not lend themselves to the power of any outsider. The victory lap may have been heady; after running it, all kinds of obstacles may have seemed easy to surmount. War lent itself to the outsider's machines and its "smart" weapons.

Routine—the routine of a stubborn, old region possessed of its own furies—is an altogether different world. There, the outsider can be conned, waited out, humored, its writ ignored, or altered beyond recognition: "To the Sublime Porte in Washington from your humble servant in the provinces: Your instructions were received. They are being carried out, but, Your Eminence, I wish you knew how difficult it is to establish your New World Order among these truculent tribes. Please send more treasure and ammunition and ignore reports of our cruelty; you know the ways here."

If the past is any guide, the future of arms control in the region must face impossible odds; the Middle East is likely to remain a boom market for the arms trade. Between 1973 and 1984 the arms-exporting nations sold $150 billion worth of weapons in the Middle East and another $50 billion between 1985 and 1989. That region alone is the destination of 50 percent of the world arms trade. There are now pledges that past ways will be repudiated. The "Big Five" of the United Nations Security Council met in Paris last July to agree to "rules of restraint" on transfer of weapons to a region that it described as "a primary area of tension." Sweeping promises of a more restrictive attitude toward the transfer of weapons were put on paper. The Big Five proposed the following: (1) a freeze and "ultimate elimination of ground to ground missiles" in the region; (2) a ban on the "importation and production of nuclear weapons usable materials"; (3) an agreement by all the states of the region to become signatories of the Chemical Weapons Convention "as soon as it is concluded in 1992"; and (4) submission by all nations in the region of all of their nuclear activities to the International Atomic Energy Agency.[16] But the Big Five themselves are the principal marketers. Skepticism is in order about whether that pushers' huddle was really serious in its call for abstinence. Nor can the "second tier" suppliers be expected to go along. Scuds could be bought from North Korea. Brazil, South Korea, and Argentina have challenged the old oligopoly of the established exporters.

What restraint we are likely to see will be dictated by the financial circumstances of the powers of the region in the aftermath of the war. The wealthiest of the players, Saudi Arabia, ran a deficit of $15 billion and incurred some $60 billion in external obligation as a result of the Gulf War. On balance, though, the past is not reassuring: previous wars in the region have always spurred arms races. Money constraints aside, it is hard to see why this war should prove radically different. The access of Iraq to the weapons markets will be curtailed for the foreseeable future. Beyond that, the pledges of a region rid of its deadly ways are sure to be forgotten. The "smart" weapons that demolished Saddam Hussein's army were like the artillery with which Napoleon Bonaparte's army obliterated the Mamlukes of Egypt in 1798—The glamour weapons of a more advanced world; wars are their best advertisements.

Operation Desert Storm—forgive the metaphor—was desert warfare, out in the open. The alleys of the casbah in Nablus twist and turn. President Bush had rejected "linkage" between the struggle in the Gulf and the Israeli-Palestinian issue, but in a curious shift, soon after victory he asserted his own linkage. Perhaps it was that heady victory lap, or that sense of imperial burden. America had secured an Arab imperium, it would thus deliver a solution to the Israeli-Palestinian conflict for the Arabs. Brushed aside during the military campaign against Iraq, pan-Arabism made a comeback in the aftermath of the war. There was something of a return to that old axiom that the stability of Arab politics required a tolerable solution of the Palestinian question. Or perhaps it was Bush's inclination all along to overturn the status quo on the West Bank and Gaza; the war in the Gulf may have given him the chance and the self-confidence to do what he had always wanted. Ample evidence suggests that the status quo on the West Bank and Gaza concerned President Bush and Secretary of State James Baker in ways that it had not concerned the Reagan administration. A newly elected George Bush and his designated secretary of state had pushed for the "dialogue" with the Palestine Liberation Organization (PLO) to which the Reagan administration had given consent during its final days in office. Bush had sought the rehabilitation of Yasser Arafat and the PLO. He had devoted to Israel's settlements on the West Bank the sort of attention that was not in Ronald Reagan's nature and style. The dialogue with the PLO had aborted; the Bush administration called it off in June of 1990. But Bush's hand had been forced by Arafat's unwillingness to dissociate himself from acts of terror pulled off by operatives close to him. With the conclusion of the Gulf War, Bush would try again.

It was Bush's call, and he made it in the face of a bleak set of circumstances on the ground. The Palestinians had hectored Bush and his campaign—on the West Bank, in Jordan, and in the exile Palestinian communities everywhere. Their celebrated *intifada* had turned on itself and had begun to devour its own children. The stones were thrown, but the world had stood still on the West Bank. The status quo had not been overturned. That green line between pre-1967 Israel and the West Bank and Gaza had not been redrawn. Furthermore the Arab lands of the Gulf and the peninsula were in no mood to reward the Palestinians for the ride they took with the Iraqi claimant. Indeed, if anything, the Arabs of the Gulf wanted no high-profile diplomatic venture on the Palestinian issue. Nothing from the Likud government in Israel suggested a willingness to make major concessions to the Palestinians or to the Syrians. The Egyptians alone were sure to welcome a major American diplomatic initiative, but Egypt was not a direct party to the conflict. There was not much it could deliver.

A policy of "benign neglect" of the Israeli-Palestinian conflict would have had a lot to recommend it. We know the reasons: the Palestinians whose moral and political case rested on delegitimizing military occupations hailed the conqueror of Kuwait; their leaders broke faith with their Arab patrons and financial backers and never really came to terms with the enormity and the stupidity of what they had done; and the Israelis turned away from the Palestinians to concentrate on the influx and settlement of vast numbers of Soviet Jews. Nothing here suggests the possibility of a breakthrough, but victory is rarely cautious. The American president was now possessed of a conviction that American "credibility" could sweep away the things that stood in the way of a settlement.

Two factors strengthened the Bush administration's belief in its new authority: a bet that the PLO was severely weakened and that the Palestinians on the land, in the West Bank and Gaza, might now be ready for a break with the exiled leadership of the PLO; and a sense that Israel's pressing need for higher levels of American aid would force Prime Minister Yitzhak Shamir's hand. He could not afford to be the holdout; he would have to go along. The Palestinians had not been fans of this New World Order, but they stood in line in the aftermath of the war to receive the largess of the imperial power that they had hectored. Their nationalist narrative, the way they tell and write their history, gives them hope that deliverance may come at the hands of an imperial benefactor. In the Palestinian narrative, Israel was the gift of Pax Britannica—the Balfour Declaration, the mandate period serving as a nursery for the incubation of the Yishuv. In that narrative, little is determined on the ground: Great Powers dispose of local matters. Were it only so, that the work of empire was so easy to pull off.

The question of democracy remains. Can America export it to Arab and Muslim lands? Does it travel well, that democratic yearning? Should America's wards be made to honor it?

Bush has remained (appropriately in my view) dubious of the need, let alone the ability to export democracy. His is a conservative sensibility on these matters. Other lands, other systems: old cultures cannot be reinvented or taught dangerous new ways. Allies should be taken as they come—so long as their ways are not particularly notorious, and even if they were to err, they ought to be rehabilitated. The traffic of nations should continue—witness the way the Bush administration handled China after Tiananmen Square. For the states of the Gulf and the peninsula, Bush has a set of attitudes that parallel his outlook on the Chinese: the foreign world living by its own codes. Bush prides himself on knowing the Arabs of the peninsula. He appears to regard the House of Saud with something approaching benevolent affection. Bush's attitude toward the dynastic states of the Gulf has something of the appreciation that the British took to distant realms before "reform" caught up with empire. Love of pageantry, a fascination with an exotic style merge with an acceptance of the sly ways of the place and with the ability of its custodians to make and see through quiet bargains. It is a sensibility that galls liberals and liberalism. But that is the kind of bond Bush has forged with the "friendly royals."

Bush did not launch Desert Storm to force the al-Saudis to get their women to drive or get the Sabahs to trade their old ways for some "reform" and "power sharing." At no time in the preparations for war or in the war's aftermath did Bush venture into the internal arrangement of the dynastic states of the Gulf. Bush must have known that King Fahd did not bring a vast foreign army into his country to squander his father's realm or to willingly hand over the prerogatives of his family. Quietly, the Kuwaitis—always the Kuwaitis, for they lack the dexterity of al-Saud—were told to put an end to the trials of those accused of collaboration with the Iraqis, and that major American weapons sales would be made easier if they were to undertake political reforms. For the most part, though, the internal order of the states of the Gulf was not a matter that greatly concerned George Bush.

The truth of Arab politics is straightforward: There is a standoff between the dynasties (Al-Saud, al Sabah, the Hashemites, the other small states of the Gulf) and the despots (Saddam Hussein, Hafiz al-Assad, Mu'ammer Qaddafi). In between, in a place like Egypt, the hand of political power does not suffocate as much as it does in Baghdad and Damascus, but there, too, it is a military autocracy with the army as final arbiter. Say what you will about the dynasties and the monarchies, this much should be granted them: Saudi Arabia and the states of the Gulf are held together by a social contract between the dynasties and the societies they rule. There is a "fit" between ruler and ruled. There is enough wealth in the dynastic states (Jordan aside) to buy off the disgruntled and to strike a time-honored bargain between ruler and ruled: the ruler keeps the peace, the citizenry minds its own concerns. No "visitors of dawn" haul people off to political prisons in the dynastic states; men do not "disappear" as they do in Damascus and Baghdad. This is not quite democracy, but it is a benign political order.

Trouble came, it is true, to Kuwait: A gap opened between the al-Sabahs and their critics, between "the runners" and those who stayed behind and endured the Iraqi occupation. Leaflets and pamphleteering came to Kuwait in the aftermath of its liberation. A "bourgeois opposition" of sorts developed—merchants, academics, former parliamentarians. But if a bet has to be placed, the bet should be made on an accommodation between the ruling order and its critics. The wealth of the state is a great source of power, the divisions of the place (the Sunnis, the Shia, those without citizenship) yet another. The play between prince and merchant is an old one in Kuwait. Favors and contracts could be given or withheld. Men grumble but they make their peace. It is hard to see Kuwaitis of ease and comfort manning the barricades. The cruel security dilemma of Kuwait shores up the hold of the state. Men are reluctant to play with fire. Larger players hover over Kuwait–Iraq, Iran, Saudi Arabia. The temptation to tinker with the ways of the vulnerable city-state has to pay heed to what the neighborhood permits.

The states of the Gulf are *sui generis*. They are truly a world apart. The authority that Saudis accord their rulers may jar a modern liberal sensibility, but it is indigenous and true to the place. The Arabian peninsula was a land of anarchy and hunger. Its history—known to those old enough and transmitted to the young—is of plunder and cruelty, the bedouin raid, the insecurity of life and of possession. In 1928, at a critical juncture in the Kingdom's history, Ibn Saud was challenged by his zealous followers, the *Ikhwan* (a religio-military brotherhood). The *Ikhwan* had provided the shock troops with whom Ibn Saud had achieved his major territorial conquests in the 1920s. But the true believers had gotten out of hand. They wanted a permanent campaign, godly warfare, war against the "infidel" regimes in Transjordan and Iraq. Ibn Saud, however, now sought order and the consolidation of the realm. He assembled the leading figures in his realm and laid out his claim to rule. "Might is for God alone and you will remember that when I appeared to you you were parties and sections killing each other and robbing each other, and all those whom God caused to rule you whether Arabs or non-Arabs used to make intrigues amongst you to keep you separated to decrease your power and to make you vanish away."[17] Some sixty years later, as Saddam Hussein massed his forces on the Saudi-Kuwaiti border, Ibn Saud's son and fourth successor, King Fahd, would remind his people that the realm had been built out of "bush and stones," that the great disorder that had visited what had been happier and more prosperous places—Iran, Lebanon, Iraq, etc.—had passed them by. This is not the stuff out of which modern politics is made. But an outsider swaggering in with preconceived notions of change and reform will be humbled in the peninsula.

The war was short and was fought at the edge of a vast peninsula. The social structure of the place—its habits, its old ways—was left largely undisturbed. It had been a campaign between an Arab despot and a foreign savior. Men did not have to change to be rescued. The rescue came from afar. This great storm would not uproot the place. The expectations of a profound change in the ways of the Saudi realm were not to be fulfilled. The war did embolden some Saudis to step forth and ask for more participatory politics. The same forty-three men who had warned of the dangers of a permanent American presence in the Gulf submitted a "reform" petition in the aftermath of the war. This time, their demands were those of "modernist" Muslims. Their protest was against the zeal of the religious class, the dreaded ways of the *mutawwa* (the religious police who patrol the streets and sometimes venture into private homes to harass men and women over all facets of religious and social observance), prayer, the veiling of women, and even the length of a man's *thoub*. (The zealots see a long *thoub* that touches the ground as a sign of vanity.)

A distinction was drawn by these petitioners between the infallible *Sharia* (Islamic law) derived from the Koran and the ways of the Prophet on the one hand and the interpretations given Islam by mortals who could err, who interpret Islam "in accord with their knowledge and judgment with the time and the place" on the other hand. These latter interpretations, the reformers said, are "subject to error, to give and take." No one ought to be allowed to "claim for himself a monopoly over what God and the Prophet had intended." The "committees," that oversee the *mutawwa*, the Committees for the Propagation of Virtue and the Prevention of Vice, were specifically targeted in the reformers' petition. These committees were in need of a "thorough overhaul that would regulate their functions in a precise manner," that would select for these the right caliber of leaders and members for them. The reformers wanted a "dialogue" in an "open Muslim society."[18]

The petitioners were men of the society, but they pressed for some novel things. The place of women in the social order was brought up by the petitioners: "Many realms in public life could be opened to women" even as they continued with their "high duty" of "raising future generations." The message to the ruler was a plea to rein in the power of the zealots and check their intrusions into the lives of others. These committees work with the ruler's indulgence and with the treasure of the state—halfway between volunteerism and state employment. The technocrats with foreign degrees and a desire for normalcy could not take on the *mutawwa* and the strict sensibility that sustains the *mutawwa*—hence the appeal to the monarch. A *bay'ah*, an oath of allegiance was made to the King by the petitioners, an affirmation of loyalty to the "ruling family." But the custodian of political power was invited to side with change, to tip the balance of power against zealotry and obscurantism. It is a fragile terrain on which the would-be modernizers stand, and they know it. The threat to them does not come from the ruling political authority, but from the larger social order, its xenophobia, and its aversion to great changes.

It is not such an intolerable dilemma for the dynasty: on one side the zealots, that vast "Koran belt" in the heartland of Najd with its austere brand of Islam and tradition, on the other the "reformers," touched by foreign ways and ideas. And there stands the House of Saud, brokering the two worlds. On their own the zealots would self-destruct: that was the fate of the first Saudi realm (1745–1818), which burned with religious fury and wrath, tempted the fates, and was broken by foreign intervention when it ran afoul of the Ottoman imperial order. Someone will have to pick up the tab of zealotry, keep the oil flowing, and do business with the foreign world. In the House of Saud the zealots have all the "tradition" and piety they can hope for. The traditionalists, and the *ulama* who lead them in the Saudi realm, are spared the massive assaults that have been launched by "modernizing" Muslim elites against religion and its place in the social order in Turkey, Iran, Egypt, and elsewhere in the Muslim world. No "modernist" utopia is given a free run in the peninsula. The indignities heaped on the *mullahs* of Iran by the Pahlavis, and the erosion of the powers of the official religious institution in Egypt since 1952 are unthinkable in the Saudi state. One-third of the educational curriculum is devoted to religious topics—an unrelieved tedium that gives the *ulama* vast authority and power. The *ulama* have done well by the dynasty.

But the reformers, too, know they cannot go it alone. They know the weight of custom and tradition; they know the odds against them in a battle with the traditionalists; and in the dynasty, they have a buffer. The reformers are shrewd enough to know that power, ultimate power, cannot be theirs. One-quarter century or so earlier, it was possible to think that monarchy is of the past and that men who dispose of it (as they had in Egypt, Iraq, and Libya) would be delivered into a better world: even some rebellious young princes within the ruling family (dubbed the "Free Princes") thought that way and took their campaign against the dynasty to Beirut and Cairo, dissociating themselves from their own family and its right to rule. But that was before the terrible failures of the "new politics" of radical nationalism. The conviction that Arabs who break with the past will create a better political order has been shattered.

The failure has been most acute in the republics of the Arab world, among men who had a chance to build modern politics. It was not lost on these more "modern" Arabs that the last democratic wave, which hit all kinds of unlikely shores, bypassed the Arab world. It left the republics in the Arab world largely untouched. There, as Arabs would put it, the states have eaten the green and the dry, devoured competing centers of power—the bazaar, the religious institution, the guilds, the labor unions. There is no indication that a change is in the offing, or that the coattails of a great liberal power will help. The great concerns of the Arab world have been those of thwarted nationalisms; the security of the realm, national independence, the power of an encircling, superior civilization, and then that consuming concern of half a century over Palestine and the fate of the Palestinians. Democracy was not the public good for which men and women fought. The self-confidence that a civil society needs if it is to grope for participatory politics is nowhere to be found in Arab politics. Better sixty years of tyranny than one day of anarchy, goes a Muslim maxim. History here remains a chronicle of kings and would-be kings.

Where the ballot made its appearance in Arab politics recently (Jordan and Algeria), it went the way of the fundamentalists. The inspiration of the fundamentalists is the millennium, not democracy. And besides, the fundamentalists were incapable of unseating the entrenched states at the end of the day. The fundamentalists who beat the ruling *nomenklatura* in Algeria's municipal elections, in the summer of 1990, fed off the familiar troubles of a command economy, a heavy debt burden, unemployment, a crippling bill for food imports, and a growing gap between a ruling elite steeped in the past and legions of half-educated young men and women for whom the great anticolonial battle against France was like a legend from bygone medieval times. But the Islamicists who promised to make Algeria "as green as California" could not go very far. They lacked the skills and the experience. They devoted their energy and efforts to the policing of morals and the enforcement of rituals. They bullied the people of the municipalities they controlled, cracked down on music concerts, and tried to turn their domains into small realms of virtue. They frightened off the professionals and the emancipated. Two forms of escape were on full display in Algeria: back to Islam, and a flight of those who could get out to France. Thousands of professionals quit the country for France—a special kind of "boat people" was the way they were described. Islam could drape the failure and the hurt, but it could not find a way out of the postcolonial dilemma. One year after the municipal elections, the ruling party struck back and ended the half-hearted experiment with democracy.

The same story line played out in Jordan. An embattled monarch held an election in the fall of 1989. During the preceding spring, riots had swept the country—a massive wave of unrest over cuts in public spending and curtailment of subsidies of basic commodities. The country was living beyond its means. The election was one way of implicating the society in the new austerity. The result was an embarrassingly strong showing by the Islamicists. The Islamicists picked up thirty-four of eighty parliamentary seats. Cabinet seats that matter to the Islamicists, like education and social welfare, were then given to them. Here, too, the Islamicists whose rallying cry was "Islam is the solution" soon reached a dead end. The Gulf War and its outcome demoralized them; there was no treasure to spread, no resources with which utopian ideas could be carried out. As the monarch who had opened up the political life of the country sought his country's rehabilitation in the aftermath of the war, the cabinet with strong Islamicist representation was dissolved only months after it had been formed. No illusions were entertained in Jordan as to where political authority resided. Amman was "a village" when his grandfather came to the wilderness of Transjordan seven decades ago, the Jordanian monarch is prone to reminding his countrymen. The problem of authority—

its sources, its limits—is the intractable problem of Arab political life. Is it any wonder that George Bush stuck to order and the balance of power?

IV

In one of his arresting (and ambivalent) essays on imperial burden, "Shooting an Elephant,"[19] George Orwell tells of an incident that occurred while he was with the Imperial Police in Burma. The episode speaks to George Bush's task when he set out to confront the rampaging Iraqi claimant. An elephant had gone "must" and was ravaging the bazaar. Would the sahib do something about it? To be on the safe side, the sahib takes a Winchester rifle. "The Burmese had no weapons and were quite helpless" against the elephant. A crowd gathered. The crowd had not shown much interest in the elephant; "it was different now that he was going to be shot." The sahib had not intended to shoot the elephant, but the crowd was there. "And suddenly I realized that I should have to shoot the elephant after all. . . . To come all that way, rifle in hand, with two thousand people marching at my heels, and then to trail feebly away, having done nothing—no, that was impossible." The elephant is shot; the crowd that hated the policeman descended on the elephant with "dahs and baskets" and stripped its body "to the bones."

Never mind that Bush shot but did not kill his elephant. Bush did not "trail feebly away" after he took out his big rifle and set out before a large crowd to the Arabian peninsula. No gratitude was assured at the end of the day; the crowd could take and hoot at the same time. But the elephant had to be shot. This came with the turf. That was what manning a distant place required. Between the sahib and the crowd with no weapons and no way of dealing with the raging elephant, there was no love, only a convergence of interest, an accord that the elephant had to be shot if routine is to return.

ENDNOTES

1. Robert W. Tucker and David Hendrickson, "The Ideological Origins of the New World Order," unpublished manuscript, 1991.
2. Bob Woodward, *The Commanders* (New York, NY: Simon and Schuster, 1991).
3. Ibid.
4. The range of the debate on the crisis is reproduced in Micah Sifry and Christopher Cerf, *The Gulf War Reader: History, Documents, Opinions* (New York, NY: Random House, 1991).
5. John Stuart Mill, "A Few Words on Non-Intervention," *Dissertations and Discussions*, Volume III, 1864–67, p. 169.
6. *New York Times*, August 20, 1991.
7. *Wall Street Journal*, August 1,1991.
8. The distinction was made by my colleague, Rober W. Tucker, at the Foreign Policy Round Table, the Council on Foreign Relations, June 20, 1991.
9. Field notes, Kuwait and Saudi Arabia, May–June 1991.
10. Mostapha Amin's statement was in *Al Akhbar*, (English weekly) May 10, 1991; *Al Ahram*, May 11, 1991. See also *Al Ahram*, May 16, 1991, particularly an article titled "Some Like It Foreign."
11. The British attitude toward Kuwait during that crucial period is summarized by Jacob Goldberg, *The Foreign Policy of Saudi Arabia: The Formative Years, 1902–1918* (Cambridge, MA: Harvard University Press, 1986).
12. The Saudi petitions are leaflets in my possession. The dissidents' petition was submitted to King Fahd on May 18, 1991. The rebuttal by Hay'at Kibar al Ulama was issued on June 3, 1991.
13. The "reformers'" petition cited here was circulated in the fall of 1990; and leaflet in my possession.
14. *New York Times*, April 29, 1991.
15. Nadav Safran, *Saudi Arabia: The Ceaseless Quest for Security* (Ithaca, NY: Cornell University Press, 1988), p. 447.
16. *U.S. State Department Dispatch* (Washington, DC: Department of State), July 15, 1991.
17. Christine Helms, *The Cohesion of Saudi Arabia* (Baltimore, MD: Johns Hopkins University Press, 1981), pp. 254–255.
18. "Reformers'" petition.
19. George Orwell, *Shooting an Elephant and Other Essays* (London and New York, NY: Harcourt, Brace and World, 1950).

Part III

ECONOMIC/ POLITICAL LESSONS

6

OIL, THE MIDDLE EAST, AND THE WORLD ECONOMY

Richard N. Cooper

Iraq's invasion of Kuwait in August 1990 reminded the world once again of its dependence on the Middle East for oil, and of the decisive role of oil in the world economy. Fortunately, that disturbance to the world oil market occurred at a time of ample excess capacity, such that oil production in 1990 modestly exceeded production in 1989 despite the loss of the Iraqi and Kuwaiti supply for over four months of the year (effectively less, however, because of the long "pipeline" of oil at sea on its way to market). An invasion by Iraq in 1994 or 1995 would have been much more serious, partly because of an advance in the quality of Iraq's weaponry, but mainly because of the much tighter world oil market that is likely to exist in the mid-1990s. Despite the excess capacity, which with a short lag was brought into production, world oil prices were double the preinvasion price in late August and September, from which they gradually receded. It will be argued that Iraq's invasion along with the Bush administration's mishandling of the strategic petroleum reserve (SPR) tipped the United States into recession, with a loss of output greatly exceeding the direct costs of military action.

Some projections of world energy demand, with emphasis on oil, are presented first. Then the implications of growing dependence on the Middle East for macroeconomic management of the world economy are discussed. A final, briefer, section addresses the possible implications for energy demand of growing concerns about the possibility of global climate change.

THE OUTLOOK FOR ENERGY DEMAND

For reasons that will be given, few analysts venture long-term *forecasts* of energy demand, e.g., by the year 2000. They do however produce *projections* or "scenarios." We will focus here on two scenarios developed by the International Energy Agency (IEA), a Paris-based organization of the governments of the industrial democracies created in 1975, following the first major Organization of Petroleum Exporting Countries (OPEC) price increase. Long-term projections provide a useful starting point for thinking about the future, a baseline against which the implications of alternative events or policies can be compared. A good projection requires analysts to be clear about their assumptions and compels a certain degree of consistency in assumptions.

The standard technique starts with projections of economic growth rates, drawn from demographic (labor force) and productivity trends, and derives the implications for different sectors of the economy (e.g., industry, transportation, housing). Energy coefficients are then applied to these sectoral growth rates. These may then be decomposed to different fuels by informed guesses about fuel composition. This decomposition is of course influenced by the relative prices of fuels, the key to which, in the next decade or two, is the price of oil. An assumption must therefore be made about oil prices (this assumption is partially, but only partially, dependent on the projected growth in demand for oil). The demand for different fuels, and for energy in general, is then adjusted on the basis of past behavior in response to relative price changes. Energy prices in turn may feed back on the initial rate of growth so the entire set of projections in principle is interdependent. Controversy among specialists attends each element of the projection, but the ranges of informed opinion are limited and can themselves be illuminating.

The IEA in mid-1991 offered two scenarios for world energy demand to the year 2005, with intermediate stops at 1995 and 2000.[1] They differ mainly in their assumption about the future of oil prices. The first scenario assumes that crude oil prices rise steadily from $21 a barrel in 1992 to $35 a barrel (in 1990 dollars—that is, abstracting from general inflation) in 2001 and then level out. That price is well below the $52 a barrel (in 1990 dollars) reached in 1981 but represents a near doubling from the levels of the late 1980s. The second scenario assumes that crude oil prices remain about $21 a barrel (in 1990 dollars) throughout the period 1992–2005.

Under the first scenario, world energy demand grows from 8,727 million metric tons (mmt) oil equivalent in 1989 to 12,498 mmt in 2005, or 2.2 percent a year (see Table 1). This growth is predicated on an average annual economic growth of 2.7 percent in the industrial democracies (Organization for Economic Cooperation and Development [OECD] countries), 3.1 percent for the Soviet Union and Eastern Europe, and 4.6 percent in developing countries. Since demand for energy rises less rapidly than economic growth, in contrast to historical experience before 1973, considerable conservation of energy is built into this projection.

Demand for oil under this scenario increases from 3,183 mmt to 4,147 mmt, or 1.7 percent a year over the period as a whole, slowing to 1.2 percent a year during the five years 2000–2005.[2] All other forms of energy, including nuclear, grow more rapidly,

Table 1 Energy Requirements and Oil Consumption

World Primary Energy Requirements
(million metric tons oil equivalent)

	1989	*1990*	*2000*	*2005*
World Total	8.7	10.0	11.1	12.5
OECD	4.1	4.5	4.8	5.1
USSR and E. Europe	1.9	2.2	2.4	2.7
Developing Countries	2.1	2.7	3.3	4.1

World Oil Consumption
(million metric tons oil equivalent)

	1989	*1990*	*2000*	*2005*
World Total	3.18	3.65	3.90	4.15
OECD	1.79	1.93	1.92	1.97
USSR and E. Europe	0.54	0.62	0.67	0.71
Developing Countries	0.86	1.11	1.32	1.46

Source: International Energy Agency (IEA), *Energy and Oil Outlook to 2005*, (Paris: May 1991), Table 2.

with natural gas taking the lead at 3.7 percent a year. Nonetheless, the world demand for oil rises about 30 percent over the period, from 64.5 million barrels a day (mbd) in 1989 to 83.6 mbd in 2005. Where is the additional oil to come from?

Even with the postulated increase in oil prices, production in the OECD countries (mainly the United States and North Sea) is projected to decline over the period, especially after 1995. Soviet production is assumed to be flat at 11+ mbd, its estimated 1990 level. Production in developing countries outside the Middle East is projected to rise by about 8 mbd, but half of this merely offsets the declines of 4.5 mbd (from 1989) in the OECD plus the Soviet Union. So the bulk (80 percent) of the required increase of 19 mbd must come from the Middle East, mainly Iraq, Iran, and the Arabian peninsula. On this basis, 39 percent of the world's oil supply would come from the Middle East in 2005, up from 26 percent in 1989 (see Table 2). No doubt the Middle East could provide such additional amounts of oil by 2005 with appropriate investment, but will the investments be made? And does the rest of the world want to live with the consequential increase in dependence on Middle East oil? We return to these topics below.

The second scenario assumes an oil price that rises slightly to $21 a barrel (1990 dollars) in 1992 and remains unchanged at that level through 2005. Under these circumstances world demand for oil would be just over 1 percent higher than under the previous scenario in 1995 but would be nearly 15 percent higher in 2005, 97.5 mbd rather than 85 mbd.[3] Most of the increased demand (8.6 mbd) would be in the price-sensitive OECD coun-

Table 2 Sources of World Oil Supply (percentage share)

	1989	*1995*	*2000*	*2005*
World supply (mbd)*	64.5	73.7	78.7	83.6
OECD	25	20	17	15
USSR & E. Europe	19	15	14	14
Middle East	26	34	36	39
Other Developing Countries	30	31	32	33

*Excluding processing gain of 1.3 to 1.4 mbd.

Source: Calculated from IEA, *Energy and Oil Outlook to 2005*, Table 1.

tries, which would consume nearly 21 percent more. Moreover, the lower price would discourage oil development in the high cost areas of the world so OECD production would be 11 percent lower, and Soviet production 5 percent lower, than in the first scenario. Dependence on the Middle East would therefore be even greater, with that region providing 48 percent of the world's oil by 2005, compared with 26 percent in 1989.

These projections are global in scope. The U.S. Department of Energy (DOE) undertakes projections for the United States, as does the highly-respected Gas Research Institute (GRI). Their projections are broadly consonant with the IEA scenarios. DOE has undertaken four projections to the year 2010—two similar to the IEA price scenarios, each with the U.S. economy growing on average 2.1–2.2 percent a year, one with world oil prices rising to $34 a barrel (1990 dollars) by 2010, the other with oil prices rising no higher than $23 a barrel by 2010. In addition, DOE undertakes a scenario with higher growth (2.8 percent a year) in the United States and a scenario with an even greater rise in oil prices (to $45 a barrel), most of which occurs early in the period.[4] The latter two scenarios are less plausible and will not be considered here.

Under the higher price scenario, demand for energy grows at 1.1 percent a year, just over half the growth rate. (This "energy elasticity" at 1.3/2.7=48 is just under half in the IEA scenario for the OECD as a whole, including the United States.) U.S. oil production falls by over 3 mbd under the higher price scenario (and over 4 mbd under the lower price scenario). Falling production combined with rising consumption implies a rise in imports from 1989 to 2010 of 6 mbd under the higher price scenario (and 8.6 mbd under the lower price scenario), implying in turn an oil import dependence of 64 percent by 2010 (72 percent on the low price scenario), up from 42 percent in 1989.[5]

Every other year the GRI produces a "baseline" projection of U.S. energy requirements and production, from which various excursions can be taken. GRI's most recent baseline projection assumes U.S. growth of 2.3 percent a year between 1989 and 2000, slowing to 2.0 percent between 2000 and 2010.[6] Crude oil prices (U.S. average refiner acquisition cost) are expected to rise at an accelerating pace over the next twenty years, from $18.62 a barrel in 1989 to $20.13 in 1995, $22.76 in 2000, and $35.30 in 2010 (all in 1990 dollars). These assumptions are thus similar to, but not identical with, the IEA and DOE higher price scenarios. In particular, GRI oil prices rise considerably more rapidly in the second half of the period than in the first.

Total U.S. primary energy requirements rise at 1.4 percent a year, for an energy elasticity of 1.4/2.2=.64, somewhat higher than that of DOE (for the United States) or IEA (for OECD). While the rate of energy conservation is assumed to slow from the past fifteen years, substantial energy conservation is still assumed to take place compared with pre-1973 experience, when the energy elasticity was around unity. Consumption of petroleum products grows at 1.5 percent a year, slightly higher than total energy (and again in contrast with IEA and DOE projections). Domestic oil production declines by about 1.5 mbd (half the decline that DOE projects). The combined result of declining production and increased consumption is a sharp rise in oil imports, by 7 mbd between 1989 and 2010, resulting in an oil import dependence of 64 percent in the latter year, the same as DOE projects.

The overall picture that these projections paint is one of a sharp increase in U.S. dependence on imported oil and of a sharp increase in world dependence on Middle East oil. Moreover, the lower the price increase for oil, the higher those dependencies become. Like all projections, they rest on particular assumptions about the future that could be, and indeed are likely to turn out to be, wrong. The record of long-term projections as forecasts is not outstanding.[7] Nonetheless, they embody the best information that is available today and thus inform business decisions and policy planning. Where are the major uncertainties, focusing on the next decade rather than the first decade of the next century?

UNCERTAINTIES IN THE PROJECTIONS

Small differences in average annual growth rates and in energy elasticities can cumulate to large differences over a long period of time, but they are not so important over a few years. They can of course be overwhelmed by business cycles in the short run of 2–3 years, but all these projections abstract from business cycles and embody growth rates that are sustainable over a longer time period.

A second source of uncertainty concerns oil and gas production in the Soviet Union, the world's largest producer of oil. The Soviet fields are now in decline. IEA assumes that the decline will be halted by the mid-1990s but that production beyond then will simply recover the (modest) loss until then. It is possible to imagine, however, much sharper declines there than IEA assumes, such that little is available for export (i.e., a serious collapse of the Soviet industrial economy). Such an eventuality would deprive the rest of the world of about 1.5 mbd of Soviet oil, which would have to be made up from conservation and fuel switching induced by oil price increases, or by increased production elsewhere, largely the Middle East.

On the other hand, it is said that with an injection of Western capital and technical knowledge about oil field management, Soviet oil production could be increased by 2 mbd by the mid-1990s. Increased gas production that can substitute for oil within the Soviet Union could increase the exportable oil surplus even more. This proposition must be largely conjectural since little is known outside the Soviet Union about Soviet potential although the flow of information has greatly improved. Moreover, extensive price reform in the Soviet Union may lead to the outcome that some Soviet oil, while technically accessible, is uneconomic because of the high cost of bringing it to market. Between the two possibilities is a swing of perhaps as much as 3 mbd, a substantial amount, 5 percent of current world output.

A third source of uncertainty, acknowledged in the scenarios themselves, concerns the price of oil. This source does not involve sharp but temporary disruptions to oil flow, a topic taken up below, but rather the basic investment strategy of a few oil-producing countries, especially Saudi Arabia. The problem here is that known and probable oil reserves are heavily (nearly two-thirds) concentrated in the Middle East, and from a technical and economic point of view, these are easily accessible compared with other sources of oil (e.g., western Siberia or the outer continental shelf). If oil exploration and development were left entirely to private parties, without government interference or political disturbance, Saudi Arabian and Kuwaiti oil fields would be much more heavily developed than they are today because of their low costs of development and extraction, and some higher cost sources around the world would not have been developed. For this reason, the alternative price scenarios depend, in the final analysis, predominantly on Saudi Arabian investment decisions. In terms of the IEA scenarios, if the Saudis and others in the Arabian peninsula decide to increase their production (from 1989) by 29 mbd by 2010, and make (or allow) the investments required to do so, world oil prices will remain in the vicinity of $21 a barrel. If their investment decisions permit a production increase of only 15 mbd, prices will rise (relative to the general price level) by about 3.5 percent a year. That critical question involves a series of political decisions by a few countries, impossible to determine on economic grounds alone.

Yet these decisions are of considerable importance to the rest of the world. All other things being equal, oil-importing nations (the vast majority) would presumably favor higher rather than lower Saudi investment in oil production, which would also increase world dependence on Middle East oil, and hence vulnerability to political disturbances in that part of the world.

A final source of uncertainty, the possibility of a dramatic change in energy policy in OECD countries brought about by environmental concerns, will be deferred until the final section.

OIL AND THE MIDDLE EAST

The Middle East has been and remains a politically turbulent and insecure area. Roughly twice a decade since 1950 have developments in this part of the world threatened the oil supplies, and thus the economic well-being, of the rest of the world. In 1951, during the Korean War, the Mossadegh government in Iran nationalized Iranian oil, leading to a boycott by Western oil firms. In 1956 President Gamal Abdel Nasser of Egypt closed the Suez Canal on which Europe was crucially dependent for flows of Middle East oil. In the Six-Day War of 1967 the Suez Canal was again closed and blocked by scuttled ships, not to be reopened for over a decade. The Yom Kippur War took place in October 1973, emboldening OPEC to raise prices sharply in December of that year. A fundamentalist revolution occurred in Iran in early 1979, resulting in a sharp and enduring reduction in Iranian oil production. In September 1980 Iraq invaded Iran, again closing down the Iranian oil fields temporarily and disrupting shipment from the Persian Gulf for a longer period. Then in August 1990 Iraq invaded Kuwait, and the United Nations imposed an economic embargo on trade with Iraq and Kuwait.

Fortunately, on most of those occasions alternative sources of supply were or soon became available so the economic damage was limited. The United States was able to supply Europe with oil temporarily in 1951 and in 1956–57. Supertankers were just becoming available in the mid-1960s, requiring a trip around Africa and reducing Europe's dependence on the Suez Canal for oil. Large world oil stocks had been built during the crisis of 1979–80, so a further temporary disruption to Iran's oil fields in late 1980 was less problematic, and, in any case, the world was sliding into recession, reducing its demand for oil. In 1990, as we have seen, there was enough excess productive capacity to compensate for the loss of Iraqi and Kuwaiti oil.

On two occasions, however, in 1974 and 1979–80, the world was not in a good position to absorb a major shock to oil markets, and the consequences were economically devastating, causing or greatly aggravating the two deepest recessions since the 1930s and leading to "stagflation" in the world economy.

A sharp increase in oil prices simultaneously increases the general price level (e.g., "inflation") and in the short run leads to a reduction in output arising from the large change in the distribution of income between oil consumers and oil producers. Macroeconomic management is thrown into confusion as countries try at the same time to fight both inflation and unemployment, but with different emphases, giving rise to secondary balance-of-payments problems. In many countries around the world the adverse consequences of these two major oil shocks continue to this day in the form of slow growth and high external debt.

Even the 1990 disturbance, while hardly devastating, was economically very costly. During the period 1988–1990, the Federal Reserve had been trying to ease the U.S. economy into a "soft landing." The economy had grown at an unsustainable 4.5 percent in 1988, which threatened to revive inflation. The objective was to lower growth to the long-run sustainable rate of 2–2.5 percent, and by mid-1990 this policy seemed to be enjoying some success. The economy was clearly slowing, but recession did not seem to be in the cards. As late as July 1990 the blue chip average forecast for growth in the coming four quarters was 2.1 percent.[8] One of the leading and widely used forecasters, Data Resources (DRI), has the nice characteristic of attaching probabilities to its main forecast and offering several alternatives. On this occasion DRI was forecasting growth of 2.2 percent over the next four quarters; it attached a probability of 55 percent to this forecast and a probability of only 20 percent to an early recession.

Months later July 1990 was "officially" designated (by the National Bureau of Economic Research) as the turning point of the economy. There is little doubt that Iraq's invasion of Kuwait, followed almost at once by an embargo on Iraqi and Kuwaiti oil and a sharp increase in spot oil prices, recalled to many the oil turbulence of 1979, with its uncertainty of availability and rapidly rising prices. Consumer confidence plummeted, and consumer purchases, particularly of durable goods, declined dramatically. Thus the recession began.

The psychological reaction to Middle East developments and the sharp rise in oil prices (from $19 on July 31 to $28 a barrel on August 6, the highest in five years) were compounded by the Bush administration's mishandling of the strategic petroleum reserve, which had grown to 597 million barrels and existed precisely to deal with prospective oil shortages. The United Nations Security Council called for economic sanctions against Iraq on August 6. President Bush should have stated on August 7, when he announced that by agreement with Saudi Arabia the United States would send troops to that country, that the administration also stood ready, if necessary, to draw on the SPR and that it was initiating the paperwork required for sales. Instead, he said nothing about SPR. When asked about SPR, an administration spokesman said there were no plans to draw on it. Oil futures prices subsequently rose briefly above $40 a barrel in late September and early October.

Today, unlike in 1979, much of the world's oil trades at "spot" prices, where spot prices are really near term futures prices. When a foreign tanker is unloaded in the Delaware River, the oil will very likely be priced at the near-term futures price on that day, adjusted as appropriate for the time difference. Futures prices in turn are closely linked to financial contracts in oil futures. Thus there is a direct connection between financial markets and the market for oil. Fears of a shortage get translated immediately into higher crude oil prices. Some of this psychologically damaging price increase could have been avoided if the administration had promptly offered market access to the SPR.

Why it did not remains something of a mystery. Three reasons have been given. First, the Germans and the Japanese had not yet agreed to release their (considerably smaller, but still substantial) stocks. It would be nice to have such an agreement, but nations can rarely act rapidly in concert, and Japan is especially unable to act quickly in an ambiguous situation; such a precondition implies that the SPR will never be used as it should be—to avoid macroeconomic damage to economies—since that may require dispatch.

Second, Saudi Arabia had not yet agreed to increase oil production. Increased Saudi production was certainly essential to maintaining order in world oil markets. Under the circumstances, with Saudi Arabia having asked for U.S. protection, and with the United States having agreed to provide it, increased Saudi production could hardly have been in doubt (Secretary of Defense Dick Cheney was in Saudi Arabia on August 5–6 and could have asked for assurances; the first troops arrived the day of President Bush's announcement). In any case Saudi Arabia publicly announced its willingness to increase production by 2 mbd on August 18.

A third reason advanced is that the SPR should be reserved for a *real* emergency, such as physical damage to Saudi oil production capacity, which might occur with military hostilities or as a result of terrorism. Any stockpile held against a variety of contingencies can only be used once, and the next contingency might be worse than the current one. But the SPR has a physical limit on extraction of about 3 mbd, even under extreme emergency, so any drawdown that occurred in August or September would not have prejudiced its use in October or even January. Moreover, an offer to make the SPR available might have had a market-calming effect without actually requiring a drawdown since in fact ample oil was available at least for the next ninety days because of the extensive amount of oil in transit, augmented by Saudi Arabia's policy, known to the market, of keeping at least 45 million barrels of oil at sea outside the Persian Gulf.

Whatever might have been, the United States did slide into recession. It can plausibly be called Saddam Hussein's recession. The total cost in foregone U.S. output—labor willing but unable to work, and capital available but underutilized—will be over $200 billion by the time full recovery occurs, and unemployment is back in the neighborhood of 5.5 percent. This cost is far greater than the direct outlay on military expenditures associated with the Gulf War.[9]

At this point it is perhaps worthwhile to digress on the reasons for U.S. and allied intervention in the Gulf. Contrary to widespread impression, it was not about oil, except indirectly. It was mainly about aggression and about the future aggressions that Saddam Hussein's possession of Kuwait would make possible. President Bush on several occasions likened Saddam Hussein to Adolf Hitler, and whatever the tactical wisdom of the analogy, it was appropriate. Hitler through bluster succeeded in intimidating his neighbors into yielding German-speaking Czechoslovakia to Germany in 1938, and after a brief interval he simply took the rest, gambling (correctly) that the great powers would not respond. This and other grave errors are etched into the minds of those who lived through or studied closely the Second World War, a group that included Bush, then-British Prime Minister Margaret Thatcher, and French President François Mitterrand, leaders of the three leading non-Arab members of the coalition. The sanctions provisions of the United Nations Charter were designed specifically to prevent a repetition of those events. Hussein's intelligence services erred seriously in not drawing his attention to this parallel.

If Saddam Hussein, like Hitler, had succeeded in keeping his prize, he almost certainly would *not* have sequestered the oil. He did not want the oil. He wanted the revenues from the oil. The most likely strategy, had he succeeded in his bluff, is that he would have produced Iraqi and Kuwaiti oil in abundance, but he would have used his military power to intimidate Saudi Arabia and the other Arab Gulf states into trimming their production to secure an oil price of, say, $25 a barrel—considerably higher than the $17–18 price that had prevailed since 1987, but not so high as to alarm the major oil consumers. Such a strategy would have more than doubled Iraq's oil revenue, from about $25 billion a year before invasion to nearly $55 billion after securing Kuwait's oil and Saudi Arabia's "cooperation." The larger revenues would have been devastating in the hands of a leader so ambitious, ruthless, and bold. The international community had a strong interest in preventing that from happening.

ECONOMIC VULNERABILITY

The Iraqi invasion of Kuwait and the subsequent events demonstrate *again* the dependence of the world on oil from a politically unstable area of the world. The vulnerability arises because oil has become the single most important material input into modern economies and because scope for substituting for oil in the short run is distinctly limited. The combination means that any large and rapid change in oil prices represents a major disturbance to entire economies. A sharp rise in oil prices both creates inflationary pressures and at the same time reduces aggregate demand in oil-importing countries, as oil users cut back their expenditures on other goods and services in order to pay their higher oil bills. The latter consequence can be avoided by borrowing to cover the increased oil bill, but full coverage runs against most canons of sound finance and generally simply postpones and prolongs the pressures for economic contraction. Paradoxically, a sharp decline in oil prices may also impose contractionary pressures on the world economy, as oil producers move to cut their expenditures quickly, and oil-consuming beneficiaries take longer to increase their expenditures. Of course a price decline helps reduce inflationary pressures so the policy dilemma is not so acute.

It is worth noting that a large price increase spread over a long period of time is not nearly so damaging. In the long run, possibilities for conserving oil or finding substitute fuels are considerably greater than they are in the short run. And of course the beneficiaries of higher oil prices will spend their higher incomes, thus avoiding global contractionary pressures. Some subtle arguments can be made for why high oil prices will discourage growth, but the quantitative effects are generally small.[10] Large *rapid* changes in oil prices cause the problem, but such changes are more likely to result from political disturbances than from strictly economic factors.

Since 1973 there has been a substantial reduction in the energy requirements of the U.S. economy, relative to gross national product (GNP). This energy productivity improvement is due in part to genuine conservation and in part to changing the industrial structure of the U.S. economy away from high energy intensive activities, such as the basic metals industry. Compared with the early 1970s, Americans now import relatively more of their energy in the form of finished goods than in the form of oil. Reduction in the oil and gas content of GNP has been even greater than for total energy, with a nearly 40 percent decline between 1973 and 1989. As with other industrial countries, the decline has been especially great, nearly 70 percent, in the industrial sector, with much smaller reductions in transportation and in residential and commercial buildings (heating, cooling, and lighting). So the economy is less vulnerable to disturbances in the oil sector than it used to be.

It is noteworthy, however, that in early 1990 retail gasoline prices were no higher in real terms (i.e., corrected for general inflation) than they were in 1973, before the first oil shock. The real rise in oil prices was offset by a decline in the inflation-corrected value of gasoline taxes. This phenomenon was partly corrected in late 1990 with the five cent a gallon increase in federal excise taxes plus tax increases in many states so retail gasoline prices in mid-1991 were modestly above their level (in real terms) of 1973, but still lower than they were in 1974, after the first but before the second oil shock.

The vulnerability of the economy to oil shocks does not depend, except possibly in the shortest of runs, on the amount of oil imported directly from the Middle East. The world oil market is integrated, and shortfalls anywhere will affect prices and availability around the world. It does depend in part on the total amount of oil imported (relative to GNP), and it depends in part on the total amount of oil (and close substitutes for oil) consumed, even if it is not imported.

The amount of oil imported determines the impact of a rise or fall in world oil prices (a change in the country's international terms of trade) on the total real income of the country since a rise in price represents (after allowing for some responsive decline in imports) a transfer of wealth to the foreign suppliers. Given the price rise and response in reduced demand, this loss of wealth cannot be recovered within the country, no matter how hard workers may try to protect their real wages by demanding higher money wages, and no matter how hard firms may try to protect their profits by raising their prices. Ordinary firms and households do not understand this point, however, and may try to restore their real incomes. That effort, or the prospect of it, may induce the economic authorities, and especially central banks, to pursue relatively tight macroeconomic policies in order to forestall or limit a wage-price inflationary cycle. Such action reinforces the contractionary impact of the oil price increase itself.

This problem is especially acute if imported oil is an important input to the economy. But it is not entirely absent even if all the oil is domestically produced, provided the domestic oil market is tied in with the world oil market, as it was, for example, in the United Kingdom during the oil price increases of 1979–80. A disturbance elsewhere in the world will still lead to a sharp increase (say) in domestic oil prices (unless they are held down by price controls, as they were in the United States and a number of other countries after the 1974 oil shock). That in turn will redistribute income away from oil consumers to oil producers within the country and may induce oil consumers to try to restore their real incomes through wage or price increases. Moreover, a sudden, large redistribution of income even within a country might have recessionary tendencies, as losers must cut their non-oil expenditures quickly, and gainers can increase their spending at a more leisurely pace. The recessionary tendencies will probably be less pronounced than when the redistribution is across national boundaries, and especially when the gainers are foreign governments rather than private parties since governments generally take longer to readjust their spending behavior.

In summary, the negative macroeconomic effects of world oil price shocks are a function mainly of the share of oil in total consumption and of the share of imported oil in total oil consumption; the origin of the foreign oil is of negligible importance. As we have already experienced three times in the past two decades, the cost of these oil shocks can run into hundreds of billions of dollars of lost output.

Vulnerability of modern economies to oil shocks can be reduced by the following four ways: 1) by reducing the likelihood of the shocks, mainly through skillful foreign policy; 2) by reducing the likely magnitude of oil shocks, e.g., through diversifying global sources of supply; 3) by reducing the magnitude of the price effects of a given shock, e.g., by timely use of official oil stocks in the short run; and 4) by reducing the share of oil in national consumption. "Energy independence," apart from being unrealizable at acceptable cost for most countries, including the United States, is not the issue; for the reasons cited above, energy independence, even if it could be achieved, would not insulate the country from world oil shocks unless the country disconnected itself altogether from world markets, an action not to be recommended.

Since 1973 the United States has reduced substantially its dependence on oil, mainly in the industrial sector, but dependence on imported oil is expected to grow sharply during the next two decades, from 42 percent to 64 percent on the DOE and GRI projections. World dependence on Middle East oil, the most likely source of oil shocks, is also expected to grow significantly, from 26 to 39 percent over the next fifteen years on the IEA's projection. These trends suggest increased vulnerability in the future. It is time again to think about seriously reducing the dependence of the United States and other economies on oil. Success over the next several years would postpone the time by which the world oil market tightened again to the degree it was in 1973 or 1979. It would also increase the relative importance (import coverage) of the SPR, although that can also be done at some expense by adding to the existing stock of roughly 600 million barrels. Most importantly, however, it would reduce the impact on the U.S. economy itself of an oil shock of a given size.

In February 1991 the Bush administration released its National Energy Strategy (NES).[11] It contains many fine elements. While it covers the entire field of energy production and consumption in the United States, it focuses mainly on oil and on reducing the country's future dependence on imported oil. If fully enacted and if the analytical assumptions of its projections are correct, the NES would increase U.S. oil production by 3.8 mbd by 2010. This increase would be brought about partly and controversially by opening to exploration new areas in Alaska and on the continental shelf, but mainly and less controversially through enhanced oil recovery from existing wells, to be induced by tax incentives already agreed as part of the November 1990 budget compromise.

The NES would reduce oil consumption by 2010, relative to projected consumption, by 3.4 mbd, brought about in part by energy conservation, but mainly through fuel switching, especially for private and public automobile fleets, which would be required to use alcohol, compressed gas, electricity, or other nonpetroleum-based fuels. Taken together, increased production and reduced consumption of oil would reduce imports (relative to projection) by over 7 mbd by 2010, roughly offsetting the projected increases discussed earlier.

The NES however explicitly rejects higher fuel efficiency standards for new automobiles, and it also rejects (by omission) additional taxes on gasoline, motor fuel, petroleum products, or carbon emissions. While extolling the role of the market as an allocative mechanism and suggesting moves to lighten regulation substantially, especially with respect to natural gas, the NES thus rejects the policy instruments that could mobilize the market mechanism most effectively for reducing consumption of oil. Apart from some oil-exporting countries, the United States maintains the smallest tax on gasoline of any major country, even after the increases of late 1990.

The NES also does not consider "feebates," whereby buyers of automobiles with rated fuel efficiency higher than the current required average of 27.5 miles per gallon (mpg) would get a rebate whose magnitude depended on the extent of the difference, for example $100 per one mpg difference, while buyers of automobiles with rated fuel efficiency lower than the current average would be required to pay a corresponding fee (the proceeds of which would be used to pay the rebates). This represents another market mechanism for encouraging oil efficiency, one that recognizes that those who drive vehicles with low fuel efficiency are imposing higher potential costs on society both through pollution and increased oil vulnerability.

There are many opportunities for energy conservation in commercial, government, and residential buildings, and NES does not give as much attention to them as they deserve. Most of them, however, would reduce demand for electricity, and while meritorious on other grounds would not contribute greatly to reducing the demand for oil.

The NES calls for substantial increases in research and development of alternative energy sources, some of which if successful would displace oil in the distant future. The principal deficiency of the NES is its unwillingness to invoke market forces, guided mainly by higher gasoline taxes, to reduce demand for oil in the next decade.

ENERGY AND THE ENVIRONMENT

A final source of uncertainty in projections of demand for energy a decade or two ahead involves growing concern of publics in many industrialized countries with environmental degradation and, in particular, with the possibility of global climate change resulting from the so-called greenhouse effect. At present, political pressure is especially strong in Europe, where several countries have already established formal objectives for reducing their contribution to the greenhouse effect. Many human activities emit gases that trap the (re)radiation that naturally occurs from the earth, thus tending to warm the atmosphere at the surface of the earth. Among these gases is carbon dioxide (CO_2), up until recently considered a colorless, odorless, and harmless gas consumed by plants in photosynthesis. It has lately been demonized. It is a natural end product of all carboniferous fuels, including wood, coal, oil, and natural gas, as well as of human respiration. As public concern with greenhouse warming grows, attention will be drawn from this quarter to the huge quantity of energy that modern societies consume in the form of carboniferous fuels.

It is conceivable that during the next decade political pressures to forestall greenhouse warming—which holds out the possibility, but by no means the certainty, of raising the average equilibrium surface temperature of the earth by 1–3° C by the middle of the next century—will result in public policy actions toward much greater energy conservation than is now contemplated. As noted above, many opportunities for conservation remain, especially in the building and transportation sectors.[12]

How such a development would affect the demand for oil is unclear. A concern with greenhouse warming draws attention to CO_2 emissions, and this varies considerably from fuel to fuel per unit of energy provided, as Table 3 shows.

Relative to the energy produced, coal emits considerably more carbon dioxide than does crude oil, which in turn emits more than natural gas. Solar and nuclear energy do not involve oxidizing carbon and thus do not emit CO_2. Concern with greenhouse warming leads naturally to an emphasis on solar or nuclear energy, but the former is not at present economically feasible on an adequate scale, and the groups concerned about global climate change have not yet been able to bring themselves around to favor nuclear energy, although some of them are less hostile to nuclear energy than others. This leads logically to an emphasis on energy conservation. The fuel most in need of conservation under this heading is coal, not oil. One public policy

Table 3 Carbon Emitted per Unit of Energy

	Kilograms per Barrel of Oil Equivalent
Solar and nuclear energy	0
Natural gas	83
Crude oil	116
Coal	150
Synthetic oil	187–256
Oil shale	292

Note: Synthetic oil and oil shale include emissions from both production and consumption.

Source: Adapted from U.S. Congress, Office of Technology Assessment (OTA), *Changing by Degrees: Steps to Reduce Greenhouse Gases,* OTA-O-482, (Washington, DC, 1991), p. 333; and G. Marland, "The Impact of Synthetic Fuels on Carbon Dioxide Emissions," in W.C. Clark, ed., *Carbon Dioxide Review 1982,* (New York, NY: Oxford University Press, 1982), pp. 406–410.

action mentioned with increasing frequency is a tax on emitted carbon. If sufficiently high to influence behavior, it would lead to a reduction in demand for coal, which is used mainly for electricity generation, some reduction in demand for electricity (because of its now higher price), and some substitution of lesser taxed fuels for coal—nuclear if it can pass the regulatory and economic hurdles—and natural gas. Demand for oil could go either way, depending on the availability of nuclear power and natural gas for power generation. If the latter were relatively unavailable, the demand for oil could rise.

Of course, oil today is used mainly for transportation, for industrial fuel and chemical feedstocks, and for heating buildings. A carbon tax would presumably lower demand for oil in these uses, partly by reducing demand for energy and partly by encouraging substitution of natural gas where that is easily done. On balance, the demand for oil would probably decline with a carbon tax. If the oil price reflected this decline, high cost sources of supply of oil would be closed down, thus increasing the share of oil, but not necessarily the absolute amount, coming from the Middle East. If the Middle East countries reduced their oil investment and production in order to maintain oil prices, the share from the Middle East would decline.

The IEA has calculated the impact on OECD consumption of oil and other fuels of an OECD-wide carbon tax of $65 and $130 a metric ton of carbon, equivalent to about $8 and $16 a barrel of oil, or a tax of roughly 40 percent and 80 percent on oil at prices of mid-1991. The lower tax would reduce oil consumption by 3 percent from the high price scenario projection for 2005, and total fossil fuel consumption by 5.2 percent (the greatest reduction, not surprisingly, being in coal consumption, and natural gas consumption actually increasing, despite a stiff tax on it as well).[14] The higher tax would reduce fossil-fuel consumption by 9.1 percent from the 2005 projection, and oil by 7 percent. The impact of even these rather high taxes on carbon emissions in the IEA model would be substantial, but not overwhelming. The lower tax would reduce carbon emissions by 7.5 percent, the higher tax by 12.7 percent. Even the higher tax would leave OECD carbon emissions 7 percent higher in 2005 than they were in 1990 (compared with 22 percent higher with no carbon tax).

The higher tax would reduce OECD oil demand by nearly 3 mbd by 2005. On the assumption that the Middle East remains the residual supplier, that would reduce world dependence on Middle East oil in 2005 from 39 to 35 percent. So to this extent (dependent on Saudi Arabian investment strategy), environmental policies and energy security policies are complementary. A tax on petroleum products alone rather than all fossil fuels would of course reduce dependence on Middle East oil even more, at some sacrifice in emission of carbon dioxide (since coal consumption would be modestly encouraged rather than discouraged by such a tax). But the major point for this discussion is that future environmental policies may influence future energy consumption significantly.

ENDNOTES

1. International Energy Agency, *Energy and Oil Outlook to 2005* (Paris: IEA, May 1991, processed).
2. One metric ton of oil contains about 7.7 barrels so one million barrels a day is the equivalent of about 48 mmt a year.

3. These figures include a "processing gain"—the result of chemicals added during the refining of oil—of about 1.5 mbd.
4. Department of Energy (DOE), *Annual Energy Outlook 1991, with Projections to 2010* (Washington, DC: EIA, March 1991, processed).
5. Petroleum declines slightly as a share of total U.S. primary energy consumption on the higher price scenario, with the result that dependence on oil imports as a percentage of total primary energy requirements rises from 18 percent in 1989 to 26 percent in 2010. On the lower price scenario the rise is to 30.5 percent. Calculated from Ibid.,
6. *1991 Edition of the GRI Baseline Projection of U.S. Energy Supply and Demand in 2010* (Chicago, IL: Gas Research Institute, April 1991).
7. See Richard N. Cooper, "Resource Needs Revisited," *Brookings Papers on Economic Activity*, No. 1 (Washington, DC: Brookings, 1975), which reviews the twenty-five year projections of the Paley Commission made in 1951.
8. The Blue Chip survey on the tenth of each month covers fifty-two professional forecasters. On July 10, 1990, *none* of the fifty-two forecast a year-over-year recession from 1990 to 1991—the lowest forecast was for growth of 1.0 percent—and only one of the fifty-two forecast a recession of 1990 over 1989, with a forecast decline of 0.6 percent.
9. It is perhaps unfair to attribute the entire cost of the recession to Iraq's invasion since in July 1990 some forecasters foresaw a "growth recession," that is, an economy with positive growth rates but with some rise in unemployment. Even cutting our estimate in half leaves a figure twice the size of the military expenditures.
10. For instance, in the DOE energy scenarios, the constant price scenario increases U.S. growth by less than 0.1 percentage point a year compared with the scenario where oil prices rise by 3.5 percent a year between now and 2010.
11. Department of Energy (DOE), *National Energy Strategy*, First Edition 1991/1992 (Washington, DC: U.S. Government Printing Office [U.S. GPO], February 1991).
12. One estimate suggests that a systematic program geared toward energy conservation could reduce U.S. energy consumption by nearly 30 percent at no serious economic cost, by which is meant that the investments required would yield a real rate of return of 10 percent or higher, roughly that earned by U.S. industry. Calculated from the report of the National Academy of Sciences, *Policy Implications of Greenhouse Warming* (Evans Report) (Washington, DC: National Academy Press, 1991), pp. 106–107. Since the cooperation of millions of economic agents would be required to achieve these results, a major public information and promotion campaign would be required, especially in the absence of material incentive, such as a fuel tax.
13. IEA, *Energy and Oil Outlook to 2005.*

7

THE UNFETTERED PRESIDENCY

David R. Gergen

From the day Saddam Hussein's army smashed into Kuwait until the day it left, George Bush was far more preoccupied with managing the international dimensions of the Persian Gulf crisis than the array of forces at home. Congress, public opinion, and the press were usually afterthoughts—problems to be addressed after making hard, military choices about Saddam Hussein, people to think about after exhausting the overseas rolodex. As is often the case with the Bush presidency, domestic management by the administration was not pretty either. It rarely inspired. It often seemed uncertain of purpose. It lacked the sure, deft touch the president showed abroad.

Yet by the end of the ground war in late February, it was clear that Bush had achieved almost as complete a mastery of the domestic scene as of the foreign. Congress had acquiesced at every important point along the way; the public awarded him the highest approval ratings of any president in history; and the press had been overwhelmed by the executive branch.

What happened? How did the administration succeed with such relative ease at home? A large part of the answer lies, of course, in the nature of the crisis. From the beginning, Saddam Hussein was the perfect villain, the man everyone could easily hate, and his aggression was perfectly unambiguous. On the morning after his invasion of Kuwait, the *Los Angeles Times* published an editorial that captured the U.S. view of the invasion for the next seven months. "The aggression was undisguised, the greed was naked, the operation was swift, vengeful and effective. In just a few hours, Iraq's dictator Saddam Hussein wolfed down all of Kuwait and sat back to gloat." After the gas lines of the 1970s, Americans hardly had to be reminded that if Saddam Hussein advanced into Saudi Arabia, he would greatly disrupt their lives and might cost them their jobs. Thus it was not hard to persuade most Americans that Saddam Hussein had to be stopped and, better yet, driven from power.

The story of the administration's domestic management does not stop there. While they occupied the high ground from the beginning, Bush and his key advisers also showed a resourcefulness that kept them on top for the duration. They showed that in the new post-cold war era—Bush rarely calls it a "New World Order" these days—the president may enjoy some new powers that were beyond the command of his predecessors. Those new powers more than compensated for the periodic sloppiness of his domestic team. By skillfully pulling levers on the international scene, Bush was able to keep Congress out of the game and then to box it in as the war approached. In taking initiatives unilaterally from the Oval Office, he demonstrated that a president need not be tied down by the latest public opinion polls but can transform them in his favor. Through a reformed military command, newly savvy in media management, he was able to dominate and shape press coverage to his advantage. Many have written of late that the presidency is a diminished institution; some have called it "fettered." In the Persian Gulf crisis, Bush proved to be an unfettered president—an assertion of power that is likely to shape his remaining years in the White House.

The pages that follow look more closely at the administration's management of domestic affairs from the day of the invasion in August until the end of the ground war in February. Obviously other lessons can be drawn from the period after the war ended when the United States let Saddam Hussein off the hook, and Congress and the press began asking tougher questions; the later months suggest that when a president loses control overseas, he also begins to lose his mastery at home. This paper will concentrate on the seven key months until the coalition drove Saddam Hussein's army from Kuwait.

PINNING DOWN CONGRESS

One of the most striking features of the Bush management style is how consistently he left Congress out of the decision loop until the nation was on the brink of war. The administration spoke positively of consultation, but in practice, it engaged only in notification and more often than not, after the fact. The president's door was open, but after listening patiently to his critics, he usually ignored them. While Bush is an easy and affable man, he is also secretive and likes to rely upon a closed circle, even within the executive branch. He is disinclined to trust Congress on sensitive foreign policy questions because he thinks it is incapable of keeping a secret and, like several of his recent predecessors, he believes that partisanship infests the institution. In the months since the Gulf crisis, Bush has harshly attacked Democrats in Congress for faintheartedness during war and asserted that if he had listened to their counsel, Iraq might now occupy both Kuwait and Saudi Arabia. It is apparent that over time, divided government has taken a heavy toll on comity between branches.

Among the president's key advisers during the Gulf crisis, White House Chief of Staff John Sununu only reinforced the president's distrust of Congress. Defense Secretary Dick Cheney counts many friends on Capitol Hill, but since his days as Gerald Ford's chief of staff, he has felt strongly that Congress encroaches too much upon presidential discretion in foreign affairs. Cheney is a strong opponent of the War Powers Resolution. Secretary of State James Baker is more inclined toward working with Congress, but even he testified in the fall of 1991 that the president could certainly go to war in the Gulf without consulting Congress. Colin Powell, chairman of the Joint Chiefs of Staff, worried during the Gulf crisis that the White House was not building enough bridges to Capitol Hill, and he maintained some links of his own, but on general questions of consultation, he deferred to civilians. Only Brent Scowcroft, national security adviser, kept a regular pipeline working to Capitol Hill, occasionally slipping an opponent of the president's policy, like Senator David Boren (D-Okla.), in to see Bush for a private heart-to-heart or quietly meeting Congressman Les Aspin (D-Wis.) to talk through options—efforts that did not go unrewarded. In general, Bush's high command formed a stout wall against Congress, and the gates opened only when it seemed convenient.

A review of key presidential decisions from August through January 1991 will help to sketch out the relationship with Congress and also lay the groundwork for a later analysis of public opinion and the press.

When the Iraqis invaded Kuwait on August 2, Bush worked intensively with his advisers and with foreign leaders before announcing five days later that the United States was deploying 125,000 troops to Saudi Arabia in a defensive measure. Beyond his tight, inner circle, he paid serious attention to only a handful of foreign leaders he trusted. Congress was on the sidelines. Indeed, throughout the crisis, Margaret Thatcher and Prince Bandar of Saudi Arabia had far more influence on the president's thinking than did George Mitchell (D-Maine) and Tom Foley (D-Wash.). The Senate and House adopted resolutions on August 2, condemning the Iraqi invasion and supporting the president's initial economic sanctions, but then both chambers left Washington for August recess and remained far from decision-making. After Bush announced the deployment on August 7, Senate Majority Leader George Mitchell said that the president failed to notify him in advance. "The president attempted to call me a couple of times," he said, "but we weren't able to make contact." Senator Sam Nunn (D-Ga.) said he also learned of the deployment "after the fact," although he added that he had no complaints. "The president has to be the one to make these decisions, and I think in this case things moved so fast that he had to do it." August turned out to be a critical month in the crisis, the time when the administration built a framework for all that followed; Congress being away from Washington made it both easy and convenient to ignore Capitol Hill.

The second milestone in the crisis was reached in late October when the president decided to double the size of the U.S. forces. Early hopes that Saddam Hussein might leave Kuwait voluntarily or that sanctions would quickly force him out were fading in the administration. From the beginning, the president's men had also worried far more about holding together the international coalition than their domestic supporters did, and now that concern was deepening. The clash at Temple Mount in Jerusalem on October 8 convinced at least one of the president's top advisers that if the administration waited too long in evicting Saddam, outside events in places like Israel could split apart the unwieldy group of nations opposing Iraq. On October 30, the president decided to increase the U.S. commitment by 200,000 troops. Again, Congress was not seriously consulted, but this time, the administration nearly paid a fatal price. In the week leading up to the decision, Cheney testified before the Senate Armed Services Committee and said nothing about a potential buildup. On three television shows the next morning, however, he hinted that as many as 100,000 additional troops might be sent, and word leaked from the administration that troop rotations might be canceled. Aides from the Senate Armed Services Committee, angry to be kept in the dark, called to ask what was happening and were told that nothing new was underway. On the morning of October 30, Bush and his top advisers met with congressional leaders and never broached the subject of a buildup. That afternoon, the president signed off on the Schwarzkopf plan to double the troop commitment. He also decided to delay a public announcement by over a week, allowing the November elections to pass quietly and giving Baker time for another overseas trip to round up international support in advance.

Against that backdrop, it is understandable that Senator Sam Nunn was furious Thursday afternoon, two days after the election, when Cheney told him for the first time of the president's decision to double the troops and that the decision would be publicly announced within less than an hour. Nunn was not even accorded the courtesy of a private conversation, so that he could discuss the implications, because Cheney's telephone call reached him in a restaurant. Les Aspin, chairman of the House Armed Services Committee, was reached by phone in Kinosha, Wisconsin. Other congressional leaders had similar experiences. Nunn was the most deeply aggrieved. "I was not consulted. I was informed," he said curtly. He also remembered that in early briefings in August, Powell had assured him and other senators that in any battle, the United States would rely primarily upon air power, and Powell said nothing about a large ground commitment. Now Nunn worried that by doubling the troop commitment and canceling rotations, Bush was forcing the United States to fight within a matter of a few months and not waiting for sanctions to work. Nunn was concerned that U.S. ground forces would be thrown headlong into a fray. He soon ordered public hearings that almost turned the tide of congressional opinion against the president in December.

In retrospect, some of the president's advisers believe their handling of Congress on the buildup decision represented some of their worst mistakes in domestic management. "We screwed up," one adviser says ruefully. "We had some mixed signals about consulting on the Congress, and different people thought other people were doing it. . . . Nunn was upset because he clearly thought we had changed our objective and hadn't consulted him. And there were a number like that." While Nunn had genuine disagreements with the administration at the time, it is widely believed among Nunn-watchers that had he been included in the president's inner sanctum from early on in the crisis—and especially in later October—he would never have become such a dangerous opponent. His thunderous objections gave cover to many other Democrats, who were worried about the troop buildup and could now go public. Democratic opposition was also fueled by a sense that Bush was newly vulnerable after a budget debacle in October and off-year election losses in November. Capturing the spirit of the moment, Senator Daniel Patrick Moynihan (D-N.Y.) warned on November 12, "If George Bush wants his presidency to die in the Arabian desert, he's going at it very steadily."

In the weeks that followed, while sticking to its course, the White House began to pay more attention to assuaging Congress and the public as it undertook the third stage of the crisis: passage of UN Resolution 678, authorizing military action against Saddam Hussein unless he evacuated Kuwait by January 15. The administration wanted the resolution primarily for military purposes and to bind the international coalition together. As Baker pointed out to his colleagues, passage of a war powers resolution by the UN would make it almost impossible for Congress to reject it. At Thanksgiving, Bush pulled off a minor coup against Congress, inviting the leadership to accompany him in a visit to the troops. Despite heartfelt misgivings about a possible war, Speaker Foley decided he had no choice but to go, as did Majority Leader Mitchell. Their presence lent a bipartisan aura to the president's policies and showed just how easily Bush could force Congress to support him. A critical moment in congressional relations came in the last week of November. That Tuesday and Wednesday, two former chairmen of the Joint Chiefs of Staff, William Crowe and David Jones, along with former defense chief James Schlesinger opened the Nunn hearings with strong appeals to give sanctions more time. Many in the press and Congress thought that for the first time, the domestic opposition had the president on the defensive and might upend his policies. That Thursday, the UN Security Council adopted its resolution authorizing military force by a 12–2 vote with China abstaining, and that Friday, Bush made his surprise announcement that he was inviting Tariq Aziz, Iraq's Foreign Minister, to Washington and sending Baker to Baghdad to make one last stab at a peaceful withdrawal. The two initiatives paid off: Bush once again had the upper hand over his domestic opponents, and he never lost it thereafter.

Bolstered by his Gulf visit, Bush returned to spend part of December at Kennebunkport, where he crossed his own Rubicon: aides said that in his days alone—again, without consulting Congress—the president resolved that if Saddam Hussein had not left by the January deadline, the battle should begin. Coming back to Washington, Bush also soon found that he had one more hurdle to cross at home: to keep the public firmly behind him, he had to seek congressional authorization before he ordered up a first strike. Aides insist that Bush all along had preferred a congressional vote of approval in advance, but in the fall, he did not want a vote unless he could be sure he would win massively. Anything less, he felt, would send a signal of weakness to Saddam Hussein. Leaders of Congress told him correctly that they could not guarantee that outcome, so that he carefully avoided calling Congress back into session, as some in his own party demanded. As he returned in January, the President was still disinclined to seek congressional authorization, a feeling reinforced by his Chief of Staff John Sununu. A leading GOP ally on the Hill, Bob Michel (R-Ill.), soon sent a message, however, that Congress had come back determined to vote and that unless the White House got in front of the parade, it might lose control. Shortly thereafter, Bush submitted a formal request for congressional action. By now, he thought that approval by a single vote would be enough.

From the outside, Bush seemingly cruised to victory on Capitol Hill. Among insiders, however, there was anguish over the outcome less than seventy-two hours before the final vote as once again, the president's domestic management failed to match his international operations. The White House had no trouble lining up Republican support, but it left to friendly Democrats responsibility for rounding up members of their party. Late Wednesday afternoon before the Saturday vote, a key Democratic ally called the White House in alarm to report that unless the president himself exercised a full-court press, they might lose by default. The White House had a compelling argument, he said, but was not making it heard. That call apparently helped to mobilize a much more aggressive lobbying effort, and by Thursday night, the White House could count on a majority in each chamber. But the ham-handedness of the domestic operations, stretching all the way back to the snubbing of Nunn and the consistent failure to consult with the leadership, almost cost the White House the vote. Many members of Congress said it turned out to be the toughest vote of their careers. As Elizabeth Drew pointed out later, however, one should distinguish between the difficulty of the decision versus the vote.[1] Most members of Congress could easily decide how to vote, "but few favored actually casting it" because they knew it might kill their careers among voters. Many floor speeches during the debate, widely applauded as among the finest in recent congressional history, were not intended so much to sway opinion in Washington as back home, where constituents were avidly watching.

The crucial factor in the congressional vote—and indeed, in considerations from August through January—was that the president had placed Congress in a corner. At every step, he first lined up international support for his initiatives and left Congress no choice but to come along for the ride. The deftness of his international moves made up for the clumsiness of his domestic management. Most members were genuinely supportive of the president's policies in the early months when they were defensive in character, but after the White House changed to an offensive posture, a growing number opposed him and wanted to give sanctions more time. By December, some top Democrats were experiencing enormous personal anguish—"I've never been as upset in twenty years," one leader said privately—but they felt boxed in by the international coalition and by the January deadline. A number also felt set up by the White House. Many of those who voted with Bush (e.g., Senator Al Gore [D-Tenn.]) felt the decision had been lifted from their hands: if they voted against Bush, the international coalition might fall apart, Saddam Hussein would emerge victorious, the United States would suffer a devastating defeat. And who would bear the blame?

Critics, especially on the left, argue that in its approach to the war, Congress once again revealed itself as a pusillanimous body that insists upon having a voice but always ducks responsibility, a patsy that timidly defers to the executive branch on sensitive foreign points beyond its control. "Everybody here checks their spines in the cloakroom," Rep. Patricia Schroeder (D-Colo.) has said. Typical of the criticism of Congress in the fall was an article by Richard E. Cohen in the *National Journal* arguing that "well-placed Members have displayed the common congressional traits of cold feet and hot air." The situation, he added, reinforces the view of Yale law professor Harold Hongju Koh that "Congress has persistently acquiesced in executive efforts to evade strictures" of post-Vietnam legislation, such as the War Powers Resolution. One wonders whether that is too facile an explanation for the refusal of Congress to block the president in the Persian Gulf. Senate Majority Leader Mitchell and House Speaker Foley knew they had it within their power to upend the president in the late fall if they summoned their colleagues back to Capitol Hill for a vote. They never exercised that power for the same reason that they decided to accompany Bush to Saudi Arabia over Thanksgiving and that they allowed the January ballot to be a vote of conscience, not party: they felt the country has only one chief executive at a time, and he had committed the nation to a grand coalition. They strongly disliked the president's policy but felt U.S. leadership in the world was on the line. Unless and until that effort began to fail, they felt they should not try to derail it. That seems less an act of timidity than of honorable patriotism.

PUBLIC OPINION: AN EXERCISE IN OLD-FASHIONED LEADERSHIP

If anything, the White House found it easier to manage public opinion than did Congress. Americans instantly backed the president in the first days of August, and a majority stuck with him for the next seven months. Indeed, the public was far more bellicose than Congress and to the degree that people did criticize Bush, many thought his mistake was in moving too cautiously. Everett Carl Ladd, executive director of the Roper Center for Public Opinion Research at the University of Connecticut, wrote in September, "In the 45 years since World War II, I can find no other instance when so large a segment of the public has endorsed committing U.S. troops prior to their actual engagement."[2]

When the war ended, the Roper Center published a review of polls taken between August 1990 and early March 1991.[3] The Gulf crisis, it reported, was "the subject of an unprecedented barrage of polling—easily the greatest number of questions ever asked of any focused event." Altogether, major polling organizations posed some 4,000 questions of the American people, 80 percent of which dealt directly with the Gulf. Among the key findings:

- Approval of President Bush's handling of the Gulf crisis was in the 70–85 percent range during August, dipped in October and November to the 50–70 percent range, and then in

December and January began climbing modestly. When war broke out, support shot up from about 60 percent to over 80 percent. Such public enthusiasm greatly enhanced the president's position both overseas and in dealing with Congress; it also encouraged the U.S. press to serve as more of a cheerleader at times, though the press was far more critical of the prewar buildup than the public.

- The breakdown among demographic groups followed predictable lines. Since the beginning of polling, women have been less disposed toward the use of force than men. For example, nearly half of the women surveyed in the Vietnam War described themselves as doves, compared to about one-third of men. During the seven months of the Gulf crisis, support among men for the use of force ran between 7–18 points higher than among women, according to *ABC-Washington Post* surveys. It should be pointed out that even among women, support tended to be in the 60–75 percent range. Only among one group, blacks, did support for the Gulf effort fall below a majority. A *CBS-New York Times* poll in mid-February, for example, found that only 33 percent of blacks thought the United States was right to start military action, compared to 68 percent of all respondents.

- Strikingly, the months of October and November found that support for the president's policies began to crumble among members of Congress and the public, but for different reasons. Congress was increasingly convinced that Bush was rushing too rapidly toward war and wanted to slow him down. Among the 36 percent of the public who disapproved of Bush's handling of the crisis in mid-November (after the troop buildup was just announced), some 37 percent said he was moving too quickly. A larger number, 44 percent, said he was moving too slowly! That sentiment showed up in a variety of other polls and flourished at the end of the war, when many Americans felt the fighting ended too soon and that the coalition should have forced Saddam Hussein from power.

It is frequently argued in the press that support for the war would have evaporated if U.S. body bags had begun piling up and if the battle stretched for more than a few weeks. Commentators point to a poll by *ABC-Washington Post* taken in early January, showing that 63 percent of Americans favored a war, but then, when asked how they would feel if 1,000 of their countrymen and women died, support sank to 44 percent. That poll, it is said, proves that, just as in Vietnam, Americans are impatient and will not accept many casualties. While superficially appealing, this argument is wrong both in its premise and conclusion. Contrary to current myth, support for the Vietnam War did not disappear quickly but was sustained during nearly three years of bloody fighting. Everett Ladd points out that as late as February 1968, just after the Tet offensive, 61 percent of Americans said they were hawks compared to 23 percent who identified themselves as doves. Support for the Vietnam War ebbed only when the public concluded that the Johnson administration either could not or would not win the war. Similarly in the Korean war, it was not body bags or long fighting that soured the public, but a view that the United States was heading for a stalemate. Franklin Delano Roosevelt showed in World War II that U.S. presidents can sustain public support for a long, bloody war so long as they can convince the public they know what they are doing and that the United States is on the road to victory. Given the extraordinary levels of support for the Persian Gulf effort from the first days of August, it is highly probable that the public would have stuck it out a lot longer than most commentators assume.

Several obvious factors contributed to the deep public support in the Gulf: the raw, naked nature of Iraq's invasion, the apparent threat to Saudi Arabian oil fields, the typical "rally round the President" effect when U.S. forces are sent overseas, and the universality of international opinion against Saddam Hussein. As he did with Congress, Bush was cleverly able to influence opinion at home by first mobilizing support overseas. To an extent that no one can measure, Bush also benefited because Americans already held his foreign policies in high esteem. As of July 11, before Saddam Hussein struck, Gallup found 62 percent of Americans approved of the president's conduct of foreign policy compared to 40 percent who approved of his handling of the economy. Once people decide that a president is highly capable in a field, as it had with Bush on foreign policy, they tend to give him considerable leeway thereafter in that area (though not necessarily in other fields, as Bush has found in his management of the U.S. economy).

The more central story of public opinion during the war was how successful Bush was in generating grass roots support through a series of bold, unilateral actions at key points along the way. As Charles Krauthammer recognized in a column in January, "Bush managed to rally a reluctant nation to a successful war not with inspiring words or soaring visions, but with a series of shrewd and forcing actions. Military schools will long be studying Schwarzkopf's march through the Gulf. Government schools will be studying Bush's march through Washington." In the first days of August, for example, the public praised Bush for imposing economic sanctions, just as Congress did, but 56 percent told a Gallup poll that they opposed sending U.S. troops to defend Kuwait. Then Bush acted, casting the deployment as a defense of both Kuwait and Saudi Arabia, and 81 percent immediately expressed approval. Bush had in effect created "new facts," and the public swung in line behind him. Similarly, during the fall, Americans supported the president's general policies in the Gulf, but many were reluctant to back a war unless all other means had been exhausted. The president told his aides as early as August that a war could well be the only way to evict Saddam Hussein. Yet he also saw that in order to bring the public and Congress with him, he first had to convince them that he had tried other options. Thus he ran through a series of measures such as sanctions, repeated trips to Baghdad by intermediaries, and finally, the Baker-Aziz attempt at diplomacy. All seemed to fail, and Aziz also managed to insult the United States by refusing the Bush letter. The Soviets first proposed setting a deadline, but in embracing it, the White House also conditioned the public to see January 15 as an end point in negotiations. With the deadline approaching and peaceful means of resolution at a dead end, public willingness to go to war rose sharply in late December and early January. An *ABC-Washington Post* poll on January 9 found 75 percent ready to take all actions necessary, including war, up some 10 points from the previous month. Through its international actions, the White House had thus laid the groundwork well at home. The next test came over a ground war. As the air war opened with such apparent success, the public was extremely positive but remained apprehensive about ground fighting. A *CBS-New York Times* poll found less than two weeks before the ground war began that only 11 percent of Americans were in favor of a ground attack. But the day after the coalition troops launched their assault, 75 percent of the public approved. Once again, a presidential initiative—strong, decisive, unilateral—transformed public opinion in favor of the White House.

In sharp contrast, the president's attempts to persuade the public through the bully pulpit were much less successful. The White House repeatedly stumbled as it sought to define the stakes in the Gulf. Rather than making a case for collective security, Bush tended to personalize the affair, promising to "kick ass" if Saddam Hussein failed to withdraw. So great was the frustration of James Baker at White House ineptitude that he tried to take the lead on the subject, but then he, too, blundered as he argued that the deployment was intended to protect U.S. jobs. Rhetoric had been a sore point for Bush since the Reagan days, when he thought that the former President was excessively scripted. When Bush took over the White House, Sununu significantly downgraded White House speech writers, cutting their pay and even denying them access to the White House mess. As a result, Bush has delivered some of the least memorable speeches since Warren Harding. His address to the nation during the budget debacle in the fall of 1990 was so poorly received that he was exceedingly cautious in using televised speeches to mold public opinion during the Gulf crisis. Ronald Reagan could shift opinion as much as twenty points through an Oval Office address, as he did with regard to marines in Lebanon, but Bush barely sways the needle. What Bush did do well during the Gulf period was to remain a visible presence in the media by frequent daytime press conferences, which instilled confidence in the public that he was on top of the problem and was moving toward a solution. Through constant repetition, he also turned the lessons of two past wars to his advantage, driving home the point that the United States must not appease a tyrant and that it must never again fight a war it is not determined to win. It can be argued that Bush set himself up with the frequent Hitler analogy: if Saddam Hussein is Adolf Hitler, why did Bush leave him in power? But his promise to fight a quick, successful war did help to exorcise the ghosts of Vietnam. It was one of his few victories from the bully pulpit.

Summing up, the chief lesson to emerge from the Gulf experience is that contrary to widespread thinking of recent years, a president's foreign policy need not be a creature of public opinion polls. Defense Secretary Caspar Weinberger, in his formulation of 1984, said that before going to war, a president must be reasonably assured of support from the public. His views were not atypical; many in the military concluded after Vietnam that they could never fight again unless the polls were on their side in advance. In effect, many in the defense establishment had become intimidated by public opinion. Bush showed in the Gulf that public opinion is remarkably malleable and that a president can mobilize it in his favor through old-fashioned leadership. On most foreign policy questions, as Daniel Yankelovich[4] has shown, the public is uncertain and is willing to be lead if it trusts the president in charge. Bush is not as effective at rhetorical persuasion as his predecessors; Jimmy Carter was better at it as he demonstrated when he turned opinion around about the Panama Canal treaty. But Bush is willing to act decisively, especially in the use of military force, and he showed in the Gulf that action can be liberating. A president does not have to hold his finger in the breeze before he moves; he can move first, and if he does so skillfully, the breeze will shift in his direction.

MANAGING THE PRESS

While concerns over press coverage of the Gulf crisis were of course heavily intertwined with efforts to manage Congress and public opinion, the press did present a discrete set of challenges for the administration. Once the war started, for example, the administration could forget about Congress, but the press demanded far more attention. The press, by its nature, would also be far more independent-minded and less sympathetic to a Gulf war than Congress or the public might be. Most important, the press is still remembered as an enemy from the United States' last war. Despite persuasive evidence to the contrary, many officers in the military—and a good many conservative Republicans—still believe that Vietnam was lost not on the battlefield but in the living room. Not surprisingly, the military approached the press challenge far more seriously than the White House, and eventually, the military's management proved decisive.

The White House at first treated the Gulf as it would any other major news event, making the president more available for impromptu press conferences and providing more background briefings. The focus in the early fall was largely on the domestic audience. It soon became apparent, however, that the reach of CNN to 124 different countries introduced new and complicating factors into diplomacy. The magnitude of the problem came home to the White House soon after Bush announced the doubling of troops, and Congress began attacking the president. According to one White House source, a distraught President Turgut Ozal phoned Bush from Turkey, saying he had just seen some members of Congress on CNN proclaiming that the Constitution did not permit Bush to use force. Was that true? Bush reassured Ozal that there is a natural tension between the executive and legislative branches but that as president, he had full authority to order up a battle. Ozal, though still puzzled, reportedly took the president at his word. The White House realized that if Ozal was wondering about U.S. resolve, Saddam Hussein was too since he was a devotee of CNN. In effect, Bush and his advisers learned that they had to communicate through the press to two different audiences who needed to hear different messages: they had to convince Saddam Hussein that they were ready and eager to hit him if he did not get out, but they also had to convince the U.S. public that they would be prudent. "Every time we score with one, we set ourselves back with the other," complained one presidential aide. The proposal for a Baker-Aziz duet, for example, placated the doves at home but the United States worried it might send the wrong signal to Saddam Hussein; thus Baker was sent on his mission with a very short leash. (Hawks say that Baker was also restricted so that he would not give away the store.) Throughout the crisis, the White House was unable to find a formulation that would satisfy both audiences and thus tended to be schizophrenic in its communications through the press.

As the war started, Bush advisers worried that Saddam Hussein might use the press to twist U.S. opinion to his own advantage. By focusing attention on military hostages, for example, he might make Americans wonder if the war was worth it. Another concern was how he might exploit damage to his own people. "We thought about this a lot (before the war), that Saddam Hussein was bound to hold up babies and show the horrors of a genocide attack on them and so on," recalls one adviser. That concern reached its heights when U.S. air attacks were decimating many parts of Iraq, and the Baghdad regime permitted international networks to film the aftermath, complete with scenes of dead women and children in a bunker. (Fortunately for the administration, U.S. television showed much less gruesome pictures from that bombing than did European television.) The administration concluded that it could not match Saddam Hussein image for image; rather, the United States had to win a smashing victory as quickly as it could. Success, argued one Bush adviser, would be the best antidote to Saddam Hussein's media manipulation.

As it did in Grenada and Panama, the White House left the bulk of media management during the Gulf crisis to the Pentagon. The White House answered questions about presidential activity and international diplomacy, but on all military matters both inside the United States and in the Gulf, Cheney's office along with the military command planned and executed the day-to-day handling of press coverage. While presidential Press Secretary Marlin Fitzwater kept a watchful eye, he rarely interfered with Pentagon officials. Nor did Scowcroft and Bush, by all accounts. As far as the administration was concerned, that turned out to be a wise decision, as the military completely overwhelmed the press and greatly shored up public support during the crucial stage from January through February.

From the beginning, the military saw the press as a potential threat to its assignment and worked assiduously to turn journalists to its own advantage. Disinformation is a time-honored part of war and quickly became a weapon here. In August, Schwarzkopf was terribly worried that Saddam Hussein might overrun Dhahran before the United States could have a sizable defense force in place. Bush himself was staying awake all night at Kennebunkport worrying about the same problem. To confuse Saddam Hussein, *Newsweek* reported later, "The Pentagon orchestrated a stream of public announcements of units deployed on the gulf; the statements left out the fact that only elements of these units had actually been sent. Saddam Hussein had no satellites or spy planes to watch the buildup; he got much of his intelligence from CNN. So Schwarzkopf made sure television crews were out each day shooting the giant C-5 Galaxy transports that landed every few minutes in Dhahran." Later on, in the days leading up to the ground war, the United States repeatedly let the press film practice landings by amphibious forces, trying to convince Saddam Hussein that he faced a frontal attack from the sea. A good number in the U.S. press knew it was a phony plan. The U.S. press also knew with considerable precision where coalition ground forces would actually strike, but in a tradition that is also long but not well appreciated, the press withheld the information in order to protect allied troops.

In retrospectives on war coverage, many have argued that the military was successful in managing the press because it engaged in censorship and allowed far less access to the troops than it did in Vietnam. Certainly, the Pentagon did both and, indeed, carried those practices far beyond necessity. Very few reports from the field were actually changed (occasionally, locations were excised), but there were a number of unjustified delays. More infuriating for journalists were barriers placed on access. Journalists like to roam, talking with unofficial sources so they can compare and contrast that information with what they hear from official, canned briefings. In Saudi Arabia, a journalist could not talk with a sergeant without a commissioned public affairs officer monitoring the conversation. Most field reporting took place through pools, but pools were restricted to a small number and their reports often lacked insight. Since most of the early action was in the air, not on the ground, on-scene reporting was also inhibited. And of course, the press always had to contend with the social strictures of Saudi Arabia, which were especially onerous for the many female correspondents covering their first conflict. "The sad fact is that we 'covered' the war, but we didn't report the war," concludes media critic Jonathan Alter. "There was very little independent journalism until the last hours of the conflict. Pool coverage is not journalism." The Pentagon has defended the system on the basis that the press sent some 1,400 reporters to the Gulf and that pools were its only choice. But the press believes that the Pentagon intentionally allowed in hordes of reporters so that it could hide behind the pool system. Had the Pentagon accredited reporters more selectively, allowing national news organizations a certain number of slots and regional news teams a smaller number, the flow would have been smaller, and more reporters could have traveled out with units in the field, instead of staying back in Riyadh. Only when the ground war actually began did the pool system finally start to crumble. Still fuming, some seventeen major news organizations have petitioned the Pentagon for a radical overhaul of the rules for the next military engagement. Ideally, many news organizations would like to scrap the rules altogether, but in a practical sense, the press needs the cooperation of the military to work out arrangements for satellite transmission and other logistical details.

The argument over pools, as important as it is, unfortunately misses the larger significance of what the military achieved in press management during the war: an unprecedented dominance over the pictures and words conveyed by the media. In conflicts stretching back to the Civil War, independent photographs taken by the press have provided the most memorable images of the battlefield. From Vietnam, the pictures that linger in the mind's eye are of a little girl running down a village road, her body afire from napalm, and of a Vietnamese general cocking a pistol to the head of a Vietcong prisoner. Those pictures haunted the public, but they haunted the military, too. In the Persian Gulf, the military came ready to provide its own home videos, better than anything the press could concoct, and the pictures that burned their way into the public psyche were of precision-guided bombs homing in on their targets—perfect bull's-eyes, no blood, thank you. The U.S. military films so captured the public imagination that soon the British and French were producing films of their own. The press simply could not compete. Similarly, the press gave the crisis such extraordinary attention that it had enormous amounts of airtime and copy holes to fill. The military knew exactly how to take advantage: by preventing reporters from gaining access to the troops in the field so they could write their own stories and by providing daily, open briefings in both Riyadh and Washington, the military monopolized the airwaves and directed press attention to the stories that it wanted to reach the public. According to the Pentagon press office, there were some 119 briefings in Washington and at least 98 in Riyadh from August through March. As noted by Larry Grossman, former head of PBS and of NBC News, "The screen was filled up by material—briefings, press conferences, videotapes—that was supplied by the government. The issue was not so much keeping things away, but how much one perspective dominated the screen. This was the ultimate in the cheerleading war."

It is not difficult to figure out what happened. Angry and humiliated by Vietnam, the military has for the past fifteen years worked hard to reform itself; its transformation has been the most successful of any institution in the country, a lesson that others should learn. Among the top priorities for the military was to master press relations. Many officers thought reporters were as much of an enemy as the army on the other side. War colleges across the country began calling in leaders of the press to address their conferences and training future generals and admirals to handle the press. Schwarzkopf has never liked the press, but he learned how to deal with it in the jungles of Vietnam. One of the attractions in selecting Powell as chairman of the Joint Chiefs of Staff was his ease in working with Congress and the press (although the White House later came to regret his conversations with Bob Woodward of *The Washington Post*). Before heading up the marine operations in the Persian Gulf, General Walter Boomer had spent his last assignment as chief public affairs officer for the Marine Corps. Thus, the military was fully prepared to overwhelm the press in the Persian Gulf, and it was no contest because the press was totally unprepared. In past wars, most of those carrying pencils or cameras have seen previous military service, but in this war, the only thing most reporters knew about a platoon was what they saw in the movie. When the draft ended in 1973, the vast majority of would-be journalists decided they would rather write than fight. Few reporters today under thirty-five have ever worn a uniform. Moreover, the press corps that covers the Pentagon on a regular basis is small, usually about three dozen. When news organizations geared up to send 1,400 correspondents and technicians, they naturally sent a lot of greenhorns. It was not long before "Saturday Night Live" began running spoofs of the military briefings—only this time, the jokes were on the press. Major news organizations, as noted, are now asking the Pentagon to overhaul its rules on pools and access. Far more important is that the press examine itself, learning how it can achieve more independent, balanced reporting of future wars, rather than turning its channels over to the government. The government has a legitimate need to communicate directly with the public, especially in wartime, but the essence of a free press is that it provide a second, independent look. In the Persian Gulf, the military snookered the press.

CONCLUSION

In one of the many ironies of the Gulf crisis, the performance of a Republican president validated the writings of liberal scholars far more than those of conservative ones. For several years, the right has bitterly complained that the power of the executive branch has been excessively curtailed by an arrogant Congress, a vacillating public, and a hostile press. Most of the attacks have been aimed at Capitol Hill. In *The Imperial Congress*,[5] conservatives set forth a host of charges about congressional micromanagement of the Defense Department and interference with the war-making authority of the executive, starting with the War Powers Resolution. In *The Fettered Presidency,* editors L. Gordon Crovitz and Jeremy A. Rabkin describe a plethora of legal constraints imposed by Congress that has allegedly manacled the executive branch.[6] Crovitz has also led a campaign on the editorial pages of the *Wall Street Journal* to reassert presidential prerogatives, especially in national security. By contrast, liberals have argued that the president has excessive, unrestrained powers. Harold Koh's book, *The National Security Constitution,* paints a dark, lurid picture of executive authority.[7] Michael J. Glennon sees Congress as utterly weak and supine; he is among many who believe that there is an urgent need for the 1973 War Powers Resolution to be repealed or revised. Louis Henkin offers a more moderate view, believing the president cannot go to war without a clear, unambiguous indication of congressional approval in advance. Essentially, these scholars object to what Bush demonstrated in the Gulf: that under current circumstances, a popular president who so chooses may ignore the War Powers Resolution and indeed, the Congress, in pursuing his foreign policy goals.

Two questions remain to be answered: Is the Gulf experience likely to serve as a model for the executive branch in potential conflicts of the future? Should it? To the first question, most commentators assume that Congress and the public would have been far more opposed to the use of U.S. force if the crisis had occurred anywhere else but the Gulf. If Kuwait grew broccoli, so the saying goes, the United States would never have been willing to fight, and to that extent, the war was arguably *sui generis,* devoid of meaning for the management of future crises. Yet just as Vietnam cast a long shadow, the lopsided, almost costless victory in the Gulf is sure to influence the domestic response to trouble spots in the future. So long as the United States has not disarmed itself and does not feel economically decimated, a future overseas crisis is likely to find that dovish Democrats will be apt to give a hawkish president, Republican or Democrat, a great deal of leeway to use limited force. Having been burned once, dovish Democrats will be loath to wind up on the wrong side of history again. Nor can Democrats afford to let their party become further identified as soft on national security. If anything, the party is likely to move toward the center on military affairs during the next several years. By the same token, the public will probably be less frightened about the prospects of limited wars in the future. Not that Americans are eager to go to war: a *Time* survey after the war found 70 percent rejecting the idea of the United States playing world policeman. But the dazzling display of power by the air force in the Gulf will likely reduce public apprehension about using force in the future. Vietnam haunted the public psyche before the Gulf; it does no longer.

During the summer of 1991, Bush's warnings to Saddam Hussein that the United States and its allies might strike him again in order to destroy his nuclear capacity caused barely a ripple of protest in Congress and the public. Polls showed a distinct lack of public enthusiasm, but it was clear that Bush enjoyed a relatively free hand. Had he launched an attack, it is likely that both the public and Congress would have rallied behind him. What this suggests is that having won so handily in the Gulf, Bush has enhanced the powers of his office for future conflicts: as long as he can make a credible case that U.S. interests are at stake, a president during the 1990s should find it even easier to carry the nation into a limited battle.

Just because the president has enlarged powers does not mean that he should exploit them; the fact that the Bush administration so easily managed domestic forces in the Gulf does not mean its performance should serve as a model. A decent respect for constitutional arrangements and, indeed, for self-interest dictates otherwise. The Constitution certainly envisions a greater comity between the branches than shown in the Gulf crisis. Michael Glennon argues in a recent *Foreign Affairs* article: "Starting from President Bush's unilateral commitment to defend Saudi Arabia and proceeding to Congress' jury-rigged approval, the episode represented a textbook example of how an audacious executive, acquiescent legislature, and deferential judiciary have pushed the Constitution's system of separation of powers steadily backwards toward the monopolistic system of King George III."[8] In his hyperventilation, Glennon goes too far, but he has a point. While a president must of necessity take the lead in a military crisis, he is at least expected to consult Congress, taking into account the views of the coequal branch, not simply inform after the fact.

By opening its decision-making process to domestic forces, the administration could have served its own ends, too. Had Bush truly consulted the congressional leadership more often in the Gulf, he would not have jeopardized his power or authority; if anything, he would have enjoyed more support from Nunn and other Democrats. Good fortune stayed with Bush in the Gulf, but if the war had gone badly, the Congress that he treated so summarily in the fall would have jilted him in the spring. The press that so willingly triumphed the videotapes of successful air strikes would have begun screaming about military deception and cover-ups. The administration would have been far better prepared for a nasty turn in the war if it had built a more durable consensus at home: if Democrats felt they had been part of the decision making, if the public had a clearer, more persuasive explanation of the war's purpose, if the press had been granted greater freedom to cover the crisis at the front, all would have been better prepared to stick with the president. Bush threw the dice repeatedly in this crisis and always won; the next president may not be so blessed.

Looking ahead, the country has an opportunity to restore a precious asset in foreign policy: a bipartisan consensus on the role of the United States in the world. Such a consensus was enormously valuable to U.S. policymakers in the formative years after World War II but was lost, of course, in the jungles of Vietnam. Now, both parties can begin moving toward a new set of understandings: the Republicans need not be so preoccupied with the Soviet menace, and the Democrats need not be so fearful of a limited use of U.S. force. Both can begin to redefine the security interests of the United States without baggage from the past. That process requires both sides to engage in give-and-take. In the run-up to the 1992 presidential election, rank partisanship is once again asserting itself on both ends of Pennsylvania Avenue, but after the election is over, it may be possible to build a more durable understanding between the White House and

Congress. In his book, *A Question of Balance: The President, Congress and Foreign Policy,* editor Thomas E. Mann sets forth a sensible proposition: the two branches should negotiate a new arrangement in national security whereby Congress abandons its detailed, restrictive, and often punitive approach to foreign policy measures after the fact in exchange for the president bringing Congress more fully into the setting of broad policy goals in advance.[9] The Senate Intelligence Committee and the intelligence agencies within the executive branch have struggled successfully to achieve greater comity, and their progress should serve as an example of what can be achieved in other areas of foreign policy. To assure the future strength of U.S. leadership overseas, a new balance needs to be struck at home.

ENDNOTES

1. Elizabeth Drew, "Letter from Washington," *New Yorker,* February 4, 1991, p. 86.
2. Everett Carl Ladd, "The American Public and the Gulf Crisis," *Christian Science Monitor,* December 7, 1990; also reprinted in "U.S. Public Opinion on the Gulf Crisis: The Story in Stages," prepared by the Roper Center for Public Opinion Research, University of Connecticut, from the pages of *Public Perspective.*
3. "U.S. Public Opinion on the Gulf Crisis."
4. See the Daniel Yankelovich Group, *Americans Talk Security* (ATS) (Winchester, MA: ATS).
5. Gordon S. Jones and John A. Marini, eds., *The Imperial Congress: Crisis in the Separation of Powers,* The Heritage Foundation (New York, NY: Pharos Books, 1988).
6. L. Gordon Crovitz and Jeremy A. Rabkin, eds., *The Fettered Presidency: Legal Constraints on the Executive Branch* (Washington, DC: American Enterprise Institute for Public Policy Research, 1989).
7. Harold Hongju Koh, *The National Security Constitution: Sharing Power After the Iran-Contra Affair* (New Haven, CT: Yale University Press, 1990).
8. Michael J. Glennon, "The Gulf War and the Constitution, *Foreign Affairs,* Vol. 70, No. 2 (Spring 1991), pp. 84–101.
9. Thomas E. Mann, ed., *A Question of Balance: The President, Congress and Foreign Policy* (Washington, DC: Brookings, 1990).

PART IV

STRATEGIC LESSONS

8

WAR BY MISCALCULATION

Bernard E. Trainor

Demere rebus tumultum

— *Seneca*

INTRODUCTION

It is far too early to draw conclusions fully from the Gulf War and project their implications for the future. But it is possible at this early date to see the shadow that the events cast on future politico-military considerations. This paper will address these considerations by concentrating on key events and issues of the war itself. Based upon extensive interviews with the intelligence community and operational commanders, this paper will also advance a best guess as to what was going on in the mind of Saddam Hussein and his high command at critical junctures in the Middle East drama. The paper is divided into four parts corresponding to the sequence of major events in the war and a fifth part consisting of observations and conclusions.

THE OPENING MOVES

Since the advent of the nuclear age, U.S. military policy has been to deter conflict by maintaining military strength in such proportions as to convince a potential enemy that it has more to lose than gain if it risks conflict with the United States. The policy serves to intimidate enemies and support friends. It is made up of two elements: capability and credibility. Capability is the raw military power that can be brought to bear against an enemy. Credibility is the willingness to use that power.

The policy has been most successful in dealing with the main threat to U.S. interests—the Soviet Union—but has been less successful against lesser threats, as the series of limited wars over the past four decades attest. With the exception of the Korean War, where the military capability of the United States itself was discounted by North Korea, the failure of the deterrence policy on the level below the superpower confrontation has always been a function of the credibility part of the equation. Adversaries like Mu'ammar Qaddafi and Manuel Noriega, who have gotten into fights with the United States, simply misjudged either U.S. interest or resolve.

From the evidence available it appears that Saddam Hussein miscalculated on both counts. He apparently convinced himself that the United States would not react to an inter-Arab dispute, and if it did, it did not have the capability to reverse the Iraqi conquest of Kuwait at a price that would be acceptable to the American people. Saddam Hussein also misjudged the ability of the United States to form a solid coalition of Western and Arab states to oppose him. In addition, he overestimated his own capability to fight a modern war. These miscalculations were fatal to countless Iraqis.

How the Iraqi leader could have so badly misjudged the U.S. temper is still to be speculated, but the evidence suggests that U.S. overtures of friendship and cooperation during and after the Iran-Iraq War played a part. The United States government came to view Iraq as a bastion of stability in the region and a counter to a weakened, but still revolutionary, Iran.

The unsavory and aggressive nature of the Ba'athist regime was accepted as a fact of life, but apparently the Arabists in the State Department believed that if they built commercial and diplomatic ties with the Baghdad regime, it would moderate its behavior over time. Saddam Hussein thus overestimated the willingness of the United States to accede to Iraq's goals in the interest of Iraq's geopolitical importance to the United States.

Self-delusion was not restricted to the executive branch as evidenced by the fawning visit of Senators Robert Dole (R-Kans.), Howard Metzenbaum (D-Ohio), and Arlen Specter (R-Pa.) to the Iraqi leader only months before his invasion of Kuwait.

The U.S. intelligence community was not as sanguine as the State Department about Iraq. It had mixed feelings. On one hand, as early as 1988, it warned that Iraq was a potential regional aggressor because the Iraqis failed to demobilize after the war with Iran as was expected. On the other hand, it watered down the threat a year later by observing that the threat was mitigated by Iraq's preoccupation with its postwar recovery.

The Defense Department formally hewed to the administration line that Iraq should not be viewed as an enemy. No mention of Iraq as a potential aggressor was made in the defense guidance issued by the secretary of defense to the joint chiefs of staff as the guideline for planning. However, in 1989, within both the office of the undersecretary of defense for policy, and the Central Command in Tampa, Florida, which had military responsibility for the Middle East, reassessments of regional threats in the Middle East got under way.

Iraq replaced the Soviet Union as the most likely aggressor, and Saudi Arabia was seen as the target. Within Central Command a new contingency plan was drawn up with Iraq as the enemy. The State Department got wind of the plan and complained to the chief of staff that Iraq was not an enemy and that it was totally inappropriate to be making plans to fight Iraq. Needless to say, Central Command continued its planning and war-gaming it in an exercise called "Internal Look" just a month before Iraq's invasion of Kuwait took place.

The plan was not complete, but it did provide the framework for the August deployment of U.S. forces to Saudi Arabia under what came to be known as Desert Shield. Under the plan, the command was prepared to trade space for time if the Iraqis marched south. Kuwait and northern Saudi Arabia were written off, and the front was to be stabilized north of Jubayl before Iraq could reach the key oil fields and port facilities in the vicinity of Dhahran. Air force and navy air strikes were viewed as critical to the success of the defense.

Despite the early efforts to come up with a feasible plan for the defense of Saudi Arabia, there is little evidence to suggest that Central Command planners thought of it as more than a routine precaution. The command's head planner said that the Iraqi invasion of Kuwait came as a surprise. It is clear, in retrospect, that the evidence was there to warn of the attack, but it was not taken seriously. Satellites spotted Iraqi combat units massing on the Kuwaiti border, but this was interpreted as posturing by the Iraqis to intimidate Kuwait in their ongoing oil dispute. However, alarm bells went off in the third week of July when a massive logistics buildup began behind the frontline units. Civilian trucks were also reported being requisitioned for military use, a move the Iraqis could ill afford economically unless they were serious about military action. Still, many intelligence analysts remained skeptical of Iraq's hostile intent. For one thing, no invasion rehearsals had been spotted, and such exercises were viewed as a precondition for anything larger than a border incursion.

Toward the end of July, however, some senior-level analysts within the intelligence community said Iraqi preparations were too extensive to be judged a bluff. They forecast an imminent attack against Kuwait and credited the Iraqis with the ability to seize all of Kuwait and unseat the al Sabah regime. The Iraqis were not, however, judged capable of extending their attack into Saudi Arabia without reorganizing and resupplying at the Saudi border.

The analyses of the Iraqis' capabilities and intentions were based almost exclusively on technical intelligence, such as satellite imagery because there was virtually no human intelligence to fill out the picture. At the policy-making level at the Defense Department, Central Intelligence Agency, the State Department, and in the White House, the warnings were discounted. There appear to be several reasons for this. The first reason is the inclination of senior policymakers to take warnings from intelligence officers with a grain of salt because of the latter's traditional propensity to exaggerate the significance of indicators and warnings as insurance against underestimating a threat. Second, the moderate Arab leaders of the Middle East were themselves apparently convinced that Saddam Hussein was posturing for negotiating purposes only and would not attack. They gave these assurances to President George Bush, and he evidently gave these Arab views greater weight than he gave Israeli concerns over Iraqi belligerence. Third, the administration was apparently convinced that the Iraqis were weary of war and more interested in rebuilding their country than in aggression. Finally, and perhaps most importantly, there appears to have been widespread self-delusion among senior officials who were seeking to build bridges to Iraq. They would not believe that Saddam Hussein would attack, for to do so would make a sham of the conciliatory policy toward him that was set in motion at the conclusion of the Iran-Iraq War.

It can only be concluded that there was a failure in policy, diplomacy, and intelligence in the years between the end of the Iran-Iraq War and the invasion of Kuwait. Because of this, no signal was sent to Saddam Hussein that he risked confrontation with the United States if his army crossed the Kuwait border.

THE BUILDUP

Once the invasion took place the president acted quickly, which must have come as a surprise to Saddam Hussein, given the conciliatory exchange he had with the U.S. ambassador to Iraq in late July. U.S. forces were immediately deployed to the Gulf while the president adroitly mustered international support and, not as adroitly, domestic support for opposition to Iraq.

A key feature of the early deployments, which must be taken into account when building a future force structure, was that it was a remarkably effective four-service response. Within seventy-two hours an aircraft carrier was in the North Arabian Sea to protect the deployment of an army airborne brigade to Saudi Arabia, which in turn provided ground protection to air force tactical fighters flying into Saudi airfields. Within three more days another carrier was in the Red Sea prepared to strike Iraq from a different direction, while air force F-111 bombers were deployed to Turkey to provide an attack capability from a third direction. Shortly thereafter a flotilla of ships loaded with prepositioned equipment, heavy weapons, and logistic support, sailing from Diego Garcia in the Indian Ocean, joined up in Saudi Arabia with 18,000 marines flown in from the United States. In less than three weeks the United States had dispatched a balanced military force made up of all services, capable of delaying but not stopping any Iraqi attack into Saudi Arabia.

In addition, the first concrete manifestation of coalition cooperation emerged as warships from Britain and France arrived to institute the sanctioned embargo of Iraq by the United Nations. In the interim, the first contingent of Egyptian troops also arrived in Saudi Arabia as the precursor of what was to become a coalition army of Westerners and Arabs.

Other than worrying about an Iraqi attack south, which became increasingly doubtful as the allied buildup gained momentum, General H. Norman Schwarzkopf, the U.S. theater commander during the Desert Shield phase of the overall campaign, faced the problems of logistics and command and control for coalition warfare.

The movement from the United States and Germany, of what turned out to be over one-half million troops with their weapons and equipment, was a daunting task. It fell to the Transportation Command, established in the wake of the Goldwater-Nichols military reform act, to do the job.

Logistic support for an inter-theater lift consists of three parts: the facilities and expertise at the port of embarkation (ports and airfields), the means of transportation (ships and planes), and the facilities and experts at the receiving end of the logistics line. For airlift, all three elements proved adequate once the Civil Reserve Air Fleet was activated. Airfields and equipment in both the United States and Saudi Arabia were exceptionally good. Since most of the air force units and their ground support equipment went by air, their movement was relatively easy. Ammunition, which went by sea, posed few problems as most bulk carriers could accommodate the standard ammunition and supply loads.

For the marines and the navy also, the task was not onerous. Since they were configured for overseas and expeditionary deployments, most of their requirements were met by navy ships, prepositioned equipment already afloat, and by airlift. Moving the army was a different story. Aside from rapid reaction forces such as the paratroops, Army units were not trained for expeditionary deployment. Troops and critical equipment could go by air to Saudi Arabia, but tanks, artillery, and other heavy items had to go by sea. Confusion at ports of embarkation was compounded by the inadequacy of the ports and cargo-handling equipment and personnel. In addition, the sealift assets were a catchall because of the neglect of maritime shipping in the United States. Dedicated fast sealift ships were few, short on maintenance and crews. Ships, taken up from trade, both domestic and foreign, frequently were only marginally suitable. Fortunately, port facilities in Saudi Arabia were outstanding, so unloading and turnaround time in theater was rapid. Despite these headaches, the Transportation Command and soldiers and sailors involved in the sealift operations were innovative and ultimately managed their resources well.

While the theater commander fretted about the pace of the heavy buildup of his forces, he had the additional worry of cobbling up a coalition strategy as well as the command and control apparatus to hold it together and direct it. Not only did technical and operational differences between the nations, and indeed the services, need to be resolved, but political sensitivities and prerogatives also had to be taken into account.

General Schwarzkopf never quite managed to truly integrate the coalition forces, but he did the next best thing; he got all his disparate warriors to cooperate. He commanded the Americans and the British Division, which put itself under his command. The Arabs worked out their own command arrangements but agreed to conform to U.S. operational plans. The French, although initially operating with the Arab command, accepted membership in the American XVIII Corps once the allied ground offensive took place in February.

For both defensive and offensive operations, the U.S. theater commander resorted to the simple expedient of giving each nation its own sector in which to operate. He did the same with the two division Marine Corps ashore in Saudi Arabia, whose modus operandi differed from the army's. In this way the field commander and his staff could devote their energies to coordinating what promised to be concurrent but separate operations within an overall strategic framework. This was a feasible solution, and it worked well in the defense and in the offense. But in both phases of the campaign the command arrangements were never tested under stress. How well the arrangement would have worked in the face of unexpected operational reverses will forever remain unknown. At any rate, the Schwarzkopf solution should not be considered the ideal for coalition warfare.

By late summer the dangers of an Iraqi invasion of Saudi Arabia were minimal. This gave the field commander the luxury of emplacing his electronic gadgetry, building up his logistic infrastructure unimpeded, training his troops for desert warfare, and developing plans for offensive operations from a position of relative strength. General Schwarzkopf set the time lines and controlled the pace of events with minimal outside interference from either the enemy or the heads of state. Few commanders enjoy such luxury in coalition warfare, and this too should not be used as the norm for the future.

As the logistic buildup, training, and interallied dialogue continued, the shape of the coming war also began to emerge. Other than in numbers, the allies had all the advantages. Their troops, equipment, logistics, and command and control were vastly superior to the those of the Iraqis. The terrain and sparse population in the theater lent itself to the maneuver and fire doctrine of the U.S. combined arms combat formations. The Iraqis were isolated and beset by enemies on all sides. Their command system and lines of communications were vulnerable. The U.S. Navy controlled the Gulf, and when called upon, allied air forces were certain to gain air superiority and in short order deliver punishing blows both in Iraq and against Iraqi forces in Kuwait. It was a war that could not be lost. The only question was the price to be paid in winning it.

To answer that question, the intelligence community carefully analyzed the strengths and weakness of their opponent. The Iraqi military command was judged to be professional and competent. But it was rigid in its procedures, unaccustomed to reacting to the unexpected, and experienced in fighting primarily defensive set piece battles against the Iranians, whose only advantage on the battlefield had been numbers. The Iraqis had never experienced concentrated air attacks or the blows that could be delivered by powerful maneuverable armored forces supported by air strikes.

The command and control within the Iraqi armed forces was sophisticated but was overly centralized. Little initiative could be expected from subordinate commanders if their source of direction was cut off. Modern air defenses were thick around Baghdad but weak in the Kuwaiti theater. Low-level air defenses were rated formidable because of the number and variety of antiaircraft weapons. The Iraqi Air Force was large and modern for a Third World nation, but its competence was rated low.

Ground forces varied in quality. The Republican Guards, both armored-mechanized and infantry, were rated good and were considered to be combined arms organizations complete with their organic supporting arms and ancillary combat support units. The regular army infantry, reserves, and conscripts were rated poor, as were the armored forces. Iraqi artillery was respected because of the number of guns and Iraq's proven ability in the war with Iran to use it effectively. The Iraqi combat engineers were highly rated because of their ability to build sophisticated fortifications, obstacles, and intra-theater roads. Overhead imagery confirmed the quality of their work. However, the Iraqis were seen as logistically vulnerable. They had long lines of communications and little in the way of a flexible tactical logistic system.

Perhaps the fatal weakness on the Iraqi side was its intelligence collection capability. It was nil, a weakness that the allies used both for deception and to achieve surprise.

While the coalition built its forces, the Iraqis did nothing to interfere: no spoiling attacks, air raids, or commando attacks. One explanation derives from Iraq's lack of precise targeting information necessary for such actions. The most probable explanation, however, is that Saddam Hussein did not think the United States would go to war because of its fear of casualties. This belief was fostered by Saddam Hussein's reading of Vietnam and Beirut and U.S. anguish over "body bags," as reflected in the daily television coverage available to him. Additionally, he apparently found it hard to believe that the United States was willing to bleed over what was an internal Arab dispute. Under these circumstances he probably thought it wise not to take action that would force a U.S. military response.

THE AIR WAR

On January 17, 1991 (local time), the air war began, and Desert Shield became Desert Storm. The air campaign was designed to be the crown jewel in the U.S. war plan, and it was designed to cripple the Iraqis to such an extent that if Saddam Hussein did not withdraw from Kuwait, the subsequent ground war would be swift and have a minimum of casualties. The air attacks were also designed to destroy Iraq's nuclear weapons potential.

Air force planners had carefully analyzed Iraq's strengths and weaknesses and conceived a very effective strategic air campaign, which was war-gamed in the Pentagon under a simulation known as "Checkmate." Initially the air commanders in Saudi Arabia were cool to the plan because it was drawn up by outsiders 1,000 miles from the battlefield, but in time the plan was adopted, refined, and finally put into action. A feature of the campaign was that it treated the bombing of Iraq and Kuwait as part of the same package. For example, the bombing of bridges and electrical grids around Baghdad related directly to the Iraqis' ability to exercise command and control of their forces in Kuwait.

In drawing up the air plan, the air force sought to identify Iraq's "center of gravity," i.e., that part of the Iraqi war machine that would, if successfully attacked, lead to decisive results. The planners focused on Saddam Hussein's elaborate command, control, and communications system as the critical node. With it destroyed, Iraqi air defenses would be useless, and their troops in Kuwait would be deaf and dumb in addition to being blind for lack of intelligence. Even if the Iraqi Air Force rose to do battle, it would do so lacking direction, thus making it extremely vulnerable to allied fighters.

Because of the precision of the bombing, the strategic attacks on Iraq avoided inflicting massive casualties on civilians. But the economic infrastructure of Iraq was devastated in the process. Electrical systems that were critical to Saddam Hussein's command and control were also critical to civilized urban life. Iraq was not quite bombed back to the Stone Age, but the philosophy behind the bombing was in the Curtis LeMay tradition, and it has had a deplorable impact on the civilian population. A medical team from Harvard University, assessing the damage during a visit to Iraq last spring, forecast that with the destruction of utilities, transportation, and fuel refineries, and the concomitant breakdown in sanitation systems, a minimum of 170,000 children will die as the indirect victims of the air war during this year.

The impact on civilians of a strategic air campaign remains controversial. It has the potential of being politically counterproductive. Before a strategic air campaign is launched, it should be subjected to a rigorous political and ethical cost-benefit analysis in addition to a military one.

Having quickly shut down Iraq's command, control, and communications infrastructure and taken command of the air, the coalition air forces were then free to attack military targets critical to ground operations. These included supply and logistic facilities, artillery and rocket launchers, tanks and armored personnel carriers, command posts, and ultimately fortifications in the path of the impending ground offensive.

While the air campaign was a brilliant success, it was not perfect. The Iraqis proved adept at deception and camouflage. In addition, intelligence on the numbers and whereabouts of critical targets was imperfect. As is now known, the intelligence community was unaware of the extent of Iraq's nuclear program and facilities. The same was true of its Scud inventory. A good deal of the air effort, which should have been attacking more important targets, was diverted to search for and attack these missiles that were of little military significance but turned out to have enormous political and psychological value. The Iraqi Air Force, although it never contested the allies by its very existence, engaged the attention of allied aircraft that might otherwise have been used in ground attacks. That the Iraqi planes constituted a potential threat throughout the war can be seen from data provided by a Central Command official. Of the 685 fixed-wing combat aircraft in the Iraqi inventory at the outset of the war, only eighty were destroyed: 102 had fled to Iran, leaving 503 available for operations.

Precision guided missiles were stars in the war and proved their worth, as did unguided bombs used with modern target acquisition and releasing systems. B-52 bombers, however, had a spotty record. Used against area targets, they were expected to have the same devastating effect that they had had in Vietnam, but the dispersion and nature of Iraqi protective revetments reduced the impact of the B-52 bombing raids.

Organizationally, and from a command and control standpoint, the air campaign went smoothly. Even though the air traffic within the theater was extremely heavy with different types of aircraft and helicopters from different services and countries, the air space management systems were able to coordinate the comings and goings, and remarkably, there were no air-to-air collisions.

There were doctrinal differences between the services in the conduct of the air war. These were resolved satisfactorily, but usually in favor of the air force, which was clearly in charge of the campaign. Interoperability problems also arose, primarily due to incompatibility of similar equipment. Thus the thirty page daily air tasking order specifying missions for the upcoming twenty-four hours had to be flown by helicopter to the navy carriers in the Gulf because air force and navy computers could not talk to one another.

The length of the air campaign was a function of many considerations and not tied to a specific timetable. On the strategic level, some targets had to be revisited, new targets emerged, and the Scud hunt had to be pursued. On the operational and tactical level, the aim was to reduce the overall Iraqi combat capability in the Kuwaiti theater by roughly 50 percent, however long that took. Bad weather, smoke, and difficulty in assessing bomb damage made it difficult to measure precisely the progress of the campaign. Another factor affecting the length of the air war was the readiness of the ground forces to go over to the offensive.

With little in the way of opposition, the allied air forces had the luxury of carrying out their attacks at their own pace.

Psychological operations were closely tied to the air campaign within the Kuwaiti theater and were quite successful. For example, individual Iraqi units would be informed by leaflets dropped from the air, that they would be bombed on the following day. After the bombing, they would be reminded of the warning and given the schedule for the next time they would be struck. The leaflets suggested, of course, that the soldiers see to their own safety by fleeing from their posts. Many did just that.

Deception, too, was very effective. While the air campaign was under way, Central Command created the impression that should a ground war follow, it would consist of an amphibious attack along the coast in conjunction with a direct assault across the Saudi-Kuwaiti border. The Iraqi army disposed itself to defend against just that type of attack. In fact, the Allied Command had decided that the Republican Guard units in southern Iraq were to be the objective of the coming offensive. With the guard units destroyed, Iraqi resistance was expected to collapse. All other ground operations were to be subordinate to that one single objective.

It was clear that the air bombardment of the Iraqis had weakened their war-making capability to a critical degree. Targets throughout Iraq had been destroyed, the 50 percent level of destruction of heavy weapons and equipment was being reached in the Kuwaiti theater, and the battlefield itself was being prepared for the allied ground offensive. Although there was hope that Saddam Hussein would quit without the need for a ground war, even ardent air power advocates began to concede that a ground attack would be necessary to end the war.

Iraqi morale was low: although ammunition was plentiful, there was serious maldistribution of food and water among frontline units. Desertions and defections were also rife, but the intelligence community concluded that within the Iraqi military, there was still too much fear of the regime for a wholesale collapse of the army to occur.

Within the Iraqi high command, doubts apparently began to arise over the Iraqi army's ability to fight successfully an Iran-

Iraq war type defense against the coalition. The air campaign was far longer and more effective than they anticipated. But they still believed that the United States was loath to suffer heavy casualties in a ground war. The static defenses that they had established facing Saudi Arabia and along the east coast of Kuwait were designed to channel any allied attacks into killing zones where Iraqi weapons were still expected to take a heavy toll on the attackers. But the battlefield bombing was destroying those defenses and weapons. Evidence suggests that Saddam Hussein concluded that unless the allies attacked soon, there would be no defenses. It also suggests that the Iraqis decided to launch a limited attack south to provoke the Americans into battle in the hopes of starting the bloodletting that would lead to an antiwar outcry in the United States. Thus the battle of Khafji came to pass.

The three-pronged attack launched on the night of January 29 was no minor affair. Three heavy Iraqi divisions and three infantry divisions from two separate corps were earmarked as part of the attacking force. They were to follow in the wake of lighter brigades, whose job it was to locate the enemy and engage it, at which time the six divisions would attack. The object was not to seize terrain but to create a bloody brawl. Even though the Iraqis did not know the location of the allies, they knew an attack of corps-size was bound to elicit a response.

Khafji was a defining moment in the war. Whatever illusions the Iraqi high command had of punishing the allies and perhaps stalemating the war went up in smoke and flames at Khafji. The main attack never got off the mark. The advanced guard brigades were spotted early in their movement and taken under immediate air attack. The one that succeeded in reaching Khafji found itself being decimated by a combination of air, artillery, rocket, and finally ground attack.

From that point on, according to intelligence analysts, the Iraqis knew they were beaten. The best that Saddam Hussein could hope for at that point was to preserve what forces he could and survive as a ruler. For almost one month more the Iraqis hunkered down in their bunkers while the air campaign turned its fury on frontline positions, the armored reserve forces near Kuwait City, and most of the Republican Guards along the border between Kuwait and Iraq. The grand plan of enmeshing the allies in the mine fields and barbed wire on Iraqi land and coastal defenses while artillery pounded the allies and reserves counterattacked was diminished. Desertions, abandonments, and surrenders became widespread. Air power had been stunningly successful.

THE GROUND CAMPAIGN

When the ground campaign was launched, General Schwarzkopf was careful to give the Arab units recognizable and meaningful roles, with the exception of the Syrians, who were held "in reserve." But the Americans, and to a lesser extent the British and the French, predominated, and the less sophisticated Arab units were hard put to keep up with them. As part of the deception plan, a marine attack through the center of the Iraqi defenses, where an attack was expected by the defenders, led the way. All of this was to focus the attention of the Iraqis while the main attack was made in the west against the Republican Guards by heavily armed divisions. The Marine attack up the middle was so quick and successful that the timetable for the enveloping heavy armored corps' attack on the western flank was moved up to take advantage of Iraqi disarray. On the coast the Iraqis waited for the amphibious landing that never came. Deceived into facing eastward, they were taken on land from the west. There was no cohesive defense. Republican Guard divisions were taken completely by surprise when attacks came at a time and place not provided for in their defensive plans. They were astounded that the Americans could navigate with such precision over the featureless desert. The key, of course, was the Global Positioning System (GPS), which made use of satellite fixes to determine locations.[1]

The feared Iraqi use of chemical weapons never materialized during the allied offensive. This remains a mystery of the war. The Iraqis had a large inventory of chemical munitions, including thirty Scud warheads, but no chemical weapons were fired and no weapons were found in Kuwait. Ancillary equipment and artillery dispositions associated with chemical warfare were identified by coalition intelligence, but apparently no chemical weapons were actually brought south of the Euphrates. It is likely that both Saddam Hussein and his field commanders were inhibited by the possibility of retaliation and, in the case of unit commanders, the added concern of being held personally responsible at the conclusion of a war that they were clearly going to lose. Another more practical inhibition was the Iraqi's inability to locate lucrative targets for chemical attack for lack of a target acquisition capability.

Within a day of the opening of the offensive, the Iraqi army was in complete rout, with only a few units standing to fight in uncoordinated and unsuccessful efforts to slow the attack. Of the major Republican Guard divisions, the Tawakalna, Medina, and Adman were destroyed, but 70 percent of the Hammurabi division made it safely across the Euphrates line around Basra. It was quickly reorganized and joined five other escaping divisions in Basra to put down the Shia uprising in southern Iraq.

When the cease-fire went into effect on February 28, a substantial portion of the Iraqi occupation army was still fleeing north across three bridges remaining in the vicinity of Basra. But at that point nobody on the allied side had a clear picture of what remained of the Iraqi order of battle.

The theater commander's directive at the outset of Desert Storm was as follows: "USCINCCENT [U.S. Commander in Chief Central Command] conducts offensive operations to eject Iraqi forces from Kuwait and destroy the Iraqi war fighting capability." In forty-three days of an air war and 100 hours of a land campaign, he achieved the first objective, but whether he fully achieved the second is open to argument.

Any analysis of the ground war, however, must conclude that it was as impressive as the air campaign, notwithstanding the lack of opposition. In retrospect, logistic problems were more formidable than Iraqi defenses. The intra-theater logistic nightmares had the same roots as the inter-theater ones that marked the buildup and primarily plagued the army. Configured to fight in Europe, where host nation support and logistic infrastructure was in place, the army was not immediately prepared to operate in a remote desert environment. The problem was compounded when the theater commander decided to envelop the Iraqis with a wide swing through the western Iraqi desert. The logistic and supply problems thus created were enormous. The critical shortages were in trucks and tank transporters. Every available civilian truck that could be rented on the Arabian peninsula was pressed into action. Tank transporters were leased or purchased from European countries, including those of the former communist bloc. Through creativity and prodigious effort at all ranks, the army officer in charge of the effort managed to muster the wherewithal to support the combat units. It is not without justification that the adage goes "amateurs talk tactics, professionals talk logistics."

Without detracting from the brilliance of the campaign, it should again be noted that the forces involved were only loosely federated and not integrated. They each did their own thing in accordance with their own doctrine and in their separate zones of action. It worked well because the opposition was negligible.

Even within the U.S. ranks there were some problems. The most serious ones concerned mines (both on land and at sea), the difficulty of identifying friendly forces during air attacks in a war without front lines, and lack of responsive air support. The problem with land mines was due to the Iraqi propensity to make extensive use of their large inventory of mines as a key element in their defensive strategy. This required the allies to employ an abnormally large number of mine field breachers. As was the case with the procurement of trucks and tank transporters, the allies scoured military inventories of several countries for mine-clearing and breaching equipment.

The navy's lack of an adequate mine countermeasure capability was more serious and greatly impacted on its ability to execute a contingency plan for an amphibious operation around Kuwait City if one became necessary.[2] This weakness was an outgrowth of the U.S. military orientation against a Soviet threat in Europe. The navy saw its role as providing powerful aircraft carrier battle groups to attack the Soviets from seaward locations in the event of war. Under NATO division of labors, the continental navies were responsible for inshore mine clearance.

While the navy was without peer on the high seas, it was as ill-prepared for operations in shallow and confined waters during the Gulf War as it had been in the same location during the Iran-Iraq tanker War.

The identification friend or foe (IFF) problem for close air support aircraft caused casualties in both the ranks of the Americans and the British. Operating at night, in bad weather, over featureless terrain, while being shot at from the ground makes it difficult for all but the most experienced pilots to distinguish between a friend and an enemy. The same is true for tank crews. A series of ad hoc systems minimized the problem once the ground war got under way, but a permanent solution to prevent fratricide has yet to be found.

In the context of the victory, these problems fade, but in a tougher war they could have been quite troublesome. The ground campaign has also been hailed as a classic example of the joint air-land battle doctrine of the army and air force (Marine Corps operational doctrine is different). But it was not air-land, it was air and land. It was only a marginally integrated effort. The army did not find the air force system of battlefield support sufficiently responsive. The air force required too much lead time for requests for air support and frequently modified the requests to conform to their own assessments. Every corps commander within Central Command complained about air force tactical support.

Ground commanders are never satisfied that they have enough information about the enemy to their front, and the Kuwaiti campaign proved no exception. Despite high-technology intelligence systems, the process of collecting, evaluating, and distributing intelligence to the consumer in a timely and usable fashion continues to elude U.S. forces. As one infantry company commander remarked, "I knew more about what was happening in Baghdad than I did about what was happening to my front." It was not that the intelligence was not available. On the contrary, the allies were supported by the best tactical intelligence of any war in history. The problem lay in the timely distribution of that intelligence to the consumer.

CONCLUSIONS

Any assessment of the Gulf War must start with the question, "Was the war preventable?" At first blush, the answer seems to be yes. It is likely that Saddam Hussein would have been deterred if he knew that the United States would intervene and if he had fully realized how quickly and effectively the United States could project armed forces to the region and rally international support to oppose him. But that is too easy an answer.

As noted earlier, Saddam Hussein did not demobilize after the war with Iran. On the contrary, he improved his armed forces and undertook to modernize them with the purchase of foreign arms. He also initiated a domestic arms manufacturing program with results that impressed outsiders at an arms fair in Baghdad in 1989. In addition, he continued to improve his ballistic missile, chemical, and biological inventories. Most ominously of all, he was racing to produce nuclear weapons, an effort whose scope is just now being understood.

There can be little question that Saddam Hussein was placing Iraq in the position to use force to achieve whatever long-range goals he had in mind, if other means of achieving them were insufficient. In that sense, a war at some point was probably not preventable, particularly if Saddam Hussein grew stronger while the United States reduced its military capability, as it was in the process of doing in the wake of the Cold War. Saddam Hussein made the fundamental mistake of going to war at a time when the United States was at the height of its strength and no longer had to worry about a Warsaw Pact threat. However, he had not achieved his military potential, particularly in the field of nuclear weaponry.

As for using sanctions rather than military force, as many argued in the early days of the crisis, this seems naive in retrospect. The U.S. Navy and other navies within the coalition established a near-leakproof blockade of Iraq, which is still in place. It has hurt Iraq, but even with its economic infrastructure devastated and its economy and quality of life reduced to a primitive state by the air war, Saddam Hussein remains defiant. It is not likely that sanctions alone would have brought him to his senses.

The question of sanctions then brings up the issue of whether the war achieved its objective. In a narrow, legalistic sense it did, in that it ejected Iraq from Kuwait, but it only diminished Iraq's threat to the region; it did not eliminate it. The Baghdad regime's attempt to salvage its nuclear weapons development program, in contravention of the United Nation's imposed terms under the cease-fire, suggests an unchastened Saddam Hussein, who remains a potential threat to the region. In that sense the nonlegalistic objective of restoring stability to the region was not achieved, and Iraq remains a potential threat to tranquility in the Middle East.

In a broader sense, Saddam Hussein's actions during the war opened a Pandora's box. The world watched aghast as Scud missiles with outdated technology flamed into Israel and Saudi Arabia. While most of them were intercepted by Patriot missiles, the value of ballistic missiles for political and psychological purposes as well as military ones was self-evident. The message for future would-be aggressors is that ballistic missiles are good to have. They are even better if they carry a warhead of "mass destruction," such as chemicals or biological or, most importantly, nuclear payloads. One need not speculate long on how different the Gulf crisis might have been if Saddam Hussein had nuclear warheads for his missiles at the outset of the crisis. This, of course, raises the issue of ballistic missile and nuclear proliferation. Establishing a regime to prevent the production and fielding of mass destruction ballistic missiles must be a priority for the international community in the aftermath of the war.

On the positive side, Iraq's aggression was not allowed to stand, and the world community within the framework of the United Nations (UN) showed remarkable cohesiveness. This bodes well for the future. Notwithstanding the reluctance of the United States to subscribe beforehand to any arrangement that might limit its freedom of action when its defined interests are involved, the coalition effort opens the door for exploration for greater use of the UN.

Chapter 7, Article 43 of the UN charter provides for armed intervention and collective military action in the interest of international order. With the end of the Cold War, which inhibited its invocation in the past, it might be wise to consider creating a military infrastructure to be activated under Article 43 in time of crisis. In this regard, the dormant Military Staff Committee of the UN could be energized to develop doctrine, training standards, and procedures to integrate national forces operating under Article 43, should a multinational force again be activated.

In addition to creating the framework for an enforcement arm for the UN Security Council members might also consider creating a "peace watch" capability. Similar to past and existing UN observer teams, peace watch teams could be dispatched as an early warning mechanism to troubled international borders during times of tension and when aggression appears to threaten. Here again the Military Staff Committee could be useful in supporting such an effort.

Notwithstanding any potential value in the future of building on the success of coalition warfare in the Gulf, the success of U.S. arms in the war is bound to have a profound effect on international behavior. The power and effectiveness of U.S. troops, weapons, equipment, and operational art was so impressive as to leave little doubt that the United States is the most powerful military nation on earth. The willingness to use that military might well gives comfort to friends and pause to potential foes for a long time to come. But the effects will be transitory if the United States allows its superiority to erode.

The war gave credence to the observation of Soviet Marshal Nicolai Ogarkov in 1984 that high technology had wrought "a revolution in warfare." The United States brought to the battlefield an integrated system of sensors, stealth, electronic suppression techniques, and precision munitions designed to counter Soviet-style warfare on the European continent. This system proved its worth in the desert. High technology is a key to U.S. military dominance, and sufficient investment must continue to be made in research, development, and procurement of high-technology weapons and equipment. This need not be a search for ever more exotic technology, just enough to ensure that superiority is maintained across the board in both quality and quantity.

The other strong suit that the United States brought to the battlefield was the quality of its armed forces. Never in the history of the republic has a more competent and proficient military been fielded. The high quality displayed by all the services is a function of four factors: high caliber personnel, professional education, realistic and continuous training, and the unique concepts of leadership and management to which the services subscribe. The first three factors are self-evident; the last is less apparent yet equally important. The U.S. military operates with a pyramidal organizational structure. At successive levels from the peak of the structure to the bottom of the pyramid, somebody is clearly in charge to provide explicit articulation of the mission to be achieved in relation to the objective of the next higher level of responsibility. While the structure is rigid, the execution is flexible in that subordinates are expected to take the action necessary to meet the mission goals. This fosters innovation and creativity as opposed to mindless fulfillment of task, irrespective of its value to the overall goal.

The effectiveness of this system was demonstrated in countless ways during Desert Storm and Desert Shield as service personnel coped with the unexpected. Without such a system of leadership and management, even the best weaponry and equipment in the hands of well-trained troops would not have been brought to bear effectively.

As the result of this system, the logistic and operational deficiencies that emerged during the course of the deployment and war were solved on an ad hoc basis. Needless to say, however, those deficiencies, such as sealift, mine warfare, and integration of the air-ground effort must not be left to ad hoc solutions in the future but must be remedied while shaping the military for a future that will see smaller armed forces with fewer dollars to spend.

While the strictly military problems that were highlighted during the war are correctable by the Defense Department alone, the major problem of comprehensive, accurate, and timely intelligence is a far greater problem. General Schwarzkopf stressed this in his testimony on Capitol Hill. The problem of intelligence extends beyond the military and needs improvement at every level. The need ranges from better human intelligence, in order to forecast intentions, to improved means of doing such things as bomb damage assessment. It is clear from the crisis and the war that there needs to be greater integration of U.S. intelligence efforts.

In summary, the United States must ensure that it maintains a high-quality and balanced military force of air, ground, and sea components as it draws down in size. As overseas bases disappear, logistics to support force projection must be improved. Personnel, weapons, training and leadership, and intelligence are the ingredients of effectiveness, and while they can be maintained at lower costs, capability must never be sacrificed on the altar of economy. With smaller forces, the United States must foster new concepts and procedures for coalition warfare, and weaknesses in joint operating procedures within its own armed forces must be corrected.

Most of all, the U.S. armed forces must not rest on their laurels in the afterglow of their dramatic victory in the Gulf. It is well to remember that a British expeditionary force armed with the high-technology weapons of the day achieved a similar striking victory at low cost at Omdurman in the Sudan in 1898. A year later that same force was pinned down in South Africa, being embarrassed by a motley army of Boer farmers.

ENDNOTES

1. The Republican Guards were quite familiar with the desert over which the U.S. Army's VII Corps attached. It was on the edges of the training area customarily used by the guards, but Iraqi units rarely ventured into it for fear of getting lost.
2. The contingency plan was used as part of the overall theater deception plan.

9

THE IMPACT OF THE PERSIAN GULF WAR ON MILITARY BUDGETS AND FORCE STRUCTURE

Lawrence J. Korb

INTRODUCTION

To understand fully the impact of the Gulf War on the size and shape of the defense budgets and the military force structure of the United States, it is necessary to go back to the spring of 1990. At that time, the Bush administration apparently had not accepted the fact that the Cold War had ended and was trying to maintain the Cold War force structure of the U.S. military. Despite the fact that in late 1989, the Soviet Union had allowed its Eastern European empire to crumble and the Warsaw Pact to dissolve, Secretary of Defense Dick Cheney argued that the changes in the Soviet military threat to the West had not diminished enough to justify significant reductions in the Cold War force structure or Cold War levels of defense spending. Accordingly, throughout the first half of 1990, Cheney vigorously argued that defense spending should not be reduced by more than 10 percent in real terms over the fiscal year (FY) 1991–95 period.

Cheney's position was supported by almost no one in the executive or legislative branches. Even members of his own party, like Senators John McCain (R-Ariz.) and William Cohen (R-Maine), found his response to events in Eastern Europe rather timid.[1] Senator Sam Nunn (D-Ga.), the chairman of the Senate Armed Services Committee (SASC), criticized the Department of

Defense for basing its spending plans on outdated assumptions about the military threats facing the United States.[2] The then director of Central Intelligence, William Webster, argued that the Soviet Union had made a historic turn away from militarism, that the changes were irreversible, and that the Soviets therefore no longer posed a significant military threat to Western Europe.[3] Even such hard-liners as former defense officials Richard Perle and James Schlesinger agreed with Webster.[4] So, too, did current military leaders like General Colin Powell, chairman of the Joint Chiefs of Staff (JCS), and Admiral David Jeremiah, vice-chairman of the JCS. Both these military officers found Cheney's stand unrealistic. Powell felt that the military forces could easily be reduced by 20 to 25 percent over the first half of the 1990s, while Jeremiah argued that it would take the Soviets two years to put themselves again in a posture to threaten the West militarily.[5] It appeared to longtime participants in the defense debate, like Les Aspin (D-Wis.), chairman of the House Armed Services Committee (HASC), and John Warner (R-Va.), ranking member of the Senate Armed Services Committee, that Cheney's ideas had become irrelevant to the debate.[6]

At the same time that the Soviet military threat was crumbling, the projected size of the federal deficit was growing by leaps and bounds. When he presented the administration's FY 1991 budget to the Congress in February 1990, Budget Director Richard Darman estimated that the deficit for FY 1990, the budget year ending in September 1990, would be about $90 billion. The actual deficit was $220 billion, an increase of $130 billion or 144 percent. Similarly, Darman had initially projected the FY 1991 deficit to be about $60 billion. By the spring of 1990, Darman had reestimated the deficit for FY 1991 at $160 billion, an increase of 167 percent in just three months. (It actually was $279 billion.)[7]

The combination of the decline in the Soviet threat and the growth in the size of the projected deficit put the defense budget into a political free-fall. Because the civilian leadership of the Department of Defense (DoD) seemed unable to articulate what constituted a clearly defined military threat to the security of the United States, and because the defense budget was the largest source of discretionary funds in the federal budget (about 60 percent), the various congressional committees with oversight over the DoD proposed slashing the president's FY 1991–95 program throughout the spring and early summer of 1990.

The Senate Armed Services Committee proposed cutting $128 billion from the FY 1991–95 Bush program, and its chairman, Senator Sam Nunn, gave a series of speeches trying to "fill in the blanks" in what he argued was Cheney's antiquated Cold War military strategy. The House Armed Services Committee argued that the proposed budget could be reduced by at least $200 billion in the first half of the 1990s, while the House and Senate Budget Committees argued that as much as $250 billion could be slashed from the five-year defense plan.

When the president and congressional leaders agreed to hold a summit on the entire federal budget, it was clear that the defense budget would be reduced substantially over the 1991–95 period. Even Richard Darman, budget director and chief administration negotiator, had accepted that fact. Going into the negotiations, it appeared that the best the DoD could hope for would be the budget reduction proposed by the HASC. Indeed, Cheney presented an illustrative 25 percent force structure reduction to Congress in June 1990. Although the secretary of defense argued disingenuously that his proposal was illustrative and that the 25 percent force structure reduction would translate only into a 10 percent budget reduction, no one took him seriously.[8] Senator Nunn argued that Cheney had given his implied consent to the force reduction,[9] and Congressman Aspin showed how the Cheney force structure reductions could bring real budget reductions of between 18 and 27 percent over the FY 1991–95 period.[10]

THE IMPACT OF THE WAR

Before the budget negotiators completed their task, Saddam Hussein invaded Kuwait and President Bush, vowing that Saddam Hussein's invasion would not stand, quickly ordered military forces from all five armed services to the Gulf. The invasion led to a quick agreement among the budget negotiators to take three steps in regard to the defense program. First, they accepted for FY 1991–95 the defense budget totals proposed by Senator Nunn. Second, the conferees agreed that through FY 1993, defense spending levels would be segregated from the two other categories of discretionary federal spending, domestic and international. Third, the costs of military operations in the Gulf would be placed "off budget" and would be funded by a supplemental budget, supported primarily with foreign contributions.

Each of these three actions, which were a direct result of Saddam Hussein's invasion, will have long-term benefits for the DoD. As indicated in Table 1, the budget summit cuts only $128.9 billion from the president's proposed five-year program, almost exactly the amount proposed by Senator Nunn. Had the negotiators accepted the proposal of the HASC, defense spending would have been reduced by an additional $80 billion.

Similarly, separating defense from domestic or international programs means that new programs in areas like health and environment, or aid to Eastern Europe, cannot be funded in FY 1992 and FY 1993 by reducing defense below the $291 billion agreed to at the summit for each of those years. If Congress wants to add a new domestic program, it must cut an old one or raise taxes. It cannot pay for it, as it has in the past, by cutting a program like the B-2 bomber. Any reductions in defense below the agreed upon levels can go only to reducing the overall federal deficit. This provision will mean about $20 billion more for defense in FY 1992 and FY 1993, because in recent years Congress had always revisited (cut) the out years. For example, the Congressional Budget Resolution of 1986 agreed that DoD would receive $303 billion in FY 1988 and $323 billion in FY 1989. Congress actually authorized only $284 billion and $290 billion, or $52 billion less.

Finally, placing the Desert Shield and Desert Storm operations off budget meant that none of their costs would have to be absorbed in the baseline defense budget. Normally some or all of the cost of military operations, like the blockade of Cuba during the missile crisis of 1962 or the invasion of Panama in 1989, are borne by the regular defense budget. Moreover, since the Bush administration was able to get foreign nations to contribute approximately $55 billion to this account, substantially more

Table 1 National Defense Budget Authority in Billions of Dollars

	FY 91	FY 92	FY 93	FY 94	FY 95	Total FY 91–95	Cumulative Real Reductions (%) FY 90–95
President's Request	306.9	312.5	317.5	321.6	325.7	1584.2	8.7
Nunn Proposal	289.0	290.5	291.5	292.0	293.0	1456.0	21.0
Compared to President	-17.9	-22.0	-26.0	-29.6	-32.7	-128.2	
House Armed Services Committee	283.0	280.5	275.4	270.4	265.6	1374.9	26.5
Compared to President	-23.9	-32.0	-42.1	-51.2	-60.1	209.3	
Budget Summit	288.3	290.9	291.1	292.0	293.0	1455.3	21.0
Compared to President	-18.6	-21.6	-26.4	-29.6	-32.7	-128.9	

than the Congressional Budget Office (CBO) and the General Accounting Office (GAO) estimated the incremental costs of the forty-three-day war to be, the Pentagon was actually able to shift some of its baseline budget into the supplemental account. For example, before the war, the projected baseline defense budget for FY 1992 was supposed to buy 6,500 high speed, anti-radar (HARM), Patriot, Tomahawk, and Hellfire missiles (the glamour weapons of the Gulf War). However, when the actual FY 1992 budget request was sent up to the Hill, it requested only 1,500 of these missiles. The proposed war supplement initially called for funding another 5,000, far more than the number actually fired in the Gulf.[11]

All told, Saddam Hussein's invasion stopped the defense free-fall and provided defense with a "bonus" of at least $100 billion over the FY 1991–95 period. These additional funds are enough to fund the entire 650 Advanced Tactical Fighters (ATF) and the remaining 60 B-2 bombers or maintain and operate two heavy army divisions, two tactical air wings, and two carrier battle groups for the entire FY 1991–95 period.

Moreover, as the massive buildup of the U.S. forces continued throughout the fall and winter of 1990, many observers expected the Pentagon or the Bush administration to seek to renegotiate the defense portion of the Budget Summit Agreement. Indeed people like Henry Kissinger argued that this nation was fortunate that the invasion of Kuwait occurred before the force reductions, which were going to be brought about by the Budget Summit Agreement, took place. In their opinion, the 1995 force structure would not have been capable of evicting the Iraqi army from Kuwait.[12]

Nonetheless, the Bush administration did live up to the Budget Summit Agreement. On February 5, 1991, three weeks before the war ended, Secretary Cheney and Chairman Powell did propose a 22 percent real budget reduction and a 25 percent force structure reduction for the FY 1992–97 period.[13] The DoD spending plan for the next five years is outlined in Table 2. It indicates that after rising by almost 55 percent between FY 1980 and FY 1985, and dropping by approximately 22 percent since then, defense authority will fall another 22 percent by

Table 2 National Defense Budget Authority and Outlays, FY 1980–FY 1996 (in billions of current dollars)

	Fiscal Year								
	1980	1985	1990	1991*	1992*	1993*	1994*	1995*	1996*
Budget Authority	143.9	294.7	303.3	285.6	290.8	290.9	291.9	295.1	297.8
Real Growth (%)		54.9	-12.9	-10.3	-1.0	-3.8	-3.3	-2.5	-2.7
Outlays	134.0	252.7	299.3	298.9	295.2	292.0	286.7	288.6	293.2
Real Growth (%)		35.7	1.3	-5.1	-4.2	-4.9	-5.5	-2.9	-2.0

*Office of Management and Budget (OMB) estimates

FY 1997. This plan follows the Budget Summit Agreement and will bring defense spending in real terms back to the level of FY 1980 by FY 1997.

The Cheney-Powell force structure plan is outlined in Tables 3 and 4. As indicated in Table 3, it calls for reducing both active duty and reserve personnel levels by 20 percent below their 1990 levels, with the heaviest reductions coming in the army, and the smallest in the navy and Marine Corps. Active duty end strength in the army would be reduced by almost 30 percent, in the Air Force by 19 percent, and in the navy and Marine Corps by only 13 percent. The Bush administration also proposes to cut selected reserve forces by 20 percent. The reserve forces of the army, navy and Marine Corps will all be reduced in excess of 20 percent, while the air force reserves will actually increase by 2 percent.

These personnel reductions also meant sizable reductions in force structure. As indicated in Table 4, the army's Total Force will be reduced from 28 to 18 divisions, the navy from 15 carriers and 545 ships to 13 carriers and 451 ships, and the air force from 36 to 26 tactical air wings. Overall, the reserve component of the ground forces combat units would remain roughly the same as 1990, i.e., 33 percent of the army and 25 percent for the marines. However, the reserve portion of the tactical air forces will rise substantially, i.e., from 33 percent to 42 percent, of the air force's tactical air wings, and from 13 to 16 percent of the navy's carrier air wings.

Table 3 Military Personnel Strength (Strength at end of fiscal year, in thousands)

	1980	1987	1990	1991*	1993*	1995*
ACTIVE DUTY MILITARY						
Army	777	781	751	702	618	536
change since FY 90 (%)				-7	-18	-29
Navy	527	587	583	570	536	510
change since FY 90 (%)				-2	-8	-13
Marine Corps	189	199	197	194	182	171
change since FY 90 (%)				-2	-8	-13
Air Force	562	607	539	509	458	437
change since FY 90 (%)				-6	-15	-19
TOTAL ACTIVE	2,055	2,174	2,070	1,975	1,794	1,654
change since FY 90 (%)				-5	-13	-20
SELECTED RESERVE						
Army	580	766	736	776	621	551
change since FY 90 (%)				5	-16	-25
Navy	97	148	149	153	127	118
change since FY 90 (%)				3	-15	-21
Marine Corps	36	42	45	44	39	35
change since FY 90 (%)				-2	-13	-22
Air Force	156	195	198	203	202	202
change since FY 90 (%)				3	2	2
TOTAL SELECTED RESERVE	869	1,151	1,128	1,176	989	906
change since FY 90 (%)				4	-12	-20

*Department of Defense projections

Would this 1995 force structure have been capable of handling the Gulf situation? Is Kissinger correct that we were lucky that Saddam Hussein confronted the Cold War military force structure, as opposed to the 1995 force structure? The United States deployed some 540,000 people to the Gulf. As indicated in Table 5, this force was composed of ten ground divisions (eight army and two marine divisions), ten tactical air wings, and six carrier battle groups. While substantial, this deployment represented about 17 percent of the 3.2 million people in today's Total Force of active duty and selected reserve personnel. It would

Table 4 Force Structure FY 1990–95

Force	FY 1990 Active	FY 1990 Reserve	FY 1995 Active	FY 1995 Reserve	Reductions FY 1990–95 Active	Reductions FY 1990–95 Reserve
Army Divisions	18	10	12	6	-6	-4
Marine Divisions	3	1	3	1	—	—
Aircraft Carriers	13	—	12	—	-1	—
Carrier Wings	13	2	11	2	-2	—
Battle Force Ships	545	—	451	—	-94	—
Tactical Fighter Wings	24	12	15	11	-9	-1

have represented only 21 percent of the 1995 Total Force. Similarly, even after the planned reductions, the U.S. armed force will still have twenty-two ground divisions, twenty-six tactical air wings, and twelve carrier battle groups, substantially more than the force deployed to the Gulf, even if one makes the assumption that all the forces deployed to the Gulf were necessary to attain the military objective.

As was planned before the Gulf War, the reduced forces will be grouped into three conventional packages: Atlantic, Pacific, and Contingency. In addition, there will be a Strategic Force package. These proposed packages are outlined in Table 6. The Atlantic Force will be composed of forces based in Europe and the Middle East, backed up by continental United States (CONUS)-based forces whose primary missions are in those theaters. As indicated in Table 6, the Atlantic package would consist of six

Table 5 Forces Deployed to the Gulf as a Portion of the Total Force

Force	1990	1995	Number Deployed to the Gulf	Percentage of Force 1990	Percentage of Force 1995
Army Divisions	28	18	8	29	44
Marine Divisions	4	4	2	50	50
Aircraft Carriers	13	12	6	46	50
Battle Force Ships	545	451	100	18	22
Fighter Wings	36	26	10	28	38

Table 6 Proposed U.S. Force Packages

	Army	*Navy*	*Marine Corps*	*Air Force*
ATLANTIC FORCES				
Europe	2 divisions	1 CVBG	MARG in Med. MPS	3 wings
CONUS	4 active 6 reserve (+2 cadre) divisions	5 CVBGs and support ships	2 MEBs (plus 1 RC)	2 active 11 reserve wings
PACIFIC FORCES				
Korea	1 division			1–2 wings
Japan		1 CVBG	1 MAGTF (TBD)	1–2 wings
Hawaii/ Alaska	1 division (light)		1 MEB	1 wing
CONUS		5 CVBGs and support ships	1 MEB	
CONTINGENCY FORCES				
	4 divisions	Forces from Atlantic and Pacific 8 SL-7s and rest of RRF		7 wings inter-theater airlift

Plus special operations forces of all services

STRATEGIC NUCLEAR FORCES

SSBNs	18 Trident submarines
ICBMs	500 Minuteman III missiles and 50 MX
Bombers	B-52H + B-1 + 75 B-2s

CVBG = Carrier Battle Group
MAGTF = Marine Air-Ground Task Force
MARG = Mediterranean Amphibious Ready Group (Marine Expeditionary Unit)
MEB = Marine Expeditionary Brigade
MEF = Marine Expeditionary Force
MPS = Maritime Prepositioning Ships
RC = Reserve Component
RRF = Ready Reserve Fleet
TBD = To Be Determined

Source: Testimony of Admiral David E. Jeremiah, vice-chairman of the Joint Chiefs of Staff, before the House Armed Services Committee, March 12, 1991.

of the army's twelve active divisions, six of the navy's twelve carrier battle groups, five of the air force's fifteen tactical air wings, and one-third of the Marine Corps' active force. This large portion of the 1995 active force would be augmented by all of the army and air force's reserve combat forces (six divisions and eleven wings). The Pacific Force would be primarily a maritime force. It would consist of the remaining six carrier battle groups and the other two-thirds of the marines, plus two army divisions and three air force wings. The remainder of the active forces (four divisions and seven wings) would be assigned to a U.S.-based Contingency Force. These army and air force units would be supplemented by naval forces from both the Atlantic and Pacific. By 1995 the strategic package will consist of 18 Trident submarines with 432 missiles, 550 land-based intercontinental ballistic missiles (ICBMs), and some 300 B-52H, B-1, and B-2 bombers.

While the overall force structure level does not appear to be affected by the war in the Gulf, three specific aspects of it appear to be: The heavy-light ground force mix, the active-reserve mix, and the readiness level of the active force. Before the Gulf War, many army leaders and defense experts argued that the army should shift the bulk of its heavy divisions, which were structured primarily to fight the Soviets, to the reserves as a hedge against a resurgent Soviet threat, while the active army should be oriented toward light forces, which would be moved quickly into places like Grenada and Panama.[14] However, the new administration plan actually increases the percentage of heavy divisions in the active force. In 1990, ten of the army's eighteen active divisions, or 55 percent, were classified as heavy. Eight of the twelve divisions, or 66 percent of the army's 1995 active force, will be heavy.

Before the war there was also considerable sentiment for moving the active reserve mix of army combat divisions from two-thirds active/one-third reserve, to one-half active, one-half reserve. However, the performance of the three round-out brigades that were called to active duty during the Gulf crisis was so poor that the 1995 army will attempt to preserve the two-thirds/one-third army active/reserve combat mix.[15] Conversely, the Air National Guard units performed so well that the number of guard wings will be reduced by only one, while nine active tactical air force wings will be cut over the next five years.

Finally, before the Gulf War there were suggestions that the end of the Cold War meant that the readiness levels of many of the active forces could also be reduced significantly. In April of 1990, Senator Nunn argued that the DoD could introduce a concept of flexible readiness that would keep only those forces that might have to fight on short notice at high levels of readiness, e.g., strategic, forward-deployed, special operations.[16] However, the FY 1992–1997 defense program keeps all of its active forces at current or Cold War levels of readiness by funding the same levels of flying hours, steaming days, and vehicle miles. (The operations and maintenance account for FY 1992 is slightly higher than FY 1991 in nominal terms.)

Congress has accepted the Budget Summit Agreement, as modified by the Gulf experience, with regard to spending levels and force structure issues, except in the area of the active reserve mix. Congress appears set to authorize the entire $291 billion requested for FY 1992, and to approve the active duty force levels proposed by the Pentagon. However, the House has refused to reduce selected reserve end strength for FY 1992 by 9 percent, as the administration requested. Instead, it approved a cut of only 3 percent, opting to keep another 69,000 reservists on active duty. The House has thus placed in jeopardy the Pentagon's plan to reduce reserve personnel by 20 percent by 1995 at a cost of $12 billion over the next five years.[17]

The war in the Gulf has also revived the debate about the value of continuing to purchase costly high technology systems, originally designed to counter primarily the Soviets, in the post-Cold War period. Prior to U.S. involvement in the Gulf, many questioned the need for proceeding with the next generation of advanced weapons systems. Programs that appeared to be on the "bubble" because of the end of the Cold War were the B-2 strategic bomber, the Advanced Tactical Fighter (ATF), the Advanced Tactical Aircraft (ATA), the Advanced Medium Air-to-Air Missile (AMRAAM), the Tacit Rainbow antiradar cruise missile, the Strategic Defense Initiative (SDI), the C-17 airlift aircraft, the Joint Surveillance and Targeting Radar System

(JSTARS), the Army Tactical Missile System (ATACMS), and the *Milstar* Satellite System. Indeed, all of these systems had been recommended for reductions or cutbacks at one time or another by the Armed Services or Defense Appropriations Subcommittees. For example, in the spring of 1990, the Senate proposed canceling *Milstar;* the House proposed canceling JSTARS and B-2. Moreover, on the eve of the war, the Pentagon itself cancelled the ATA and the Tacit Rainbow antiradar cruise missile because of cost and performance problems.

However, the spectacular performance of U.S. advanced weaponry in the Gulf seemed to tilt the debate in favor of moving ahead with the next generation of advanced technology. Superior U.S. technology not only enabled the coalition to win the war rapidly, but also with a remarkably low number of casualties. Fewer Americans were killed in liberating Kuwait than in trying to maintain order in Lebanon in 1983. The air force and navy lost fewer planes to combat in the Gulf than they do in normal peacetime training operations. The Iraqis shot down only eleven navy and Marine Corps attack planes, while they succeeded in destroying seven air force combat planes.

Proponents of advanced technology, such as William Perry, former undersecretary of defense for research and engineering, argued that U.S. advanced technology gave the U.S.-led coalition unprecedented command, control, and communications over its forces, and almost unlimited intelligence about the enemy forces. In addition, it allowed coalition forces to suppress enemy defenses so thoroughly that the Iraqis were essentially blind and defenseless while the allies knew what was happening throughout the theater. Finally, U.S. superior technology allowed the United States to attack Iraqi forces and facilities with such precision that their will was broken.[18]

Almost from the onset of the war, proponents of high technology attempted to capitalize on the success of certain systems employed in the Gulf to bolster the case for the new generation of systems currently on the bubble. Proponents of the B-2 pointed to the success of the F-117A Stealth Fighter as the reason for going ahead with the final 60 B-2s. Supporters of the B-2, such as Air Force Secretary Donald Rice, noted that the F-117As flew 2 percent of the combat sorties in the Gulf, but hit over 40 percent of the strategic targets without a single loss. While the B-2 costs five times as much as the F-117A, it has over five times the range and ten times the punch. Moreover, had the B-2 been available in the Gulf, two B-2s could have done the work of seventy-five planes, that is, thirty-two fighter bombers, twenty-eight escort and electronic warfare planes, and fifteen tankers, at one-fifth the cost.[19]

Similarly, supporters of SDI pointed to the fact that the Patriot Anti-tactical Ballistic Missile System intercepted forty-one out of the first forty-two Scuds fired against Saudi Arabia and Israel, as proof that defense against ballistic missiles is possible and that this nation should therefore revive Ronald Reagan's dream of undertaking a crash program to provide this nation with a defense against ballistic missiles.

For some endangered high-tech weapons, no transference was necessary. Even though JSTARS was still in its developmental stage and not due to be fully operational until the mid-1990s, the Pentagon hastily sent the two existing developmental models to the Gulf. Despite concerns about its premature deployment among senior air force officials, the modified Boeing 707s performed spectacularly.[20] The JSTARS E-8A aircraft, flying trouble-free, alternate nighttime twelve-hour shifts, detected troop movements, monitored battles, and obtained clear imagery of sites located behind Iraq's front lines, including Scud sites. Similarly, even though ATACMS was not yet in full-scale production when Saddam Hussein invaded Kuwait, its production was accelerated, and it was whisked to the Gulf in time to counter Iraqi artillery fire in mid-January.

Will the success of the high-tech weapons in the Gulf save these advanced technology weapons from the budget ax? The Bush administration hopes so. In its FY 1992 defense budget, it requested that Congress appropriate $4.8 billion for the next four B-2s and increase production so that by FY 1995, the bomber reaches its peak production rate of twelve a year at a cost of $5.7 billion.[21] The Bush administration also seeks to increase SDI funding from $2.9 billion in FY 1991 to $4.6 billion in FY 1992 and $4.9 billion in FY 1993. While the president also has added a Tactical Missile Defense Initiative (TMDI) to SDI, which will add an additional $0.6 billion to SDI in FY 1992 and $0.7 billion in FY 1993, the focus is still on readying phase one of SDI for deployment. This will consist of roughly 1,000 space-based "brilliant pebbles" interceptors, a like number of ground-based interceptors, and space and ground sensors.

Finally, the Gulf War also renewed the debate about the lack of mobility of U.S. forces. Although the United States has unrivaled military power, it took more than six months for this country to deploy to the Gulf the necessary men, women, and matériel sufficient to liberate Kuwait. One of the reasons that the ground war could not begin until late February 1991 was that all of the ground forces thought to be necessary were not in place until then.

All told, the Pentagon moved 3.9 million tons of cargo and 540,000 people to the Gulf between August 1990 and February 1991. While most of the equipment came from the United States, some was shipped from Europe or moved from ships prepositioned near Diego Garcia. About 90 percent of the people and 13 percent of the cargo was moved by air. This required about 15,000 airlift missions to the Persian Gulf, and another 7,000 within the theater. Ninety percent of the C-5 and C-141 cargo aircraft and the first and second stages of the Civil Reserve Air Fleet (CRAF) had to be used.

Sealift carried only 10 percent of the people, but 87 percent of the matériel. Although the Military Sealift Command operated an average of 210 cargo ships a day during the crisis, only eight fast sealift ships (SC-7) were employed; only 20 percent of the equipment delivered to the Gulf was shipped on U.S. commercial vessels; and only 14 of the first 41 ships in the ready reserve fleet reached their loading ports on schedule. Not only did the United States have sufficient time to deploy its men, women, and matériel, its principal ally, Saudi Arabia, had a well-developed logistic infrastructure, that is, many big, state-of-the-art airfields and ports.[22]

The need for increasing airlift capacity was recognized over a decade ago, and the Gulf crisis should give new life to the C-17, which has been troubled by cost overruns, performance retrogrades, and production delays since its inception. The administration hopes to purchase 18 of these planes in FY 1992 and FY 1993 at a cost of $7 billion, and eventually buy 120 at a cost of $35.2 billion, or almost $300 million per aircraft.

The Gulf situation demonstrated the value of maritime prepositioning. Because the marines placed $1.4 billion worth of equipment on thirteen ships that cost $2 million a month to operate, the Marine Corps was able to move enough equipment to the Gulf for one expeditionary force very rapidly. Before the end of August, the marines had moved enough supplies to Saudi Arabia to support 32,000 marines for 30 days. As a result of the Gulf War, the DoD is now considering prepositioning enough equipment in the Middle East to support a heavy army division.[23] The navy supports this idea, but the marines are opposed to it. Rather than having two Marine Corps, marine generals would prefer that the navy buy more fast sealift ships.[24]

Congress would also like to see the navy buy more fast sealift. Indeed, it has appropriated $1.3 billion for fast sealift over the past two years. Not only has the navy not yet obligated the money, the DoD was trying to reprogram the funds during the deployment to the Gulf. However, as a result of the Gulf War, the DoD plans to begin a fast sealift program but because it has not yet defined mission requirements, it will not seek funds for the program until FY 1993.

CONCLUSION

Were it not for the Gulf War, defense spending for the FY 1991–95 period would undoubtedly be somewhat lower. Congress would not have accepted the relatively benign reductions proposed by Senator Nunn for FY 1991, nor would it have protected defense from the potential raids of the domestic and international sectors in FY 1992 and FY 1993. However, beginning in FY 1994, when the DoD can again become a source of funds for domestic programs, defense spending will probably give back some of the gains it received from the Budget Summit Agreement.

The Gulf War has also marginally increased the priority given to active duty forces, heavy forces, and the overall readiness of the forces. It has also increased somewhat the chances of obtaining funding for the next generation of high-tech weapons and the share of the defense budget given to mobility forces. However, it has not changed the baseline force structure and force packages that will provide the framework for the reduced levels of defense spending.

It is not even clear how long-lasting these impacts will be. The reserve lobby is resisting vigorously the reductions in reserve forces and may use its clout with Congress to diminish the priority given to active forces. Moreover, the House Armed Services Committee has cut more than 50 percent from the administration's FY 1992 request for B-2 and SDI and transferred the money to such low-tech programs as V-22 and F-14D. Finally, the marines are opposed to army maritime prepositioning while the navy is fighting funding for fast sealift.

What is clear is that the Gulf War has not altered in any fundamental way the fact that the Cold War has ended, that, as a result, the United States will reduce its military forces and level of defense spending substantially over the next decade, and that even this smaller force is more than capable of handling a Persian Gulf-type war. Indeed, while the United States focused its attention on the Gulf, the Conventional Forces in Europe Treaty was concluded; the Warsaw Pact was dissolved; the Soviets announced further decreases in the level of defense spending; and the staunchest military ally of the United States in the Gulf, Great Britain, slashed its own defense budget even more deeply than it had projected before the Gulf War. Moreover, after the failed mid-August coup in the Soviet Union, attempts were renewed to reduce the FY 1992 and FY 1993 defense budgets or to transfer funds from the defense budget to the Soviet Union for emergency relief. Furthermore, in late September 1991, President Bush responded to the events in the Soviet Union by unilaterally terminating land- and sea-based tactical nuclear weapons and land-based mobile missiles. Finally, given the parochial tendencies of Congress and the services, and the continuing pressures of the federal deficit, the Gulf War may be seen as no more than a slight perturbation in the flow of events.

ENDNOTES

1. Helen Dewar, "GOP Senators Propose Doubling Bush's Defense Cuts," *Washington Post*, April 6, 1990, p. 4.
2. "Defense Floor Speeches by U.S. Senator Sam Nunn," March 22, March 29, April 19, and April 20, 1990, in *Congressional Record* (Washington, DC: U.S. Government Printing Office [U.S. GPO], 1990).
3. "Cheney Finds CIA Director is No Comrade in Arms," *Washington Post*, March 6, 1990, p. A21.
4. R. Jeffrey Smith, "Schlesinger Urges Radical Cuts in Europe," *Washington Post*, January 31, 1990, p. A12, and *Defense Daily*, January 25, 1990, pp. 124–125.
5. R. Jeffrey Smith, "Powell Says Defense Needs Massive Review," *Washington Post*, May 7, 1990, p. 1.
6. Patrick Sloyan, "Pentagon Chief on Defensive," *Long Island Newsday*, April 1, 1990, p. 13.
7. All budget figures are from the *Budget of the United States Government* (Washington, DC: U.S. GPO) for the appropriate year.
8. Michael R. Gordon, "Cheney Gives Plan to Reduce Forces by 25 Percent in 5 Years," *New York Times*, June 20, 1990, p. 1.
9. Rick Maze, "Cheney's Cut Scenarios Taken as Fact By Lawmakers," *Air Force Times*, July 9, 1990, p. 3.
10. William J. Eaton, "$270 Billion 5-Year Defense Cut Urged," *Los Angeles Times*, June 29, 1990, p. 35.
11. "Bush Seeks to Buy 900 More Missiles," *Philadelphia Inquirer*, February 26, 1991, p. 9.
12. Kissinger warned in an op-ed piece in the *Washington Post*, on February 26, 1991, "Had Kuwait been invaded two years later, the American defense budget would have declined so as to preclude a massive overseas deployment."
13. Barton Gillman, "Cheney, Powell Support Cutbacks With Caution," *Washington Post*, February 22, 1991, p. 4.
14. Tom Donnelly, "Army, Marines Butt Heads Over Contingency Role," *Army Times*, March 26, 1990, p. 3, and Jeffrey Record, "The Army Goes to War With the Marines, *Baltimore Sun*, February 16, 1990, p. 15.
15. "Sullivan Hints Army Reservists Aren't Prepared to Handle High-tech Army," *Inside the Army*, June 24, 1991, p. 1.
16. Nunn, "Defense Floor Speeches."
17. Eric Schmitt, "House Votes Military Budget, Cutting Arms Programs," *New York Times*, May 23, 1991, p. 20.
18. Les Aspin, "Understanding Technology on the Battlefield," speech before the American Institute of Aeronautics and Astronautics, May 1, 1991, summarizes William Perry's testimony before the House Armed Services Committee on this subject. See also William J. Perry, "Desert Storm and Deterrence," *Foreign Affairs*, Vol. 70, No. 4 (Fall 1991), pp. 66–82.
19. Donald Rice, "Deterrence Argued as Chief Mission for Bomber in 21st Century," *Knoxville News Sentinel*, June 2, 1991, p. F-1.

20. John Boatman and Barbara Stars, "Eyes of the Storm," *Jane's Defence Weekly*, May 4, 1991, p. 735.
21. The analysis of the Bush administration's proposed defense budget is drawn from *Responding to Changing Threats*, a report of the Defense Budget Project's Task Force on the FY 1992–FY 1997 Defense Plan (Washington, DC: The Defense Budget project, June 1991).
22. David Morrison, "Logistics War's Long Long Lines," *National Journal*, March 2, 1991, pp. 514–515, and Carol Matlock, "Barely Afloat," *National Journal*, April 27, 1991, pp. 988–992, summarize the logistic aspects of the Gulf War.
23. Department of Defense (DoD), Joint Military Net Assessment (Washington, DC: DoD, 1991), Section II, p. 29.
24. Rick Atkinson, "Gulf Crisis Poses Dilemma for U.S. Military Facing Cutbacks," *Washington Post*, December 23, 1990, p. 1.

10

DESERT STORM AND DETERRENCE IN THE FUTURE

William J. Perry

INTRODUCTION

In Desert Storm, the United States employed for the first time a new class of military systems that gave its forces a revolutionary advance in military capability. Key to this new military capability is a new generation of military support systems—intelligence sensors, defense suppression systems, and precision guidance subsystems—that serve as force multipliers—that is, they multiply the effectiveness of U.S. weapon systems. An army that has this capability has an overwhelming advantage over an army that does not, much as an army equipped with tanks would overwhelm an army with horse cavalry.

This new conventional military capability adds a new and powerful dimension to the ability of the United States to deter war. While it is certainly not as powerful as nuclear weapons, it is more credible as a deterrent in some applications, particularly in regional conflicts that are vital to U.S. national interests. In particular, it has the potential to play a very significant role in deterring those regional conflicts that would involve the confrontation of armored forces (as opposed to guerrilla wars). With the increasing proliferation of modern weapons in politically unstable parts of the world, those types of conflicts otherwise might be expected to occur with increasing frequency. It also can serve as a credible deterrent to a regional power's use of chemical weapons. Finally, it should strengthen the already high level of deterrence of a major war in Europe or Korea. In particular, the United States can now have high confidence that the defeat of a conventional armored assault in those regions could be achieved by conventional military forces so that the role of U.S. nuclear forces could be limited to the deterrence of nuclear attacks.

THE U.S. ADVANTAGE

That the United States really has achieved a revolutionary advance in military capability is suggested by the results of the war. One overall measure of performance is the relative losses: tanks lost, prisoners taken, and casualties. These relative losses were so lopsided—almost a thousand to one—that there is almost no historical precedent. It is tempting to conclude, as some have done, that this lopsided result was attributable simply to the incompetence of the Iraqi military. Indeed, Alexander Bessmertnykh, appearing before the Supreme Soviet to discuss the performance of Soviet-supplied air defenses in Iraq, said that the failure was " . . . not a reflection of a weakness of combat equipment. Ultimately, equipment is good when it is in good hands." This explanation ignores two important realities: the size and capability of the Iraqi armed forces and the devastating assault to which they were subjected during the air war.

Prior to the war, Iraq had perhaps the fourth largest army in the world and was one of the most formidable regional military powers. It had over a million men in its army, almost one-half of whom were in the Kuwaiti theater. Most Iraqi officers had gained recent combat experience in the Iran-Iraq War. Iraqi forces were armed with large quantities of Soviet matériel, much of it modern, as well as some Western equipment, including Mirage aircraft and Exocet missiles. They had a very dense, internetted air defense system, a large number of mobile missiles, 4,000 tanks, 3,000 modern long-range artillery pieces, and a demonstrated capability to deliver chemical weapons both by air and artillery. And the Iraqis had a unitary force operating within a few hundred miles of its supply base while the United States led a disparate coalition some 6,000 miles from its primary supply base. So why were the coalition forces, under U.S. leadership, able to defeat the Iraqis so quickly, so decisively, and with so few losses?

Many significant factors favored the coalition forces, some of which were peculiar to Desert Storm and cannot be counted on in any future conflict. Two of the foremost factors were the quality and quantity of Saudi air bases and the ready supply of fuel in the theater. And, of course, Saddam Hussein made a political misjudgment about his ability to ride out the international outrage over his invasion of Kuwait; this misjudgment gave the coalition forces more than five months to get to the theater and get organized. The combination of buildup time and bases available largely offset what otherwise would have been a significant geographical advantage for the Iraqis.

Other factors favoring the coalition will be applicable to a wide variety of military contingencies—the foremost factor being a great advantage in leadership. The leadership of the coalition was superb, and the diverse military forces operated with an unprecedented unity, which was greatly facilitated by the command authority given General Colin Powell and General H. Norman Schwarzkopf by the Goldwater-Nichols Defense Reorganization Act. The Iraqi leadership, on the other hand, made serious strategic blunders (most notably, allowing the five-month buildup). Even at a distance of 6,000 miles, U.S. air logistics support was outstanding, and, after a slow start, the 13,000-mile sealift also became effective. In contrast, the Iraqi supply lines were essentially cut off early in the air war by the coalition's successful interdiction campaign.

Of course, no military operation can be successful with poorly trained troops, and the U.S. military demonstrated that its forces were superbly trained. With an average service time of seven years and training time of two years, this all-volunteer force was notably better trained and motivated than the draftee force that the United States had fielded in the Vietnam War. More generally, the coalition forces had a very significant advantage in training and motivation over the Iraqi forces, whose combat experience with Iran prepared them for a war very different from the one waged by the coalition and whose initial doubts about the wisdom and justice of their cause were greatly amplified by the pounding they took during the air war.

All of these advantages combined do not account for a thousand-to-one discrepancy in performance. A significant part of that edge can be attributed to the revolutionary new military technology used for the first time by U.S forces in the Gulf War.

U.S. MILITARY TECHNOLOGY

What was this technology, why was it so effective, to what extent can it be generalized to other situations, and to what extent can it be effective as a deterrent to war? This new military technology, built and deployed during the 1980s, was largely conceived and developed during the 1970s. It was developed as part of what Secretary of Defense Harold Brown called the "offset strategy" in response to the then-perceived threat of an armored assault by the Warsaw Pact forces in Central Europe. A key part of the strategy was to use the technology advantage of the United States to offset the quantitative advantage of Soviet forces. At that time NATO estimated that if it had to face a surprise armored assault from the Warsaw Pact, it could be outnumbered three to one in personnel and armored equipment and so NATO and, in particular, the United States, sought to use technology as an equalizer, or "force multiplier."

Much of the debate this past decade surrounding the offset strategy has been based on the incorrect assumption that its primary objective was to use "high technology" to build better weapon systems than those of the Soviet Union. Higher quality tanks or guns or aircraft, by themselves, could not likely offset a three-to-one disadvantage, particularly considering the high quality of the counterpart Soviet weapons. The offset strategy was based instead on the premise that it was necessary to give these weapons a significant competitive advantage over their opposing counterparts by supporting them on the battlefield with newly developed equipment that multiplied their combat effectiveness. This strategy was pursued consistently by five administrations during the 1970s and 1980s, all the while being carefully observed by the Soviet Union. In 1983, Marshall Nikolai Ogarkov, then chief of general staff of the Soviet Union, said that the Americans were developing a "reconnaissance strike complex," and tried, with limited success, to move the Soviet military in that direction.

Most of the new military support systems in the offset strategy are designed around modern electronics and computers. Three components of this new support capability were most critical to the remarkable success of coalition forces in the Gulf War: command, control, communications, and intelligence (C^3I), defense suppression, and precision guidance.

C^3I gives any field commander what the military calls "situation awareness." In Desert Storm, coalition battlefield commanders gained a remarkable awareness of the situation on the battlefield: to an unprecedented degree, they knew where relevant opposing forces were located (to target or avoid these forces); they knew where supporting friendly forces were located (to synchronize combat actions with these forces); and they knew their own location precisely. This awareness was achieved by employing a diverse set of intelligence sensors, navigation systems, and communication systems.

For the first time in a war, the United States made effective use of all of its satellite systems to support field commanders. Most of these systems were designed to support national objectives, not military operations. During Desert Shield, this diverse set of systems was used to generate data for maps, locate military units, identify equipment, and pinpoint the location of the air defense and command and control installations of the Iraqi forces—data crucial to the planning that preceded the beginning of the air war. During Desert Storm, all of these systems plus weather satellites were dedicated to the support of coalition forces, and communication systems and procedures were put in place to transmit their outputs to military commanders in the theater.

Satellite systems, for all of their capabilities, are constrained by the laws of orbital mechanics to orbit the earth periodically while the earth rotates underneath them. As a consequence, low-altitude satellites cannot "hover" over a region of interest to get continuity of coverage of that area. Rather, each satellite collects "snapshots" several times a day according to the periodicity of its orbit and subject to weather conditions. Also, in Desert Storm, the data from satellites were subject to communication delays in getting to military commanders. All of these factors adversely affected the timeliness of data necessary for the planning of military operations or targeting.

Therefore it was necessary to supplement the satellites with airborne reconnaissance systems capable of maintaining station and "staring" at a given region for many hours. In Desert Storm, U.S. forces used a wide variety of tactical reconnaissance aircraft, both manned and unmanned and including the aerial reconnaissance cameras used in previous wars. The older systems entailed reporting delays because of the time required to return and process the collected data (film, for example). However a new generation of tactical reconnaissance systems was also used with great effectiveness. Two systems, both manned airborne radars, illustrate the new capability: AWACS (Airborne Warning and Control System) and JSTARS (Joint Surveillance and Targeting Radar System). Each of these systems is a converted Boeing 707 transport aircraft carrying a very large radar, advanced computers, and communication equipment to relay the data to the ground. Because the target acquisition sensors on these systems are radars, they can operate day and night and in nearly all weather. Because of the on-board computers and communication equipment, the output of the systems can be provided as it is collected to intelligence command centers and to relevant military commanders, who thus learn where their targets of interest are at that time, not where they were a day earlier—a typical reporting delay with aerial reconnaissance cameras, which were also a source of targeting data in Desert Storm.

One AWACS aircraft can instantaneously survey the air space over an area larger than Kuwait and detect and locate every aircraft flying in that area (except for stealthy aircraft). The availability of this air order of battle data gave coalition aircraft a significant advantage over Iraqi fighters in the air-to-air combat that occurred during the first week of the war, and thereby contributed, along with the superb training of coalition pilots, to the lopsided results and brief duration of that phase of the war.

After the Iraqi Air Force gave up combat operations, AWACS served exclusively as an airborne air traffic controller, effectively controlling 2,000 to 3,000 sorties a day, remarkably with no midair collisions. It is noteworthy that Iraq had an AWACS-type aircraft but because of the coalition's air supremacy was not able to use it, which makes the point that AWACS both contributes to, and is facilitated by, air superiority.

JSTARS performs a similar function in the detection and location of ground vehicles, both moving and stationary. JSTARS was still in developmental test and evaluation when Desert Shield began. Because of the obvious importance to the impending military operations of real-time targeting data on ground vehicles, two JSTARS aircraft were pulled out of their test program for emergency deployment to the Kuwaiti theater. During Desert Storm, JSTARS was used in three different missions. It detected and located the vehicles trying to resupply the in-theater Iraqi forces and passed these target data to strike aircraft with devastating effect. As a result, the Iraqi forces in Kuwait essentially became cut off from their supply base. JSTARS was also used to target Iraqi tanks when they came out of their bunkers. This role was performed first during the battle of Khafji when JSTARS targeted all of the tanks in the Iraqi force for successful attack by coalition aircraft as well as providing assurance to ground force commanders that the Iraqis were not reinforcing their initial probe. Later, during the five-day ground war, targeting data from JSTARS contributed significantly to the destruction of the Iraqi tank forces with almost no loss of coalition tanks.

On a few evenings, the JSTARS aircraft was diverted from coverage of Kuwait to coverage of the Scud launching areas in western Iraq. This mission had some limited success in detecting and targeting Scud launchers. However, only one JSTARS aircraft was available on any given evening, and it was generally positioned so that it could target the Iraqi vehicles carrying supplies to their forces in Kuwait. If a larger JSTARS force had been available, it is likely that some portion of this force would have been dedicated to searching for Scuds as they were transported to their launch areas. Had that happened, it is possible that JSTARS could have developed a reasonably reliable signature of Scud activities, so that it, together with a small force of strike aircraft, could have become an antiballistic missile system, attacking the missiles on the ground before they were launched.

Besides the radar systems, many U.S. reconnaissance systems and combat vehicles were equipped with night vision devices (infrared detectors that form images by measuring small differences in temperature in the scene). Iraqi night vision devices were neither as numerous nor as effective. As a result, coalition military forces "owned the night" and made very effective use of that advantage. Infrared detectors, for example, were used to determine which bunkers had tanks inside (surveillance was conducted at dusk when the desert sand had cooled down but the metal in the tank still held its heat); this contributed to the large-scale destruction of the Iraqi tank force that took place before the ground war started. After the ground war started, the night vision devices in U.S. tanks, infantry fighting vehicles, and helicopters were used to direct fire against Iraqi tanks often before the Iraqis even knew coalition forces were present.

Coalition forces also made very effective use of navigation data from the global positioning satellites (GPS). Many U.S. aircraft, ground vehicles, and infantry units were equipped with GPS receivers, which gave them their precise location on the battlefield, as well as the precise time (for synchronization purposes). The GPS System was important to coalition ground forces because it enabled them to locate their units accurately on the map, which otherwise would have been difficult in the desert because of the absence of natural identifying features. GPS was important to coalition air forces because it allowed them to update the accuracy of their inertial guidance systems, and to improve the delivery accuracy of unguided ("dumb") bombs against fixed-coordinate targets. The GPS System provides location accuracies of about ten meters, which is more than a tenfold improvement over previous generation navigation systems.

Some of the intelligence data collected was processed at sites in the United States. Therefore it was necessary to make extensive use of satellite communications systems for communicating large volumes of data, including high resolution pictures, from the United States to the theater daily. Most of this traffic was carried by the Defense Satellite Communication System, which was operating at capacity and, because of the heavy load (on the order of 100 million bits per second!), still had to be supplemented with commercial satellites and couriers.

A new generation of digital radios was used for the first time to supplement the standard military radios in communicating within the theater. The purpose of the in-theater command and control system was to permit transmission to the field commanders of commands and relevant intelligence data as it was collected. For example, as JSTARS operators detected armored vehicles, they would transmit the coordinates of these vehicles to the army command post on the ground, which used it to assign targets to artillery, rockets, and attack helicopters. JSTARS also received data from AWACS on the locations of aircraft in the theater. Thus an air force fire control officer on board the JSTARS aircraft was able to select a high-value ground target detected by JSTARS and transmit its coordinates directly to the strike aircraft that AWACS data indicated was closest to that target.

This combination of intelligence sensors, precision navigation data, and communications gave the coalition field commanders an ability to understand what was going on in the field to a degree that had never been achieved in any previous military operation.

During the first few weeks of the air war, coalition air strikes crippled the Iraqi C^3I system. This was achieved by making the collection of detailed data on this system a top collection priority before the beginning of the air war and by attacking its elements with precision guided weapons during the air war. A large part of the "multiplier" effect achieved during Desert Storm came from the remarkably effective situation awareness of coalition forces, for which Iraqi forces had neither an effective counterpart nor an effective countermeasure.

DEFENSE SUPPRESSION

Defense suppression was another major component of the offset strategy. Defense suppression is the name that the military gives to the complex of systems whose function is to destroy or render ineffective the opposing air defense system before it can function. When General Colin Powell testified to the House Armed Services Committee in December, just before the war started, he gave them a prospective view of what a war with the Iraqis could involve. He noted that the Iraqi air defense was dense, equipped with a large number of Soviet-built missiles, thousands of antiaircraft artillery guns, and internetted with a hardened and redundant communication system. U.S. air operations against Vietnam, and Israeli air operations against Egypt and Syria experienced attrition rates in the range of one-third percent to 2 percent against less capable air defense systems. An attrition rate of 1 percent (one loss per 100 sorties) is less than the average rate in previous wars, but in the very intensive air operations conducted in the Gulf War, (about 100,000 sorties in six weeks), such an attrition rate would have led to unacceptable losses: 1,000 coalition aircraft destroyed and more than 1,000 crew members killed or captured. If losses had in fact occurred at that rate, coalition air forces probably would not have conducted 100,000 sorties and the whole war would have changed its nature.

Coalition air forces did not suffer historical attrition rates because the United States had developed novel and very effective defense suppression systems. Because of the use of these new systems during Desert Storm and because of the early achievement of air supremacy, coalition forces incurred losses of about one in 3,000 sorties instead of one in 100. Even if this calculation is revised to exclude support aircraft, the loss rate is still less than one in 1,000 combat sorties.

Defense suppression systems used in Desert Storm were of two different generic types: precursor systems and escort systems. The role of precursor systems can best be illustrated by describing their performance on the first night of the war. The Stealth attack bomber (F-117A) and the Tomahawk (a ship-launched cruise missile) were sent in first to destroy the radars and the command and control network of the Iraqi air defense. Stealth fighters were chosen for this mission because their low radar cross sections make it very difficult for radar fire control systems to engage them. Tomahawks are also difficult to engage because of medium-to-low radar cross sections plus a very low altitude of flight. Special operations forces (including Army Apache helicopters) also played a role in the precursor attack that first night, clearing a swath in the Iraqi air defense network fence.

After these attacks disabled the Iraqi air defense, the main strike was initiated by standard (non-stealth) attack bombers. The attack bombers were accompanied by escort aircraft, equipped with radiation-seeking missiles (which attack radars by homing on their transmissions) and electronic countermeasures (ECM) systems (which degrade radars by transmitting signals that mask the legitimate target return), to suppress any radars that were still operating. In the first few days of Desert Storm, U.S. forces fired hundreds of radiation-seeking missiles; as a consequence, the operators of those air defense radars that were still functional became increasingly reluctant to turn them on. Without tracking data from their radars, the Iraqi gunners could be compared to a duck hunter on a dark, moonless night armed with a rifle instead of a shotgun and shooting at ducks flying at 400 miles an hour.

Under these circumstances, the Iraqi air defense operators reverted to World War II tactics: during night operations over their cities, they put up barrages of antiaircraft gun fire (flak); during daytime operations over their army units, they used optical controls to direct shoulder-fired missiles and guns (including the Soviet-built ZSU-23 gun, which has an optical sight that is very effective in clear weather).

In order to minimize losses against these tactics, coalition air forces generally flew at night and at altitudes above the reach of the antiaircraft guns. This of course required that the coalition's strike aircraft be equipped with night vision devices and armament that could hit targets accurately from high altitude delivery. Most of the coalition strike aircraft are so equipped. The British Tornado aircraft suffered significant losses to antiaircraft fire in the early phases of the war delivering runway cratering munitions from low altitudes. After these initial losses, the British shifted to the high level delivery of laser-guided bombs.

The A-10 aircraft, which is designed to attack hard, defended ground targets, such as tanks, has as its primary armament a

30 mm cannon that is typically fired at low altitudes. Indeed, the A-10 is intended to get "down in the dirt" with the infantry that it is supporting. Unlike other U.S. strike aircraft, it has substantial armor plating to give it some protection from ground fire. Even so, during the course of Desert Storm, seven A-10s were lost, three of them to shoulder-fired missiles. The A-10s used their 30 mm cannon to attack directly ground vehicles at short ranges and low altitudes, but the A-10s in Desert Storm were also equipped with Maverick missiles, which they used to attack heavily defended targets beyond the reach of the targets' antiaircraft guns. With this combination of tactics, armor, and armament, A-10s played a major role in the destruction of Iraqi armored forces and supply vehicles.

The net result was that coalition air forces were able to conduct 2,000 to 3,000 sorties a day with losses that averaged less than one aircraft per day. The outstanding performance of defense suppression was one of the most important factors in the military success of the coalition.

PRECISION-GUIDED WEAPONS

Precision-guided weapons comprised the third component of the offset strategy used to great advantage in Desert Storm. Laser-guided bombs, laser-guided missiles, and infrared guided missiles were dramatically more effective and caused far fewer civilian casualties than the area bombing that characterized previous wars.

The effectiveness of precision weapons can be illustrated by the results of the F-117A (the Stealth attack bomber), since nearly all of the weapons it used were precision guided (in contrast to the F-16, for example, which delivered mostly "dumb" bombs). In Desert Storm, the F-117A typically carried two laser-guided 2,000 pound bombs. Because of their greatly reduced vulnerability to radar-directed fire, F-117As were used in night operations to attack heavily defended targets, such as nuclear, chemical, and biological facilities, command and control nodes, air defense radars, command centers, and military production facilities.

They flew 1,300 sorties and delivered about 2,100 bombs (some bombs were held back because of cloud cover over the target area). Of the 2,100 bombs delivered, the preliminary assessment of the U.S. Air Force is that 1,700 fell within 10 feet of the intended aim point. Considering the destructive force of a 2,000 pound bomb, it is likely that well over 80 percent of these 2,100 bombs destroyed their assigned targets. This is a remarkably high rate of effectiveness, particularly considering that Stealth fighters typically flew at medium altitudes to avoid the antiaircraft barrage fire prevalent around the highly defended targets that they were attacking. During the 1,300 sorties, no F-117As were shot down or even damaged.

It is important to emphasize the interdependence and interaction of intelligence, defense suppression, and precision guidance. No one of these capabilities was sufficient by itself. The effectiveness of the coalition's defense suppression tactics depended on the precision-guided weapons used to disable the Iraqi air defense; the effectiveness of the precision-guided weapons, in turn, depended on the intelligence data that provided the identification and location of targets; and the very survivability of the tactical intelligence systems depended on the effectiveness of the coalition's defense suppression systems. All of these critically depended on—and contributed to—the ability of the coalition to achieve air supremacy early in the air war. All of these were links in the chain of effectiveness, and if any one link had been removed, the overall effectiveness of the chain would have been significantly diminished. Operating together, these systems made a vital contribution to shortening the war, to dramatically reducing coalition casualties, and to reducing Iraqi civilian casualties.

EFFECTIVENESS OF NEW TECHNOLOGY

Although U.S. military leaders made very effective use of these new support systems, it appears that even they underestimated the remarkable increase in military capability that these systems provided. While the effectiveness of the new systems has been demonstrated on proving grounds for the last few years, they had never been used in a war before, and the American military and certainly the public did not fully understand the extent to which they would dominate military operations. There have been, of course, no shortage of defense critics arguing that this new technology would not work in a war.[2] The critics made a number of persuasive arguments.

First, they argued that the new technology was too expensive and therefore would result in too few weapons. Of course, the answer to this argument is that it does not take as many weapons to achieve the desired military effect if each weapon hits the target.

The second argument was that the new technology was so complex that it would be unreliable, particularly in the field. The preliminary reports on reliability of U.S. equipment in Desert Storm refute this argument. The air force has reported that the combat readiness rate of the F-16 was 96 percent, which means that when the military commander tasked an F-16 for a combat mission, 96 percent of them were ready to conduct that mission. In fact, the services have reported readiness rates higher than 90 percent on the F-117A, the F-18, the Tomahawk, the AH-64, the Patriot, the Abrams tank, and the Bradley fighting vehicle. It is appropriate to withhold final judgment on this issue until the final operational statistics are available, but when they are, I expect them to demonstrate that the increasing use of modern electronic subsystems in military systems actually *increases* reliability and maintainability (because microelectronics subsystems are inherently more reliable than the electromechanical subsystems that they replace).

The third argument of the critics was that because of the complexity of the technology in these new weapon systems, they would be too difficult to operate. This was an explicit criticism of the weapon system designers, suggesting that they did not know how to design weapons systems that took human factors adequately into account, and an implicit criticism of U.S. military personnel, implying that they were incapable of operating equipment embodying modern technology. On the contrary, this war has demonstrated that the U.S. military is both capable and well trained and that the designs of the new systems were entirely compatible with that level of training.

Finally, the critics expressed a general concern that the new systems would lose their effectiveness because of the "fog of war," that is, the confusion on the battlefield. In fact, there were many factors, both physical and psychological, that caused confusion in this war. Coalition troops faced desert sand and dust, they contended with unseasonable rainstorms, and they fought combat missions under the cloud of an unprecedented man-made catastrophe—the smoke from hundreds of oil wells set on fire by the Iraqis. Additionally, the Iraqis tried in various ways to confuse, misdirect, and demoralize coalition forces.

Coalition forces were able to deal with these problems by a combination of tactics and technology. Effects of the physical fog were minimized by the use of a diverse set of sensors in different frequency bands, and the effects of the psychological fog were minimized by previous training under simulated combat conditions, most notably the combat training carried out at Nellis Air Force Base and the National Training Center at Fort Irwin, where U.S. and allied units conduct mock battles against units trained in Soviet tactics and equipped with real or surrogate Soviet weapons. Key to coalition success, however, was the intelligence information that enabled coalition commanders to cut through the "fog."

MILITARY SHORTCOMINGS

After such a successful military outcome, it is psychologically hard to focus on shortcomings of the U.S. military, but nonetheless necessary, in order to plan intelligently future defense programs. Some of the areas where shortcomings have been reported concern the relative lack of readiness of U.S. sealift and some of the ground reserve units. Also, evidently there were some failings in strategic intelligence, or U.S. planners would not have been surprised by Iraq's invasion of Kuwait, or the status of their chemical weapons, or the number and disposition of their ballistic missiles. These failings suggest that the quality of the intelligence community's analytical capability does not match the quality of its sensing systems.

U.S. tactical intelligence systems achieved mixed results: JSTARS was very effective in the timely reporting of the quantity and location of enemy equipment, but is not designed to locate or count enemy personnel or do bomb damage assessment. Photographic systems partially filled these gaps but were subject to weather blackouts and a built-in reporting delay for film processing and delivery. Also, in the communication of intelligence data within the theater, significant problems exsisted both in the capacity of the data links and their ability to operate from service to service. As a result, the services had to work around these problems, primarily by making extensive use of couriers, which sometimes led to significant delays in the availability of data whose timeliness was operationally significant.

These shortcomings argue for three high priorities in the ongoing defense modernization program: proceeding with the production and deployment of JSTARS, providing real-time data links for aerial reconnaissance cameras, and developing equipment, software, and operating procedures that achieve real service-to-service interoperability in tactical data links.

There were serious shortcomings that were only latent, that is, they did not seriously affect military operations in Desert Storm but could have serious consequences in future operations. Because the U.S. C^3I was so significant, it will be carefully studied by other nations, not only to learn how to emulate it, but also to learn how to counter it. Many of the C^3I systems used in Desert Storm could be degraded by foreseeable countermeasures. Additionally, most of the communication systems were already stretched beyond their capacity; response to countermeasures would have reduced the capacity further. Partly because of the surprise effect of the first use of these new systems, and partly because of the shock effect of coalition air raids in the first week, the Iraqis never mounted a meaningful countermeasure program, even though their forces were equipped with moderately capable countermeasure equipment. As a result, U.S. C^3I systems got a "free ride" to some extent, which is unlikely to happen again. Therefore a critically important part of the U.S. future defense program should be dedicated to the "hardening" of these C^3I systems, that is, modifying them so that they are less susceptible to countermeasures.

While precision-guided weapons were used with great effectiveness during Desert Storm, they represented only a fraction of the total bombs dropped. Because of the high density of antiaircraft guns in Iraq, most of the bombs were released at high altitude, which decreased the accuracy of delivery of the "dumb bombs." Therefore, a clear lesson from Desert Storm is to increase the inventory of precision-guided weapons, whose accuracy is independent of the altitude of delivery. This need is particularly urgent for the navy. The navy's relative lack of emphasis in this field did not pose a serious problem in Desert Storm, because the availability and proximity of Saudi airbases resulted in most of the air strikes being launched from ground bases instead of carriers. However, a future war, with different geographical conditions, might necessitate launching the majority of air strikes from carriers. Therefore it is important that carrier-based strike aircraft increase their capability to deliver precision-guided weapons.

Most of the current generation of both air force and navy precision-guided weapons require that an operator guide them all the way to impact, which increases the risk to the operator during that period. The Iraqis were not able to take significant advantage of this vulnerability, but "lessons learned" analyses of other nations will certainly highlight the twin lessons of the devastating effect and the vulnerability of these precision-guided weapons. Therefore another important emphasis in the U.S. defense program should be the expedited development of next-generation "fire-and-forget" weapons, which would be autonomously guided to the target after initial identification by the operator. This new generation would have the precision but not the vulnerability of the current generation weapons, and some would have all-weather capability.

U.S. chemical defense systems and air defense systems were not given significant combat tests although they did pass important tests of deployability and operability. The U.S. air defense system (Patriot) never had to face Iraqi attack aircraft, but it did operate many times against an Iraqi modification of the Scud missile. While these operations will be subjected to intense analysis and further debate in the months ahead, it seems clear that the Patriot operated with high reliability, that it was quite capable of hitting an incoming missile, but that it did not effectively deal with relatively simple countermeasures.

It appears that the Iraqis, when they modified the Scud to extend its range and payload, created an inadvertent countermeasure. This modification introduced an instability that made the missile vulnerable to breaking up during reentry into the atmosphere. As a result, the Patriot was presented on many engagements with a multiplicity of targets, one of which was the warhead, and the rest of which were pieces of the missile, creating the same effect as decoys. On some of these engagements, it appears that the Patriot attacked the missile debris, missing the warhead. The Patriot results offer a straightforward lesson for defense planning, namely, that any program to develop a ballistic missile defense system will require serious attention to the development of counter-countermeasures, and even then some "leakage" can be expected.

Of course, implementing a program to upgrade U.S. defense capabilities in the years ahead depends not only on these suggested judgments, but on the size of the defense budget. The President's long-term defense plan, unveiled at Aspen last year and reaffirmed by Secretary Dick Cheney subsequent to Desert Storm, calls for a real decrease in the defense budget of three to four percent a year over the next six years and a reduction of more than 400,000 military personnel and a proportionate number of civilian personnel. In conjunction with this personnel reduction, it is important to review the role of U.S. reserves and national guard forces, some of which demonstrated a very high degree of readiness and effectiveness in Desert Storm, but others of which were still not fully combat ready after five months. It is crucial to maintain the research and development (R&D) strategy that contributed to the advantage that U.S. forces enjoy today. This will require a continuing exploration of new military technology, a vigorous program to build and test prototypes, and a constrained acquisition program to modernize the forces selectively. I believe that it is possible to construct a defense program that can maintain the military advantage of the United States into the next century and, at the same time, be entirely compatible with the reduced defense budget proposed in the president's plan.[3]

It is certain that countries all over the world will conduct their own analyses of the coalition's military success and that some will try to emulate the technical systems critical to that success. There is no secret about how these systems were developed in the United States. In the 1970s, U.S. defense officials saw the opportunity to exploit the new developments in microelectronics and computers to very great advantage in military applications. Then, during the course of five administrations and in the face of substantial public debate, the Department of Defense conceived, developed, tested, produced, and deployed the systems embodying the new technologies. Finally, the U.S. military developed the tactics for using the new systems and conducted extensive training with them, much of the training being under simulated field conditions.

To sustain the U.S. position of leadership in this new military capability, it is neither necessary nor sufficient to control the sale of technology or components. Indeed, even if it tried, the United States could not control this technology. With the exception of stealth, the underlying technology of these new weapon systems as well as the components embedded in them can be found in commercial products that have been on the market for five to ten years. (Commercial products lead defense in the incorporation of most new technology because of the agonizingly long development cycle in the defense procurement system.) The U.S. advantage in this new military technology is not in components, but in systems, training, and operational experience.

To sustain this advantage, the United States must control the sale of the systems that are key to the offset strategy: intelligence sensors, stealth aircraft, and precision-guided weapons. Even if the United States maintains strict control on the sale of these systems, other nations will gain this capability in time, but not without a substantial investment over many years. Just how long the United States maintains its advantage depends on how consistent it is in constraining the sale of this current generation of weapons and how effective it is in developing the next generation.

DETERRENCE

This new military capability adds an important dimension to the ability of the United States to deter war. Deterrence is a complex issue that involves political and psychological factors often more important than the military dimension. Only the military dimension of deterrence, and in particular, the extent to which the new military capability changes the deterrence calculus, which has been in place for the past four decades, will be assessed here.

The fact and perception that the United States has a powerful new conventional military capability raises the nuclear threshold; that is, the level at which the United States might escalate from a conventional defense to a nuclear defense. Since the late 1950s, this threshold has been low because NATO believed that Warsaw Pact forces had a substantial advantage in numbers and (with respect to U.S. forces) geography and that they posed a serious threat of launching a short-warning armored assault on Western Europe. NATO has responded to this threat by deploying nuclear forces in Europe that could be used against a nonnuclear as well as a nuclear attack against NATO. However, the threat of such an attack has diminished because of the dissolution of the Warsaw Pact, the dramatic political changes in the Soviet Union, and the reduction in Soviet military forces.

Indeed, based on these changes alone, a panel of the National Academy of Sciences has recommended[4] that the United States limit the role of its nuclear weapons to being a deterrent against nuclear attack only. The demonstration of this powerful new conventional military capability adds important new support for that recommendation. That is, this new capability in U.S. forces gives NATO the ability to defend Western Europe against any plausible attack by the Soviet Union with its present or projected conventional forces. Therefore, the United States would no longer need to extend its nuclear forces to deter nonnuclear attacks. Such a policy change would lead to a profound change in the size, composition, and deployment of U.S. nuclear forces. In particular, it would permit the removal of ground-based nuclear weapons from forward bases in Europe and Korea, thereby reducing the (already small) danger of nuclear weapons being used accidentally or inadvertently.

The new military capability also provides a credible response to a regional power that uses chemical weapons. Therefore it can provide a component of deterrence against the use of such weapons. Indeed, the Iraqis were deterred from using their formidable arsenal of chemical weapons in Desert Storm by a complex set of factors not fully understood, but which certainly included their calculus of the effectiveness of the military responses available to the United States without resorting to a response with chemical weapons. Their calculus also probably was influenced by the extent to which the military power of the United States prevented any effective application of their tactical chemical weapons. Coalition air supremacy precluded their dispensing chemical weapons by air, and the coalition's crippling of their C^3I net forestalled their ability to locate targets for chemical artillery shells.

The assessment that the United States can respond effectively to a regional power that used chemical weapons should strengthen the argument that the administration can agree to a complete ban on the possession of chemical weapons. Because of the credibility of its nonchemical response, it should not be necessary for the United States to maintain a small chemical force to respond to nations who either refuse to sign the proposed treaty or who cheat on it.

Desert Storm demonstrated that the new military capability is very effective in dealing with a regional power that attacks a neighbor with modern weapons (missiles, strike aircraft, and armored forces). This demonstrated effectiveness makes it quite credible that the United States has the military component of a deterrent to regional conflicts. The actual deterrent effect will depend, of course, on the potential aggressor's assessment of the political will of the United States, which, in turn, will depend on whether the United States has made security guarantees to the threatened nation and if not, then the extent to which there is strong international support for a military response. One of the unusual aspects of Desert Storm was the near unanimity of the international community in condemning Iraq's aggression and the coherence with which the United Nations was able to act. It remains to be seen whether Desert Storm will be a model for the United Nations in facing down aggressors or whether it will be a singular event.

CONCLUSIONS

While this new military capability will add a new dimension to deterrence, it also has significant limitations. It will not add to the ability of the United States to deter a nuclear attack; for the foreseeable future, that deterrence will depend on the strength of U.S. nuclear forces. Also, the new capability will be quite limited in its effectiveness in any regional conflicts that are basically civil wars or are dominated by guerilla warfare. No one should be deluded into believing that the military capability that can easily defeat an army with 4,000 tanks in the desert is going to be the decisive factor in a jungle or urban guerrilla war.

A central national security issue for the United States in the 1990s will be how to use this remarkable new military capability wisely. The United States will be required to formulate a national security policy that constrains the sale of systems critical to the offset strategy so that the U.S. advantage is protected, manages the declining defense budget with an investment strategy that extends U.S. advantage, guards against the hubris of believing that this new military capability solves all national security problems, and positions foreign policy so that the United States does not become either the world's policeman or the world's bully. Clearly, the United States does not want to spend the rest of the decade fighting regional conflicts. The key to avoiding such entanglements is for the United States to use its new strength to deter these conflicts rather than fight them.

ENDNOTES

1. This paper is an extended version of William J. Perry's article, "Desert Storm and Deterrence," which was published in *Foreign Affairs*, Vol. 70, No. 4 (Fall 1991), pp. 66–82.

2. See, for example, James Fallows, *National Defense* (New York, NY: Random House, 1981).
3. Such a program is described in William J. Perry's "Defense Investment Strategy," *Foreign Affairs*, Vol. 69, No. 2 (Spring 1989).
4. Committee on International Security and Arms Control, The National Academy of Arts and Sciences, *The Future of the U.S.-Soviet Nuclear Relationship* (Washington, DC: National Academy Press, 1991).

PART V

POLICY RECOMMENDATIONS

11

U.S. STRATEGY AFTER THE STORM

Bobby R. Inman, Joesph S. Nye, Jr., William J. Perry, and Roger K. Smith

The first lesson of the Gulf War is to be very wary of any so-called "lessons" of the Gulf War. To say that the Gulf War was unique is to cloud its central and defining characteristic with a gross understatement. One is hard pressed to recall a more unambiguous act of aggression that was so pregnant with dark possibilities by a large state against a small neighbor. In fact, so dark were the possibilities raised by Iraq's act of aggression that the five permanent members of the United Nations Security Council agreed on a series of remarkable, indeed historic, resolutions—resolutions that encouraged over thirty nations to lend their might to reversing Iraq's occupation of Kuwait.

Further, it is hard to imagine a more clumsy or cynical villain. In a bizarre attempt at crisis management just a few days after invading Kuwait, Saddam Hussein, president of Iraq, poured gasoline on the fire he had ignited by detaining foreign nationals as "guests" of the Iraqi state. Three days after he began to take hostages and four days after he announced the "eternal merger" between Iraq and its long-lost nineteenth province, Saddam Hussein cloaked himself in the mantle of Palestinian nationalism by proclaiming that the resolution of the Kuwait crisis was inextricably linked with the Palestinian cause.

In addition, a more compliant adversary may never be found. Saddam Hussein did not attempt to interfere with the coalition's efforts to marshal and train its forces, to test, adjust, and make fully operational its high-tech weapon systems, and to work out the command and control links for a coordinated multinational campaign. Not only did the coalition have the luxury of months of unfettered preparation, but it was also able to decide when and where the coming battle would be fought. No less rare in the annals of far-flung military expeditions was a readily available infrastructure (ports, air bases, fuel, and prepositioned equipment) to support the deployment of half a million men and women. Consequently, the first lesson of the Gulf War is clear: the Gulf War was exceptional.

But here is the rub: there is no rule to which a war may be an exception. All wars are extraordinary. Whether the war be large or small, brutally long or mercifully short, it is frozen in its own particular constellation of political forces and actors. Yet, for all this singularity, lessons, sometimes quite sweeping lessons, are drawn from wars. Over time, as these lessons become internalized and institutionalized into the body politic, they fence off the areas of acceptable discourse and silently determine the range of reasonable policy. Minutes after the 100-hour ground campaign had ended, experts were sifting through the sands searching for lessons. Already, we have heard that the Gulf War has either exposed the hollowness of U.S. power or confirmed its unrivaled strength; it has either demonstrated the supremacy of land-based air power or proven—by its uniqueness—the continuing need for naval projection forces.

Two points should be acknowledged about the process of drawing lessons. First, it is an entirely natural and necessary process. Although it is true that those who remember the past are just as likely as those who forget it to repeat it, human beings cannot go forward unless they try to make sense of history. Guides for future action must inevitably be culled, in part or in whole, from past experience. Second, just as all politics are local, so all lesson-drawing is political. Although the intensity of the process will turn on whether the war was a victory or a defeat, the act of drawing lessons is profoundly political because those lessons will affect who gets what, when, where, why, and how. Lessons about war cannot be separated from lessons about peace so conclusions about strategy or tactics inevitably involve considerations about budgets and force planning, jobs and economic prosperity. Consider, for example, the continuing saga of the B-2, a weapons platform originally designed for strategic nuclear missions. The performance of the F-117A Stealth Fighter during the Gulf War (which flew only 2 percent of the combat sorties, but 40 percent of the destruction of strategic targets) has led proponents of the B-2 to the lesson that the plane should be fully funded; after all, they argue, although the B-2 costs five times as much as the F-117A, it has over five times the range and ten times the striking power. Consequently, these proponents argue, instead of using 75 planes (32 F-117As, 28 escort and electronic warfare planes, and 15 tankers), the United States could have simply sent two B-2s to the Gulf.[1]

All this being said, what then is the purpose of this essay and what can it hope to achieve? Having posited that the process is embedded in the struggle over interests, values, and identities, a struggle that is commonly referred to as politics, we cannot claim to have discovered a set of apolitical lessons. On the contrary, the lessons that follow are very political in nature, but not partisan. Our lessons are political in that they are designed to clarify U.S. interests. They are nonpartisan in that they are not intended to advance the interests of any political party or interest group. What we hope to achieve is not the entry of one more laundry list of "dos" and "don'ts" into the ever-expanding debate on the meaning of the Gulf War. Rather, we hope to improve the quality of that debate by considering methods as well as conclusions.

When searching for the lessons of a war, there is a tendency to assume that history both ends and begins with that conflict, that the opening salvos signal the close of one era and the eventual armistice announces the advent of an entirely new one. Because the Gulf War so closely followed the ending of the Cold War,[2] this tendency has become more pronounced. Instead of seeing the Gulf War as the baseline for a "New World Order" (which might be better dated from 1989), we prefer to see it as part of an unfolding post-Cold War system. Or to put it another way, although the Gulf War was a unique event, it was also just the most recent in a series of unique events. We have tried to look at the Gulf War and the policy choices that now confront U.S.

decision makers as though they were already part of history. By bringing a sense of the past and the future to a reading of the Gulf War, the limits and opportunities of U.S. diplomacy become more discernible. It is this perspective, we hope, that makes the following lessons both valid and valuable.

The essay will proceed in a simple and direct manner. It will look at the lessons that can be derived from the prewar period, from the war itself, and finally from the war's immediate aftermath.

WHAT CAN BE LEARNED FROM THE PERIOD BEFORE THE WAR?

Preventive Diplomacy

The first substantive lesson of the Gulf War is the same lesson that follows every war, the need for better preventive diplomacy. Explaining the flawed course of U.S. diplomacy toward Iraq prior to August 1990 has become a cottage industry of sorts. Dozens of analysts have painstakingly reconstructed the U.S. failure to deter Iraq, the failure to recognize and respond to a dangerous threat.[3] There is no use belaboring the discussion; in the clear light of hindsight, the events speak for themselves: the failure to heed Saddam Hussein's long, angry analysis of world events given to the Arab Cooperation Council (ACC) in February 1990, the unwillingness to impose economic sanctions or cut off food aid after Saddam Hussein threatened to "burn half of Israel" with chemical weapons, the reprimanding of a "Voice of America" journalist after an editorial critical of Saddam Hussein was published, and, of course, the meeting of Saddam Hussein with U.S. Ambassador April C. Glaspie on July 25 and the congressional testimony of John Kelly on July 31 that told Saddam Hussein that the United States would not intervene in "inter-Arab matters."

Better preventive diplomacy is one of those many things that are easier said than done. However, in the aftermath of the war, the Bush administration has taken useful steps to deter further aggression in the Gulf region. The United States has entered into a set of negotiations with the nations of the Gulf Cooperation

Council (GCC) (Saudi Arabia, Kuwait, Qatar, Bahrain, Oman, and the United Arab Emirates).[4] The negotiations are specifically designed to establish a firm basis for joint exercises, prepositioned equipment, and U.S. access to air bases and port facilities. More broadly, these negotiations are designed to cement a long-term alliance system for the Gulf.

The Regional Balance of Power

The new alliances and the announcement of arms sales to U.S. Middle East allies are indications that a successor to the Pax Britannica (which ended in 1971) has arrived. The twenty-year hiatus following Britain's withdrawal from east of Suez was an uneasy interregnum during which the local powers tried and failed to strike an enduring regional balance. Having turned back the second challenge to regional stability in little more than a decade (the first was the Ayatollah Ruholla Khomeini's), the small Gulf states and the United States have now decided to enter into a more formal set of entangling relationships.

Although alliances and arms sales are traditional and well respected tools for maintaining the balance of power, they also have some inherent limitations. For example, the arms you sell to your friends today may be the arms your adversary carries tomorrow. More fundamentally, this new relationship rests on weak institutions. The history of formal and informal treaty organizations in the Middle East has been, as Fred Halliday puts it, "one of weakness, incompleteness and failure."[5] The Central Treaty Organization (CENTO), established by the Baghdad Pact, was little more than a paper alliance; the Arab League was ineffective in Lebanon, merely providing a veil of legitimacy for the gradual imposition of Syrian hegemony over that country; and the GCC and the ACC did nothing to protect one of their member states when it was threatened in the summer of 1990. This trend has continued. The Damascus Declaration issued by Egypt, Syria, and the GCC has already become a footnote in history. In March 1991, just days after the Gulf War had ended, the foreign ministers of these eight states met to hammer out an agreement on postwar security and economic arrangements. Although the details of this pact were never revealed, the basic bargain was clear: Egypt would be the Gulf's new protector; in return, Egypt would receive Saudi aid for the ever-ailing Egyptian economy. As it became evident just how thoroughly destroyed Saddam Hussein's war machine was, however, the Saudis began to rethink this strategic bargain. Remembering the last time the Egyptians were on the Arabian peninsula in the early 1960s and (due to the high cost of the war) being forced to borrow for the first time on the international capital markets, the Saudis apparently decided by summer to rely on a low-cost and low-profile arrangement with the United States.

The sand on which this new alliance system is being built is soft for reasons other than history. One should not confuse a new set of alliances with a new regional security structure. These new alliances do not include Iran or Iraq, the two most powerful states along the littoral of the Persian Gulf. Any viable, long-term security structure must be integrative; it should not, as one observer points out, "gratuitously perpetuate or harden, let alone create divisions."[6] At present there is a quiet division in the GCC that may be quite important down the road. Although most of the junior members of the GCC favor closer ties with Tehran, Saudi Arabia is far more reluctant. Saudi Arabia sees its neighbor across the Gulf as not only a geopolitical rival in the quest for dominance of the Gulf region, but also as a rival for the leadership of Islam. A security arrangement that does not incorporate Iran (and Iraq) will be tenuous, if the United States reduces its role.

The emerging security order in the Gulf is an order with the United States at its center. It is an order premised upon the United States acting as the balancer; it is premised on the United States being willing and able to intervene when and where necessary. To maintain a balance of power in the Gulf, the United States will need to do the four things that all previous balancers have done. First, it must remain ever vigilant. Second, ideology cannot be allowed to muddle the calculus of U.S. interests, there must be flexibility in the selection of allies and adversaries. Third, the United States must be willing to "compensate" allies and neutral bystanders. And finally, the United States must be willing to go to war again to preserve the balance. Can the United States play this role? The judgment of history is not optimistic.[7]

In regard to constant vigilance, the record of 1990 is enough to give one pause. Although there was no shortage of technical intelligence documenting Iraq's hostile intentions toward its neighbor, the administration miscalculated.[8] To this miscalculation can be added other notable missteps. Over the last decade and a half there have been a number of turning points in the Gulf region, and in each instance the United States has been slow to react, always a step behind the action. In the late 1970s, the United States was slow to adjust to the revolutionary changes in Iran. During the early and mid-1980s it was hesitant and indecisive in who it backed in the Iran-Iraq War, simultaneously giving intelligence aid to Iraq and selling weapons to Iran in exchange for hostages. When the United States finally "tilted" unambiguously toward Iraq in the late 1980s, through the reflagging and escorting of Kuwaiti tankers, it was slow to realign away from Iraq after the war, a realignment that should have seemed self-evident after Saddam Hussein gassed his own Kurdish population in 1988 and threatened in the spring of 1990 to visit the same destruction on Israel.

A number of reasons have been offered for why the United States did not react more forcibly in the summer of 1990: the judgment that Saddam Hussein could be, to quote John Kelly on his trip to Baghdad in February 1990, a "force for moderation,"[9] the assurances from President Hosni Mubarak and King Fahd that Iraq would not invade Kuwait, the unflappable complacency of Kuwait itself in the face of Iraq's threats, and a general inclination to wait for regional disputes to "ripen" before attempting a resolution.[10] These reasons imply that U.S. failure in the summer of 1990 was *sui generis* and unlikely to be repeated. However, two other reasons for the deterrence failure that led to the Gulf War cast doubt on U.S. abilities to fine tune a balance of power in the Middle East.

The first is Washington's preoccupation with other issues, most notably the Soviet withdrawal from Eastern Europe and the reunification of Germany. These tumultuous events were extraordinary, but the effect they produced was not. Decision making in Washington often hinges on the struggle for a senior decision maker's time. As Anthony Lake describes it, even the most important issues seem like sounding whales to presidents, national security advisers, and secretaries of state: "They are viewed and pursued but rarely dealt with definitively before they dive again as events bring another issue to view. The policymaker must deal with these issues when they are in crisis and on the surface."[11] In short, policymakers will always be distracted by other concerns. The Carter administration was slow to react to the changes in Iranian politics, in part because of underlying assumptions about the Shah that had become woven into the structure of policy—much the way that assumptions about Saddam Hussein had become part and parcel of U.S. policy in the Gulf—but also because throughout most of 1977 and 1978, the senior decision makers were preoccupied with the Middle East peace process, the strategic arms limitation negotiations (SALT II), and the Panama Canal treaty.

The second reason why the United States failed to balance Saddam Hussein's power was the animus felt in Washington toward Iran. The embassy hostage crisis, the failure at Desert One, the hostage holding in Lebanon by Iranian-backed terrorists, and the Iran-Contra affair all made international realignment difficult due to domestic considerations. This reason calls into question the U.S. ability to meet the second requirement for a balance of power. An effective balance of power system requires more than discerning judgment and constant scrutiny. It also requires the insulation of foreign policy from domestic politics. Because domestic politics in the Middle East are volatile and changes in regime, as well as policy, commonplace, U.S. diplomacy will have to be agile if it is to be effective. Will Congress and the public permit the executive to ally with the devil whenever it is necessary, to make the subtle distinctions, complex choices, and precarious manipulations that balancing requires? Even if this constancy in approach can be carried through the course of one administration, can it be sustained from one administration to the next, or will every new occupant of the Oval Office reset U.S. priorities? These same questions can be applied to the third criterion for an effective balancer: the willingness and ability to "compensate" allies and neutrals. U.S. acquiescence in Syria's takeover of Lebanon in the fall of 1990 ruffled few domestic feathers at the time because it was overshadowed by the Gulf crisis; but there will not always be the convenient cover of an international crisis behind which the United States can cut the necessary deals of realpolitik.

The point here is not to suggest that a traditional approach is inappropriate; it is not. Nor is the point to suggest that it is impossible for the United States to play the balancer in the Gulf; it is possible. Rather, the point is to show that such a course is fraught with difficulty, that alliances and arms sales are necessary but not sufficient to establish a durable balance of power in the Gulf. What is needed are mechanisms that will keep the balance steady when the United States is distracted by events in other regions, when the United States is unable to realign because it has demonized or romanticized another state, and when the United States is unwilling to sacrifice principle for power. By themselves these additional mechanisms will also be insufficient to hold the balance. There is a synergy, however, that makes the whole greater than the sum of its parts. In short, the United States must design its security arrangements in the Gulf as it does its nuclear command and control system, with layered redundancy. The goal should be a regional security system that is able to stabilize itself. This is prudent not simply because of the conflicts between the demands of balance-of-power politics and the character of the U.S. political system, but also because of the challenges that will eventually arise in the Middle East due to the presence of yet another dominating power from outside the region. As Martin Indyk has argued, American foreign policy must start with the balance of power, but not stop there. It must also lean in the direction of arms control, development, and supporting peace in the region.[12]

Arms Control

Stripped down to the essentials, Saddam Hussein invaded Kuwait because he could. Not only had the United States and others dropped the deterrence ball, but his army, at least in the abstract, could present him with a *fait accompli,* without fear of any regional riposte and, given the size and battle-tested strength of that army, Saddam Hussein could expect to deter any outside power from reversing his gain. Clearly, he miscalculated the will of the United States and the difference between having the world's fourth or fifth largest army and having the world's most technologically sophisticated and well-trained military force. Saddam Hussein was not, however, alone in his mistaken assumptions; in the fall of 1990, estimates of allied casualties in a war to dig him out of Kuwait ran into the tens of thousands. In short, there is no getting around the fact that Saddam Hussein's relentless buildup of his country's conventional and nonconventional forces contributed mightily to the onset of the crisis. Consequently, if the United States hopes to provide better arrangements for preventive diplomacy, then the control of arms in the region must be a principal complement to alliances and arms sales.

Global as well as local measures can help.[13] The Chemical Weapons Convention, the global ban on chemical arms, should be signed and ratified and its international inspectorate operating as soon as possible. The Missile Technology Control Regime (MTCR) should expand to include all the major missile suppliers, such as China, and then be transformed from an informal suppliers' agreement into a formal treaty with a secretariat in place to ensure implementation. The Biological Weapons Convention should have a protocol and procedures for verification. An agreement on steps toward a formal treaty creating a nuclear-free zone for the region would be helpful. And then the best of all worlds would have an agreement similar to the Treaty on Conventional Forces in Europe (CFE) to stabilize the conventional balance in the Middle East.

Clearly, this is what the president had in mind when he outlined a plan for a comprehensive Middle East arms control regime in May 1991.[14] The president's plan put particular emphasis on formal arms control agreements. The plan called for a freeze on the purchase, production, and testing of surface-to-surface missiles with an eventual ban on ballistic missiles, as well as chemical and biological weapons, and a verifiable ban on the production and acquisition of enriched uranium and weapons-grade plutonium. Formal arms control agreements have a number of very distinct advantages, the most important of which is that a formal obligation creates a stronger presumption in favor of compliance. Not only has a nation staked its reputation on a highly visible and formal pledge, but a treaty establishes a basis for domestic and international mechanisms, such as new bureaucracies and monitoring organizations, to help assure compliance by increasing transparency. Given the sensitivity and importance of military security, formal agreements are very desirable. However, there are several reasons why formal arms control will face difficulties at this time.

First, the Middle East is not like the Central Front in Europe; for each state in the region there is not one single threat, but multiple and overlapping security threats. Second, unlike the U.S.-Soviet strategic balance, there is nothing approaching parity in either the size or sophistication of military forces in the Middle East. Third, the Treaty on Conventional Forces in Europe and the Strategic Arms Reduction Treaty are the products of over twenty years of dialogue and background negotiations; there is no comparable background for arms control in the Middle East. And finally, even if there were a comparable set of precedents for serious arms negotiations, the process of arriving at ratifiable treaties is long and slow. Setting aside for the moment the oft-noted problem with formal arms control—that the slow pace of negotiations is frequently overtaken by advances in technology—the United States cannot afford to have its primary focus be formal agreements.

Multilateral Measures

"Unipolar moments" are both fleeting and illusory.[15] The United States is the only military superpower, but it is one of three global economic powers, as the financing of the war demonstrated. Unipolar illusions usually end sooner rather than later. Although the United States is clearly the world's pre-eminent military and diplomatic power (able to move vast armies tremendous distances and win, able to forge diverse and resilient coalitions), there are, at present, sharp limits on its autonomy of action. The dependence on foreign creditors and the domestic political impasse on the issue of taxation, as well as the continuing economic strength of Europe and Japan, will ensure that the political bounce the United States received from its victory in the Gulf will be shorter than the one it received from its victory in 1945. The United States, if it wants to build a durable security structure in the Middle East, must move fast before the dust settles. It must move quickly if it wants to influence *how* the dust settles. What can the United States do that will be both quick and effective?

The first thing that the United States must do is something the administration is already hard at work at doing: ensuring rigorous Iraqi compliance with the terms of United Nations (UN) Resolution 687. The resolution requires Iraq to destroy, under international supervision, all chemical and biological weapon stocks, to remove all nuclear-weapons-grade material, and to destroy all ballistic missiles with a range greater than 150 kilometers. If the terms of this resolution are met, the ability of Iraq to upset the balance of power will be sharply curtailed. Enforcement of this resolution is also required for the beneficial impact it will have on future efforts at arms control in the Middle East. Ensuring compliance with Resolution 687 will be a difficult undertaking; already it has involved the United States and France in threatening to use force if Iraq resumes its nuclear weapons program[16] and the threat of military escorts for UN inspection teams.[17] If the United States enforces the resolution successfully, it will set the tone for other steps that can be quickly achieved.

Second, the United States can establish a number of "way stations," informal arms control agreements that will establish momentum for later, more formal, more complicated agreements. For example, the United States can build on its enforcement of the nuclear proliferation clauses of resolution 687 by urging a change in the safeguard procedures of the International Atomic Energy Agency (IAEA). One of the lessons from the revelations about the extent of Iraq's nuclear program is the need for "challenge" inspections by the IAEA of suspicious facilities. This change need not involve amendment of the Non-Proliferation Treaty, just a vote by the Governing Board of the IAEA authorizing a change in the information circular on safeguard procedures (INFCIRC 153). Another expedient way to improve efforts at nuclear nonproliferation would be to have the Nuclear Suppliers Group become a part of the IAEA; this would encourage membership in the group by the so-called "second-tier suppliers."

One of the more unambiguous lessons of the Gulf War is the need to shore up export controls. Iraq took full advantage of deliberate loopholes, sloppy legislation, weak enforcement, and poor supplier coordination to arm itself to the teeth. For example, Iraq was able to acquire over $500 million worth of arms and military-related high technology from Germany between 1982 and 1989 despite policies banning exports of weapons to countries engaged in regional conflict. Germany and the United States have begun to take active measures to tighten their laws.[18] But unilateral efforts are not enough. One simple and informal way to improve the international control over dual-use items is to improve each country's ability to control exports. Long before any formal treaty, such as a ballistic missile nonproliferation treaty, is negotiated, model export control laws should be cooperatively developed and disseminated to ensure effective second-level enforcement. International standards would greatly help the MTCR because, as an export agreement, it is open to different interpretations by each of its member states.[19]

Another way to increase first- and second-level compliance with international standards and norms is to increase the sharing of intelligence and the discussion of "problem" states. It would be an easy matter for the United States to inaugurate meetings with its key allies, who also happen to be the principal suppliers of modern weapons and dual-use technology—semiannual meetings devoted to proliferation concerns. Institutionalization of regular nonproliferation meetings with allies would accomplish a couple of very important things. First, the preparation necessary for such talks would keep the president and his secretary of state actively engaged in integrating nonproliferation and foreign policy without making excessive demands on their time. One of the principal problems dogging U.S. nonproliferation efforts over the years has been the relatively low priority it has received from senior decision makers. Second, such meetings would play to the natural strength of international summits and negotiations. As Gilbert Winham has argued, international negotiations are inherently more an effort to reduce complexity and develop common perceptions than to direct efforts at exchanges of benefits and concessions.[20]

Formal international nonproliferation regimes are critically important, but their evolution can be aided by certain informal arrangements. These arrangements will not only be important on their own merit; they are also needed as indications of intent. It is very important that the United States be clear about the messages it sends on the formation of these regimes. Mixed signals, especially now, when there is an unparalleled opportunity to make significant progress in a short period of time, are to be avoided at all costs. In May 1991 the Bush administration gave the negotiations for a Chemical Weapons Convention (CWC) a powerful boost when it announced that it would forswear the use of chemical weapons for any reason and unconditionally commit to the total destruction of its stockpile within ten years of a chemical weapons convention being signed. Under the previous policy, the United States would have retained two percent of its chemical arsenal as a deterrent until all chemical-weapons-capable states had signed the convention. Unfortunately, the Bush administration gave the CWC a shove in the opposite direction when it exchanged a tough on-site challenge inspection scheme to support the chemical weapons ban for a less intrusive one in August 1991.[21] The United States should seek a tougher verification scheme.

Another area in which quick and informal cooperation among weapons suppliers can help stabilize the balance of power in the Middle East is through restraint on arms sales. Although a ban on any transfers of advanced delivery systems, such as fighter bombers and missiles, is highly desirable, it will be difficult to put in place immediately.[22] In the meantime, as Geoffrey Kemp argues, a suppliers' agreement simply to slow down delivery of advanced combat aircraft and subsystems would send an "important political statement of intent."[23] And it may be possible to develop a COCOM (Coordinating Committee for Multilateral Export Controls)-like agreement to slow the export of certain advanced technology systems that proved so important during the war.[24]

The Peace Process

Preventive diplomacy in the Middle East must go beyond alliances, arms sales, and arms control. It needs to include the peace process. On the one hand, the United States must be careful not to breathe life into something that the Gulf War had diminshed—the belief in pan-Arab nationalism. The revived myth of a pan-Arab cause will erode the ability of the United States to play the balancer in the region. If that were not enough of a disincentive to vigorous pursuit of a peace conference, then surely the fact that prospects for success are slim should encourage caution. Unlike the situation in the mid-1970s, no implicit deal needs to be formalized; nothing in the works approaches the specificity of an exchange of some land (Sinai) for some recognition. Nonetheless, the Bush administration is right in pushing the peace process along on grounds of realpolitik. One of the keys to stability in the Middle East is keeping Syria in the Egyptian-Saudi axis. At first glance, this should be a relatively easy thing to do; for the time being, Hafiz al-Assad has nowhere else to go. With the destruction of Iraq's offensive striking power and the withdrawal of Soviet power from the region, the only way Syria can balance Israel is by aligning itself with the U.S.-led coalition of Arab states. The price for better relations with the United States, however, is Syrian participation in the peace process. By making Syria pay that price, the United States can further stabilize the region.

As intimated above, there is, at present, little likelihood of a deal between Syria and Israel over the Golan Heights. There are, however, more limited, but still quite valuable arrangements. A U.S.-brokered disengagement in Lebanon and the implementation of some interim autonomy for the Palestinians on the West Bank and in the Gaza Strip would bring two very important benefits. First, it would improve the Arab-Israeli balance by reducing tensions and flash points along Israel's northern border. Second, it would stabilize the inter-Arab balance by drawing the Syrians further into the Egyptian-Saudi axis. The further Syria is enmeshed in the Western camp, the greater the likelihood that Western-led efforts at arms control will succeed. Given the Soviet Union's withdrawal and the absence of complicating positions on the peace process put forward by the West Europeans, now is an opportune moment to push the peace process along.

Energy Security

Iraq's invasion of Kuwait brought to the attention of the U.S. public, in a way that no amount of statistics, or charts, or expert testimony could, the fact that the United States is increasing its dependence on foreign oil, primarily oil imported from the Persian Gulf. For over a year now, energy experts have warned that U.S. dependence on foreign sources was growing at an increasing rate; a relatively conservative estimate holds that by the beginning of the next century, absent any changes in policy, U.S. dependence on imported oil will reach above 60 percent.[25] What makes this trend worrisome is that by the end of the 1990s, the number of major oil exporters outside the Gulf region will have shrunk; countries such as Algeria, Venezuela, and Nigeria will consume domestically much of what they produce. By the end of the decade, half the world's oil will come from the Gulf, compared with only 25 percent today. This problem will be exacerbated because although demand for electricity is growing in the United States, there is also growing opposition to either coal or nuclear power, leaving only oil and natural gas as economically efficient sources. Compounding this problem even further is the great likelihood that political disruptions in the supply of oil from the Persian Gulf are to be expected. Roughly twice a decade since 1950, from Mohammed Mossadegh's nationalization of Iranian oil to the invasion of Kuwait and the UN-sponsored embargo on trade with Kuwait and Iraq, developments either in the Gulf directly or the Middle East more broadly have threatened the oil supplies and thus the economic well-being of the world.

The Gulf War suggests two lessons for U.S. action in future crises. First, the greatest damage from oil comes not from physical shortages, but from the "stagflation" effects on the economy of rapid price rises. Early use of the strategic petroleum reserve (SPR) could help to dampen market effects that escalate prices. A strong argument can be made that the 1990 economic slowdown tipped into a recession only after Iraq invaded Kuwait.[26] The invasion and annexation of Kuwait and the almost immediate embargo on Iraqi and Kuwaiti crude resulted in a sharp increase in spot oil prices. This increase in the spot price sent a fragile consumer confidence in the national economy plummeting, resulting in a sharp decline in the purchase of consumer durables. If President Bush had announced on August 8 that not only would the United States send troops to Saudi Arabia, but would also be prepared to draw on the SPR, fears about an oil shortage would have been eased, and with them fears about the economy (especially since Saudi Arabia did not announce for another ten days that it would increase production). Because of this omission, the Gulf War was far more costly than most people think. The total cost in forgone output—labor willing to work but unable, capital available but underutilized—may be in the hundreds of billions of dollars by the time full recovery occurs. The war itself, measured in direct outlays for military expenditures, only cost about $50 billion.

The second lesson is that the United States needs to insulate itself better from crises in the Gulf. Energy independence is not possible at any acceptable cost, but reducing the share of oil in national consumption is possible and at acceptable cost, and it will increase the credibility of the SPR. In February 1991 the Bush administration released its National Energy Strategy (NES). Although the NES has a number of innovative and worthwhile elements, such as encouraging conservation through fuel switching, it is notably deficient in one key area: it is unwilling to invoke market forces to reduce demand for oil. The NES uses market forces in the form of tax incentives to increase U.S. oil production through enhanced recovery from existing wells, but it rejects by omission the use of the policy instruments that could mobilize the market mechanism most effectively for reducing consumption. If the United States wants to be serious about reducing the degree of its political and economic vulnerability to domestic and international upheaval in the Middle East, then it must raise taxes on gasoline, motor fuels, petroleum products, or carbon emissions. Apart from a few of the oil-exporting countries, the United States has the smallest tax on gasoline of any major country, even after the increases of late 1990.

WHAT CAN BE LEARNED FROM THE WAR ITSELF?

Two analysts have boldly ventured the claim that the victory in the Gulf was a "defining moment in military history; a campaign as momentous in operational terms as Cannae, Agincourt, Waterloo, the Somme, or Normandy."[27] Although it remains to be seen whether the Gulf War, as these two analysts predict, will "long be studied as a classic," a number of very definite lessons have already been drawn. Probably the most obvious, obvious to anyone with a television during the six weeks of hostilities, was that "high tech" works. The persistent questions about the effectiveness of advanced military technology, questions fueled by a series of scandals over fraud, mismanagement, and cost overruns at the Pentagon, have seemingly been put to rest by the systems conceived and developed during the 1970s. The "offset strategy," fathered by Harold Brown during his days as secretary of defense, had at its core the notion that high technology could be used not only to build better weapons than the Soviets could field, but actually to offset the large numerical advantages of the Warsaw Pact; high technology could act as a force multiplier. In the Gulf this complex of reconnaissance and strike technologies gave the U.S.-led coalition unprecedented command, control, and communications over its forces and vast intelligence about the enemy's forces. In addition, it allowed coalition forces to suppress enemy defenses so thoroughly that the Iraqis were essentially blind and defenseless, while the allies knew what was happening throughout the theater. Finally, superior U.S. technology allowed the coalition to attack Iraqi forces and facilities with such precision that it broke their will. As Clausewitz argued long ago, the destruction that matters in battle is not physical but moral—the destruction of the enemy's capacity to resist. "The killing of his courage rather than his men" is the object of battle.[28]

Less obvious, but no less significant, are the lessons being drawn by the Pentagon in regard to the composition of the nation's force structure. Although it will keep the same force level totals agreed to before the war, the Pentagon has decided to change three specific aspects of its forces. First, before the war there was a growing consensus that the army should shift the bulk of its heavy divisions to the reserves, while the active army would be oriented toward light, rapid reaction forces. That judgment has since been reversed. In 1995, as a percentage of the active force, heavy divisions will constitute 66 percent as opposed to 55 percent in 1990. Second, before the war there was considerable sentiment in favor of changing the active-reserve mix from two-thirds active, one-third reserve to a fifty-fifty split. Because the performance of the three round-out brigades sent to the Gulf was so poor, the army is attempting to retain the two-thirds active, one-third reserve combat mix, though congressional pork barrel politics may get in the way. The third lesson involves readiness levels. Earlier it was widely believed that flying hours, steaming days, and vehicle miles could all be reduced due to the ending of the Cold War; only those forces that would have to fight on short notice would retain the same level of readiness. The current defense program (fiscal years 1992–97) keeps all active units at their Cold War readiness levels.[29]

These are just some of the lessons from the war that are being learned. There are two other lessons that have not received as much attention but have very profound political consequences, both at home and abroad. The first concerns the size, not the shape, of the U.S. military. Throughout the debate in the fall of 1990, there was a recurring theme: fervent relief that Saddam Hussein had decided to invade in 1990 and not five years later when the United States would not have had the forces necessary to evict the invader. This appears to be a needless worry. In retrospect, it is now clear that if this crisis had occurred in 1995, the United States could have easily deployed the same number of forces. Table 5 in Chapter 9, "The Impact of the Persian Gulf War on Military Budgets and Force Structure" by Lawrence J. Korb, explains why. In terms of personnel, the Gulf deployment represented about 17 percent of today's Total Force; under the 1995 plan, it would have constituted only 21 percent of the Total Force.

The second lesson, which is generally unacknowledged, is not as optimistic. It concerns commitments in excess of resources. During the 1960s there was talk about U.S. ability to fight two and a half wars simultaneously. After the Vietnam War, that goal was dropped to one and a half. During the early Reagan years, there was some rhetoric that implied a goal of three and a half wars. During all this time there was a sneaking suspicion that the United States could probably only fight one war at a time. The Gulf War has confirmed that suspicion. In the Gulf the United States mobilized a force structure that was designed to fight at least one and a half wars simultaneously to fight a Third World contingency—something that has always gone under the heading "half war"—under near ideal conditions. One of the reasons why the United States could fly so many sorties and keep so many tanks up and running during the Gulf War was because maintenance and supply units from everywhere else were stripped of their personnel and supplies. Although it may be true in retrospect that the United States brought more force to the Gulf than was necessary, it is also true that if the United States had had to fight even another "half war" somewhere else it would have been sorely pressed.

WAR TERMINATION AND WORLD ORDER

Whatever the success of the campaign, there has been far less evidence of careful preparation for war termination. The first lesson after the shooting stopped was that there was considerable ambiguity about objectives. Despite occasional lapses during the war, the Bush administration generally defined the purpose of Desert Shield and Desert Storm as the removal of Saddam Hussein from Kuwait. The Bush administration also referred to the creation of a New World Order. Here the rhetoric was often confused, sometimes referring to cosmopolitian concepts like "justice for all peoples," and sometimes to more traditional principles of interstate order like the rule of law, collective security, international control of arms, and peaceful settlement of disputes. In practice, the traditional view prevailed, and rather than a New World Order the administration pursued a concept of collective security that might have been called "world order delayed," because the concept so closely resembles what the UN system was supposed to provide if the Cold War had not intervened. The ambiguity came to the surface at the end when the administration tried to operationalize the term in the weeks following Iraq's defeat.

The Bush administration's initial reluctance to intervene on behalf of either the Shiites or the Kurds, who were being brutally suppressed by Saddam Hussein's military forces, showed that the "New World Order" was in essence the very old Westphalian system with a few garnishes. Rather than threatening air attacks against any Iraqi forces that left their garrisons, the United States left Saddam Hussein unconstrained. The decision to let Saddam Hussein use helicopter gunships in his suppression of the rebellions was probably motivated by a fear of Iraq's possible "Lebanonization," and the implications that this might have for the regional balance of power. However, domestic and international pressures altered this bias for state sovereignty and noninterference. The Bush administration then sought to create a safe haven for the Kurds north of the 36th parallel and it aggressively pursued adherence to the terms of UN resolution 687. This ambivalence about the Westphalian and post-Westphalian principles of world order is likely to be the rule, not the exception in U.S. diplomacy after the Gulf War. The question is not whether this ambivalence was or is a mistake, but rather how the United States can best deal with a very turbulent period. The world is in transition; it is caught between the old Westphalian system and an undetermined successor. What is not ambiguous is that the outlines of this successor system cannot be produced in 100 hours or 100 days; it will take decades.

DOMESTIC POLITICS AND FOREIGN POLICY

In such an environment, the process by which U.S. foreign policy is determined is as important as the actual content. In this regard the Gulf War offers a number of hopeful lessons.

The first such lesson is that the myth from the Vietnam era about a crippled presidency has been firmly laid to rest. Throughout the Gulf crisis the president was able to lead, mobilize, and shape public opinion to support his actions; at every turn he was able to garner international support and then turn and use it to mobilize approval from Congress and from the general public. President Bush's handling of the crisis was an exercise in good, old-fashioned leadership.[30] Although the executive branch clearly emerged from the crisis with its powers enhanced, Congress also improved its position by accomplishing a precedent-setting action: it made the administration put to a vote in Congress the decision for war. It is highly unlikely that this precedent will be ignored the next time that the United States confronts a serious military challenge.

The Gulf War also clarified the relationship between war, public opinion, and casualties. The supposed lesson from Vietnam was that the U.S. public withdrew its support for the war when the casualties began to mount. A closer reading of the polls from then and now indicates something very different. The U.S. public will support a war for a just cause, even one that may promise high casualties, as the Gulf War conceivably did in the autumn of 1990 and early winter of 1991. It will withdraw its support when there does not appear to be any end in sight.

These "lessons" about process are perhaps the most encouraging lessons from the Gulf War. In 1947 Harry Truman was facing a very uncertain and dangerous international situation, and he asked Dean Acheson what was the best way to mobilize the U.S. public for a long struggle. Acheson answered, "Scare the hell out of them, Mr. President." Today, the United States is facing a very different, but an equally troubling world. The lessons about process seem to indicate that it is possible for the United States to craft a policy that finds the middle ground between indiscriminate isolation and equally indiscriminate internationalism, the two poles between which U.S. foreign policy has historically oscillated. For only in that middle ground between the two poles will the United States be able to address its domestic and international challenges.

CONCLUSION

The collective act of drawing lessons from what nations go through is akin to a group effort at backyard brewing. The goal is to distill from certain raw elements a bracing tonic composed of just the most essential elements. Unfortunately, what is all too often extracted is a heady mixture that is quite intoxicating, if not blinding. For most Americans, the wars of the last half century have spawned at least three 150-proof "lessons" of history; so concentrated have these lessons become that they are now bumpersticker sized: "Munich," Munich's cold war corollary "the domino theory," and, of course, "No more Vietnams." Because the Gulf War occurred at a moment of such fundamental uncertainty about the future of the United States, both at home and abroad, the potential for a very potent and ultimately blinding mixture is quite real.

We have tried to guard against drawing extravagant lessons by trying to view the Gulf War from a distance. Viewing time as a stream makes one recall Heraclitus's observation that "you can never step into the same stream twice." Keeping the uniqueness of the Gulf War uppermost in our minds has forced us to be humble before the complexities of history. This should encourage us to look for those lessons that will yield marginal improvements in how international security can be provided in the aftermath of the Gulf War. We have self-consciously looked for ways to make small adjustments because our reading of history tells us that small changes can make a difference, and that attempts to rewrite history at a single stroke are likely to cause, not prevent, pain.

ENDNOTES

1. See Donald Rice's comments in "Deterrence Argued as Chief Mission for Bomber in 21st Century," *Knoxville News Sentinel*, June 2, 1991, p. F-1; Rice's arguments were echoed by Senator Sam Nunn (D-Ga.) during an interview on "Meet the Press," September 15, 1991.
2. A very persuasive case can be made that the ending of the Cold War simultaneously made the beginning and ending of the Gulf crisis possible. The end of the Cold War made the Gulf crisis possible by loosening the restraints that Moscow had placed on Baghdad's freedom of action. At the same time, the end of the Cold War made Soviet cooperation with the U.S.-led effort possible; it is hard to imagine the same level of international and domestic support for the war if the Soviet Union had opposed United

Nations resolution 678 in November 1990. See Chapter 1: "Status Quo Ante: The United States and its Allies" by Strobe Talbott and Chapter 4: "The Postwar Balance of Power in the Middle East" by Martin Indyk.

3. One of the most detailed is by Paul Gigot, "A Great American Screw-Up," *National Interest*, No. 22 (Winter 1990/91), pp. 3–10.
4. The first of these agreements, a ten-year security pact between Kuwait and the United States, was signed in mid-September. See Eric Schmitt, "U.S. and Kuwait Sign Pact on Troops," *New York Times* (September 20, 1991), p. A10.
5. Fred Halliday, "The Gulf War and Its Aftermath: First Reflections," *International Affairs*, Vol. 67, No. 2 (April 1991), p. 230.
6. Shahram Chubin, "Post-war Gulf Security," *Survival* Vol. 33, No. 2 (March/April 1991), p. 153.
7. On the narrower question of the U.S. ability to extend deterrence successfully to its allies in the Middle East, the record is equally grim. According to one scholar, of the seven occasions between 1960 and 1988 when the United States tried to deter the use of force against an ally in an ongoing regional conflict, it succeeded only twice. See Janice Gross Stein, "Extended Deterrence in the Middle East: American Strategy Reconsidered," *World Politics* Vol. 33, No. 3 (April 1987), pp. 326–352; and Janice Gross Stein, "The Wrong Strategy in the Right Place: The United States in the Gulf," *International Security* Vol. 13 No. 3 (Winter 1988/89), pp. 142–167.
8. The United States, it appears, made two separate miscalculations. First, it was assumed that Saddam Hussein was or could be made to be a force for moderation in the region. As Brent Scowcroft explained nearly a year after the invasion, the administration believed that Saddam Hussein could be a "reasonably responsible member of the international community." CNN interview with Brent Scowcroft, July 14, 1991, cited in John Goshko, "State Department Sees No Problem in Glaspie's Cables on Saddam Meeting," *Washington Post*, July 16, 1991, p. A-14. The second miscalculation was to think that even if Saddam Hussein were to be immoderate, he would never be so rash as to annex a neighbor. According to Bob Woodward, the director of the Defense Intelligence Agency, Lieutenant General Harry E. Soyster, did not believe one of his analyst's predictions that Iraq would invade Kuwait because it was inconceivable that "Saddam would do something so anachronistic as an old-fashioned land grab. Countries didn't go around doing things like that anymore." Bob Woodward, *The Commanders* (New York, NY: Simon & Schuster, 1991), p. 217.
9. As cited in John K. Cooley, "Pre-war Gulf Diplomacy," *Survival* Vol. 33, No. 2 (March/April 1991), p. 126.
10. Before going on to become the director of the National Security Council's staff for the Middle East, Richard Haass wrote a book giving pride of place to the notion of "ripeness" in international disputes; see Richard N. Haass, *Conflicts Unending: The United States and Regional Disputes* (New Haven, CT: Yale University Press, 1990).

11. Anthony Lake, *Somoza Falling. The Nicaraguan Dilemma: A Portrait of Washington at Work* (Boston, MA: Houghton Mifflin, 1989), p. 39.
12. See Martin Indyk's essay on the balances of power, Chapter 4: "The Postwar Balance of Power in the Middle East."
13. For further discussion of these and other specific suggestions on how the United States can improve its efforts at stemming the proliferation of missiles and nonconventional weapons, see Aspen Strategy Group, *New Threats: Responding to the Proliferation of Nuclear, Chemical, and Delivery Capabilities in the Third World* (Lanham, MD: University Press of America, 1990).
14. Andrew Rosenthal, "Bush Unveils Plan for Arms Control in Middle East," *New York Times*, May 30, 1991, p. A-1.
15. Charles Krauthammer, "The Unipolar Moment," *Foreign Affairs*, Vol. 70, No. 1 (America and the World 1990/91), pp. 23–33.
16. Maureen Dowd, "France Backs U.S. on Using Force if Iraq Pursues Nuclear Weapons," *New York Times*, July 15, 1991, pp. A-1, A-5.
17. Paul Lewis, "U.N. Considering a Troop Escort in Iraq," *New York Times*, September 18, 1991, p. A-3.
18. The U.S. effort began with the issuance of a new Executive Order, No. 12375, the Enhanced Proliferation Control Initiative (EPI), which set further controls on precursor chemicals and dual-use equipment and technology related to chemical weapons, biological weapons, and missiles, as well as setting civil and criminal penalties for those who knowingly participated in the proliferation of such weapons. In August 1991 the Commerce Department, after a long battle with the State Department, imposed strict new licensing rules for exports; the Commerce Department estimates that these new rules will affect between $50 and $70 billion in annual U.S. exports. See Clifford Krauss, "Export Curbs on Allies: Baker's Hard Choice," *New York Times*, March 6, 1991, p. A-17; and Eduardo Lachica, "US Curbs Sale Abroad of Items Used to Build Arms," *Wall Street Journal*, August 15, 1991, p. A-10. For discussion of German efforts, see Stephen Kinzer, "Germany Says It Seeks to Curb Its Arms Exports," *New York Times*, February 7, 1991.
19. For other recommendations on how the evolution of nonproliferation regimes can be encouraged through informal means, see Chapter 3 by Antonia Handler Chayes and Abram Chayes, "Arms Control in the Middle East."
20. Gilbert R. Winham, "Negotiation as a Management Process," *World Politic*, Vol. 30, No. 1 (October 1977), pp. 87–114.
21. Gerald F. Seib, "Bush Fires Up Critics of Chemical Arms Treaty by Forsaking His Tough Site Inspection Scheme," *Wall Street Journal*, August 15, 1991, p. A-10.
22. One of the more difficult problems with an immediate ban on weapons such as fighter bombers, is that it would freeze certain destabilizing imbalances—countries with large existing air forces would be able to ride out the moratorium far better than countries on the verge of modernizing

or refurbishing depleted forces. Moreover, there is the more intractable problem that one country in the region, Israel, has its own sophisticated aerospace industry. Finally, there is the problem with critical subsystems. Significant increases in capability can come from new avionics suites; a country does not need to buy a whole new aircraft to gain added striking power. Consequently, any moratorium would have to include subsystems as well. This does not make a moratorium impossible, only more difficult to arrange.

23. Geoffrey Kemp, "The Middle East Arms Race: Can It be Controlled?" *Middle East Journal*, Vol. 45, No. 3 (Summer 1991), pp. 450–451.
24. For more on the technological lessons from the Gulf War see William J. Perry's essay in Chapter 10: "Desert Storm and Deterrence in the Future," which is an elaboration of his article "Desert Storm and Deterrence," *Foreign Affairs* Vol. 70, No. 4 (Fall 1991), pp. 66–82.
25. For more on this subject, see the papers by Richard N. Cooper and Charles A. Zraket in Aspen Strategy Group, *Facing the Future: American Strategy in the 1990s* (Lanham, MD: University Press of America, 1991).
26. See Richard Cooper's contribution on the economic lessons of the Gulf crisis in Chapter 6, "Oil, the Middle East, and the World Economy."
27. William J. Taylor, Jr., and James Blackwell, "The Ground War in the Gulf," *Survival* Vol. 33, No. 3 (May/June 1991), p. 245.
28. Carl von Clausewitz, *On War*, transl. and ed. Michael Howard and Peter Paret (Princeton, NJ: Princeton University Press, 1976), pp. 230–232.
29. In Chapter 9: "The Impact of the Persian Gulf War on Military Budgets and Force Structure," Lawrence J. Korb gives a detailed analysis of how the Gulf War has affected the U.S. defense budget and force planning debate.
30. For more on how Bush mobilized the public and boxed the Congress in during the months before Desert Storm, see David Gergen's analysis in Chapter 7: "The Unfettered Presidency."

APPENDICES

Appendix A

THE PERSIAN GULF CRISIS: A CHRONOLOGY OF EVENTS

Joao Resende-Santos

HISTORICAL NOTE

The latest crisis in the Persian Gulf did not emerge full-blown on August 2, 1990. The events of August 2 were a violent culmination of a long-standing historical dispute between Iraq and Kuwait dating back to the early part of the twentieth century. Nor was it the first time that Iraq had invaded neighboring Kuwait. In narrow terms, there are two facets to the Iraq-Kuwait quarrel leading up to the August 2 invasion.

The first facet centers on Iraq's accusations that Kuwait and the United Arab Emirates (UAE) were intentionally producing oil in excess of their Organization of Petroleum Exporting Countries (OPEC) quotas with the explicit purpose of undermining the Iraqi economy. Even prior to Saddam Hussein's July 17 veiled threats and accusations, Iraqi officials had shown growing concern over the consequences of falling oil prices for Iraq's war-devastated and debt-straddled economy. In addition, Iraq also accused Kuwait of "stealing" oil from the Rumaila oil fields, of which over ninety percent lie on the Iraqi side of the border.

The second facet of the Iraq-Kuwait dispute revolves around Iraq's long-standing territorial claims on Kuwait, principally regarding the Bubiyan and Warbah islands, the two uninhabited but strategically located islands controlling access to Umm Qasr, Iraq's only port in the Persian Gulf. While its immediate, preinvasion claims had centered on the islands, after the invasion, Iraq revived historical claims on the whole of Kuwait, which it asserted had formed part of Iraq since the Ottoman Empire.

Territorial claims and counterclaims in the Middle East are not uncommon. Iraq has territorial disputes with all of its immediate neighbors, including Syria, Turkey, and Iran. The most flagrant example of the animosity and violence generated by outstanding territorial dispute (among several other factors) was the bloody and protracted Iran-Iraq War of 1980–88. The territorial dispute between Iraq and Kuwait dates back to the early 1920s when stateless, boundary-less tribal politics on the local level meshed with Great Power politics and competition to divide the moribund Ottoman Empire. The Sykes-Picot agreements of 1916 between Britain and France, and subsequent agreements, did not resolve inter-Arab territorial claims and the ambiguities surrounding tribal boundaries. By 1922 the colonial powers had agreed to the concept of fixed boundaries but failed to resolve the uncertainties surrounding the borders between Iraq, Kuwait, and Saudi Arabia. The boundaries of Iraq had been drawn by the British in 1920, encompassing the three former Ottoman provinces of Basra, Baghdad, and Mosul, becoming independent (albeit British-dominated) in 1932. British-occupied Kuwait is said to have existed as an independent entity since the early 1700s, only nominally controlled by the Ottoman Empire as part of Basra province. On June 19, 1961 Kuwait became a fully independent state, but within weeks Iraqi forces invaded the sheikhdom, claiming full sovereignty over the country. Iraqi leader, Abdel Karim Qassem, announced his intention to annex Kuwait, but British troops, later replaced by an Arab contingency force, quickly returned to Kuwait to deter a consolidation of the invasion. In October 1963, the new Ba'athist Iraqi regime recognized Kuwait as an independent state, thus technically and legally giving up any territorial claims on Kuwait. Yet despite its apparent recognition of Kuwait, Iraq continued to lay claim on Bubiyan island, and in March 1973 Iraqi troops and armored columns moved across the border and occupied the Kuwaiti outpost of As Samitah along the depopulated border. Iraqi forces finally withdrew a year later under pressures from Saudi Arabia and the Arab League, but the historical animosity and disagreements merely subsided with the shifting sands of Middle East politics.

What follows is a chronology of the events leading up to and beyond Iraq's invasion of Kuwait on August 2, 1990. The ordering of events within each date entry does not necessarily imply any chronological ordering.

THE PERSIAN GULF WAR: CHRONOLOGY*

August 1988

- Iran and Iraq agree to a UN-sponsored cease-fire. Kuwait begins to procure advanced weaponry from the United States and France and sends emissaries to both Iran and Iraq as part of its efforts to seek a "balance" in its relations with the two countries.

February 24, 1990

- Saddam Hussein in a speech to the Arab Cooperation Council warned that with the decline of Soviet power, "the Arab Gulf region will be governed by the wishes of the United States." In his speech, Hussesin implied that no "good" Arab would want this and consequently, the Arabs had to look for ways to undermine U.S. influence in the region.

April 2

- Saddam Huessin declares that Iraq possesses binary chemical weapons and that "By God, we will make the fire eat up half of Israel, if it tries to do anything against Iraq."

May 1

- Iraqi oil minister reaffirms need for OPEC member countries to adhere to the established production quotas to maintain oil prices—during extraordinary session of OPEC Ministerial Committee in Geneva. Agreement is reached by 13 oil ministers to collectively cut back production by 1.445 million barrels per day (mbd).

May 2

- Hosni Mubarak visits Syria; the two countries restore relations, signaling the end of Egypt's estrangement from the Arab world.

June 26

- Deputy Prime Minister of Iraq, Sa'dun Hammadi, arrives in Kuwait for talks over oil policy. Hammadi says Iraq spoke out because "the knife has reached the bones after penetrating the flesh." Hammadi delivers message to Kuwaiti emir from Hussein, warning that Iraqi interests are being hurt by excess oil production.

May 30

- During a closed session of the extraordinary Arab League Summit in Baghdad, Hussein says that, "The cause of this confusion is the failure by some of our Arab brothers to abide by the OPEC decisions when they flooded the world market. . . . For every dollar drop in the price of a barrel of oil, our loss amounted to $1 billion annually. . . . War is fought with soldiers and much harm is done . . . but it is also done by economic means. . . . I say to those who do not mean to wage war on Iraq: This is in fact a kind of war against Iraq. . . . We have reached a point where we can no longer withstand the pressure. "Final statements support Iraq's "right to take all necessary measures to guarantee and defend its national security."

July 1

- In response to a question about oil policy during an interview with the *Wall Street Journal,* Hussein calls on producers and consumers to pursue policies that do not harm others. "Who is responsible for this injustice? They are some of the Western states, and some of my friends in the region who do not see beyond their noses."

July 12

- Saudi Arabia secures UAE agreement to observe the OPEC quota of 1.5 mbd and to adhere to the Jiddah resolutions.

July 15

- In a letter sent to Chedli Klibi, the Arab League secretary-general, Iraq's Deputy Prime Minister and Foreign Minister, Tariq Aziz, criticizes "Kuwaiti behavior outside the framework of pan-Arab concepts. . . . Kuwaiti Government officials have encroached on Iraq and systematically, deliberately, and continuously harmed it . . . and tried to weaken it. . . . There are two issues. . . . Since the colonial era . . . an issue has remained in abeyance between Iraq and Kuwait on the demarcation of borders. . . . [Secondly] For many months . . . the Kuwaiti Government began to adopt an unjust policy aimed at harming . . . Iraq. . . . The Governments of Kuwait and the UAE implemented an intentional scheme to glut the oil market . . . [resulting] in grave losses [to Iraq]. . . . In addition to these premeditated abuses, the Kuwaiti Government . . . set up oil installations in the southern section of the Iraqi Rumaila oil field and extracted oil from it . . . [amounting] to $2.4 billion. We put on record . . . that Iraq has every right to retrieve the funds stolen from it. . . . Kuwait has committed aggression against Iraq and its rights by encroaching on our territories and oil fields and by stealing our national wealth. Such behavior amounts to a military aggression."

July 17

- In a speech delivered on the 22nd anniversary of the Iraqi revolution, Hussein denounces the "subversive policy" of "certain rulers of the Gulf states" to wage economic harm on Iraq. He adds that "evildoers" are in the service of the United States, which seeks to undermine Arab interests and dominate the oil market. Hussein threatens to use force. "If words fail to protect Iraqis, something effective must be done to return things to their natural course and to return usurped rights to their owners." Hussein's comments are viewed by observers as part of his recent campaign to impose his will on the region. For thr first time since the Iran-Iraq War, Hussein has threatened to use force against another Arab state.

July 18

- Kuwait denies the Iraqi charges, instead accusing Iraq of violating Kuwaiti territory. In separate official statements, Kuwait calls for an Arab League arbitration panel on border demarcations. Kuwait affirms that part of the Rumaila oil fields belongs to Kuwait and that Iraq is drilling inside Kuwaiti territory.

July 19

- Iraqi National Assembly denounces "conspiracy" against Iraq, saying Kuwait and the UAE are "stabbing [Iraq] in the back with a poisoned dagger." It calls on Iraqis to bring "pressure to bear by all available means on the rulers of Kuwait and the UAE."
- U.S. Defense Secretary Richard B. Cheney says that U.S. commitment to protect Kuwait during the Iran-Iraq War if it is attacked remains in force.

July 19–22

- Mubarak receives Kuwaiti envoy, announces that Egypt will seek to resolve dispute between Iraq and Kuwait. Mubarak says Hussein gave "assurances" Iraq will not attack Kuwait.
- King Fahd of Saudi Arabia telephones both the emir of Kuwait and Saddam Hussein and appeals for conciliation.
- Senior Kuwaiti official says it is premature to call an emergency session of the Gulf Cooperation Council (GCC) in light of Iraqi complaints. Kuwaiti ambassador to the United Nations, Muhammad A. Abu al-Hassan, delivers a message from the emir of Kuwait to UN Secretary-General Javier Perez de Cuellar, explaining the Kuwaiti position in the political crisis with Iraq.

July 24

- The *Washington Post* reports that the Bush administration and Arab sources say that Iraq has moved nearly 30,000 troops along the border with Kuwait over the weekend; troop movements are spotted by Western military attaches. Kuwait is also reported to have moved troops and Soviet-made missiles to the border. Arab diplomats and outside observers regard Iraq's move as a show of force rather than preparation for an invasion.
- Responding to requests from the UAE, the Bush administration, after warning Iraq against the use of coercion and intimidation and calling for a peaceful solution, announces the dispatch of combat ships and aerial refueling planes to the UAE in rare joint exercises following Iraqi threats to use force against the Emirates and Kuwait. Pentagon Spokesperson Peter Williams says the U.S.

"would take very seriously any threat to U.S. interests or U.S. friends in the region."

- Mubarak flies to Iraq, Kuwait, and Saudi Arabia in an effort to defuse tensions.
- Pentagon spokesman declares that the U.S. is determined to defend its "friends in the Gulf" and ensure the free flow of oil.
- Western diplomats in the region report that Iraq has moved two armored divisions of about 30,000 men near the border with Kuwait over the weekend.
- Iraq condemns American-UAE joint exercises as part of the "conspiracy against the Arab nation and against Iraq in particular by U.S. imperialism and Zionism."

July 25

- OPEC meeting in Geneva agrees to raise oil prices. Mubarak says Hussein agreed to a peaceful settlement of the dispute.
- Bush administration officials say that Iraq has bolstered its troops on the Kuwaiti border to over 100,000.
- Kuwait agrees to face-to-face talks with Iraq concerning oil and the border dispute, retreating from earlier position calling for an Arab League arbitration. Senior OPEC officials say Iraq's recent actions are meant simply to intimidate Kuwait and the UAE to lower their production.
- Hussein summons U.S. Ambassador April C. Glaspie to send message to President Bush that "nothing will happen." He tells Glaspie that there was no need for a U.S. military response, adding that dispute with Kuwait was a "family matter." Accounts of the meeting differ. According to Iraq, Glaspie says the U.S. has "no opinion" on inter-Arab disputes, while Glaspie maintains she warned Iraq against using force.
- Arab sources in Cairo disclose that Hussein promised Mubarak during their meeting on 24 July that Iraq will not take any military action against Kuwait but demanded that Kuwait send an official memorandum containing the basis for a settlement before the two countries meet in a summit.
- Mubarak says, "I believe [Saddam Hussein] is interested in resolving this issue and has no intention of attacking Kuwait or any other party."

July 26

- The Bush administration steps up policy review of Iraq and is considering sanctions and export controls. Review began earlier this year in light of evidence that Iraq was accelerating efforts to build chemical and nuclear weapons.

July 27

- OPEC ministers agree to a target price of $21 per barrel, fixing daily output at 22.5 mbd, with expectations that it will rise to $25 in the fourth quarter of the year.
- U.S. Congress votes to impose sanctions on Iraq.

July 30

- Senior Kuwaiti and Iraqi delegations arrive in Jiddah, Saudi Arabia, for talks concerning their border and oil disputes. King Hussein arrives in Kuwait for talks.
- Western diplomats in Kuwait say that Iraq has deployed about 100,000 troops along the border, including 300 tanks and 300 artillery pieces. Observers view latest troop movements as consistent with Hussein's tough negotiating style rather than a sign of imminent invasion.

July 31

- Iraqi and Kuwaiti representatives hold closed session meetings in Jeddah, with King Fadh as mediator for the talks. The Kuwaiti prime minister and crown prince expresses hope for a quick end to the "passing crisis."
- Assistant Secretary of State John H. Kelley tells the House Foreign Affairs Subcommittee on Europe and the Middle East that Iraq has a "very large, significant military force" along Kuwait's border. He says the U.S. will do all it can "to support [its] friends when they are threatened and to preserve stability," but emphasizes that the U.S. has no treaty obligations to any Gulf state.

August 1

- Iraqi-Kuwaiti talks in Jeddah break down after first session. Iraq's Deputy Prime Minister, Sa'dun Hammadi, says, "No agreement has been reached on anything because we have not felt that the Kuwaitis are serious about redressing the grave damage inflicted on Iraq."

August 2

- At around 02:00 hours Thursday morning (Gulf time) Iraqi troops invade Kuwait, reaching Kuwait City within hours after overrunning Kuwait's 20,000-strong army. The Kuwaiti ruling family and government officials flee to Saudi Arabia. Iraqi troops are said to be moving south toward the Kuwaiti oil ports. Despite Kuwait's appeals to its Arab neighbors for assistance, Arab response to invasion is muted and divided.
- Hours after the invasion, the Iraqi Revolutionary Command Council (RCC) announces the invasion of Kuwait, stating that "the sons of dear Kuwait appealed to the Iraqi leadership to provide support

and backing to prevent any possibility by those who may think of foreign interference." The RCC decided to respond to "the request made by Kuwait's free provisional government. . . . We will withdraw when the situation becomes stable."

- Kuwaiti radio broadcast appeals to Kuwaitis to "respond to the homeland's call" and to repel "barbaric invasion"; radio appeals to Arab states and the GCC for military assistance. The radio broadcast appeals to other Arab states and to the United Nations for a military intervention.
- Sa'dun Hammadi, Iraq's deputy prime minister, asserts in Cairo that the crisis is an internal matter and added that the provisional government in Kuwait had requested Iraqi assistance.
- The self-declared "Provisional Free Kuwaiti Government," in a radio broadcast, denounces the "despotic, corrupt family rule." "Tyrannical ruling clique . . . were the servants of the foreigner . . . that contemplate ambitions in Kuwait and the entire region." The statement promises to hold free and fair elections, to protect the rights of foreigners, and to abide by external agreements and financial obligations. The head of the "provisional government" is later disclosed to be Colonel Ala' Hussein 'Ali, formerly Iraq's military attaché to Libya.
- The fifteen terrorists imprisoned in Kuwait since a December 1983 bomb attack on the U.S. and French embassies are reportedly transferred to Baghdad.
- The Arab League Council holds an emergency session in Cairo at the request of Kuwait following the entry of Iraqi forces into Kuwaiti territory. The League adopts a resolution, with Jordan and five other Arab states abstaining, condemning the invasion and requesting immediate withdrawal of Iraqi troops. Hammadi, the Iraqi delegate, terms the resolution "illegal," noting that it did not receive unanimity. Kuwait asks conference for a joint Arab force to protect it from the Iraqi invasion in accordance with the League's defense agreement. Mubarak holds two-hour session with the President of the UAE, Sheik Zayid Ibn-Sultan al Nuhayyan.
- King Hussein of Jordan arrives in Egypt for discussions with Mubarak. During their meeting both presidents received a telephone call from President Bush.
- The UN Security Council, in a three-hour emergency session, condemns the Iraqi invasion and calls for the immediate, unconditional withdrawal of Iraqi forces (Resolution 660). Yemen abstains from voting.

- The U.S., Britain, and France call for the immediate withdrawal of Iraqi forces from Kuwait; three countries freeze Iraqi and Kuwaiti asset, and stop arms deliveries to Iraq.
- Bush administration officials say initially that President Bush is not contemplating military action and that no Arab state, including Saudi Arabia, has yet asked for assistance. After meeting with British prime minister Margaret Thatcher, President Bush declares that the U.S. is not "ruling out any options" and condemns the Iraqi invasion as "naked aggression"; he announces that the United States will impose a near total economic embargo on Iraq. The U.S. freezes $30 billion in Iraqi assets in the country. American and allied governments freeze Kuwaiti assets, estimated at $45–50 billion in the U.S. and $100 billion worldwide, to keep them from falling into Iraqi hands. Congressional leaders call for multilateral sanctions, warning against Iraqi hegemony over the entire region. The carrier battle groups *Independence* and *Eisenhower* are ordered to sail towards the Gulf. Additional U.S. forces are ordered into the region, but administration officials say that a major deployment would take several weeks.
- The Soviet Union, Iraq's major arms supplier, announces the suspension of military sales to Iraq.
- World market oil price reaches $21.50 per barrel.

August 3

- U.S. intelligence reports buildup of 100,000 Iraqi troops south of Kuwait City and near the border with Saudi Arabia. Fresh Iraqi troops are said to be arriving in Kuwait.
- President Bush warns Iraq not to attack Saudi Arabia, declaring that the "integrity of Saudi Arabia" is a "vital interest" to the United States. Bush calls Iraq's occupation of Kuwait "unacceptable," warning that "further expansion" would trigger U.S. military response. He stresses that the U.S. will help any way it can if Saudi Arabia asked. The U.S. steps up naval deployment in the region. Several congressional leaders make blunt warnings to Saddam Hussein against possible attack on Saudi Arabia. The House and Senate vote unanimously to impose trade sanctions and cut off credits to Iraq. The Senate approves a resolution calling for collective military action under UN auspices to restore international security. The United States begins to press for multilateral sanctions against Iraq through the United Nations. While expressing concerns that the Arab states may agree to a compromise with Iraq, Bush hints that the U.S. will try to get Iraq's oil pipelines in Turkey and Saudi Arabia closed.

- President Mubarak of Egypt, stressing that "Arab leaders are capable of finding a solution to this problem without any foreign interference," asks President Bush to halt any plans for an American military intervention, stressing the need to keep the crisis from being internationalized.
- Secretary of State James A. Baker III and Soviet Foreign Minister Eduard Shevardnadze, in an unprecedented joint statement, call on the world community to impose an arms embargo on Iraq. The joint American-Soviet statement warns of "very serious consequences" if Iraq did not withdraw its forces immediately.
- The European Community (EC) imposes an immediate oil and arms embargo, warning that if Iraq does not withdraw, it will press for comprehensive, mandatory sanctions.
- Fourteen of the 21-member Arab League, meeting in Cairo, finally endorse a resolution condemning the Iraqi invasion, and call for an immediate withdrawal. The resolution is opposed by six members, including Jordan, Yemen, Libya, and the Palestine Liberation Organization (PLO). King Hussein announces that a special Arab summit would be held on August 5 in Saudi Arabia; he leaves for Iraq to meet with Saddam Hussein.
- Iraq announces that its troops will withdraw from Kuwait on August 5.
- Kuwait's ambassador to Britain appeals to the international community for "any aid they can give."
- The Gulf Cooperation Council (GCC), in emergency meeting, condemns "the Iraqi aggression" and calls for unconditional withdrawal.
- The ruling Ba'ath Party of Iraq applauds "the glorious national uprising in Kuwait." Baghdad radio warns that Iraq will make the Persian Gulf "a graveyard for all those who think of committing aggression, starting with these cowardly American navies."
- Israeli Defense Minister, Moshe Arens, warns that if Iraqi forces enter Jordanian territory, Israel will view it as a *casus belli.* Foreign Minister David Levi and other Israeli officials accuse Iraq of seeking to dominate the Middle East and compare Hussein to Hitler.
- Crude oil prices rise to $23 per barrel.

August 4

- The Kuwaiti emir, Sheikh Jabir al-Ahmad al-Sabah, announces that no negotiations are possible until after Iraqi forces are withdrawn from Kuwait.
- Iraqi troops are reported to have been deployed in the oil-rich Kuwaiti-administered "neutral zone," four miles from the Saudi

border. Iraqi officials deny reports of troops approaching the Saudi border.

- The Arab League extraordinary summit, scheduled for August 5, is canceled amidst apparent divisions among Arab leaders.

August 5

- The "Provisional Free Government" of Kuwait warns outside countries "to remember that they have interests and nationals in Kuwait" if they decide to resort to "punitive measures."
- Saudi forces are put on full alert; reservists are called.
- President Bush dispatches Defense Secretary Dick Cheney to Saudi Arabia to procure air and naval installations for American forces if the need to respond militarily arises. Bush, declaring that Iraq's invasion "will not stand," says that Saddam Hussein "lied" about withdrawing troops from Kuwait, stating that intelligence reports show additional troops entering Kuwait.
- EC senior officials agree to ban oil imports and arms sales to Iraq. Japan, under pressures from the Bush administration, imposes an immediate ban on Iraqi oil imports and a general economic embargo. China announces an arms embargo on Iraq.
- King Hussein of Jordan, stressing that Jordan's refusal to condemn Iraq is based on an attempt to act as a neutral mediator, claims that the Iraqi invasion was "redrawing the boundaries between the haves and the have-nots."
- A flotilla of American, French, and British naval vessels takes up position in the Mediterranean, Arabian, and Red seas in preparation to impose a possible blockade. U.S. special forces teams are said to be assembling in the region for possible assault missions and hostage rescues.

August 6

- The United Nations Security Council, in a 13-0 binding resolution (Resolution 661), with Cuba and Yemen abstaining, votes to impose mandatory economic sanctions on Iraq.
- King Fahd of Saudi Arabia, after meeting with Defense Secretary Cheney, requests U.S. military protection.
- President Bush orders U.S. forces ("Operation Desert Shield") to Saudi Arabia and Gulf region.
- Saddam Hussein warns that if Saudi Arabia shuts down the Iraqi oil pipeline running through its territory that it will attack the kingdom.
- Several hundred Westerners are forcibly taken from Kuwait and bused to Baghdad.
- Iraq shuts down its two oil pipelines through Turkey.
- Saudi troops are reportedly entering the so-called "neutral zone,"

a buffer zone along the Saudi, Iraqi, and Kuwaiti borders. Iraqi troops are said to be within ten miles of the Saudi border. An estimated 2,000 American military personnel and four AWACS radar planes are in the kingdom.

- The Iraqi ambassador to France warns that France's decision to impose comprehensive economic sanctions will hurt France's "huge interests" in Iraq.
- The United States and Egypt quietly begin preparations for an American airlift of Egyptian forces to Saudi Arabia if requested. The Bush administration, with British support, begins considering options for a multilateral naval force to impose a blockade. A second American aircraft carrier battle group is ordered into the region. The Soviet Union, France, and Britain have ordered additional naval units into the area.
- Iraq is said to have redeployed 70,000 troops from the Iranian border into Kuwait.
- Administration and congressional members criticize the sharp rise in domestic gasoline prices, as oil prices of the world market reach a five-year high of $28.05 per barrel.

August 7

- With the approval of King Fahd, the Bush administration, warning that Saudi Arabia faced an "imminent threat" from the "offensive posture" of Iraqi troops massed along the border, begins deployment of aircraft and troops to Saudi Arabia as part of a multinational force to defend the kingdom.
- Egypt becomes the first Arab state to agree to join the multinational force; the administration approaches Morocco and Pakistan to take part in the coalition.
- Les Aspin (D-Wis.), chairman of the House Armed Services Committee, Sam Nunn (D-Ga.), and other congressional leaders declare support for troop deployment.
- Saddam Hussein vows to "pluck out the eyes" of anyone who attacks Iraq, arguing that invasion was designed to correct the flawed regional borders drawn by the colonial powers.
- The U.S. orders nonessential embassy personnel in Iraq and Kuwait to evacuate. The State Department is investigating reports that 28 Americans, among some 200 other foreigners, were rounded up by Iraqi troops in Kuwait and taken to Baghdad.
- The GCC holds an extraordinary session in Jeddah and condemns Iraq's invasion, calling for its immediate withdrawal.
- Cheney arrives in Egypt for consultations with Mubarak, reportedly requesting the use of Egyptian military facilities. Mubarak

rejects Cheney's request, stating that Egypt opposes any foreign intervention in the crisis.

- A day after Baker arrived for consultations with President Turgut Ozal, Turkey announces an economic embargo on Iraq and shuts down Iraqi pipelines.

August 8

- Declaring that a "line has been drawn in the sand," Bush announces that the deployment of U.S. forces to Saudi Arabia is to defend the kingdom from a possible Iraqi attack; the mission is "wholly defensive." Bush adds that "our overall objective is to see Saddam Hussein get out . . . and to have the rightful regime of Kuwait back in place." He compares Hussein to Hitler. Congressional leaders support the president's decision to send troops. The U.S. deployment is expected to exceed 50,000 troops, the largest deployment since Vietnam. American officials warn of severe consequences if Iraq uses chemical weapons.
- Iraq, which now has an estimated 200,000 troops inside Kuwait, announces the annexation of Kuwait, which it now calls the "19th Province." Saddam Hussein says that the "eternal merger . . . will be the pride of the Arabs."
- Mubarak, proposing an Arab "umbrella" force to facilitate an Iraqi withdrawal, calls for an Arab summit in a last-minute effort to find an Arab solution to the crisis and calls for an Arab security force to supervise the withdrawal of Iraqi troops.
- The U.S. begins diplomatic contacts with Syria and Iran to coordinate efforts to impose the UN sanctions.
- Britain sends air and naval units to Gulf at the request of Saudi Arabia.
- In a 15-0 vote, the UN Security Council declares the annexation of Kuwait "null and void" (Resolution 662). Soviet foreign ministry spokesman says that if the Security Council approves of collective military action, the Soviet Union, which has an estimated 8,000 citizens in Iraq, will comply.
- Pentagon sources say that Iraq is deepening its defensive position in Kuwait, including the introduction of surface-to-air missile systems.
- The initial wave of American forces dispatched to Saudi Arabia begins arriving, including a brigade of the 82nd Airborne Division and two squadrons of F-15 combat aircraft.
- Baker meets with Turkish president Ozal to obtain permission to use military facilities in Turkey, and promises U.S. protection in the event of an Iraqi attack.

- Iraq seals its borders and prevents the departure of foreigners.
- Israel tests an air defense missile, as Prime Minister Yitzhak Shamir warns that Saddam Hussein courts "disaster" if he attacks Israel.
- France announces dispatch of ground forces and additional naval units to Saudi Arabia. Britain sends additional air and naval forces to join the multinational force but announces it will not be sending ground forces.
- Arab summit is postponed until 10 August, as Iraqi delegation arrives unexpectedly and demands to represent Kuwait. Jordan announces that it will comply with the UN sanctions.
- Reports surface of Kuwaiti underground resistance against Iraqi troops.
- Saddam Hussein meets with Yasser Arafat. Government sources announce that borders, closed since August 2, will be open for Arabs who want to leave Iraq but will remain closed to Americans and Europeans.
- The Iraqi ambassador to Greece declares that Iraq will use chemical weapons if it is attacked by the United States or Israel.
- The Iraqi foreign ministry orders all diplomatic missions in Kuwait City closed by 24 August.
- Israeli prime minister Shamir declares that Israel is "ready" in the event of an Iraqi attack. Foreign Minister David Levi warns that any Iraqi destabilization or attempts to cross Jordanian border would be regarded as a threat and that Israel will "take necessary actions."
- King Fahd of Saudi Arabia calls Iraqi invasion "the most vile aggression known to the Arab nation" and demands the withdrawal of Iraqi forces and the restoration of the *status quo ante.*

August 10

- Emergency Arab summit opens in chaotic closed session in Cairo, attended by both the Iraqi and Kuwaiti delegations. Iraq insists that the summit should focus on the subject of foreign intervention in the region. Arab leaders, in a 12-9 majority decision of the 21-member League, agree to send an Arab military force to Saudi Arabia and other Gulf states. Libya, Iraq, and the PLO oppose the resolution, and Jordan votes in favor but with "reservations."
- Saddam Hussein calls for a "holy war" to "burn the soil under the feet of the aggressors and invaders."
- NATO foreign ministers unanimously endorse the deployment of U.S. forces to defend Saudi Arabia but disapprove of a joint NATO military action.
- Egyptian and Moroccan troops begin arriving in Saudi Arabia, with each country planning to send approximately 5,000 troops.

Jordan announces it will not send troops unless U.S. forces withdraw.

August 12

- Bush orders American naval units to block shipping in and out of Iraq.
- Saddam Hussein offers to withdraw from Kuwait on condition that: 1) Israel withdraws from the "occupied territories" and Syria withdraws from Lebanon. Afterwards negotiations are to take place over the status of Kuwait on the basis of Iraq's "historical rights", 2) American and allied forces withdraw immediately from the region, and 3) all sanctions and boycotts against Iraq are terminated.
- The Bush administration immediately rejects Hussein's withdrawal offer, rejecting any linkage between issues.
- Israeli prime minister Shamir terms Saddam Hussein's offer "cheap propaganda."

August 13

- Iraq has reportedly transferred $3–4 billion in gold, foreign currencies, and goods seized in Kuwait to Iraq.
- An estimated 500 Americans have fled to Saudi border.
- Administration officials warn that if Jordan allows Iraq to use the Jordanian port of 'Aqaba to break UN sanctions, U.S. forces will blockade the port.
- Pakistan announces that it will send troops to join the multinational force in Saudi Arabia. More than 10,000 American troops have reached the Gulf.
- King Hussein, after meeting with Saddam Hussein, accuses the U.S. of causing an "explosive situation" in the region by intervening. He says deployment of U.S. forces is part of "foreign ambitions" to take control of "Arab wealth."
- Iraqi officials suggest that Westerners trapped in Iraq and Kuwait, including 3,000 Americans and 5,000 Britons, will not be allowed to leave until the crisis is over.

August 14

- King Hussein arrives in the U.S. for talks with Bush, who warns that the U.S. will blockade the port of 'Aqaba if Jordan allows Iraqi goods to pass. Administration officials announce that the U.S. is asking West European states and Japan for financial contributions to Jordan and Syria to offset losses from the invasion.
- In a letter to Iranian president Ali Akbar Hashemi-Rafsanjani, Saddam Hussein offers to concede to Iranian terms for a peace treaty, including the withdrawal of Iraqi troops from the Iranian border. Hussein agrees to Iranian demands regarding the 1975 Algiers accord, prisoner exchanges, and troop withdrawal, stating

that "everything you wanted and concentrated upon has been realized." The Bush administration expresses concern that Iran-Iraq rapprochement may undermine the UN sanctions.

- Bush says that an Iraqi attack on Saudi Arabia threatens "our way of life."
- Iraqi foreign minister Aziz calls the detention of Americans and other foreign nationals a "temporary precautionary measure"; he accuses the U.S. of wanting to "dominate" the region.

August 16

- After meeting with King Hussein, President Bush is unable to receive assurances that Jordan will close port of 'Aqaba to Iraqi shipping.
- Pentagon officials disclose that an estimated 160,000 Iraqi troops are massed in and around Kuwait.
- A naval quarantine of Iraq begins after commercial shippers are formally notified.
- Saddam Hussein calls Bush a "liar," warning that thousands of American troops will "go home shrouded in sad coffins." He added that there is "no turning back."

August 17

- Bush announces call up of limited numbers of reservists.
- Iraqi official says that nationals from "aggressive nations" will not be permitted to leave Iraq. It is also announced that foreign nationals will be scattered around military and industrial installations to act as human shields. Officials also warn that Iraq will consider an increase in oil output by any OPEC member as an act of war.
- American naval units detain Iraqi vessels in the Gulf.
- Thirty-five Americans are taken under armed guard from a Baghdad hotel and detained in another hotel.

August 18

- Iraq declares the U.S.-led naval quarantine an "act of war" and warns that foreign nationals held captive in Iraq and Kuwait will suffer from food shortages.
- Saudi Arabia announces unilateral increase in oil output by 2 mbd, bringing its average daily output to 7.5 mbd.

August 19

- Saddam Hussein announces that Iraq will release all foreign nationals in exchange for a complete withdrawal of the U.S.-led multinational force.
- Iraqi authorities in Kuwait order the 9,000 Western nationals trapped in the country to gather at designated hotels. British, American, and other Western nationals are rounded up and taken to undisclosed locations.

August 20

- More than 200,000 Kuwaitis are said to have taken refuge in Saudi Arabia and other Gulf states.
- Defense Secretary Cheney, on five-nation tour in the Gulf, announces that the UAE has agreed to allow the U.S. to station troops. President Bush says the U.S. holds Iraq responsible for the safety of Western "hostages."

August 21

- In response to the latest Iraqi offers for negotiations, administration officials state that no talks are possible until Iraq unconditionally withdraws from Kuwait.
- Administration officials announce possible call up of 40,000 additional reservists.
- Saddam Hussein warns that if the U.S. attacks, "a grave disaster would take place, not only regarding the region, but the whole world." Aziz arrives in Jordan to present Iraqi negotiations proposals.

August 22

- Japan announces that it will provide billions of dollars in financial and technical aid to Middle Eastern countries hurt by the blockade.
- In the face of an intensifying flood of Asian and Arab refugees, Jordan announces the closure of its borders.
- Saudi Arabia begins to supply American forces with jet and diesel fuel, giving fuel free of charge to foreign forces. In addition, it begins to supply the multinational force with water and food. World market oil price is over $31 per barrel
- Iraq announces that France and Japan will be allowed to evacuate some of their nationals, estimated at 560 and 731 respectively.

August 23

- Saddam Hussein holds a televised meeting with British hostages.
- Baghdad warns that if the U.S. and other countries do not close their embassies in Kuwait Baghdad will treat it as "act of aggression."

August 24

- President Gorbachev warns Iraq of "appropriate additional" UN measures if its forces do not comply with UN demands. During the past week the Soviet Union has been at the center of a diplomatic surge to resolve the crisis.
- Iraqi troops surround remaining foreign missions in Kuwait, cutting off water and electricity to some.

August 25

- The UN Security Council approves Resolution 665, allowing for "measures commensurate to the specific circumstances" to enforce the economic embargo by a 13-0 vote, with Yemen and Cuba abstaining.

- Iraq cuts off water and electricity to American embassy in Kuwait; announces the release of diplomatic dependents in Kuwait but not the diplomats themselves.

August 26

- American officials say that while economic embargo is beginning to have an impact, a decisive impact is unlikely within months.
- Iraq releases 53 American diplomatic dependents and detains 3 at the Turkish border.

August 27

- Signs of congressional unease over Bush's Gulf policy begin to surface. Les Aspin and other Democratic leaders caution that Bush does not have a mandate to take military action. Nunn says that more Arab participation in the multinational force is needed.
- Bush reiterates there is "no flexibility" on U.S. demands regarding the crisis.
- Three dozen staff members of the Iraqi embassy in Washington are expelled.
- The price of oil drops to $26.91 per barrel.

August 28

- Saddam Hussein announces the release of all foreign women and children in Iraq and Kuwait. An estimated 11,000 Westerners are still trapped in the two countries. He challenges George Bush and Margaret Thatcher to a debate.
- The Bush administration announces plans to sell Saudi Arabia $6 billion of advanced weaponry in an emergency package, waiving a congressional limit on the sale of arms to the kingdom.

August 29

- OPEC agrees to increase oil output by 4 mbd.
- Despite promises to release Western women and children, Iraq demands that each hostage must obtain an exit visa.

August 30

- Bush asks allies to "bear their fair share" of the costs of deploying the multinational force and imposing economic sanctions.
- Iraq places new requirements on the release of women and children, demanding that they submit letters requesting permission to leave, accompanied by an Arabic translation, and proof that local taxes have been paid.
- Prime Minister Thatcher criticizes European states for their limited contributions to the multilateral effort in the Gulf, adding that "it's not what you say that counts but what you do. . . . We cannot expect the United States to go on bearing major military and defense" responsibilities.

- The Soviet Union criticizes the U.S. military buildup in the region. The Soviet deputy foreign minister adds that "the buildup of American military cannot please us. . . . The situation is becoming more explosive. . . . There are no guarantees that the United States will leave after the crisis is over."
- Iraq announces that "all foreign men, nationals of countries involved in the brutal American blockade against Iraq, are being relocated at vital installations around the country."

August 31

- Arab League foreign ministers meeting in Cairo harden anti-Iraqi position with a majority resolution demanding that Iraq pay war reparations. Divisions within the League deepen, however.
- The commander of American forces in the Gulf, General H. Norman Schwarzkopf, declares that no offensive military actions will be taken unless Iraq launches an attack first.

September 1

- The Arab Foreign Ministers Council, meeting in Cairo, issues resolutions calling for troop withdrawals, an end to human rights abuses inside Kuwait, an Arab solution to the problem, and the release of foreign nationals. Resolutions emphasize the legality of foreign diplomatic missions in Kuwait.
- Iraq finally releases 750 foreign women and children held captive in Iraq and Kuwait, including 210 Americans and more than 200 Britons. The evacuation of foreigners continues over the next several days.

September 2

- Iraqi officials announce partial rationing of food purchases.
- Perez de Cuellar says that he was "disappointed" by Iraq's unwillingness to make concessions regarding withdrawal and the release of foreign nationals.

September 3

- More than 350,000 refugees, mainly Arabs and Asians fleeing Kuwait, are said to have crossed the border into Jordan, where at least 130,000, mainly Asians, continue to encamp.
- Following the recent visit by Secretary Cheney, Bahrain, the UAE, Qatar, and Oman grant the U.S. permission to deploy combat aircraft in their territory.

September 4

- The Kuwaiti "prime minister" installed by Iraq, has reportedly been executed.
- President Bush formally announces cancellation of Egypt's debt to the U.S.

- Foreign Minister Schevardnadze calls for an international conference to be convened to discuss the "interlocking" problems of the Middle East.

September 5

- Saddam Hussein calls for a holy war against Saudi Arabia and the American and foreign forces in the region, adding that "many heads will roll." "We are duty-bound to engage in holy *jihad* so that we can liberate the two holy mosques from . . . the invading armies that have occupied and desecrated the land housing the sacred places of Muslims and Arabs."
- Aziz meets with Gorbachev in Moscow, days before a scheduled Bush-Gorbachev summit meeting.
- Bush tells congressional members that if economic sanctions fail to force an Iraqi withdrawal, the U.S. "will review options."
- The Soviet Union and Japan issue a rare joint statement condemning Iraq.
- Israeli foreign minister Levi meets with Baker in Washington, the first high level U.S.-Israeli meeting since the invasion.

September 6

- Soviet special envoy, Yevgeny Primakov, arrives in Baghdad for talks with Saddam Hussein.
- Saudi Arabia announces that it will finance the operating costs of American forces in the region, estimated at $1.5 billion per month and that it will provide several billion dollars in aid to regional countries that have joined the multinational coalition.
- Iran, India, and several other countries announce that they may send food and medicine to Iraq as humanitarian relief.
- François Mitterrand criticizes the Soviet proposal for an international conference on the Middle East, arguing that a conference "cannot substitute the decisions of the United Nations. After the liberation of Kuwait, we can examine its usefulness."

September 7

- The Emir of Kuwait, Sheikh Jabir al-Ahmad al-Sabah, announces that the Kuwaiti government-in-exile will contribute $2.5 billion dollars to the operating cost of American forces in the Gulf, with an additional $2.5 billion in aid to regional countries hurt by the embargo.
- The EC announces that it will give economic aid to countries hurt by the international embargo but that no contributions will be made for the operating expenses of American forces.
- The first large group of American women and children arrive in Jordan from Kuwait. An estimated 2,000 American men and

women are said to be in Kuwait. The State Department discloses that more than 90 American men are in detention.

September 8–9

- After meeting with Baker, President Mubarak announces that Egypt will send additional troops to Saudi Arabia, where 2,000 Egyptian troops are already deployed. Mubarak says that Iraq's chemical and missile arsenals will pose a threat to the region if it is allowed to keep them after it withdraws from Kuwait.
- In a letter addressed to presidents Bush and Gorbachev on the eve of the Helsinki summit, Saddam Hussein warns that "all invaders will be defeated"; he reiterates Iraqi position that Kuwait was a part of Iraq and that attempts to restore the *status quo ante* are "futile." Aziz leaves on an official visit to Iran.

September 9

- Presidents Bush and Gorbachev release a joint summit statement pledging to work individually and in concert to force Iraq's acceptance of the UN resolutions. "Our preference is to resolve the crisis peacefully.... However, we are determined to see this aggression end . . . and we are prepared to consider additional [measures] consistent with the UN Charter." Differences remain between the two countries over the use of military force, Soviet participation in policing the embargo, and a proposed international conference linking the different issues of the region. Gorbachev makes explicit his opposition to the use of force. Bush promises that U.S. forces will withdraw once regional security has been assured. Bush also agrees to accept Soviet participation in Middle East peace efforts, reversing long-standing U.S. policy.

September 10–11

- Saddam Hussein offers free oil to Third World countries that break with the UN sanctions.
- Reports from Kuwait indicate intensified underground resistance activities. Kuwaiti military commanders hint that the remnants of the armed forces have joined the resistance.
- Iran and Iraq announce resumption of full diplomatic ties amidst reports that Iraq is asking Iran to help it circumvent UN sanctions.

September 11

- In an address before a joint session of Congress, President Bush reaffirms U.S. commitment to roll back Iraq's occupation of Kuwait, threatening to use force to achieve this objective if necessary. Bush says that the world and the U.S. "will not be blackmailed" by Iraq and that "Saddam Hussein will fail."

- Congressional leaders harden their criticism of inadequate European and Japanese contributions to the multinational coalition.

September 13

- The Security Council approves provisions regarding limits of humanitarian food supplies sent to Iraq in a 13–0 vote, with Cuba and Yemen abstaining.
- The U.S. warns that it will hold Iraq responsible for any terrorist acts committed against American forces or interests in the Gulf.
- Syria announces that it will dispatch an additional 10,000 troops and 300 battle tanks to the Gulf to join the 4,000-strong Syrian deployment already there.
- Japan announces an additional $3 billion in financial assistance to the Gulf region.

September 14

- American and Australian warships fire warning shots at an Iraqi tanker and forcibly board the ship for inspection.
- France announces that Iraqi troops stormed the French ambassador's residence in Kuwait, seizing four French nationals. Iraqi troops also break into the Belgian diplomatic compound and the Canadian ambassador's residence, where they seize but later release the American, Canadian, British, and Irish consuls.
- Baker meets with Hafiz al-Assad, president of Syria, who assures Baker that Syria will send additional forces to the Gulf. Baker says that "we share a common purpose with respect to the problems in the gulf, but we make no secret about the fact that there are still problems revolving around this question of terrorism."
- West Germany announces that it will provide an additional $2 billion in economic aid as well as transport planes and ships to the multinational force.

September 15

- Mitterrand announces that France will send 4,000 more troops and additional equipment to the Gulf. He calls for the UN to extend the embargo on Iraq to include air traffic.

September 16–17

- In a videotaped broadcast over Iraqi television, Bush warns Iraqis that Saddam Hussein is putting them on the "brink of war," adding that "there is no way Iraq can win."
- General Michael J. Dugan, the Air Force chief of staff, is dismissed following his suggestions that the only effective way to dislodge Iraq from Kuwait was heavy bombing of Baghdad to "decapacitate" the Iraqi leadership.

- A conference of Arab and Palestinian radicals in Amman, Jordan warns that it will "strike against American interests everywhere."

September 18–19

- King Hassan II, King Hussein, and President Chadli Bendjedid of Algeria gather in Rabat, Morocco for a mini-summit on the Gulf Crisis.
- Senior Iraqi officials warn that Iraq will strike at American interests anywhere in the world if it is attacked by the United States and that Iraq will destroy all the oil wells in the region.

September 20–21

- Administration officials disclose their opposition to the latest peace proposals put forth by King Hussein, calling for the simultaneous withdrawal of non-Arab forces from Saudi Arabia and an Iraqi withdrawal from Kuwait.
- Iraq expels American, West European, and Egyptian attachés and diplomatic personnel. An RCC statement read on Iraqi television declares that "there is not a single chance of retreat."

September 23

- Saddam Hussein warns that Iraq will attack the Saudi oil fields, other Arab countries, and Israel if Iraq is "strangled" by the UN sanctions. "We will turn the whole area, including the oil fields, into flames."

September 24–25

- In a speech before the UN General Assembly, Mitterrand suggests that an Iraqi withdrawal will help the settlement of other Middle East disputes.
- The Security Council adopts a resolution by a 14-1 vote, with Cuba in opposition, to impose an air embargo on Iraq. Shevardnadze warns Iraq that the UN has the legal power to "suppress acts of aggression."
- Bush announces the creation of the Gulf Crisis Financial Coordination Group, headed by Treasury Secretary Nicholas F. Brady, to coordinate multilateral aid to nations hurt by the embargo on Iraq.
- The Pentagon accuses the Soviet Union of having 500–1,000 military personnel in Iraq, charging that some are providing technical services.
- World oil price rises to $38.25 per barrel.

September 26

- Baker tells Israeli foreign minister Levi that the U.S. "remains committed to Israel's security" if it is attacked by Iraq.
- The House Foreign Affairs Committee approves a resolution endorsing Bush's handling of the Gulf crisis but warns against taking offensive military actions.

September 28

- National Security Adviser Brent Scowcroft warns that the "systematic destruction" of Kuwait shortens the time the U.S. can wait for sanctions to force Iraq to pull out.

October 1

- In an address before the UN General Assembly, Bush expresses hopes for a peaceful resolution of the Gulf crisis, adding that an Iraqi withdrawal may help "settle the conflicts that divide the Arabs from Israel."

October 5

- Soviet envoy Primakov meets with Saddam Hussein and urges him to pull out of Kuwait.

October 7

- Despite an initial reluctance, Israel begins nationwide distribution of gas masks and emergency kits in the wake of mounting fears of an Iraqi chemical attack. Kits are not to be distributed to 1.7 million Palestinians in the West Bank and Gaza Strip.

October 8

- Egyptian and Syrian military commanders in Saudi Arabia declare that their troops will not be taking part in any offensive action against Iraq but are in Saudi Arabia only to defend the Kingdom.
- Iranian president Rafsanjani warns exiled Kuwaiti leaders against any possible concessions toward Iraq that involve the transfer of Bubiyan and Warbah islands, which control access to the Shatt al Arab waterway at the head of the Persian Gulf.

October 12

- Rifaat al-Mahgoub, the Speaker of the Egyptian Parliament and loyal supporter of Mubarak, is assassinated by unidentified gunmen in Cairo.
- West Germany and Belgium announce the closure of their embassies in Kuwait. The United States, Canada, Britain, and France are the only Western countries to keep skeletal missions open despite Iraqi order of August 24.

October 13

- King Hassan II of Morocco asserts that a "moral linkage" between the Gulf crisis and the Palestinian-Israeli issue exists.
- Promising to restore the 1962 constitution, the rulers of Kuwait hint of possible political liberalizations during a gathering of Kuwaiti officials and citizens in Jeddah.

October 14

- A Soviet news agency reports that Saddam Hussein hinted that Iraq might withdraw from most of Kuwait in exchange for Bubiyan and Warbah islands. Special envoy Primakov reportedly tells Hussein that the Soviet Union would not stop a U.S. military attack against Iraq.

October 16

- In response to recent Iraqi probings for a compromise, Secretary of State Baker rejects Saddam Hussein's offer for a settlement. Baker says that the U.S. will not accept "partial solutions."
- The Japanese cabinet approves a plan to send 1,000 non-combatant Japanese troops to the Persian Gulf, marking the first foreign military venture since World War II. The plan provokes widespread domestic opposition and raises regional concerns.

October 17

- Members of the U.S. Senate Foreign Relations Committee demand that Bush obtain congressional approval before initiating any military action. During a committee hearing, Baker agrees only to consultation.

October 18

- Yevgeny Primakov, senior aide to Gorbachev, meets with Baker and National Security Adviser Scowcroft.

October 19

- The Iraqi oil minister announces gasoline rationing as a result of a shortage of refinery chemicals caused by the UN sanctions.
- The Pentagon announces that 400–500 top battle tanks, the M-1A1, stationed in Europe will be redeployed to the Gulf. The new tanks will raise the total number of American tanks to over 1,000. Iraq is estimated to have over 3,500 in Kuwait and southern Iraq. U.S. troop strength reaches over 200,000; Arab coalition troop strength at about 80,000.
- Amidst rumors that the Soviet envoy is carrying negotiations proposals from Saddam Hussein, President Bush meets with Primakov but says that the U.S. will not accept partial solutions.

October 21

- Former British prime minister, Edward Heath, on a private mission to seek the release of British citizens held in Iraq, meets with Saddam Hussein, who agrees to release an unspecified number of Britons. An estimated 8,000 male Westerners, primarily Americans, British, French, Japanese, and Italians, are still being held captive in Iraq.

October 22

- The defense minister of Saudi Arabia, Prince Sultan ibn Abdel-Aziz, the third ranking official in the country, hints at the possibility of a settlement that would allow Iraq to withdraw in exchange for some Kuwaiti territory and Saudi financial compensation. The minister's comment causes an immediate political fallout and Saudi efforts at damage control. The Saudi ambassador to the United States, Prince Bandar bin Sultan, declares that Saudi Arabia has not changed its position on the crisis.

- Saddam Hussein announces the possibility of releasing all 300 French hostages and a number of sick and elderly Americans, following French suggestions that a settlement to the crisis could lead to a settlement of the Israeli-Palestinian issue, a linkage opposed by the U.S.

October 23

- Bush, again comparing Saddam Hussein to Hitler, reaffirms that "there can never be compromise with this kind of aggression."

October 24

- Congressional leaders announce that they reserve the right to reconvene Congress should Bush decide to initiate military action in the Gulf while Congress is in recess.
- Saddam Hussein orders the release of all 327 French hostages in Iraq and Kuwait. France, with 13,000 troops and several warships deployed in the Gulf, has the second largest foreign military presence in the area.
- Primakov arrives in Cairo for talks with Mubarak.

October 25

- The Bush administration announces its intention to send an additional 100,000 troops to Saudi Arabia.
- The Congress approves Bush's request to forgive Egypt's $7.5 billion in military debt to the U.S.

October 27

- Soviet special envoy Primakov arrives in Baghdad, after stops in Egypt and Syria, for talks with Aziz and Saddam Hussein. In hopes of securing a settlement with Hussein, the Soviet Union asks for a vote delay on the Security Council calling for the collection of evidence of Iraqi war crimes, among other things.
- While hinting that Iraq may be reconsidering its refusal to withdraw from Kuwait, Mikhail Gorbachev warns that Saddam Hussein should not interpret initiatives to seek a settlement as a sign of weakness nor a split in the multilateral coalition lined up against him.
- The GCC Secretary-General says that if Iraq does not withdraw voluntarily, it will be forced to do so; "Kuwait in the end will be liberated, either through diplomacy or military means."

October 28

- Saddam Hussein reverses earlier decision to ration fuel, stating that the oil minister (who is dismissed) had miscalculated supplies.

- Presidents Gorbachev and François Mitterrand of France meet in Paris to discuss proposals to end the Gulf crisis, amidst speculations that France and the Soviet Union are considering a joint initiative to resolve the crisis.

October 29

- The Security Council approves the so-called "war crimes" resolution (Resolution 674) allowing for the seizure of impounded Iraqi assets, declaring Iraq responsible for personal and property damages caused by its invasion and occupation of Kuwait. The resolution asks member states to prepare a list of claims for financial compensation and evidence of human rights abuses by Iraqi forces. With Cuba and Yemen abstaining from voting, the resolution warns of "further measures" if Iraq does not comply with its demands, although no explicit mention is made of the use of military force.
- British officials, including Foreign Secretary Douglas Hurd, express concerns that the continued buildup of forces without the possibility of an immediate military action may undermine the credibility of the multinational force. Britain has 15,000 troops in the Gulf.
- Kuwait's ambassador to Britain accuses Iraq of torture and systematic atrocities against Kuwaiti civilians.
- Iraq's Deputy Prime Minister Ramadam says Iraq will not be the only battle zone but will include Israel.
- Prime Minister Shamir says if Iraq attacks Israel, it will pay a "terrible price"; he says Israel will not be dragged into the conflict.

October 30

- Ten American soldiers are killed aboard the assault ship *Iwo Jima* when a steam valve erupts. A marine is killed in a separate vehicle accident. Total American deaths rises to 43.
- Congressional leaders urge Bush to move slowly when considering any military action. After meeting with Bush, Senator William S. Cohen (R-Me.), vice chairman of the Senate Select Committee on Intelligence, states that there is "no impression we're moving closer to war," but that Bush's patience is growing thin.
- Saddam Hussein puts Iraqi forces on "extreme alert," warning country of imminent U.S. attack. He tells Iraqi generals to prepare for urban fighting. Hussein's actions come after recent announcements by Bush and Baker that military force may be used to remove Iraq from Kuwait, with Baker stating that the U.S. cannot "rule out a possible use of force if Iraq continues to occupy Kuwait."

October 31

- Bush warns that he has "had it" with Iraq's treatment of American hostages and dependents. Top administration officials have been increasingly stressing the hostage issue in their escalated verbal war against Iraq.
- In an interview with CNN, Saddam Hussein says Iraq will not be forced to pull out of Kuwait by the economic sanctions.
- Kuwaiti prime minister says Warbah and Bubyian islands and the Rumaila oil fields are "not subject to bargaining."

November 1

- General H. Norman Schwarzkopf cautions that the total destruction of Iraq's military may not be in the long term interests of the United States and that a regional power balance must be maintained after the crisis is resolved. He also recommends that troops be rotated every six to eight months.
- Bush retreats from latest rhetorical threats, saying that he is not trying to prepare the public for war. He says, however, that the "sand is running through the glass" for Saddam Hussein. The administration's recent mixed signals have given rise to mounting criticism that Bush has not clearly articulated American policy in the Gulf.
- In a message to Presidents Mitterrand and Gorbachev, Iraqi officials say that foreign hostages will be allowed to leave if France and the Soviet Union take a stand against the use of force.

November 2

- Saudi Arabia and Iran hold high level meetings, resuming diplomatic relations ruptured during the Iran-Iraq War.
- Three French soldiers are taken prisoners by Iraqi troops when they venture into Iraqi territory and are later released.
- Kuwaiti prime minister and heir apparent, Sheikh Saad al-Abdallah al-Sabah, says that economic sanctions have not achieved their expected results and that "the time has come for the international community to look into other options" to force Iraq out of Kuwait. Kuwait's ambassador to Britain calls for immediate military action against Iraq to liberate Kuwait.

November 3

- Baker begins 8-day trip to the Middle East, the Soviet Union, and Europe to seek support for a resolution authorizing the use of force.
- Senior Iraqi officials announce an offer to release Western and Japanese hostages if the U.S.-led coalition countries promise not to attack Iraq and commit to solving other regional problems. Offer is rejected by the United States.

November 4

- The first contingents of the long-awaited, 15,000-strong Syrian armored division arrive in Saudi Arabia, dispelling earlier speculation that Assad was having second thoughts about Syria's involvement.
- Former Japanese prime minister, Yasuhiro Nakosone, meets with Saddam Hussein to ask for the release of Japanese hostages.

November 5

- Secretary of State Baker and King Fahd agree on a framework regarding the precise lines of command and control over American and Saudi forces in a possible war with Iraq, but the agreement leaves in place current command chain with Arab forces under Saudi command and non-Arab forces under American command.
- Former West German chancellor, Willy Brandt, meets with Saddam Hussein in a private diplomatic effort to seek the release of German hostages.

November 6

- Baker meets with Mubarak during a visit to Egypt. While in Egypt, Baker also meets with the Foreign Minister of China (PRC), Qian Qichen, who indicates that China, which is seeking to improve relations with the West, will not oppose a possible Security Council resolution authorizing the use of force against Iraq.
- Saddam Hussein allows the release of 77 Japanese hostages following a meeting with former Prime Minister Nakosone of Japan, but other Japanese hostages, some held at strategic sites, remain captive.

November 7

- After meeting with Turkish president Ozal, Baker arrives in Moscow for talks with Gorbachev and Shevardnadze to discuss Soviet support for a Security Council resolution authorizing the use of force. Baker says that the "credibility of the UN is at stake" if Iraq continues to refuse to withdraw.
- Prime Minister Thatcher strongly warns that unless Iraq withdraws voluntarily from Kuwait it will be removed by force, adding that "time is running out."

November 8

- President Bush orders an additional 150,000 troops and military personnel to augment the 230,000 already in the Gulf region. In the first public acknowledgement of an offensive role of U.S. forces, Bush said that the decision was meant to give the multinational force an "offensive military option."
- Soviet Foreign Minister Shevardnadze declares that while the Soviet Union would prefer a diplomatic solution, military force

may be required to remove Iraq from Kuwait but insisted that the use of force be made under UN auspices.

November 9

- Following his meeting with Baker, Gorbachev says that he is "disappointed" that Soviet initiatives have failed to persuade Saddam Hussein to withdraw from Kuwait and says that he is not optimistic about a peaceful resolution. Gorbachev adds later during a visit to West Germany that the UN should decide now on "how to proceed further."
- The Bush administration expresses concerns that Iraq "is not taking [the U.S.] seriously."

November 10

- Baker completes mission to the Middle East, Europe, and the Soviet Union. He expresses some frustration with the French response but optimism with the Soviets. The European allies want more time for the sanctions to work.

November 11

- Democratic congressional members criticize the administration's Gulf policy and accuse Bush of rushing the country into war without public and congressional approval. Powerful members of Congress, including Nunn and Daniel Patrick Moynihan, express concerns that Bush is exceeding constitutional limits and call for a congressional approval of a decision to go to war.
- King Hassan II of Morocco calls for a "last chance" emergency Arab peace conference but his call receives lukewarm American and Arab-coalition response.

November 12

- American Catholic Bishops approve a letter to Bush stating that all-out war is immoral if nonviolent solutions are not pursued.

November 13

- Baker says that Iraq's actions are a threat to the U.S. "economic lifeline" and American jobs.

November 14

- Bush assures congressional leaders that the recent buildup of U.S. forces in the Gulf region does not mean war. Bush tells members of Congress that he will continue to consult them throughout the crisis, but says he does not intend to seek congressional authorization for the use of military force. George Mitchell (D-Maine) and Tom Foley (D-Wash.) say that a special session of Congress during the recess is unnecessary.

November 15

- Soviet envoy Primakov says that the Security Council should delay the vote on a resolution authorizing the use of force to give Hussein a "big face-saving package."

- In an interview with ABC News, Saddam Hussein says he is willing to negotiate with the U.S. but will not accept preconditions such as a pullout from Kuwait. He reiterates that all Middle East issues must be discussed as part of negotiations over Iraq's withdrawal from Kuwait.
- Bush says after the crisis "there would have to be some international guarantees" regarding Iraq's weapons of mass destruction.

November 16

- Iran and Iraq announce an agreement aimed at resolving the major outstanding disputes from the Iran-Iraq War, including prisoner exchange and the resumption of full diplomatic relations.

November 18

- German chancellor Helmut Kohl, during a brief visit by President Bush, stresses that negotiations should be pursued with Iraq and raises doubts about the wisdom of military action.
- Saddam Hussein, in an official statement, says that all Western hostages will be released by late March 1991 "unless something . . . mars the atmosphere of peace."

November 19

- Iraq announces that it is sending 250,000 more troops to the "Basra and Kuwait provinces," raising Iraqi troop strength to an estimated 680,000.
- Bush and Gorbachev meet in Paris, but Gorbachev does not give any clear indications that the Soviet Union will back a UN resolution allowing for the use of force. Bush says that "we have a conceptual agreement that force cannot be ruled out."

November 20

- Iraq announces it will release all German hostages, some of whom are being held as "human shields." The Iraqi foreign ministry says that the decision is intended to encourage European states to "take more independent actions and stand against the arrogant position of the Americans."
- Several House Democrats and one Senator, led by Rep. Ronald Dellums (D-Calif.) file a lawsuit in a Federal District Court seeking an injunction to prevent President Bush from ordering offensive military action in the Gulf, arguing that only the Congress can declare war.

November 21

- Bush arrives in Saudi Arabia, meets with the Saudi king and the Kuwaiti emir.

November 22

- Bush meets with American forces in Saudi Arabia. In a Thanksgiving Day address to the soldiers, Bush warns that Iraq may be close to acquiring nuclear weapons, for the first time invoking Iraq's military potential as a reason for the deployment of American forces. Accompanied by congressional leaders, Bush says that the troops' mission is marked by a "real sense of urgency."
- Baker is rebuffed by Yemen's president, Ali Abdullah Saleh, who denounces U.S. forces as impeding Arab diplomatic efforts, saying that the American military presence "complicated the problem rather than solved it."

November 23

- Bush meets with Syrian president Hafiz al-Assad in Geneva. Bush, who was urged by Arab leaders to meet with Assad praises Assad, and says that although the U.S. has "big differences" with Syria, Syrian participation is key. Bush dismisses Israeli criticisms of his meeting with Assad.
- Soviet foreign minister Shevardnadze and Chinese foreign minister Qian Qichen meet in China for talks on the Gulf crisis and issue a statement calling for a peaceful solution. China has repeatedly condemned the Iraqi invasion but has been reluctant to support the use of force.

November 25

- Cheney says that Iraq is closer to producing nuclear weapons than before the invasion. Scowcroft says that Iraq could develop a bomb within months and that Saddam Hussein is preparing for terrorist attacks against American targets.

November 26

- Gorbachev warns Aziz that Iraq must withdraw or face a "tough resolution," adding that the "fate of Iraq is in the hands of the leadership. Time is running out."

November 27

- Iraqi foreign minister Aziz says that Iraq "will never succumb to pressure," in reference to a possible UN resolution authorizing force against Iraq. He adds that peace talks over Kuwait could only begin if "other Middle East issues" are also discussed.
- After a four-day inspection tour, the International Atomic Energy Commission says that Iraq's stock of enriched uranium (93% pure uranium 235) has not been diverted to the production of a nuclear weapon.
- The Senate Armed Services Committee, under Chairman Sam Nunn (D-Ga.), opens hearings on the Gulf crisis; Nunn urges patience.

November 28

- Before a Senate hearing, Admiral William J. Crowe Jr., and General David C. Jones, former chairmen of the Joint Chiefs of Staff argue that the deployment of additional U.S. forces makes war more likely. Both urge Bush to give sanctions more time and say that a war would damage the U.S.'s long term interests in the region. Henry A. Kissinger testifies that the U.S. cannot wait for sanctions to work, stating that "by the time it is evident that sanctions alone cannot succeed, a credible military option will probably no longer exist."
- House Majority Leader Richard A. Gephardt (D-Mo.) says he opposes the use of military force and calls on Bush to "stick with the sanctions." Nunn says a force of 430,000 is too large to be maintained politically and logistically. Republican leaders disagree over a possible special session of Congress, which Robert Dole (R-Kans.) and Richard Lugar (R-Ind.) support.
- King Fahd of Saudi Arabia says that "no other solution will be accepted" other than Iraq's total and unconditional withdrawal from Kuwait, and if Iraq does not withdraw, it would be a "tragedy for Iraq." The King hints that the objective should also be to destroy Iraq's arsenal of unconventional weapons.

November 29

- The Security Council approves a U.S.-sponsored resolution (Resolution 678) authorizing the "use of all necessary means . . . to restore international peace and security" by a 12 to 2 vote, the first such resolution since the Korean War. The resolution authorizes member states to take military action if necessary if Iraq does not withdraw from Kuwait and release foreign hostages by January 15, 1991. The vote follows weeks of intensive international lobbying by the Bush administration, which immediately begins to stress that January 15 is not an ultimatum, but a means to put additional pressure on Saddam Hussein. Yemen and Cuba vote in opposition, with China abstaining from voting. Shevardnadze warns that those who "break the peace must know that all available means will be used against them."
- Vice President Dan Quayle says that there are "moral costs" to waiting for the crisis to resolve itself, adding that he supports a special session of Congress to approve a resolution similar to that of the Security Council.
- Hours before the Security Council vote, Saddam Hussein says that Iraq is prepared to fight against the United States. "We shall fight in a way that will make us and other Arabs hold our heads high."

November 30

- Bush orders Baker to go to Iraq to meet with Saddam Hussein at a mutually acceptable time between December 15 and January 15 in a final effort to persuade Iraq to withdraw from Kuwait. Bush says he is willing to go the "extra mile for peace" to convince Saddam Hussein that the U.S. is serious but stresses that it is not a trip of concessions or deals. Bush also invites Iraqi foreign minister Tariq Aziz to come to the U.S. for consultations during week of 10 December. In other public statements, Bush reassures the public that if war comes, it "will not be another Vietnam."
- Kuwait, Saudi Arabia, and the United Arab Emirates announce more than $3 billion in loans to the Soviet Union.
- An official Iraqi statement condemns the Security Council as a "repressive organ to implement the evil U.S. objectives," and that the U.S. and its allies will be "crushed in the battlefield."

December 1

- Iraq announces its acceptance of Bush's offer for talks, but no date is given. The same official statement calls Bush an "enemy of God" and "arrogant." Iraq suggests that the talks also include discussions about the Palestinian issue.
- Saddam Hussein, on French television, says the chances for war are 50-50. Iraq test-launches two surface-to-surface, Soviet-built Scud missiles within its own territory. Allied troops go on high alert during launch.

December 2

- Secretary of State Baker says the U.S. will not attack Iraq if Iraq withdraws from Kuwait and releases Western hostages.
- In interview, Saddam Hussein says hostages will be released soon after Bush guarantees allied forces will not attack between now and March 25.
- During Senate hearings, former Defense Secretaries, Harold Brown, Frank Carlucci, Robert McNamara, Casper Weinberger, and James Schlesinger, caution the administration against the use of force and urge the use of sanctions and diplomatic efforts.

December 3

- Secretary of Defense Cheney tells the Senate Armed Services Committee that short of military force Iraq would not withdraw from Kuwait. Cheney says that "there is no guarantee that sanctions will force him out of Kuwait," and that the U.S. did not have the time to wait for sanctions to work. Cheney adds that it is better to deal with Saddam Hussein now than later. General Colin Powell, chairman of the Joint Chiefs of Staff, tells the hearing that the U.S.

is planning a combined, overwhelming air, land, and sea campaign against Iraqi forces.

- The Iraqi health minister alleges that 1,400 children have died as a result of the lack of medicine and food caused by the UN sanctions.

December 4

- Iraq announces that all 3,300 Soviet citizens will be allowed to leave immediately.
- House Democrats adopt a nonbinding policy statement warning Bush not to undertake military action without congressional approval.
- British prime minister John Major warns Iraq to pull out of Kuwait if it wants to avoid military attack. Defense Minister Tom King says if war breaks out it will be short and quick.
- The Director of the Central Intelligence Agency, William H. Webster, tells the House Armed Services Committee that Iraq will not be able to maintain its current combat readiness beyond nine months if sanctions continue to be applied.

December 5

- Israeli defense minister Levi suggests that Israel may take military action against Iraq if the U.S. fails to force Iraq to withdraw from Kuwait and dismantle the Iraqi military machine.

December 6

- Saddam Hussein announces that all foreign, primarily Western, hostages in Iraq and Kuwait will be released immediately. President Bush says that the U.S. will maintain its pressure, however, to make Iraq leave Kuwait without condition.

December 7

- The State Department announces the embassy in Kuwait City will be evacuated once all Americans in Kuwait have been evacuated.
- Iraqi foreign minister Aziz says foreigners will be able to leave "very, very soon." Iraqi National Assembly "votes" to release "foreign guests."

December 8

- Iraqi officials say that because of his busy schedule, Hussein will not be able to meet with Secretary Baker before January 12.
- President Bush says in Caracas, Venezuela, that the evacuation of Americans out of Iraq and Kuwait "facilitates the tough decisions that might lie ahead."
- King Hussein proposes an international peace conference on the Middle East in conjuction with an Iraqi withdrawal from Kuwait.

December 9

- Over 1,000 foreigners, including 163 Americans, are evacuated out of Iraq and Kuwait. Most of the remaining 2,000 Western hostages fly out of Iraq during first two weeks of December.

- The administration accuses Iraq of trying to delay Baker's visit by refusing to agree to a date prior to January 3.

December 10

- Foreign Minister Aziz of Iraq proposes that he meet with President Bush and Secretary Baker in Washington on December 17, while Baker meets with Hussein on January 12.

December 11

- While on a private visit to the U.S., Shamir says "Israel is not Czechoslovakia in 1938. We shall not acquiesce to any deal with enemies who wish to destroy us."
- Soviet foreign minister Schevardnadze rules out any possible Soviet military participation in the Gulf and calls for a nuclear- and chemical weapons-free zone in the Middle East.

December 13

- W. Nathaniel Howell, U.S. ambassador to Kuwait, and the remaining 4-member staff, join 31 other Americans in the last U.S.-sponsored flight evacuating American hostages from Iraq and Kuwait.
- Senior administration officials say that UN sanctions should continue in force even after an Iraqi withdrawal from Kuwait to contain Iraq's military capability.

December 14

- President Bush says that direct talks with Iraq are "on hold" until Saddam Hussein agrees to meet with Secretary Baker no later than January 3.
- House Majority Leader Richard A. Gephardt and other representatives say that the allies are not contributing enough financially to support the deployment of forces in the Gulf.

December 18

- The U.S.–Iraq talks proposed by Bush is indefinitely postponed because the two sides cannot agree on a date for a reciprocal visit by Secretary Baker to Iraq.
- Baker says that the U.S. will not back away from using military force even if Iraq pulls out from only part of Kuwait. "A partial withdrawal would reward aggression."
- President Bush says he is "convinced the coalition would not fall apart" if Israel were dragged into a war by Iraq.

December 19

- Lieutenant General Calvin Waller, deputy commander of the American forces in the Gulf, says that "every unit will not be fully combat-ready" for offensive operations by the January 15 UN deadline for Iraq to withdraw voluntarily.

- President Mitterrand says a partial withdrawal of Iraqi forces from Kuwait is unacceptable.
- Cheney and Powell leave for Saudi Arabia on a five-day visit with American forces and Saudi officials.

December 21

- Cheney tells American troops in Saudi Arabia that the U.S. will have to "use force" to get Iraq out of Kuwait. Also he says that in the event of war, "there won't be any restrictions" on the military.

December 22

- Nineteen American sailors drown off the Israeli port of Haifa when a ferry boat capsizes and sinks.
- Bush is reportedly told by Pentagon officials that most American military commanders feel not all American forces will not be ready for offensive operations on January 15.

December 29

- Several Iraqi opposition groups meet in Lebanon and announce a common front to overthrow Saddam Hussein.

January 1, 1991

- The White House, under growing pressures from Congress and European allies, hints that it will accept talks with Iraq prior to January 12.

January 3

- President Bush offers to send Baker to Geneva next week to meet with Iraqi foreign minister Aziz, in a last attempt "to go the extra mile for peace," but stresses that talks will not involve negotiations or compromises.

January 4

- Iraq accepts the U.S. offer for foreign ministerial talks in Geneva scheduled for January 9. Aziz says that Iraq's priority for the talks will be to discuss the Palestinian issue.
- In an emergency meeting of the 12-nation European Community called by France and Germany, the EC assures Iraq that it will work to resolve all regional problems if Iraq withdraws peacefully. The EC invites Aziz to meet with EC foreign ministers on January 10.

January 5

- In a radio address to the nation, Bush says there will be no "secret diplomacy" when Baker meets Aziz in Geneva and says that "time is running out" for Iraq. Bush warns Saddam Hussein, in a letter to be delivered to Aziz, that Iraq faces destruction if it refuses to pull out of Kuwait.

- Aziz declines the offer for talks on January 10 by the European Community; the same official statement criticizes "subservient policy of subordination" to America followed by some European states.

January 6

- Saddam Hussein tells military commanders to prepare for "historic battle" and that the "return of Kuwait [to Iraq] is a fact and not a claim." Hussein says he will liberate Palestine and defeat American "tyranny."
- King Fahd urges Hussein to avoid "bloodshed and catastrophe" and says he expects Iraq to withdraw voluntarily. He says situation is at an "impasse."
- Baker says the U.S. cannot support the French-sponsored plan for resolving the Gulf crisis proposed by the EC on January 4.

January 7

- During meeting with some European foreign ministers in London, Baker says Iraq must "withdraw totally and completely from Kuwait or [it] will be forced out."
- Saddam Hussein says Iraq will not be the only "theater" of war and that war will not be just conventional.

January 8

- Bush asks Congress to adopt a resolution backing the use of force against Iraq.
- In a detailed report, Les Aspin, Chairman of the House Armed Services Committee, says American forces can defeat Iraq in a rapid victory and with light casualties. Aspin, who says military operations will be in phases beginning with air power, says "war is a reasonable option."
- A high-level Iraqi delegation visits Iran; the two sides agree to deploy their forces away from a one kilometer buffer zone along the border.

January 9

- After an unexpected six-hour session, U.S.-Iraqi talks end in Geneva without progress. Baker says "regrettably" Iraq was not flexible, and "if it should choose to continue its brutal occupation of Kuwait, Iraq will be choosing a military confrontation which it cannot win and which will have devastating consequences for Iraq." Bush says that Iraq's position was a "total stiff-arm . . . a total rebuff . . . nothing leads me to believe [Saddam Hussein] is going to be reasonable." Aziz refuses to accept Bush's letter to Hussein.
- Aziz says that talks were "full of threats" and reiterates threat to attack Israel.

- Saddam Hussein says that Iraq will make American forces "swim in their own blood."
- Mitterrand announces that France will seek a last-minute solution but will not back away from joining military action if Iraq refuses to withdraw.
- Mubarak says Egypt will "not permit an Israeli involvement in the gulf crisis" and that such an involvement would force Egypt to "take a different position."
- Clandestine Iraqi radio broadcast urges military to overthrow Saddam Hussein.
- Jordanian prime minister says if war breaks out, many Arab regimes will collapse because of pro-Iraq popular uprisings.

January 10

- Congress begins divisive debate on the resolution to back the use of force in the Gulf.
- Baker meets with King Fahd and Saudi officials in Riyadh.
- American and other foreign diplomatic personnel in Baghdad begin to evacuate.

January 11

- Baker tells American forces in Saudi Arabia that the U.S. is likely to begin military action soon after the January 15 deadline.
- Nunn and John Glenn (D-Ohio) say they will not support a congressional resolution backing the use of force.
- Deputy Secretary of State Lawrence S. Eagleburger leaves for Israel to assure Israeli authorities of U.S. protection in the event of an Iraqi attack. His mission is reportedly to ask Israel to stay out of hostilities if attacked.

January 12

- Congress approves a resolution authorizing President Bush to use military 1 force in the Gulf by a margin of 5 votes in the Senate and 67 in the House. Stephen Solarz (D-N.Y.), Dante Fascell, (D-Fla.) Aspin, Gore (D-Tenn.), Bob Graham (D-Fla.) support the resolution. Nunn, Mitchell, Foley, vote against.
- UN Secretary-General Perez de Cuellar arrives in Baghdad for talks with Hussein but says he is not carrying any specific proposals.
- American diplomatic personnel evacuate the embassy in Baghdad.
- President Bush says the U.S. would use military force "sooner rather than later."

January 13

- Perez de Cuellar says he was not able to achieve any progress in talks with Saddam Hussein.
- Turkey agrees to allow the U.S. limited use of Turkish air bases.

January 14

- The White House says Iraq will be living on "borrowed time" after the January 15 UN deadline.
- The nominal Iraqi National Assembly votes to back Saddam Hussein in a "showdown" against the U.S. PLO Chairman Arafat says in Baghdad that Iraq "is determined and has the capability to crush aggression and defeat it."
- France, Algeria, Yemen, and Libya appeal to Iraq to withdraw from Kuwait before the UN deadline.
- Israeli intelligence says war is inevitable. Israeli officials reiterate that Israel has the right to retaliate if attacked.
- In an open letter to King Fahd, Saddam Hussein says Saudi Arabia will be responsible if war breaks out. He condemns the King for inviting foreign troops, saying the "disgraceful" Saudi position is a declaration of war against Iraq.

January 15

- France abandons the diplomatic effort that it says was ignored by Iraq. Perez de Cuellar makes a last-minute plea to Iraq.
- In a televised address, King Hussein of Jordan says the region is on the "brink of the abyss" and that Jordan will protect its lands and skies. The region is headed for a "looming catastrophe."

January 16

- At about 18:30 hours (EDT and 02:30 Baghdad time), the U.S. and coalition Air Forces launch Operation Desert Storm, attacking Iraqi forces in Iraq and Kuwait, bombing targets deep inside Iraq, including heavy aerial bombardment of Baghdad and the Kuwaiti Theater of Operations (KTO). Coalition air forces fly under the UN flag but remain under U.S. command.
- Shortly after the war breaks out, the White House announces that "The liberation of Kuwait has begun." In a televised address to the nation, President Bush says,"We have no choice but to force Saddam from Kuwait by force. We will not fail."
- In an open message to President Bush before the outbreak of war, Saddam Hussein says Bush is wrong to think war will be quick. He says the U.S. will not define the battlefield nor the types of weapons used. He threatens that Israel "will be under the hammer" and that "heavy blood will be shed."
- Israeli defense minister Levi says Israel is in a "state of war," and an Iraqi attack on Israel will mean "certain destruction and total ruin" for Iraq.

January 17

- Iraq launches Scud missiles at Israel, but no one is seriously injured.

Despite its previous stern warnings, Israel does not retaliate. Over the next several weeks Iraq continues to launch Scud missiles at northern Israel, principally Tel Aviv and Haifa, but attacks prove militarily insignificant and cause few casualties. Iraq also launches Scud missiles at Dhahran, Saudi Arabia (where the coalition has its largest air base), but they are intercepted by the Patriot air defense system.

- Turkey's National Assembly votes to allow the U.S. to use Turkish air bases.
- One Iraqi male is killed and another injured in Manila when a bomb (apparently intended for a U.S. target) they were handling explodes.

January 19

- Bush praises Israel for showing restraint and understanding U.S. interests in keeping the anti-Iraq coalition together. U.S. technicians install and operate Patriot air defense system in Israel.
- In the first news conference since the war started, General Schwarzkopf says the allies achieved "tactical surprise" but adds that war will not be over in days.
- Bush says that the public should not get "overly euphoric" over initial successes, stating the "war isn't going to be easy all the time." He says that U.S. objectives remain the same—full implementation of all UN resolutions concerning the crisis.

January 21

- Iraqi television broadcasts interviews with downed allied airmen, who are forced to make statements criticizing the allied attack against Iraq.
- The U.S. delivers the Patriot anti-missile defense systems to Israel; the systems are to be manned by American technicians.
- Eagleburger arrives in Israel for consultations.
- Saddam Hussein says "scale of death" will rise when all weapons are used. He calls for a "holy war" against allied forces.

January 22

- Mubarak warns that if Sudan, where Iraq is reported to have deployed missiles, allows Iraq to fire missiles at Egypt from Sudanese territory, "Sudan will pay a high price."
- The Bush administration says war will last months, not just weeks or days.
- Iraq sets several Kuwaiti oil installations on fire.
- Patriot air defense systems intercept at least nine Scud missiles fired at Dhahran and Riyadh during the last day and a half.

January 23

- Two Scud missiles land in Tel Aviv, leaving three people dead and 70 wounded.

- Israel asks the U.S. for an additional $13 billion in aid.
- Iraqi television shows two more allied airmen being interviewed.

January 24

- The Chairman of the Joint Chiefs, Colin Powell, says the allied objective regarding Iraqi forces in the KTO is to "cut it off and then kill it." Cheney says the U.S. should expect surprises, and the public should not be too euphoric.

January 25–26

- Iraq deliberately releases crude oil into the Persian Gulf, creating a huge oil slick about 40 miles long. The Bush administrations accuses Iraq of "environmental terrorism."
- Bush authorizes the Pentagon to use nonlethal riot control gases against Iraqi forces.
- U.S. Marines along the border launch separate artillery attacks against Iraqi artillery positions inside Kuwait.

January 27

- The Pentagon discloses that two dozen or so Iraqi fighter aircraft and transport planes have fled to Iran for unknown reasons.
- Iran says planes will be confiscated for the duration of the conflict.
- The largest antiwar protest to date takes place in Washington D.C., with an estimated 75,000–250,000 protesters. Polls show that over two-thirds of the public support the war.

January 29

- The U.S. says more than 80 Iraqi planes have flown to Iran, some of which are more advanced tactical fighters.
- The U.S. and the Soviet Union postpone the presidential summit scheduled for February 11–13 in Moscow.
- In an interview with CNN, Saddam Hussein says Iraq will use all types of weapons if necessary.
- President Bush says when the war is over, the U.S. will undertake a major effort to "bring peace to the rest of the Middle East." He says the U.S. does not seek the destruction of Iraq and that the use of force against Iraq is "moral" and the war is a "just war."
- The Iraqi government claims that 324 civilians have died so far from heavy allied bombardment.
- In the largest ground operation to date, U.S. Marines launch artillery attacks against Iraqi positions and armor concentrations inside Kuwait.

January 30

- In his "State of the Union" address, Bush says that the U.S. is in a "great struggle" and has a "moral cause."

- Germany announces $5.5 billion more in contributions to the allied war effort.
- French defence minister Jean-Pierre Chevenement resigns; he says the allies have gone beyond the UN mandate.
- Iraqi tank battalions capture the deserted Saudi town of Khafji. Iraq releases a second oil spill into the Gulf from an offshore oil installation.

January 31

- After a 36-hour fire fight, Saudi and Qatari forces, backed by American Marines, recapture Khafji; 500 Iraqi POWs (prisoners of war) are captured.

February 4

- Powell and Cheney leave for Saudi Arabia on a fact-finding mission to assess the need and the timing for a ground offensive.

February 5

- King Hussein of Jordan says that U.S.-led war is "against all Arabs and all Muslims" and that the goal is to impose "foreign hegemony" on the region.
- Bush says he is skeptical air power alone will defeat Iraqi forces but says no final decision has been made for a ground campaign.

February 8

- Bush says he is concerned with Jordan's "shift" toward Iraq's "camp."

February 10

- In his first public announcement since the war began, Gorbachev says the war is taking on "an ever more alarming and dramatic scope" and warns the U.S. against going beyond the mandate of the UN resolutions.

February 11

- After meeting with Cheney and Powell, Bush says the air war "will continue for a while" and that no decision has been made on when to start a ground offensive.
- State Department reports about 100 terrorist incidents since January 16, but only one is directly linked to Iraq.

February 12

- In the largest combined air, naval, and ground operation to date, coalition forces launch an attack against Iraqi infantry, artillery, and armor concentrations along the southern Kuwait border.
- After meeting with Soviet envoy Primakov, Hussein says he is willing to cooperate with the Soviet Union to find a solution to the conflict but adds that Iraq will keep fighting until the "aggressors are beaten back."

February 13

- Several hundred Iraqi civilians are killed when a U.S. fighter bomber strikes what Pentagon officials say is a military command and control facility. Iraq maintains it is a civilian air raid shelter.
- Upon returning from his trip to Baghdad, Primakov says he is optimistic about a solution to the war.

February 14

- American military officials say about 1,300 Iraqi tanks, artillery pieces, and armored vehicles in the KTO have been destroyed by the air campaign.
- Twenty-seven coalition combat aircraft have been destroyed in the air war, 19 from the U.S., while 40 Iraqi aircraft have been downed.

February 15

- Declaring that "Iraq has triumphed in this duel," Hussein announces an Iraqi peace proposal, stating Iraq's "readiness to deal with Security Council Resolution 660." Among the Iraqi conditions: Saddam Hussein says a withdrawal must be linked to a comprehensive cease-fire; all other resolutions must be rescinded; the withdrawal of outside forces from the region; "Israel must withdraw from Palestine and the Arab territories"; "Iraq's historical rights on land and at sea must be guaranteed"; the reconstruction of Iraq by coalition forces; all Iraqi debts must be written off; the Gulf is to be declared a zone free of foreign military bases.
- Bush says Saddam Hussein's proposal is a "cruel hoax" and calls on the Iraqi military to "take matters into their own hands."

February 16

- Iraq claims that coalition bombers are responsible for killing 130 civilians in the city of Fallujah.

February 17

- Iraqi foreign minister Tariq Aziz arrives in Moscow for meeting with President Gorbachev. Soviet officials also meet with French, Iranian, and Kuwaiti foreign ministers.
- French foreign minister Roland Dumas says the allies are on the "eve of the ground offensive."

February 18

- Gorbachev presents Aziz with a peace proposal, the contents of which are not revealed. Soviet officials say the proposal is commensurate with the UN resolutions, but observers say that it guarantees Saddam Hussein's personal safety, the survival of his regime, no war reparations, and a conference on the Palestinian issue in return for an unconditional withdrawal. Aziz is told to return to Moscow with a response.

- The Bush administration says that despite the Gorbachev initiative, the "military campaign remains on schedule."
- Two American warships are badly damaged after being struck by Iraqi mines in the Persian Gulf.

February 19

- President Bush says Soviet peace plan "falls well short of what would be required." There is yet no formal Iraqi response to the Soviet proposal. British and French officials reiterate Bush's criticisms and rejection of the Soviet plan.
- Soviet officials urge the coalition not to begin the ground war.
- Over 86,000 sorties and missions have been flown against Iraqi targets in Iraq and the KTO by coalition forces.

February 20

- Italy and some other West European countries express support for the Soviet peace initiative.
- Baker says Iraq must withdraw totally, immediately, and unconditionally, adding that "one way or another the Iraqi army of occupation will leave Kuwait."
- U.S. ground forces mount a cross-border attack against an Iraqi troop encampment along the border, destroying several Iraqi tanks, artillery pieces, and capturing over 450 prisoners.

February 21

- In a radio address, Saddam Hussein says Iraq will keep fighting until "victory and martyrdom.... There is no other course than the one we have chosen, except the course of humiliation and darkness." His defiant speech does not reject outright the Soviet withdrawal proposal and makes no reference to linkage between Middle East issues nor to Kuwait as the 19th province.
- Hours after Saddam Hussein's speech, the Soviet Union announces Iraq has agreed in principle to the Soviet-sponsored withdrawal formula. The seven-point plan calls for Iraq's withdrawal from Kuwait beginning two days after a cease-fire, provides for an exchange of prisoners of war, and would lift all of the UN sanctions after two-thirds of the Iraqi troops have left Kuwait. Notably absent was any mention of a conference on the Palestinian issue.
- The Bush administration describes the Soviet proposal as "useful," but cited "serious concerns" over the specific terms for Iraq's withdrawal; the United States vows to continue its prosecution of the military campaign.

February 22

- President Bush announces that the coalition will give Iraq 24 hours (until noon February 23) to announce "publicly and authoritatively" a withdrawal from Kuwait or face a ground offensive; he promises only that coalition forces would not attack retreating Iraqi forces. Prime Minister Major says that the coalition position is "clear and it is not negotiable."

- Bush accuses Iraq, which has set ablaze over 140 Kuwaiti oil installations in recent days, of conducting a "scorched earth" campaign in Kuwait.
- The Soviet Union sends a revised peace proposal to Iraq.
- Up to now the number of American troops killed in action (KIA) is 23.
- According to coalition military commanders, Iraq has begun to implement a "scorched earth" policy in Kuwait, burning Kuwaiti oil facilities.

February 23–24

- Ten minutes prior to President Bush's ultimatum deadline, Iraq fires a Scud missile at Israel.
- Shortly after 20:00 hours EDT (04:00 local Gulf time on February 24), the ground phase of Operation Desert Storm begins with coalition forces racing into Iraq and Kuwait along a 300-mile front. President Bush gives the commander of coalition forces, General Schwarzkopf, full authority to conduct the war as the general sees fit.
- The coalition ground offensive has two main thrusts, with the 100,000-strong VII Corps pushing northeast into southern Iraq to cut off Iraqi forces in Kuwait and to engage the Republican Guards, and a second thrust pushing into Kuwait and toward Kuwait City. Coalition forces meet only scattered, light resistance.
- The 101st Airborne Division penetrates 50 miles into southern Iraq in a large scale, helicopter-borne operation.
- Combined British-French-American forces drive 30 miles into Iraq in 6 hours.
- Coalition forces reach the outskirts of Kuwait City before nightfall. British and American forces roll toward Basra in an effort to isolate the Republican Guards.
- More than 5,500 Iraqi soldiers are taken prisoner during the first ten hours of the ground war. Coalition commanders say the biggest problem thus far is handling the mass surrendering of Iraqi troops.
- Schwarzkopf says coalition casualties are "remarkably light" and that the operation is encountering "dramatic success," but warns that it is at an early stage.
- American military officials say retreating Iraqi troops have undertaken a "systematic campaign of executions" in Kuwait City.

- Saddam Hussein urges his troops to "show no mercy" to advancing coalition forces; he says the coalition attack failed.
- Senior administration officials say Saddam Hussein's departure from power would facilitate the situation but not alter the war objectives.
- An Iraqi radio broadcast announces the withdrawal of Iraqi troops from Kuwait. The U.S. says the war will continue until an official, formal pronouncement.

February 25

- An Iraqi Scud missile hits U.S. military barracks in Dhahran, killing 27 American reservists.
- Over 25,000 Iraq troops have surrendered to coalition forces. The coalition stops counting the number of prisoners taken.

February 26

- The Soviet Union and Iraq ask the Security Council to declare a cease-fire; the request is opposed by the U.S. and Britain, arguing that Iraq must first accept all Security Council resolutions.
- In an official radio broadcast, Saddam Hussein announces the Iraqi withdrawal from Kuwait but does not mention whether he accepts Bush's conditions. He says his forces were victorious in an "epic duel." He adds that "circumstances today have willed that [Kuwait] remain in the state in which it will remain after the withdrawal."
- President Bush, criticizing Saddam Hussein for "trying to claim victory in the midst of a rout," says the coalition will prosecute the war; he adds that Iraqi troops must lay down their arms rather than simply withdraw.
- So far in the ground war there have been only four American KIAs, with 21 wounded (excluding those killed in the Scud attack on Dhahran).
- Large numbers of Iraqi troops begin withdrawing from Kuwait, looting Kuwaiti consumer goods.
- U.S. Marines capture the Kuwait international airport outside Kuwait City. The Marines soon enter and liberate Kuwait City.

February 27

- Coalition commanders say Iraqi forces are in full retreat across the KTO.
- Two Republican Guard divisions are defeated by American forces in a tank battle near Basra.
- Declaring that "Kuwait is liberated," President Bush orders the conditional suspension of the coalition attack; the suspension would continue as long as Iraq does not attack coalition forces or

launch Scud missiles. Bush calls on Iraq to send military commanders in the war zone within 48 hours to settle the terms of a permanent cease-fire.

- 28 Americans are killed in the ground war thus far; the total since the air war and including the Dhahran Scud attack stands at 79.

February 28

- American military commanders say all 42 divisions Iraq had in the KTO have been defeated, captured, or rendered unable to fight.
- Bush says that U.S. forces will remain in southern Iraq until the coalition is satisfied that Iraq will comply with American terms for a permanent cease-fire. The president also suggested that a long-term American military presence in the Gulf region is inevitable.
- Coalition commanders stipulate that Iraqi military hardware left on the battlefield must be destroyed as a condition for the withdrawal of coalition forces from Iraq.
- Iraq agrees to abide by all 12 Security Council resolutions concerning the Kuwaiti crisis.
- Military experts estimate that some 25,000–50,000 Iraqi soldiers may have been killed in the six weeks of the war. Later it is estimated that as many as 100,000 Iraqi troops may have been killed since January 16.

March 1

- President Bush says the U.S. will move fast to resolve the problems of the Middle East. He also states that he does not want to see "one single dime of the United States' taxpayers money go to the reconstruction of Iraq."
- The formerly besieged American Embassy in Kuwait City is re-opened.
- European correspondents report the first signs of an anti government uprising in southern Iraq.

March 2

- An antigovernment uprising and generalized civil commotion break out in the city of Basra, which is reported to be in chaos with a collapsed civil government.
- In an 11-1 vote, the Security Council approves Resolution 686, which embodies Bush's demands that coalition troops remain in the Gulf until Iraq complies with the coalition peace terms. The resolution authorizes coalition forces to resume hostilities in the event of an Iraqi violation of the temporary cease-fire. Among other things, the resolution calls on Iraq to release POWs and Kuwaiti civilians, accept liability for war damages, provide maps of mine fields, and rescind its annexation of Kuwait.

March 3

- In a meeting with top coalition commanders, Iraqi military leaders accept the coalition's terms for a permanent cease-fire. General Schwarzkopf says Iraq agreed "on all matters." Among other provisions, the agreement provides for the prompt release of POWs and Kuwaiti civilians held in Iraq, the withdrawal of U.S. forces from southern Iraq after Iraq has complied with all UN resolutions, and Iraqi assistance in locating land and sea mines in Kuwait and the Gulf.
- Civil unrest and antigovernment uprisings are reported to have spread to other cities and towns near Basra, including 'Amara, Nasiriyah, and Kut. Travellers and refugees along the Iraq-Kuwait border report that government forces in Basra are trying to suppress a Shiite-led revolt.

March 4

- Kuwaiti resistance fighters, army regulars, and armed vigilante groups are said to be arresting, torturing, and generally harassing Palestinians accused or suspected of collaborating with the occupying Iraqi forces.
- Fighting in Basra between the loyalist, government forces and the largely Shiite antigovernment rebels is said to be intensifying. Regional news agencies and fleeing civilians report that Iraqi soldiers retreating from Kuwait have joined the antigovernment rebels. While Iranian involvement is suspected, it appears that the uprisings are unorganized and without any central direction. American and other Western military officials suggest that the poorly and lightly armed rebels are unlikely to succeed.
- Iraq releases the first ten coalition POWs.
- Crown Prince Sheikh Saad al-Abdallah al-Sabah returns to Kuwait from exile, the first senior member of the ruling family to return.

March 5

- In a radio broadcast, the Iraqi government announces it has rescinded the annexation of Kuwait and agrees to return seized Kuwaiti assets.
- The antigovernment rebellion in Iraq spreads to more than a dozen cities and towns in southeastern Iraq, but it is reported to be weakening; the rebels are said to be running out of ammunition and weapons. Republican Guard units are said to be moving against rebel forces in Basra.
- Increasing numbers of Palestinians in Kuwait are being killed and tortured by Kuwaiti soldiers and armed groups.
- Iraqi Shiite insurgents take control of the holy cities of Karbala' and Najaf.

March 6

- Before a joint session of Congress, President Bush says the U.S. commitment to peace in the Middle East is strong and that "the time has come to put an end to the Arab-Israeli conflict." He says that all sides must make compromises, reiterating a long-standing U.S. position supporting the principle of land for peace.
- The foreign ministers of the Arab states who joined the multinational coalition propose an Arab peacekeeping force for the Gulf, to consist of mainly Syrian and Egyptian troops.

March 7

- The Iraqi government acknowledges for the first time it is facing an internal revolt. The antigovernment uprising in Basra is said to have been quelled. American military officials say the rebellion appeared to be spreading to the Kurdish-populated northern region of the country but that the government appears poised to defeat the rebels, who have gained control of some towns and villages.

March 8

- After an American intelligence intercept of Iraqi military communications, the U.S. warns Iraq not to use chemicals weapons to put down the antigovernment rebellion but does not specify what steps it will take in the event of their use.
- Iranian president Rafsanjani calls on Hussein to resign. The Iranian news agency says the Iraqi rebellion is spreading to the Kurdish north.
- Baker meets with King Fahd as he begins his Middle East peace initiative. Saudi officials say the kingdom will play an "active" role in bringing about a peace settlement. No details are given regarding the contents of the American peace proposals.

March 9

- U.S. military officials prepare plans to bomb Iraqi military units using chemical weapons against the rebels. Iraqi government forces are said to be using helicopter gunships, tanks, and artillery to put down the rebellion. The use of helicopters is in apparent violation of the cease-fire agreement. Kurdish rebels say they have taken the provincial capital of Sulaymaniyah and accuse the government of using helicopters and tanks against the city's population.
- Kuwaiti leaders promise visiting Secretary of State Baker that Kuwait will be democratized in the near future and that Kuwait is prepared to make peace with Israel on the basis of UN resolutions.

March 10

- Eight Arab states, notably Syria, Egypt, and Saudi Arabia endorse the U.S.'s broad framework for a Middle East peace settlement, but disagreements remain between the U.S. and its Arab supporters on the specific issue of how to reach an Arab-Israeli settlement.

- U.S. military officials say loyalist Iraqi forces are having a difficult time quelling the rebellion. Heavy fighting is reported in Kurdistan. Kurdish rebels claim to have taken control of several towns and are said to be advancing towards the oil-producing center of Kirkuk. The situation remains fluid throughout the country.

March 12

- Iraqi opposition groups from various religious and political spectrums meet in Beirut to form a united front against Hussein.

March 13

- Bush accuses Iraq of violating the terms of the temporary cease-fire by using helicopters against the rebels. The Iraqi government's use of helicopters against the rebels has intensified over the last few days.
- Britain urges the Security Council to press Iraq to destroy all of its chemical and biological weapons stocks.

March 14

- Heavy fighting is reported in Kurdistan; Kurdish rebels say they control vast stretches of territory.

March 15

- Loyalist Iraqi forces appear to have regained control of important cities such as Basra, Najaf, and Karbala. American military officials say Kurdish rebels control a considerable part of Kurdistan.

March 16

- Saddam Hussein calls on the Iraqi people for support and promises democratic reforms in the near future. He acknowledges the rebellion in northern Iraq but says government forces are in control.

March 17

- Baker says the U.S. will not assist the Iraqi rebels but would welcome a change of government in Iraq.
- Kurdish rebels are said to be engaged in heavy fighting with government forces in Kirkuk.

March 18

- Pentagon officials say the U.S. will shoot down Iraqi helicopters being used against the rebels; they say the helicopters pose a threat to coalition forces.
- Bush says Iraq must pay reparations.

March 19

- Senior Kuwaiti and Arab officials say Iran has been organizing and arming the largely Shiite rebels in southeastern Iraq. Iran is also said to be arming.

- Kurdish rebels and organizing Iranian volunteers to join the uprising. Kurdish rebels take control of Kirkuk, Iraq's fourth largest city and a key oil-producing center.

March 20

- An Iraqi fighter-bomber is shot down by American warplanes over Iraq.
- American officials admit that the antigovernment uprising in Iraq is stronger than originally anticipated.

March 21

- A UN survey team reports that the results of the coalition air war against Iraq are "near apocalyptic" and that the heavy bombardment set the country back to a "preindustrial age." It calls the situation in Iraq critical and appeals for immediate mobilization of food, medical supplies, and equipment.
- Thousands of Iraqi civilians are seeking refuge in U.S.-occupied southern Iraq.

March 22

- A second Iraqi fighter-bomber is shot down by American warplanes over Iraq.
- The antigovernment revolt and unrest is said to reach Baghdad itself.
- Powell says U.S. forces will remain in southern Iraq "for some months."
- The Security Council eases the embargo on food supplies to Iraq and lessens restrictions on the delivery of certain humanitarian supplies.

March 24

- The *New York Times* reports that top administration officials are raising questions about the wisdom of Bush's decision to halt the coalition ground offensive against Iraq after only 100 hours of fighting, saying that much more armor and military equipment escaped than originally thought. These same weapons, they add, are being used to crush the Iraqi rebels.

March 25

- American officials say Saddam Hussein is about to crush the Shiite Muslim rebellion in the south. Despite U.S. warnings Iraq continues to fly helicopter gunships against the rebels.
- American officials say Saddam Hussein is close to putting down the Shiite rebellion in the south and that Iraq continues to fly helicopters against the rebels

March 26

- In an interview, Schwarzkopf says despite his recommendations to President Bush to "continue the march" into Iraq during the ground offensive, the 27 February cease-fire ordered by Bush came too soon, allowing Iraqi forces to escape with significant equipment and forces intact. The General adds that the coalition could have made it a "battle of annihilation" but the cease-fire decision provided Iraqi forces with "escape routes."

March 27

- Bush says Schwarzkopf was wrong in saying that the U.S. ended the war too soon.
- Thousands of Iraqi refugees are said to be arriving at the border camps set up by the occupying U.S. forces in southern Iraq. Refugees report atrocities by loyalist forces who are crushing the rebellion in the south; some say that loyalist forces are using chemical weapons.

March 28

- Iraqi forces begin a major offensive against Kurdish rebels in the Kirkuk area. Loyalist forces are said to have retaken Kirkuk. Rebels appeal for international humanitarian assistance.
- A Shiite rebel leader concedes that the government has retaken control of all cities and towns in the south; the rebels are operating mainly in scattered rural areas. He criticizes the Bush administration for not intervening and for "making it easy for [the government] to hold on."

March 31

- The U.S. announces it will begin withdrawing about 20,000 troops from occupied Iraq within two weeks.
- Senior Iranian officials criticize the U.S. for encouraging the Iraqi people to overthrow Saddam Hussein only to give the Iraqi government the "green light" to put down the rebellion. Iran has been calling for "international efforts to stop the massacre of the Iraqi people."
- Iraq says it has retaken Kirkuk, in addition to Dahuk and Arbil.

April 1

- Kurdish rebels are said to be retreating into the mountains in the face of the government's counteroffensive. Loyalist forces say they have retaken the city of Zakhu along the Turkish border.
- Hundreds of thousands of Kurdish people, fearing government reprisals, are said to be fleeing by foot and vehicles into the mountainsides along the border.

April 2

- More than 40,000 Iraqi refugees, mostly Shiites, are said to have fled across the border into Iran. Iranian officials describe the refugee situation as "overwhelming" and stretching Iran's capacity to assist them.

- Bush administration officials say the Kurdish rebellion is all but ended.
- Turkey announces that nearly 200,000 Kurdish refugees, mainly women and children, are heading towards its border.

April 3

- Hundreds of thousands of Iraqi refugees continue fleeing toward the Turkish and Iranian borders. Over 20,000 vehicles are said to be blocking roads leading to the Iranian border.
- Turkey says it will not allow a mass entry of Kurdish refugees into its territory.
- Loyalist forces recapture the last northern town, Sulaymaniyah, held by Kurdish rebels.
- The Security Council approves 12-1 the cease-fire resolution (Resolution 687) containing stern military and financial terms. The resolution allows for the gradual but conditional lifting of sanctions, demands that Iraq pay reparations for war damages, accept the 1963 borders with Kuwait, renounce terrorism, and permit the destruction of chemical, biological, and ballistic weapons. A UN observer team is to be sent to monitor the border.
- Senior State Department officials meet with Iraqi dissidents in the U.S.

April 4

- The U.S. urges Turkey to open its borders to Iraqi refugees. Turkey says it cannot house, feed, and protect the estimated 500,000 Kurdish refugees seeking entry into Turkey; some 10,000–80,000 refugees are said to have filtered into the country. Turkey calls for an international relief effort. Turkish president Ozal accuses Iraq of "genocide."
- Congressional criticisms mount against the administration's hands-off policy toward the Iraqi uprisings and refugee problem.
- In a message to Bush, Prime Minister Major calls for a "massive international effort" to assist the Kurdish refugees. Britain announces $1.7 million in emergency relief to be flown to Turkey.

April 5

- President Bush orders the U.S. military to begin airdropping emergency humanitarian supplies to Kurdish refugees camping along the Iraq-Turkey border. He also promises to send aid to Turkey and Iran. He leaves unclear whether the U.S. will use force to carry out the operation but says the U.S. expects Iraq not to interfere.
- Thousands of Kuwaiti refugees are said to be returning to their home towns. Some Kurdish refugees say they had been forced by Kurdish rebels to flee to the mountains.

- Iraq announces a limited amnesty to rebellious Kurds.
- The Security Council passes 10-3 a resolution condemning Iraq's repression of the Kurds and deems the uprising and refugee problem a threat to international peace and security.
- Turkey says over 100,000 Iraqi refugees have crossed its borders. Iran says 110,000 refugees are already inside its borders.

April 6

- Iraq formally accepts the Security Council cease-fire resolution but calls it "unjust."
- The U.S. warns Iraq not to use its military forces in northeastern Iraq, including helicopters.

April 7

- U.S. military aircraft begin airdropping some 36 tons of relief supplies for Kurdish refugees.
- Kuwaiti emir says parliamentary elections will be held in 1992.
- Prime Minister Major and other EC leaders call for the creation of "safe-havens" in northern Iraq for the Kurdish refugees; the enclaves are to be administered by the UN. The EC pledges $180 million in aid for the safe havens.
- An estimated two million Kurdish refugees are said to be seeking sanctuary in Turkey and Iran.
- The first major element of the 100,000-strong U.S. forces in occupied Iraq begin to pull out. The occupied southern part of Iraq is to be administered by the UN and the IRC (International Red Cross).

April 9

- The UN High Commissioner for Refugees says about 750,000 Iraqi Kurds have arrived in Iran, and another 280,000 have crossed into Turkey, with an additional 300,000 massing along the border. Relief agencies are said to be overwhelmed by the refugee problem.
- Iraq rejects the EC proposal to create UN-administered enclaves in northern Iraq to protect Kurdish refugees.

April 11

- During a meeting with EC leaders, Bush says the U.S. and the EC agreed to establish informal "safe havens" in northern Iraq. The relief effort will entail setting up camps and semipermanent structures to care for the refugees. The administration backs away from the idea of creating an "enclave," fearing it might become the basis for a Kurdish claim to nationhood.

April 13

- Bush reiterates the U.S. will not interfere in the Iraqi civil war but warned Iraq not to impede international relief efforts.

- American military aircraft intensify the airborne relief operation and extend control over other international relief operations under way.

April 14

- American military forces in occupied Iraq begin to pull back to a narrow buffer zone along the Iraq-Kuwait border.

April 16

- Iraq asks the Security Council to permit the sale of nearly $1 billion of oil to pay for the emergency importation of food and other basic supplies.
- President Bush announces that American, French, and British troops will construct secure refugee camps in northern Iraq to care and protect the more than half a million Kurdish refugees. Targeted solely for Kurds in northern Iraq, the camps would provide food and medical care for as many as 100,000 displaced Kurds, with allied troops providing security.

April 17

- Helicopter-borne American troops enter 60 miles into Iraq to secure two large zones for the construction of temporary refugee camps.
- Iraq says it has reached its own arrangements with the UN to set up "humanitarian centers" in both northern and southern Iraq to care for the refugees. Iraqi officials say Iraq will resist "with all its means" any other attempts to set up refugee camps in northern Iraq.
- The State Department and relief agencies estimate that some 500–1,000 refugees per day, mainly children, are dying in northern Iraq.

April 18

- Iraq informs the UN that a substantial stockpile of chemical and ballistic weapons survived the war. The U.S. says the inventory, which was required by the terms of the cease-fire, was faulty.

April 19

- Senior American, British, French, and Canadian military commanders meet with Iraqi generals in northern Iraq, but no details are given.

April 20

- U.S. Marines land in northern Iraq to begin constructing the first refugee camp and take control of the city of Zakho.

April 21

- Complying with allied demands, Iraqi troops begin pulling back from a 1,500 square mile zone along Iraq's border with Turkey.
- Refugees refuse to enter the U.S.-built camps in Zakhu because of the presence of armed Iraqi troops.

April 23

- Iraq asks the UN to take over the refugee camps being constructed by the U.S.

April 24

- Kurdish leaders say they have reached a broad agreement with Hussein that provides for the return of the refugees, limited autonomy for Kurdistan, and democratic reforms.

April 26

- Kurdish refugees begin leaving the mountainsides for Zakhu after the withdrawal of Iraqi troops. The UN announces it will take control of the camps soon; Kurdish rebel leaders are said to be discouraging and barring refugees from leaving the mountains.
- Bush says U.S. troops will not stay in Iraq a "minute longer" than necessary.

April 30

- Kurdish refugees begin leaving mountain sanctuaries, most of them returning home and bypassing the U.S.-built camps. American, British, and Dutch troops continue high visibility patrols.

May 1

- Allied troops begin to extend the security zone some 70 miles eastward from Zakhu. Iraqi troops are told to pull back.

May 5

- The UN observer team assumes control of the demilitarized buffer zone between Iraq and Kuwait; the last American troops leave within a few days.

May 6

- After meeting with Saudi officials, Secretary Cheney proposes that the U.S. store military equipment in Saudi Arabia and other Gulf states for future use.

May 7

- Cheney says U.S. troops will be removed from southern Iraq within two days but that U.S. forces will remain in Kuwait "for a period of months to come." Air patrols over southern Iraq end but will continue in northern Iraq.

May 8

- An American navy plane in northern Iraq is fired upon by Iraqi antiaircraft fire.

May 9

- Iraq rejects the proposed UN police force in northern Iraq.
- Another U.S. navy plane is fired upon by Iraqi antiaircraft fire during a patrol in northern Iraq.
- Kurdish refugees are overcrowding refugee camps in Zakhu. Most of the refugees are thought to be from the Dahuk area.

May 11

- American and Iraqi commanders and Kurdish guerrilla leaders inspect the city of Dahuk and reach a compromise that falls short of an allied takeover of the city.

May 12

- Kurdish tribal leaders reject the American-brokered plan for refugees to return to Dahuk, where Iraqi police are said to be on patrol.

May 13

- The UN takes administrative control of the main refugee camp in Zakhu, but allied troops will remain to provide security.

May 15

- An inspection team from the International Atomic Energy Agency (IAEA), working under the auspices of the Security Council and under the provisions of the cease-fire resolution, begins inspection of Iraqi nuclear installations under the terms of the cease-fire.

May 17

- Iraq agrees to Security Council guidelines for the inspection of its military and scientific installations.

May 18

- Kurdish leaders and the Iraqi government agree in principle to providing for limited Kurdish autonomy and democratic reforms.
- Iraqi troops withdraw from Dahuk; the UN announces it will send a small team of armed guards to the city.

May 20

- Bush says the U.S. will propose that the lifting of sanctions on Iraq be delayed until Saddam Hussein leaves power.
- A small contingent of American and British troops and technicians enter Dahuk; the presence of Iraqi police and secret police continues to dissuade refugees from returning to the city.

May 22

- The IAEA inspection team completes its inspection of Iraq's main nuclear research center (Al Tawitha), inspecting 17 pounds of the 26 pounds of enriched uranium Iraq possesses (with the rest buried in rubble according to Iraqi officials). The U.S. says Iraq has other fissionable materials hidden away.

May 23

- The UN and Iraq agree to a plan to allow a UN police force to patrol northern Iraq.

May 24

- Allied troops and technicians begin to help restore Dahuk's basic services; Dahuk remains technically out of the allied security zone and still under Iraqi authority.

May 25

- Thousands of Kurdish refugees are said to be returning to Dahuk.

May 29

- Bush announces a U.S. proposal to curb arms transfers to the Middle East by the world's largest arms exporters.

June 1

- The last Kurdish refugee camp in Turkey is closed. An estimated 50,000 refugees remain camped along the border.

June 2

- The *New York Times* reports that a classified administration study of Iraq's war damage states that Iraq's civilian economy and infrastructure were seriously incapacitated and that Iraq faces a potentially catastrophic health crisis.
- Kurdish refugees in American-occupied Zakhu stage one of a series of violent demonstrations and attacks against local Iraqi police, demanding that American troops remain to protect them.

June 4

- The Pentagon releases a heavily qualified report putting the Iraqi death toll at 100,000, with 300,000 wounded.

June 10

- Iran accuses Iraq of attacking hundreds of thousands of Shiite dissidents still encamped in southern Iraq.

June 12

- Iran says it will not remain "indifferent" to the deployment of Iraqi troops along its borders and that Iraq plans a "massacre" of Shiite Muslims in southern Iraq.

June 14

- The U.S. and the UN inspection team accuse Iraq of trying to conceal its nuclear material and weapons program.

June 21

- The U.S. and its NATO allies announce plans to station a 5,000-strong contingency force in Turkey to protect the Kurds.

June 23

- Kurdish rebel leaders say Saddam Hussein has approved a draft agreement providing for free elections for an autonomous Kurdish region.

June 25

- Iraq denies the UN inspection team full access to a military site north of Baghdad. The same team was denied access to site on June 23. Iraq is said to have removed equipment from the location while the team was kept out.

June 26

- The U.S. discloses reconnaissance photographs to back up charges that Iraq is concealing nuclear materials and equipment.

June 27

- Baker says the U.S. will not "tolerate [Iraq] trying to hide [its] nuclear capabilities."

June 28

- Iraqi soldiers block entry and fire warning shots at the UN inspection team attempting to gain access to a military installation in Fallujah. President Bush hints that the U.S. may use force to make Iraq cooperate. The Security Council condemns Iraq for its "flagrant violations" of the terms of the cease-fire resolution.

June 29

- Bush accuses Saddam Hussein of "cheating and lying" but says he has not discussed any military options.

July 3

- A UN special team says Iraq is trapping and periodically shelling several hundred thousands of Shiite dissidents in the marshlands of southern Iraq.

July 8

- Iraq discloses that it has operated three clandestine programs designed to produce enriched uranium, but that it produced only 1 lb. A recently defected Iraqi nuclear scientist says Iraq has about 90 lbs.
- Administration officials say Iraq has produced more weapons-grade material than it is disclosing and that the list is incomplete.

July 11

- Iraq withdraws the forces surrounding Shiite refugees and dissidents in southern Iraq.
- President Bush approves a list of 20 possible targets to be attacked if Iraq refuses to comply with the cease-fire resolution.

July 13

- The head of the UN inspection team says Iraq must disclose a new list of clandestine nuclear research installations and equipment.

July 14

- President Mitterrand says he supports the use of force against Iraq if it continues its efforts to develop nuclear weapons or repress Kurds.
- Iraq submits a new list of military research installations and equipment.
- Allied troops evacuate northern Iraq.

July 18

- Iraq formally pledges to the UN that there are no additional nuclear installations and that it has revealed all of its "weapons-usable" nuclear materials and equipment. Iraq also acknowledges for the first time that it was building a "super cannon."

July 20

- Reports surface of an outbreak of fighting between government forces and Kurdish rebels in Sulaymaniyah. Kurdish rebels are said to gain control of the city, and government troops withdraw.

July 28

- President Bush says Iraq is making "an enormous mistake" if it fails to disclose all of its nuclear weapons programs. He says the use of force is likely.
- Iraq provides an additional inventory listing to the UN.

July 30

- The head of the UN inspection team says the team found the quantity of Iraq's chemical weapons stock to be four times greater than Iraq originally disclosed.

August 1

- The IAEA submits a plan to the Security Council detailing a stringent long term monitoring of Iraq's nuclear technology and giving the agency virtual control over its future nuclear development, including "full and free" access into Iraqi territory.

August 5

- Iraq discloses that its nuclear scientists were able to extract weapons-usable plutonium. Disclosure is the fourth of Iraq's secret uranium processing program.

August 7

- Iraqi armed units are said to be conducting a series of raids into northern Kuwait to retrieve stockpiles of weapons left behind after Iraq's withdrawal. Raids have been taking place along the thinly monitored border for several months.
- The five Permanent Members of the UN Security Council agree to a draft resolution allowing Iraq to sell up to $1.6 billion in oil, but the resolution contains a stringent set of conditions and restrictions on the handling and use of the revenues, which would be administered by a UN escrow account.

August 9

- Iraq formally rejects the Security Council draft resolution permitting the sale of Iraqi oil.

August 13

- The Pentagon increases the number of American deaths by friendly fire to 35 out of the total 148 KIA.

August 28

- Kuwaiti border guards capture several armed Iraqis trying to infiltrate Bubiyan island and retrieve weapons.

Sources: *Foreign Broadcast Information Service* (FBIS), the *New York Times*, and the *Washington Post*.

Appendix B

UNITED NATIONS SECURITY COUNCIL RESOLUTIONS ON THE GULF CRISIS

RESOLUTION 660 (1990)

Adopted by the Security Council at its 2932nd meeting, on 2 August 1990

The Security Council,

Alarmed by the invasion of Kuwait on 2 August 1990 by the military forces of Iraq,

Determining that there exists a breach of international peace and security as regards the Iraqi invasion of Kuwait,

Acting under Articles 39 and 40 of the Charter of the United Nations,

1. *Condemns* the Iraqi invasion of Kuwait:
2. *Demands* that Iraq withdraw immediately and unconditionally all its forces to the positions in which they were located on 1 August 1990:
3. *Calls upon* Iraq and Kuwait to begin immediately intensive negotiations for the resolution of their differences and supports all efforts in this regard, and especially those of the League of Arab States;
4. *Decides* to meet again as necessary to consider further steps to ensure compliance with the present resolution.

RESOLUTION 661 (1990)

Adopted by the Security Council at its 2933rd meeting, on 6 August 1990

The Security Council,

Reaffirming its resolution 660 (1990) of 2 August 1990,

Deeply concerned that that resolution has not been implemented and that the invasion by Iraq of Kuwait continues with further loss of human life and material destruction,

Determined to bring the invasion and occupation of Kuwait by Iraq to an end and to restore the sovereignty, independence and territorial integrity of Kuwait,

Noting that the legitimate Government of Kuwait has expressed its readiness to comply with resolution 660 (1990),

Mindful of its responsibilities under the Charter of the United Nations for the maintenance of international peace and security,

Affirming the inherent right of individual or collective self-defense, in response to the armed attack by Iraq against Kuwait, in accordance with Article 51 of the Charter,

Acting under Chapter VII of the Charter of the United Nations,

1. *Determines* that Iraq so far has failed to comply with paragraph 2 of resolution 660 (1990) and has usurped the authority of the legitimate Government of Kuwait;
2. *Decides,* as a consequence, to take the following measures to secure compliance of Iraq with paragraph 2 of resolution 660 (1990) and to restore the authority of the legitimate Government of Kuwait;
3. *Decides* that all States shall prevent:
   (a) The import into their territories of all commodities and products originating in Iraq or Kuwait exported therefrom after the date of the present resolution;
   (b) Any activities by their nationals or in their territories which would promote or are calculated to promote the export or transshipment of any commodities or products from Iraq or Kuwait; and any dealings by their nationals or their flag vessels or in their territories in any commodities or products originating in Iraq or Kuwait and exported therefrom after the date of the present resolution, including in particular any transfer of funds to Iraq or Kuwait for the purposes of such activities or dealings:

(c) The sale or supply by their nationals or from their territories or using their flag vessels of any commodities or products, including weapons or any other military equipment, whether or not originating in their territories but not including supplies intended strictly for medical purposes, and, in humanitarian circumstances, foodstuffs, to any person or body in Iraq or Kuwait or to any person or body for the purposes of any business carried on in or operated from Iraq or Kuwait, and any activities by their nationals or in their territories which promote or are calculated to promote such sale or supply of such commodities or products;

4. *Decides* that all States shall not make available to the Government of Iraq or to any commercial, industrial, or public utility undertaking in Iraq or Kuwait, any funds or any other financial or economic resources and shall prevent their nationals and any persons within their territories from removing from their territories or otherwise making available to that Government or to any such undertaking any such funds or resources and from remitting any other funds to persons or bodies within Iraq or Kuwait, except payments exclusively for strictly medical or humanitarian purposes and, in humanitarian circumstances, foodstuffs;
5. *Calls upon* all States, including States non-members of the United Nations, to act strictly in accordance with the provisions of the present resolution notwithstanding any contract entered into or licence granted before the date of the present resolution;
6. *Decides* to establish, in accordance with rule 28 of the provisional rules of procedure of the Security Council, a Committee of the Security Council consisting of all the members of the Council, to undertake the following tasks and to report on its work to the Council with its observations and recommendations:
   (a) To examine the reports on the progress of the implementation of the present resolution which will be submitted by the Secretary-General;
   (b) To seek from all States further information regarding the action taken by them concerning the effective implementation of the provisions laid down in the present resolution;
7. *Calls upon* all States to cooperate fully with the Committee in the fulfillment of its task, including supplying such information as may be sought by the Committee in pursuance of the present resolution;

8. *Requests* the Secretary-General to provide all necessary assistance to the Committee and to make the necessary arrangements in the Secretariat for the purpose;
9. *Decides* that, notwithstanding paragraphs 4 through 8 above, nothing in the present resolution shall prohibit assistance to the legitimate Government of Kuwait, and calls upon all States:
   (a) To take appropriate measures to protect assets of the legitimate Government of Kuwait and its agencies;
   (b) Not to recognize any regime set up by the occupying Power:
10. *Requests* the Secretary-General to report to the Council on the progress of the implementation of the present resolution, the first report to be submitted within thirty days;
11. *Decides* to keep this item on its agenda and to continue its efforts to put an early end to the invasion by Iraq.

RESOLUTION 662 (1990)

Adopted by the Security Council at its 2934th meeting, on 9 August 1990

The Security Council,

Recalling its resolutions 660 (1990) and 661 (1990),

Gravely alarmed by the declaration by Iraq of a "comprehensive and eternal merger" with Kuwait,

Demanding, once again, that Iraq withdraw immediately and unconditionally all its forces to the positions in which they were located on 1 August 1990,

Determined to bring the occupation of Kuwait by Iraq to an end and to restore the sovereignty, independence and territorial integrity of Kuwait,

Determined also to restore the authority of the legitimate Government of Kuwait,

1. *Decides* that annexation of Kuwait by Iraq under any form and whatever pretext has no legal validity, and is considered null and void;
2. *Calls upon* all States, international organizations and specialized agencies not to recognize that annexation, and to refrain from any action or dealing that might be interpreted as an indirect recognition of the annexation;

3. *Further demands* that Iraq rescind its actions purporting to annex Kuwait;
4. *Decides* to keep this item on its agenda and to continue its efforts to put an early end to the occupation.

RESOLUTION 664 (1990)

Adopted by the Security Council at its 2937th meeting, on 18 August 1990

The Security Council,

Recalling the Iraqi invasion and purported annexation of Kuwait and resolutions 660, 661 and 662,

Deeply concerned for the safety and well being of third state nationals in Iraq and Kuwait,

Recalling the obligations of Iraq in this regard under international law,

Welcoming the efforts of the Secretary-General to pursue urgent consultations with the Government of Iraq following the concern and anxiety expressed by the members of the Council on 17 August 1990,

Acting under Chapter VII of the United Nations Charter:

1. *Demands* that Iraq permit and facilitate the immediate departure from Kuwait and Iraq of the nationals of third countries and grant immediate and continuing access of consular officials to such nationals;
2. *Further demands* that Iraq take no action to jeopardize the safety, security or health of such nationals;
3. *Reaffirms* its decision in resolution 662 (1990) that annexation of Kuwait by Iraq is null and void, and therefore demands that the government of Iraq rescind its orders for the closure of diplomatic and consular missions in Kuwait and the withdrawal of the immunity of their personnel, and refrain from any such actions in the future;
4. *Requests* the Secretary-General to report to the Council on compliance with this resolution at the earliest possible time.

RESOLUTION 666 (1990)

Adopted by the Security Council at its 2939th meeting, on 13 September 1990

The Security Council,

Recalling its resolution 661 (1990), paragraphs 3 (c) and 4 of which apply, except in humanitarian circumstances, to foodstuffs,

Recognizing that circumstances may arise in which it will be necessary for foodstuffs to be supplied to the civilian population in Iraq or Kuwait in order to relieve human suffering,

Noting that in this respect the Committee established under paragraph 6 of that resolution has received communications from several Member States,

Emphasizing that it is for the Security Council, alone or acting through the Committee, to determine whether humanitarian circumstances have arisen,

Deeply concerned that Iraq has failed to comply with its obligations under Security Council resolution 664 (1990) in respect of the safety and well-being of third State nationals, and reaffirming that Iraq retains full responsibility, in this regard under international humanitarian law including, where applicable, the Fourth Geneva Convention,

Acting under Chapter VII of the Charter of the United Nations,

1. *Decides* that in order to make the necessary determination whether or not for the purposes of paragraph 3 (c) and paragraph 4 of resolution 661 (1990) humanitarian circumstances have arisen, the Committee shall keep the situation regarding foodstuffs in Iraq and Kuwait under constant review;
2. *Expects* Iraq to comply with its obligations under Security Council resolution 664 (1990) in respect of third State nationals and reaffirms that Iraq remains fully responsible for their safety and well-being in accordance with international humanitarian law including, where applicable, the fourth Geneva Convention;
3. *Requests*, for the purposes of paragraphs 1 and 2 of this resolution, that the Secretary-General seek urgently, and on a continuing basis, information from relevant United Nations and other appropriate humanitarian agencies and all other sources on the availability of food in Iraq and Kuwait, such information to be communicated by the Secretary-General to the Committee regularly;

4. *Requests* further that in seeking and supplying such information particular attention will be paid to such categories of persons who might suffer specially, such as children under 15 years of age, expectant mothers, maternity cases, the sick and the elderly;
5. *Decides* that if the Committee, after receiving the reports from the Secretary-General, determines that circumstances have arisen in which there is an urgent humanitarian need to supply foodstuffs to Iraq or Kuwait in order to relieve human suffering, it will report promptly to the Council its decision as to how such need should be met;
6. *Directs* the Committee that in formulating its decisions it should bear in mind that foodstuffs should be provided through the United Nations in cooperation with the International Committee of the Red Cross or other appropriate humanitarian agencies and distributed by them or under their supervision in order to ensure that they reach the intended beneficiaries;
7. *Requests* the Secretary-General to use his good offices to facilitate the delivery and distribution of foodstuffs to Kuwait and Iraq in accordance with the provisions of this and other relevant resolutions;
8. *Recalls* that resolution 661 (1990) does not apply to supplies intended strictly for medical purposes, but in this connection recommends that medical supplies should be exported under the strict supervision of the Government of the exporting State or by appropriate humanitarian agencies.

RESOLUTION 667 (1990)

Adopted by the Security Council at its 2940th meeting, on 16 September 1990

The Security Council,

Reaffirming its resolutions 660 (1990), 661 (1990), 662 (1990), 664 (1990), 665 (1990) and 666 (1990),

Recalling the Vienna Conventions of 18 April 1961 on diplomatic relations and of 24 April 1963 on consular relations, to both of which Iraq is a party,

Considering that the decision of Iraq to order the closure of diplomatic and consular missions in Kuwait and to withdraw the immunity and privileges of these missions and their personnel is contrary to the decisions of the Security Council, the international Conventions mentioned above and international law,

Deeply concerned that Iraq, notwithstanding the decisions of the Security Council and the provisions of the Conventions mentioned above, has committed acts of violence against diplomatic missions and their personnel in Kuwait,

Outraged at recent violations by Iraq of diplomatic premises in Kuwait and at the abduction of personnel enjoying diplomatic immunity and foreign nationals who were present in these premises,

Considering that the above actions by Iraq constitute aggressive acts and a flagrant violation of its international obligations which strike at the root of the conduct of international relations in accordance with the Charter of the United Nations,

Recalling that Iraq is fully responsible for any use of violence against foreign nationals or against any diplomatic or consular mission in Kuwait or their personnel,

Determined to ensure respect for its decisions and for Article 25 of the Charter of the United Nations,

Further considering that the grave nature of Iraq's actions, which constitute a new escalation of its violations of international law, obliges the Council not only to express its immediate reaction but also to consult urgently to take further concrete measures to ensure Iraq's compliance with the Council's resolutions,

Acting under Chapter VII of the Charter of the United Nations,

1. *Strongly condemns* aggressive acts perpetrated by Iraq against diplomatic premises and personnel in Kuwait, including the abduction of foreign nationals who were present in those premises;
2. *Demands* the immediate release of those foreign nationals as well as all nationals mentioned in resolution 664 (1990);
3. *Further demands* that Iraq immediately and fully comply with its international obligations under resolutions 660 (1990), 662 (1990) and 664 (1990) of the Security Council, the Vienna Conventions on diplomatic and consular relations and international laws;
4. *Further demands* that Iraq immediately protect the safety and well-being of diplomatic and consular personnel and premises in Kuwait and in Iraq and take no action to hinder the diplomatic and consular missions in the performance of their functions, including access to their nationals and the protection of their person and interests;

5. *Reminds* all States that they are obliged to observe strictly resolutions 661 (1990), 662 (1990), 664 (1990), 665 (1990) and 666 (1990);
6. *Decides* to consult urgently to take further concrete measures as soon as possible, under Chapter VII of the Charter, in response to Iraq's continued violation of the Charter, of resolutions of the Council and of international law.

RESOLUTION 669 (1990)

Adopted by the Security Council at its 2942nd meeting, on 24 September 1990

The Security Council,

Recalling its resolution 661 (1990) of 6 August 1990,

Recalling also Article 50 of the Charter of the United Nations,

Conscious of the fact that an increasing number of requests for assistance have been received under the provisions of Article 50 of the Charter of the United Nations,

Entrusts the Committee established under resolution 661 (1990) concerning the situation between Iraq and Kuwait with the task of examining requests for assistance under the provisions of Article 50 of the Charter of the United Nations and making recommendations to the President of the Security Council for appropriate action.

RESOLUTION 670 1990)

Adopted by the Security Council at its 2943rd meeting, on 25 September 1990

The Security Council,

Reaffirming its resolutions 660 (1990), 661 (1990), 662 (1990), 664 (1990), 665 (1990), 666 (1990), and 667 (1990),

Condemning Iraq's continued occupation of Kuwait, its failure to rescind its actions and end its purported annexation and its holding of third State nationals against their will, in flagrant violation of resolutions 660 (1990), 662 (1990), 664 (1990) and 667 (1990) and of international humanitarian law,

Condemning further the treatment by Iraqi forces of Kuwaiti nationals, including measures to force them to leave their own country and mistreatment of persons and property in Kuwait in violation of international law,

Noting with grave concern the persistent attempts to evade the measures laid down in resolution 661 (1990),

Further noting that a number of States have limited the number of Iraqi diplomatic and consular officials in their countries and that others are planning to do so,

Determined to ensure by all necessary means the strict and complete application of the measures laid down in resolution 661 (1990),

Determining to ensure respect for its decisions and the provisions of Articles 25 and 48 of the Charter of the United Nations,

Affirming that any acts of the Government of Iraq which are contrary to the above-mentioned resolutions or to Articles 25 or 48 of the Charter of the United Nations, such as Decree No. 377 of the Revolution Command Council of Iraq of 16 September 1990, are null and void,

Reaffirming its determination to ensure compliance with Security Council resolutions by maximum use of political and diplomatic means,

Welcoming the Secretary-General's use of his good offices to advance a peaceful resolution based on the relevant Security Council resolutions and noting with appreciation his continuing efforts to this end,

Underlining to the Government of Iraq that its continued failure to comply with the terms of resolutions 660 (1990), 661 (1990), 662 (1990), 664 (1990), 666 (1990) and 667 (1990) could lead to further serious action by the Council under the Charter of the United Nations, including under Chapter VII,

Recalling the provisions of Article 103 of the Charter of the United Nations,

Acting under Chapter VII of the Charter of the United Nations,

1. *Calls upon* all States to carry out their obligations to ensure strict and complete compliance with resolution 661 (1990) and in particular paragraphs 3, 4 and 5 thereof;
2. *Confirms* that resolution 661 (1990) applies to all means of transport, including aircraft;
3. *Decides* that all States, notwithstanding the existence of any rights or obligations conferred or imposed by any international agreement or any contract entered into or any licence or permit granted before the date of the present resolution, shall deny permission to any aircraft to take off from their territory if the aircraft would carry any cargo to or from Iraq or Kuwait other than food in humanitarian circumstances, subject to authoriza-

tion by the Council or the Committee established by resolution 661 (1990) and in accordance with resolution 666 (1990), or supplies intended strictly for medical purposes or solely for UNIIMOG;

4. *Decides further* that all States shall deny permission to any aircraft destined to land in Iraq or Kuwait, whatever its State of registration, to overfly its territory unless:
   (a) The aircraft lands at an airfield designated by that State outside Iraq or Kuwait in order to permit its inspection to ensure that there is no cargo on board in violation of resolution 661 (1990) or the present resolution, and for this purpose the aircraft may be detained for as long as necessary; or
   (b) The particular flight has been approved by the Committee established by resolution 661 (1990); or
   (c) The flight is certified by the United Nations as solely for the purposes of UNIIMOG;
5. *Decides* that each State shall take all necessary measures to ensure that any aircraft registered in its territory or operated by an operator who has his principal place of business or permanent residence in its territory complies with the provisions of resolution 661 (1990) and the present resolution;
6. *Decide further* that all States shall notify in a timely fashion the Committee established by resolution 661 (1990) of any flight between its territory and Iraq or Kuwait to which the requirement to land in paragraph 4 above does not apply, and the purpose for such a flight;
7. *Calls upon* all States to cooperate in taking such measures as may be necessary, consistent with international law, including the Chicago Convention, to ensure the effective implementation of the provisions of resolution 661 (1990) or the present resolutions;
8. *Calls upon* all States to detain any ships of Iraqi registry which enter their ports and which are being or have been used in violation of resolution 661 (1990), or to deny such ships entrance to their ports except in circumstances recognized under international law as necessary to safeguard human life;
9. *Reminds* all States of their obligations under resolution 661 (1990) with regard to the freezing of Iraqi assets, and the protection of the assets of the legitimate Government of Kuwait and its agencies, located within their territory and to report to the Committee established under resolution 661 (1990) regarding those assets;

10. *Calls upon* all States to provide to the Committee established by resolution 661 (1990) information regarding the action taken by them to implement the provisions laid down in the present resolution;
11. *Affirms* that the United Nations Organization, the specialized agencies and other international organizations in the United Nations system are required to take such measures as may be necessary to give effect to the terms of resolution 661 (1990) and this resolution;
12. *Decides* to consider, in the event of evasion of the provisions of resolution 661 (1990) or of the present resolution by a State or its nationals or through its territory, measures directed at the State in question to prevent such evasion;
13. *Reaffirms* that the Fourth Geneva Convention applies to Kuwait and that as High Contracting Party to the Convention Iraq is bound to comply fully with all its terms and in particular is liable under the Convention in respect to the grave breaches committed by it, as are individuals who commit or order the commission of grave breaches;

RESOLUTION 674 (1990)

Adopted by the Security Council at its 2951st meeting, on 29 October 1990

The Security Council,

Recalling its resolutions 660 (1990), 661 (1990), 662 (1990), 664 (1990), 665 (1990), 666 (1990), 667 (1990) and 670 (1990),

Stressing the urgent need for the immediate and unconditional withdrawal of all Iraqi forces from Kuwait, for the restoration of Kuwait's sovereignty, independence and territorial integrity and of the authority of its legitimate government,

Condemning the actions by the Iraqi authorities and occupying forces to take third-State nationals hostage and to mistreat and oppress Kuwaiti and third-State nationals, and the other actions reported to the Security Council, such as the destruction of Kuwaiti demographic records, the forced departure of Kuwaitis, the relocation of population in Kuwait and the unlawful destruction and seizure of public and private property in Kuwait, including hospital supplies and equipment, in violation of the decisions of the Council, the Charter of the

United Nations, the Fourth Geneva Convention, the Vienna Conventions on Diplomatic and Consular Relations and international law,

Expressing grave alarm over the situation of nationals of third States in Kuwait and Iraq, including the personnel of the diplomatic and consular missions of such States,

Reaffirming that the Fourth Geneva Convention applies to Kuwait and that as a High Contracting Party to the Convention Iraq is bound to comply fully with all its terms and in particular is liable under the Convention in respect of the grave breaches committed by it, as are individuals who commit or order the commission of grave breaches,

Recalling the efforts of the Secretary-General concerning the safety and well-being of third-State nationals in Iraq and Kuwait,

Deeply concerned at the economic cost and at the loss and suffering caused to individuals in Kuwait and Iraq as a result of the invasion and occupation of Kuwait by Iraq,

Acting under Chapter VII of the Charter of the United Nations,

Reaffirming the goal of the international community of maintaining international peace and security by seeking to resolve international disputes and conflicts through peaceful means,

Recalling the important role that the United Nations and its Secretary-General have played in the peaceful solution of disputes and conflicts in conformity with the provisions of the Charter,

Alarmed by the dangers of the present crisis caused by the Iraqi invasion and occupation of Kuwait, which directly threaten international peace and security, and seeking to avoid any further worsening of the situation,

Calling upon Iraq to comply with the relevant resolutions of the Security Council, in particular its resolutions 660 (1990), 662 (1990) and 664 (1990),

Reaffirming its determination to ensure compliance by Iraq with the Security Council resolutions by maximum use of political and diplomatic means,

A

1. *Demands* that the Iraqi authorities and occupying forces immediately cease and desist from taking third-State nationals hostage, mistreating and oppressing Kuwaiti and third-State nationals and any other actions, such as those reported to the Security Council and described above, that violate the decisions of this Council, the Charter of the United Nations, the Fourth Geneva Convention, the Vienna Conventions on Diplomatic and Consular Relations, and international law;

2. *Invites* States to collate substantiated information in their possession or submitted to them on the grave breaches by Iraq as per paragraph 1 above and to make this information available to the Security Council;
3. *Reaffirms* its demand that Iraq immediately fulfil its obligations to third-State nationals in Kuwait and Iraq, including the personnel of diplomatic and consular missions, under the Charter, the Fourth Geneva Convention, the Vienna Conventions on Diplomatic and Consular Relations, general principles of international law and the relevant resolutions of the Council;
4. *Also reaffirms* its demand that Iraq permit and facilitate the immediate departure from Kuwait and Iraq of those third-State nationals, including diplomatic and consular personnel, who wish to leave;
5. *Demands* that Iraq ensure the immediate access to food, water and basic services necessary to the protection and well-being of Kuwaiti nationals and of nationals of third States in Kuwait and Iraq, including the personnel of diplomatic and consular missions in Kuwait;
6. *Reaffirms* its demand that Iraq immediately protect the safety and well-being of diplomatic and consular personnel and premises in Kuwait and in Iraq, take no action to hinder these diplomatic and consular missions in the performance of their functions, including access to their nationals and the protection of their person and interests and rescind its orders for the closure of diplomatic and consular missions in Kuwait and the withdrawal of the immunity of their personnel;
7. *Requests* the Secretary-General, in the context of the continued exercise of his good offices concerning the safety and well-being of third-State nationals in Iraq and Kuwait to seek to achieve the objectives of paragraphs 4, 5, and 6 above and in particular the provision of food, water and basic services to Kuwaiti nationals and to the diplomatic and consular missions in Kuwait and the evacuation of third-State nationals;
8. *Reminds* Iraq that under international law it is liable for any loss, damage or injury arising in regard to Kuwait and third States, and their nationals and corporations, as a result of the invasion and illegal occupation of Kuwait by Iraq;
9. *Invites* States to collect relevant information regarding their claims, and those of their nationals and corporations, for restitution or financial compensation by Iraq with a view to such

arrangements as may be established in accordance with international law;

10. *Requires* that Iraq comply with the provisions of the present resolution and its previous resolutions, failing which the Security Council will need to take further measures under the Charter;
11. *Decides* to remain actively and permanently seized of the matter until Kuwait has regained its independence and peace has been restored in conformity with the relevant resolutions of the Security Council;

B

12. *Reposes* its trust in the Secretary-General to make available his good offices and, as he considers appropriate, to pursue them and to undertake diplomatic efforts in order to reach a peaceful solution to the crisis caused by the Iraqi invasion and occupation of Kuwait on the basis of Security Council resolutions 660 (1990), 662 (1990) and 664 (1990), and calls upon all States, both those in the region and others, to pursue on this basis their efforts to this end, in conformity with the Charter, in order to improve the situation and restore peace, security and stability;
13. *Requests* the Secretary-General to report to the Security Council on the results of his good offices and diplomatic efforts.

RESOLUTION 677 (1990)

Adopted by the Security Council at its 2962nd meeting, on 28 November 1990

The Security Council,

Recalling its resolutions 660 (1990) of 2 August 1990, 662 (1990) of 9 August 1990 and 674 (1990) of 29 October 1990,

Reiterating its concern for the suffering caused to individuals in Kuwait as a result of the invasion and occupation of Kuwait by Iraq,

Gravely concerned at the ongoing attempt by Iraq to alter the demographic composition of the population of Kuwait and to destroy the civil records maintained by the legitimate Government of Kuwait,

Acting under Chapter VII of the Charter of the United Nations,

1. *Condemns* the attempts by Iraq to alter the demographic composition of the population of Kuwait and to destroy the civil records maintained by the legitimate Government of Kuwait;

2. *Mandates* the Secretary-General to take custody of a copy of the population register of Kuwait, the authenticity of which has been certified by the legitimate Government of Kuwait and which covers the registration of the population up to 1 August 1990;
3. *Requests* the Secretary-General to establish, in cooperation with the legitimate Government of Kuwait, an Order of Rules and Regulations governing access to and use of the said copy of the population register.

RESOLUTION 678 (1990)

Adopted by the Security Council at its 2963rd meeting, on 29 November 1990

The Security Council,

Recalling and reaffirming its resolutions 660 (1990) of 2 August 1990, 661 (1990) of 6 August 1990, 662 (1990) of 9 August 1990, 664 (1990) of 18 August 1990, 665 (1990) of 25 August 1990, 666 (1990) of 13 September 1990, 667 (1990) of 16 September 1990, 669 (1990) of 24 September 1990, 670 (1990) of 25 September 1990, 674 (1990) of 29 October 1990 and 677 (1990) of 28 November 1990,

Noting that, despite all efforts by the United Nations, Iraq refuses to comply with its obligation to implement resolution 660 (1990) and the above-mentioned subsequent relevant resolutions, in flagrant contempt of the Security Council,

Mindful of its duties and responsibilities under the Charter of the United Nations for the maintenance and preservation of international peace and security,

Determined to secure full compliance with its decisions,

Acting under Chapter VII of the Charter,

1. *Demands* that Iraq comply fully with resolution 660 (1990) and all subsequent relevant resolutions, and decides, while maintaining all its decisions, to allow Iraq one final opportunity, as a pause of goodwill, to do so:
2. *Authorizes* Member States cooperating with the Government of Kuwait, unless Iraq on or before 15 January 1991 fully implements, as set forth in paragraph 1 above, the foregoing resolutions, to use all necessary means to uphold and implement resolution 660 (1990) and all subsequent relevant resolutions and to restore international peace and security in the area;

3. *Requests* all States to provide appropriate support for the actions undertaken in pursuance of paragraph 2 of the present resolution;
4. *Requests* the States concerned to keep the Security Council regularly informed on the progress of actions undertaken pursuant to paragraphs 2 and 3 of the present resolution;
5. *Decides* to remain seized of the matter.

RESOLUTION 686 (1991)

Adopted by the Security Council at its 2978th meeting,
on 2 March 1991

The Security Council,

Recalling and reaffirming its resolutions 660 (1990), 661 (1990), 662 (1990), 664 (1990), 665 (1990), 666 (1990), 667 (1990), 669 (1990), 670 (1990), 674 (1990), 677 (1990), and 678 (1990),

Recalling the obligations of Member States under Article 25 of the Charter,

Recalling paragraph 9 of resolution 661 (1990) regarding assistance to the Government of Kuwait and paragraph 3 (c) of that resolution regarding supplies strictly for medical purposes and, in humanitarian circumstances, foodstuffs,

Taking note of the letters of the Foreign Minister of Iraq confirming Iraq's agreement to comply fully with all of the resolutions noted above (S/22275), and stating its intention to release prisoners of war immediately (S/22273),

Taking note of the suspension of offensive combat operations by the forces of Kuwait and the Member States cooperating with Kuwait pursuant to resolution 678 (1990),

Bearing in mind the need to be assured of Iraq's peaceful intentions, and the objective in resolution 678 (1990) of restoring international peace and security in the region,

Underlining the importance of Iraq taking the necessary measures which would permit a definitive end to the hostilities,

Affirming the commitment of all Member States to the independence, sovereignty and territorial integrity of Iraq and Kuwait, and noting the intention expressed by the Member States cooperating under paragraph 2 of Security Council resolution 678 (1990) to bring their military presence in Iraq to an end as soon as possible consistent with achieving the objectives of the resolution,

Acting under Chapter VII of the Charter,

1. *Affirms* that all twelve resolutions noted above continue to have full force and effect;
2. *Demands* that Iraq implement its acceptance of all twelve resolutions noted above and in particular that Iraq:
   (a) Rescind immediately its actions purporting to annex Kuwait;
   (b) Accept in principle its liability under international law for any loss, damage, or injury arising in regard to Kuwait and third States, and their nationals and corporations, as a result of the invasion and illegal occupation of Kuwait by Iraq;
   (c) Immediately release under the auspices of the International Committee of the Red Cross, Red Cross Societies, or Red Crescent Societies, all Kuwaiti and third country nationals detained by Iraq and return the remains of any deceased Kuwaiti and third country nationals so detained; and
   (d) Immediately begin to return all Kuwaiti property seized by Iraq, to be completed in the shortest possible period;
3. *Further* demands that Iraq:
   (a) Cease hostile or provocative actions by its forces against all Member States, including missile attacks and flights of combat aircraft;
   (b) Designate military commanders to meet with counterparts from the forces of Kuwait and the Member States cooperating with Kuwait pursuant to resolution 678 (1990) to arrange for the military aspects of a cessation of hostilities at the earliest possible time;
   (c) Arrange for immediate access to and release of all prisoners of war under the auspices of the International Committee of the Red Cross and return the remains of any deceased personnel of the forces of Kuwait and the Member States cooperating with Kuwait pursuant to resolution 678 (1990); and
   (d) Provide all information and assistance in identifying Iraqi mines, booby traps and other explosives as well as any chemical and biological weapons and material in Kuwait, in areas of Iraq where forces of Member States cooperating with Kuwait pursuant to resolution 678 (1990) are present temporarily, and in the adjacent waters;
4. *Recognizes* that during the period required for Iraq to comply with paragraphs 2 and 3 above, the provisions of paragraph 2 of resolution 678 (1990) remain valid;

5. *Welcomes* the decision of Kuwait and the Member States cooperating with Kuwait pursuant to resolution 678 (1990) to provide access and to commence immediately the release of Iraqi prisoners of war as required by the terms of the Third Geneva Convention of 1949, under the auspices of the International Committee of the Red Cross;
6. *Requests* all Member States, as well as the United Nations, the specialized agencies and other international organizations in the United Nations system, to take all appropriate action to cooperate with the Government and people of Kuwait in the reconstruction of their country;
7. *Decides* that Iraq shall notify the Secretary-General and the Security Council when it has taken the actions set out above;
8. *Decides* that in order to secure the rapid establishment of a definitive end to the hostilities, the Security Council remains actively seized of the matter.

RESOLUTION 687 (1991)

Adopted by the Security Council at its 2981st meeting, on 3 April 1991

The Security Council,

Recalling its resolutions 660 (1990) of 2 August 1990, 661 (1990) of 6 August 1990, 662 (1990) of 9 August 1990, 664 (1990) of 18 August 1990, 665 (1990) of 25 August 1990, 666 (1990) of 13 September 1990, 667 (1990) of 16 September 1990, 669 (1990) of 24 September 1990, 670 (1990) of 25 September 1990, 674 (1990) of 29 October 1990, 677 (1990) of 28 November 1990, 678 (1990) of 29 November 1990 and 686 (1991) of 2 March 1991,

Welcoming the restoration to Kuwait of its sovereignty, independence and territorial integrity and the return of its legitimate Government,

Affirming the commitment of all Member States to the sovereignty, territorial integrity and political independence of Kuwait and Iraq, and noting the intention expressed by the Member States cooperating with Kuwait under paragraph 2 of resolution 678 (1990) to bring their military presence in Iraq to an end as soon as possible consistent with paragraph 8 of resolution 686 (1991),

Reaffirming the need to be assured of Iraq's peaceful intentions in the light of its unlawful invasion and occupation of Kuwait,

Taking note of the letter sent by the Minister for Foreign Affairs of Iraq on 27 February 1991 and those sent pursuant to resolution 686 (1991),

Noting that Iraq and Kuwait, an independent sovereign State, signed at Baghdad on 4 October 1963 Agreed Minutes Between the State of Kuwait and the Republic of Iraq Regarding the Restoration of Friendly Relations, Recognition and Related Matters, thereby recognizing formally the boundary between Iraq and Kuwait and the allocation of islands, which were registered with the United Nations in accordance with Article 102 of the Charter of the United Nations and in which Iraq recognized the independence and complete sovereignty of the State of Kuwait within its borders as specified and accepted in the letter of the Prime Minister of Iraq dated 21 July 1932, and as accepted by the Ruler of Kuwait in his letter dated 10 August 1932,

Conscious of the need for demarcation of the said boundary,

Conscious also of the statements by Iraq threatening to use weapons in violation of its obligations under the Geneva Protocol for the Prohibition of the Use in War of Asphyxiating, Poisonous or Other Gases, and of Bacteriological Methods of Warfare, signed at Geneva on 17 June 1925, and of its prior use of chemical weapons and affirming that grave consequences would follow any further use by Iraq of such weapons,

Recalling that Iraq has subscribed to the Declaration adopted by all States participating in the Conference of States Parties to the 1925 Geneva Protocol and Other Interested States, held in Paris from 7 to 11 January 1989, establishing the objective of universal elimination of chemical and biological weapons,

Recalling also that Iraq has signed the Convention on the Prohibition of the Development, Production and Stockpiling of Bacteriological (Biological) and Toxin Weapons and on Their Destruction, of 10 April 1972,

Noting the importance of Iraq ratifying this Convention,

Noting moreover the importance of all State adhering to this Convention and encouraging its forthcoming Review Conference to reinforce the authority, efficiency and universal scope of the convention,

Stressing the importance of an early conclusion by the Conference on Disarmament of its work on a Convention on the Universal Prohibition of Chemical Weapons and of universal adherence thereto,

Aware of the use by Iraq of ballistic missiles in unprovoked attacks and therefore of the need to take specific measures in regard to such missiles located in Iraq,

Concerned by the reports in the hands of Member States that Iraq has attempted to acquire materials for a nuclear-weapons program contrary to its obligations under the Treaty on the Non-Proliferation of Nuclear Weapons of 1 July 1968,

Recalling the objective of the establishment of a nuclear-weapons-free zone in the region of the Middle East,

Conscious of the threat that all weapons of mass destruction pose to peace and security in the area and of the need to work towards the establishment in the Middle East of a zone free of such weapons,

Conscious also of the objective of achieving balanced and comprehensive control of armaments in the region,

Conscious further of the importance of achieving the objectives noted above using all available means, including a dialogue among the States of the region,

Noting that resolution 686 (1991) marked the lifting of the measures imposed by resolution 661 (1990) in so far as they applied to Kuwait,

Noting that despite the progress being made in fulfilling the obligations of resolution 686 (1991), many Kuwaiti and third country nationals are still not accounted for and property remains unreturned,

Recalling the International Convention against the Taking of Hostages, opened for signature at New York on 18 December 1979, which categorizes all acts of taking hostages as manifestations of international terrorism,

Deploring threats made by Iraq during the recent conflict to make use of terrorism against targets outside Iraq and the taking of hostages by Iraq,

Taking note with grave concern of the reports of the Secretary-General of 20 March 1991 and 28 March 1991, and conscious of the necessity to meet urgently the humanitarian needs in Kuwait and Iraq,

Bearing in mind its objective of restoring international peace and security in the area as set out in recent resolutions of the Security Council,

Conscious of the need to take the following measures acting under Chapter VII of the Charter,

1. *Affirms* all thirteen resolutions noted above, except as expressly changed below to achieve the goals of this resolution, including a formal cease-fire;

A

2. *Demands* that Iraq and Kuwait respect the inviolability of the international boundary and the allocation of island set out in the Agreed Minutes Between the State of Kuwait and the Republic of Iraq Regarding the Restoration of Friendly Relations, Recognition and Related Matters," signed by them in the exercise of their sovereignty at Baghdad on 4 October 1963 and registered with the United Nations and published by the

United Nations in document 7063, United Nations, Treaty Series, 1964;

3. *Calls upon* the Secretary-General to lend his assistance to make arrangements with Iraq and Kuwait to demarcate the boundary between Iraq and Kuwait, drawing on appropriate material, including the map transmitted by Security Council document S/22412 and to report back to the Security Council within one month;
4. *Decides* to guarantee the inviolability of the above-mentioned international boundary and to take as appropriate all necessary measures to that end in accordance with the Charter of the United Nations;

B

5. *Requests* the Secretary-General, after consulting with Iraq and Kuwait, to submit within three days to the Security Council for its approval a plan for the immediate deployment of a United Nations observer unit to monitor the Khor Abdullah and a demilitarized zone, which is hereby established, extending ten kilometers into Iraq and five kilometers into Kuwait from the boundary referred to in the "Agreed Minutes Between the State of Kuwait and the Republic of Iraq Regarding the Restoration of Friendly Relations, Recognition and Related Matters" of 4 October 1963 to deter violations of the boundary through its presence in and surveillance of the demilitarized zone to observe any hostile or potentially hostile action mounted from the territory of one State to the other: and for the Secretary-General to report regularly to the Security Council on the operations of the unit, and immediately if there are serious violations of the zone or potential threats to peace;
6. *Notes* that as soon as the Secretary-General notifies the Security Council of the completion of the deployment of the United Nations observer unit, the conditions will be established for the Member States cooperating with Kuwait in accordance with resolutions 678 (1990) to bring their military presence in Iraq to an end consistent with resolution 686 (1991);

C

7. *Invites* Iraq to reaffirm unconditionally its obligations under the Geneva Protocol for the Prohibition of the Use in War of Asphyxiating, Poisonous, or Other Gases, and of Bacteriological Methods of Warfare, signed at Geneva on 17 June 1925, and to

ratify the Convention on the Prohibition of the Development, Production and Stockpiling of Bacteriological (Biological) and Toxin Weapons and on Their Destruction, of 10 April 1972;

8. *Decides* that Iraq shall unconditionally accept the destruction, removal, or rendering harmless, under international supervision, of:
   (a) All chemical and biological weapons and all stocks of agents and all related subsystems and components and all research, development, support and manufacturing facilities;
   (b) All ballistic missiles with a range greater than 150 kilometers and related major parts, and repair and production facilities;
9. *Decides,* for the implementation of paragraph 8 above, the following:
   (a) Iraq shall submit to the Secretary-General, within fifteen days of the adoption of the present resolution, a declaration of the locations, amounts and types of all items specified in paragraph 8 and agree to urgent, on-site inspection as specified below;
   (b) The Secretary-General, in consultation with the appropriate Governments and, where appropriate, with the Director-General of the World Health Organization, within forty-five days of the passage of the present resolution, shall develop, and submit to the Council for approval, a plan calling for the completion of the following acts within forty-five days of such approval:
      (i) The forming of a Special Commission, which shall carry out immediate on-site inspection of Iraq's biological, chemical and missile capabilities, based on Iraq's declarations and the designation of any additional locations by the Special Commission itself;
      (ii) The yielding by Iraq of possession to the Special Commission for destruction, removal, or rendering harmless, taking into account the requirements of public safety, of all items specified under paragraph 8 (a) above, including items at the additional locations designated by the Special Commission under paragraph 9 (b) (i) above and the destruction by Iraq, under the supervision of the Special Commission, of all its missile capabilities, including launchers, as specified under paragraph 8 (b) above;

(iii) The provision by the Special Commission of the assistance and cooperation to the Director-General of the International Atomic Energy Agency required in paragraphs 12 and 13 below;

10. *Decides* that Iraq shall unconditionally undertake not to use, develop, construct, or acquire any of the items specified in paragraphs 8 and 9 above and requests the Secretary-General, in consultation with the Special Commission, to develop a plan for the future ongoing monitoring and verification of Iraq's compliance with this paragraph, to be submitted to the Security Council for approval within one hundred and twenty days of the passage of this resolution;
11. *Invites* Iraq to reaffirm unconditionally its obligations under the Treaty on the Non-Proliferation of Nuclear Weapons of 1 July 1968;
12. *Decides* that Iraq shall unconditionally agree not to acquire or develop nuclear weapons or nuclear-weapons-usable material or any subsystems or components or any research, development, support or manufacturing facilities related to the above; to submit to the Secretary-General and the Director-General of the International Atomic Energy Agency within fifteen days of the adoption of the present resolution a declaration of the locations, amounts, and types of all items specified above; to place all of its nuclear-weapons-usable materials under the exclusive control, for custody and removal, of the International Atomic Energy Agency, with the assistance and cooperation of the Special Commission as provided for in the plan of the Secretary-General discussed in paragraph 9 (b) above; to accept, in accordance with the arrangements provided for in paragraph 13 below, urgent on-site inspection and the destruction, removal or rendering harmless as appropriate of all items specified above; and to accept the plan discussed in paragraph 13 below for the future ongoing monitoring and verification of its compliance with these undertakings;
13. *Requests* the Director-General of the International Atomic Energy Agency, through the Secretary-General, with the assistance and cooperation of the Special Commission as provided for in the plan of the Secretary-General in paragraph 9 (b) above, to carry out immediate on-site inspection of Iraq's nuclear capabilities based on Iraq's declarations and the designation of any additional locations by the Special Commission; to develop a plan for submission to the Security Council within

forty-five days calling for the destruction, removal, or rendering harmless as appropriate of all items listed in paragraph 12 above; to carry out the plan within forty-five days following approval by the Security Council; and to develop a plan, taking into account the rights and obligations of Iraq under the Treaty on the Non-Proliferation of Nuclear Weapons of 1 July 1968, for the future ongoing monitoring and verification of Iraq's compliance with paragraph 12 above, including an inventory of all nuclear material in Iraq subject to the Agency's verification and inspections to confirm that Agency safeguards cover all relevant nuclear activities in Iraq, to be submitted to the Security Council for approval within one hundred and twenty days of the passage of the present resolution;

14. *Takes note* that the actions to be taken by Iraq in paragraphs 8, 9, 10, 11, 12, and 13 of the present resolution represent steps towards the goal of establishing in the Middle East a zone free from weapons of mass destruction and all missiles for their delivery and the objective of a global ban on chemical weapons;

D

15. *Requests* the Secretary-General to report to the Security Council on the steps taken to facilitate the return of all Kuwaiti property seized by Iraq, including a list of any property that Kuwait claims has not been returned or which has not been returned intact;

E

16. *Reaffirms* that Iraq, without prejudice to the debts and obligations of Iraq arising prior to 2 August 1990, which will be addressed through the normal mechanisms, is liable under international law for any direct loss, damage, including environmental damage and the depletion of natural resources, or injury to foreign Governments, nationals and corporations, as a result of Iraq's unlawful invasion and occupation of Kuwait;
17. *Decides* that all Iraqi statements made since 2 August 1990 repudiating its foreign debt are null and void, and demands that Iraq adhere scrupulously to all of its obligations concerning servicing and repayment of its foreign debt;
18. *Decides also* to create a fund to pay compensation for claims that fall within paragraph 16 above and to establish a Commission that will administer the fund;

19. *Directs* the Secretary-General to develop and present to the Security Council for decision, no later than thirty days following the adoption of the present resolution, recommendations for the fund to meet the requirement for the payment of claims established in accordance with paragraph 18 above and for a program to implement the decisions in paragraphs 16, 17, and 18 above, including: administration of the fund; mechanisms for determining the appropriate level of Iraq's contribution to the fund based on a percentage of the value of the exports of petroleum and petroleum products from Iraq not to exceed a figure to be suggested to the Council by the Secretary-General, taking into account the requirements of the people of Iraq, Iraq's payment capacity as assessed in conjunction with the international financial institutions taking into consideration external debt service, and the needs of the Iraqi economy; arrangements for ensuring that payments are made to the fund the process by which funds will be allocated and claims paid; appropriate procedures for evaluating losses, listing claims and verifying their validity and resolving disputed claims in respect of Iraq's liability as specified in paragraph 16 above and the composition of the Commission designated above;

F

20. *Decides*, effective immediately, that the prohibitions against the sale or supply to Iraq of commodities or products, other than medicine and health supplies, and prohibitions against financial transactions related thereto contained in resolution 661 (1990) shall not apply to foodstuffs notified to the Security Council Committee established by resolution 661 (1990) concerning the situation between Iraq and Kuwait or, with the approval of that Committee, under the simplified and accelerated "no-objection" procedure, to materials and supplies for essential civilian needs as identified in the report of the Secretary-General dated 20 March 1991, and in any further findings of humanitarian need by the Committee;
21. *Decides* that the Security Council shall review the provisions of paragraph 20 above every sixty days in the light of the policies and practices of the Government of Iraq, including the implementation of all relevant resolutions of the Security Council, for the purpose of determining whether to reduce or lift the prohibitions referred to therein;

22. *Decides* that upon the approval by the Security Council of the program called for in paragraph 19 above and upon Council agreement that Iraq has completed all actions contemplated in paragraphs 8, 9, 10, 11, 12, and 13 above, the prohibitions against the import of commodities and products originating in Iraq and the prohibitions against financial transactions related thereto contained in resolution 661 (1990) shall have no further force or effect;
23. *Decides* that, pending action by the Security Council under paragraph 22 above, the Security Council Committee established by resolution 661 (1990) shall be empowered to approve, when required to assure adequate financial resources on the part of Iraq to carry out the activities under paragraph 20 above, exceptions to the prohibition against the import of commodities and products originating in Iraq;
24. *Decides* that, in accordance with resolution 661 (1990) and subsequent related resolutions and until a further decision is taken by the Security Council, all States shall continue to prevent the sale or supply, or the promotion or facilitation of such sale or supply, to Iraq by their nationals, or from their territories or using their flag vessels or aircraft, of:
    (a) Arms and related materiel of all types, specifically including the sale or transfer through other means of all forms of conventional military equipment, including for paramilitary forces, and spare parts and components and their means of production, for such equipment;
    (b) Items specified and defined in paragraphs 8 and 12 above not otherwise covered above;
    (c) Technology under licensing or other transfer arrangements used in the production, utilization or stockpiling of items specified in subparagraphs (a) and (b) above;
    (d) Personnel or materials for training or technical support services relating to the design, development, manufacture, use, maintenance or support of items specified in subparagraphs (a) and (b) above;
25. *Calls upon* all States and international organizations to act strictly in accordance with paragraph 24 above, notwithstanding the existence of any contracts, agreements, licences or any other arrangements;
26. *Requests* the Secretary-General, in consultation with appropriate Governments, to develop within sixty days, for the approval of the Security Council, guidelines to facilitate full

international implementation of paragraphs 24 and 25 above and paragraph 27 below, and to make them available to all States and to establish a procedure for updating these guidelines periodically;

27. *Calls upon* all States to maintain such national controls and procedures and to take such other actions consistent with the guidelines to be established by the Security Council under paragraph 26 above as may be necessary to ensure compliance with the terms of paragraph 24 above, and calls upon international organizations to take all appropriate steps to assist in ensuring such full compliance;
28. *Agrees* to review its decisions in paragraphs 22, 23, 24 and 25 above, except for the items specified and defined in paragraphs 8 and 12 above, on a regular basis and in any case one hundred and twenty days following passage of the present resolution, taking into account Iraq's compliance with the resolution and general progress towards the control of armaments in the region;
29. *Decides* that all States, including Iraq, shall take the necessary measures to ensure that no claim shall lie at the instance of the Government of Iraq, or of any person or body in Iraq, or of any person claiming through or for the benefit of any such person or body, in connection with any contract or other transaction where its performance was affected by reason of the measures taken by the Security Council in resolution 661 (1990) and related resolutions;

G

30. *Decides* that, in furtherance of its commitment to facilitate the repatriation of all Kuwait and third country nationals, Iraq shall extend all necessary cooperation to the International Committee of the Red Cross, providing lists of such persons, facilitating the access of the International Committee of the Red Cross to all such persons wherever located or detained and facilitating the search by the International Committee of the Red Cross for those Kuwaiti and third country nationals still unaccounted for;
31. *Invites* the International Committee of the Red Cross to keep the Secretary-General apprised as appropriate of all activities undertaken in connection with facilitating the repatriation or return of all Kuwaiti and third country nationals or their remains present in Iraq on or after 2 August 1990;

H

32. *Requires* Iraq to inform the Security Council that it will not commit or support any act of international terrorism or allow any organization directed towards commission of such acts to operate within its territory and to condemn unequivocally and renounce all acts, methods and practices of terrorism;

I

33. *Declares* that, upon official notification by Iraq to the Secretary-General and to the Security Council of its acceptance of the provisions above, a formal cease-fire is effective between Iraq and Kuwait and the Member States cooperating with Kuwait in accordance with resolution 678 (1990);
34. *Decides* to remain seized of the matter and to take such further steps as may be required for the implementation of the present resolution and to secure peace and security in the area.

RESOLUTION 688 (1991)

Adopted by the Security Council at its 2982nd meeting, on 5 April 1991

The Security Council,

Mindful of its duties and its responsibilities under the Charter of the United Nations for the maintenance of international peace and security,

Recalling article 2, paragraph 7, of the Charter of the United Nations,

Gravely concerned by the repression of the Iraqi civilian population in many parts of Iraq, including most recently in Kurdish populated areas which led to a massive flow of refugees towards and across international frontiers and to cross border incursions, which threaten international peace and security in the region,

Deeply disturbed by the magnitude of the human suffering involved,

Taking note of the letters sent by the representatives of Turkey and France to the United Nations dated 2 April 1991 and 4 April 1991, respectively (S/22435 and S/22442),

Taking note also of the letters sent by the Permanent Representative of the Islamic Republic of Iran to the United Nations dated 3 and 4 April 1991, respectively (S/22436 and S/22447),

Reaffirming the commitment of all Member States to the sovereignty, territorial integrity and political independence of Iraq and of all States in the area,

Bearing in mind the Secretary-General's report of 20 March 1991 (S/22366),

1. *Condemns* the repression of the Iraqi civilian population in many parts of Iraq, including most recently in Kurdish populated areas, the consequences of which threaten international peace and security in the region;
2. *Demands* that Iraq, as a contribution to removing the threat to international peace and security in the region, immediately end this repression and expresses the hope in the same context that an open dialogue will take place to ensure that the human and political rights of all Iraqi citizens are respected;
3. *Insists* that Iraq allows immediate access by international humanitarian organizations to all those in need of assistance in all parts of Iraq and to make available all necessary facilities for their operations;
4. *Requests* the Secretary-General to pursue his humanitarian efforts in Iraq and to report forthwith, if appropriate on the basis of a further mission to the region, on the plight of the Iraqi civilian population, and in particular the Kurdish population, suffering from the repression in all its forms inflicted by the Iraqi authorities;
5. *Requests* further the Secretary-General to use all the resources at his disposal, including those of the relevant United Nations agencies, to address urgently the critical needs of the refugees and displaced Iraqi population;
6. *Appeals* to all Member States and to all humanitarian organizations to contribute to these humanitarian relief efforts:
7. *Demands* that Iraq cooperate with the Secretary-General to these ends;
8. *Decides* to remain seized of the matter.

RESOLUTION 689 (1991)

Adopted by the Security Council at its 2983rd meeting, on 9 April 1991

The Security Council,

Recalling its resolution 687 (1991),

Acting under Chapter VII of the Charter of the United Nations,

1. *Approves* the report of the Secretary-General on the implementation of paragraph 5 of Security Council resolution 687 (1991)

contained in document S/22454 and Add. 1-3 of 5 and 9 April 1991, respectively;

2. *Notes* that the decision to set up the observer unit was taken in paragraph 5 of resolution 687 (1991) and can only be terminated by a decision of the Council; the Council shall therefore review the question of termination or continuation every six months;
3. *Decides* that the modalities for the initial six-month period of the United Nations Iraq-Kuwait Observation Mission shall be in accordance with the above-mentioned report and shall also be reviewed every six months.

RESOLUTION 692 (1991)

Adopted by the Security Council at its 2987th meeting, on 20 May 1991

The Security Council,

Recalling its resolutions 674 (1990) of 29 October 1990, 686 (1991) of 2 March 1991 and 687 (1991) of 3 April 1991, concerning the liability of Iraq, without prejudice to its debts and obligations arising prior to 2 August 1990, for any direct loss, damage, including environmental damage and the depletion of natural resources, or injury to foreign Governments, nationals and corporations, as a result of Iraq's unlawful invasion and occupation of Kuwait,

Taking note of the Secretary-General's report of 2 May 1991 (S/22559), submitted in accordance with paragraph 19 of resolution 687 (1991),

Acting under Chapter VII of the Charter of the United Nations,

1. *Expresses* its appreciation to the Secretary-General for his report of 2 May 1991;
2. *Welcomes* the fact that the Secretary-General will now undertake the appropriate consultations requested by paragraph 19 of resolution 687 (1991) so that he will be in a position to recommend to the Security Council for decision as soon as possible the figure which the level of Iraq's contribution to the Fund will not exceed;
3. *Decides* to establish the Fund and the Commission referred to in paragraph 18 of resolution 687 (1991) in accordance with section I of the Secretary-General's report, and that the Governing Council will be located at the United Nations Office at Geneva and that the Governing Council may decide whether

some of the activities of the Commission should be carried out elsewhere;

4. *Requests* the Secretary-General to take the actions necessary to implement paragraphs 2 and 3 above in consultation with the members of the Governing Council;
5. *Directs* the Governing Council to proceed in an expeditious manner to implement the provisions of section E of resolution 687 (1991), taking into account the recommendations in section II of the Secretary-General's report;
6. *Decides* that the requirement for Iraqi contributions will apply in the manner to be prescribed by the Governing Council with respect to all Iraqi petroleum and petroleum products exported from Iraq after 3 April 1991 as well as such petroleum and petroleum products exported earlier but not delivered or not paid for as a specific result of the prohibitions contained in Security Council resolution 661 (1990);
7. *Requests* the Governing Council to report as soon as possible on the actions it has taken with regard to the mechanisms for determining the appropriate level of Iraq's contribution to the Fund and the arrangements for ensuring that payments are made to the Fund, so that the Security Council can give its approval in accordance with paragraph 22 of resolution 687 (1991);
8. *Requests* that all States and international organizations cooperate with the decisions of the Governing Council taken pursuant to paragraph 5 of the present resolution, and also requests that the Governing Council keep the Security Council informed on this matter;
9. *Decides* that, if the Governing Council notifies the Security Council that Iraq has failed to carry out decisions of the Governing Council taken pursuant to paragraph 5 of the present resolution, the Security Council intends to retain or to take action to reimpose the prohibition against the import of petroleum and petroleum products originating in Iraq and financial transactions related thereto;
10. *Decides also* to remain seized of this matter and that the Governing Council will submit periodic reports to the Secretary-General and the Security Council.

RESOLUTION 699 (1991)

Adopted by the Security Council at its 2994th meeting, on 17 June 1991

The Security Council,

Recalling its resolution 687 (1991),

Taking note of the report of the Secretary-General of 17 May 1991 (S/22614), submitted to it in pursuance of paragraph 9 (b) of resolution 687 (1991),

Also taking note of the Secretary-General's note of 17 May 1991 (S/22615), transmitting to the Council the letter addressed to him under paragraph 13 of the resolution by the Director-General of the International Atomic Energy Agency (IAEA),

Acting under Chapter VII of the Charter,

1. *Approves* the plan contained in the report of the Secretary-General;
2. *Confirms* that the Special Commission and the IAEA have the authority to conduct activities under section C of resolution 687 (1991), for the purpose of the destruction, removal or rendering harmless of the items specified in paragraphs 8 and 12 of that resolution, after the 45-day period following the approval of this plan until such activities have been completed;
3. *Requests* the Secretary-General to submit to the Security Council progress reports on the implementation of the plan referred to in paragraph 1 every six months after the adoption of this resolution;
4. *Decides* to encourage the maximum assistance, in cash and in kind, from all Member States to ensure that activities under section C of resolution 687 (1991) are undertaken effectively and expeditiously; further decides, however, that the Government of Iraq shall be liable for the full costs of carrying out the tasks authorized by section C; and requests the Secretary-General to submit to the Council within 30 days for approval recommendations as to the most effective means by which Iraq's obligations in this respect may be fulfilled.

RESOLUTION 700 (1991)

Adopted by the Security Council at its 2994th meeting, on 17 June 1991

The Security Council,

Recalling its resolutions 661 (1990) of 6 August 1990, 665 (1990) of 25 August 1990, 670 (1990) of 25 September 1990 and 687 (1991) of 3 April 1991,

Taking note of the Secretary-General's report of 2 June 1991 (S/22660) submitted pursuant to paragraph 26 of resolution 687 (1991),

Acting under Chapter VII of the Charter of the United Nations,

1. *Expresses its appreciation* to the Secretary-General for his report of 2 June 1991 (S/22660);
2. *Approves* the Guidelines to Facilitate Full International Implementation of paragraphs 24, 25 and 27 of Security Council resolution 687 (1991), annexed to the report of the Secretary-General (S/22660);
3. *Reiterates* its call upon all States and international organizations to act in a manner consistent with the Guidelines;
4. *Requests* all States, in accordance with paragraph 8 of the Guidelines, to report to the Secretary-General within 45 days on the measures they have instituted for meeting the obligations set out in paragraph 24 of resolution 687 (1991);
5. *Entrusts* the Committee established under resolution 661 (1990) concerning the situation between Iraq and Kuwait with the responsibility, under the Guidelines, for monitoring the prohibitions against the sale or supply of arms to Iraq and related sanctions established in paragraph 24 Of resolution 687 (1991);
6. *Decides* to remain seized of the matter and to review the Guidelines at the same time as it reviews paragraphs 22, 23, 24, and 25 of resolution 687 (1991) as set out in paragraph 28 thereof.

RESOLUTION 706 (1991)

Adopted by the Security Council at its 3004th meeting, on 15 August 1991

The Security Council,

Recalling its previous relevant resolutions and in particular resolutions 661 (1990), 686 (1991), 687 (1991), 688 (1991), 692 (1991), 699 (1991) and 705 (1991),

Taking note of the report (S/22799) dated 15 July 1991 of the inter-agency mission headed by the executive delegate of the Secretary-General for the United Nations inter-agency humanitarian program for Iraq, Kuwait and the Iraq/Turkey and Iraq/Iran border areas,

Concerned by the serious nutritional and health situation of the Iraqi civilian population as described in this report, and by the risk of a further deterioration of this situation,

Concerned also that the repatriation or return of all Kuwaitis and third country nationals or their remains present in Iraq on or after 2 August 1990, pursuant to paragraph 2 (c) of resolution 686 (1991), and paragraphs 30 and 31 of resolution 687 (1991) has not yet been fully carried out,

Taking note of the conclusions of the above-mentioned report, and in particular of the proposal for oil sales by Iraq to finance the purchase of foodstuffs, medicines and materials and supplies for essential civilian needs for the purpose of providing humanitarian relief,

Taking note also of the letters dated 14 April 1991, 31 May 1991, 6 June 1991, 9 July 1991 and 22 July 1991 from the Minister of Foreign Affairs of Iraq and the Permanent Representative of Iraq to the Chairman of the Committee established by resolution 661 (1990) concerning the export from Iraq of petroleum and petroleum products,

Convinced of the need for equitable distribution of humanitarian relief to all segments of the Iraqi civilian population through effective monitoring and transparency,

Recalling and reaffirming in this regard its resolution 688 (1991) and in particular the importance which the Council attaches to Iraq allowing unhindered access by international humanitarian organizations to all those in need of assistance in all parts of Iraq and making available all necessary facilities for their operation, and in this connection stressing the important and continuing role played by the Memorandum of Understanding between the United Nations and the Government of Iraq of 18 April 1991 (S/22663),

Recalling that, pursuant to resolutions 687 (1991), 692 (1991) and 699 (1991), Iraq is required to pay the full costs of the Special Commission and the IAEA in carrying out the tasks authorized by section C of resolution 687 (1991), and that the Secretary-General in his report to the Security Council of 15 July 1991 (S/22792), submitted pursuant to paragraph 4 of resolution 699 (1991), expressed the view that the most obvious way of obtaining financial resources from Iraq to meet the costs of the Special Commission and the IAEA would be to authorize the sale of some Iraqi petroleum and petroleum products: *recalling further* that Iraq is required to pay its contributions to the Compensation Fund and half the costs of the Iraq-Kuwait Boundary Demarcation Commission, and *recalling further* that in its resolutions 686 (1991) and 687 (1991) the Security Council demanded that Iraq return in the shortest possible time all Kuwaiti property seized by it and requested the Secretary-General to take steps to facilitate this,

Acting under Chapter VII of the Charter,

1. *Authorizes* all States, subject to the decision to be taken by the Security Council pursuant to paragraph 5 below and notwithstanding the provisions of paragraphs 3 (a), 3 (b) and 4 of resolution 661 (1990), to permit the import, during a period of 6 months from the date of passage of the resolution pursuant to paragraph 5 below, of petroleum and petroleum products originating in Iraq sufficient to produce a sum to be determined by the Council following receipt of the report of the Secretary-General requested in paragraph 5 of this resolution but not to exceed 1.6 billion United States dollars for the purposes set out in this resolution and subject to the following conditions:
   (a) Approval of each purchase of Iraqi petroleum and petroleum products by the Security Council Committee established by resolution 661 (1990) following notification to the Committee by the State concerned;
   (b) Payment of the full amount of each purchase of Iraqi petroleum and petroleum products directly by the purchaser in the State concerned into an escrow account to be established by the United Nations and to be administered by the Secretary-General, exclusively to meet the purposes of this resolution;
   (c) Approval by the Council, following the report of the Secretary-General requested in paragraph 5 of this resolution, of a scheme for the purchase of foodstuffs, medicines and materials and supplies for essential civilian needs as referred to in paragraph 20 of resolution 687 (1991), in

particular health related materials, all of which to be labeled to the extent possible as being supplied under this scheme, and for all feasible and appropriate United Nations monitoring and supervision for the purpose of assuring their equitable distribution to meet humanitarian needs in all regions of Iraq and to all categories of the Iraqi civilian population, as well as all feasible and appropriate management relevant to this purpose, such a United Nations role to be available if desired for humanitarian assistance from other sources;

(d) The sum authorized in this paragraph to be released by successive decisions of the Committee established by resolution 661 (1990) in three equal portions after the Council has taken the decision provided for in paragraph 5 below on the implementation of this resolution, and notwithstanding any other provision of this paragraph, the sum to be subject to review concurrently by the Council on the basis of its ongoing assessment of the needs and requirements;

2. *Decides* that a part of the sum in the account to be established by the Secretary-General shall be made available by him to finance the purchase of foodstuffs, medicines and materials and supplies for essential civilian needs, as referred to in paragraph 20 of resolution 687, and the cost to the United Nations of its roles under this resolution and of other necessary humanitarian activities in Iraq;
3. *Decides further* that a part of the sum in the account to be established by the Secretary-General shall be used by him for appropriate payments to the United Nations Compensation Fund, the full costs of carrying out the tasks authorized by Section C of resolution 687 (1991), the full costs incurred by the United Nations in facilitating the return of all Kuwaiti property seized by Iraq, and half the costs of the Boundary Commission;
4. *Decides* that the percentage of the value of exports of petroleum and petroleum products from Iraq, authorized under this resolution to be paid to the United Nations Compensation Fund, as called for in paragraph 19 of resolution 687 (1991), and as defined in paragraph 6 of resolution 692 (1991), shall be the same as the percentage decided by the Security Council in paragraph 2 of resolution 705 (1991) for payments to the Compensation Fund, until such time as the Governing Council of the Fund decides otherwise;

5. *Requests* the Secretary-General to submit within 20 days of the date of adoption of this resolution a report to the Security Council for decision on measures to be taken in order to implement paragraphs 1 (a), (b) and (c), estimates of the humanitarian requirements of Iraq set out in paragraph 2 above and of the amount of Iraq's financial obligations set out in paragraph 3 above up to the end of the period of the authorization in paragraph 1 above, as well as the method for taking the necessary legal measures to ensure that the purposes of this resolution are carried out and the method for taking account of the costs of transportation of such Iraqi petroleum and petroleum products;
6. *Further requests* the Secretary-General in consultation with the International Committee of the Red Cross to submit within 20 days of the date of adoption of this resolution a report to the Security Council on activities undertaken in accordance with paragraph 31 of resolution 687 (1991) in connection with facilitating the repatriation or return of all Kuwaiti and third country nationals or their remains present in Iraq on or after 2 August 1990;
7. *Requires* the Government of Iraq to provide to the Secretary-General and appropriate international organizations on the first day of the month immediately following the adoption of the present resolution and on the first day of each month thereafter until further notice, a statement of the gold and foreign currency reserves it holds whether in Iraq or elsewhere;
8. *Calls upon* all States to cooperate fully in the implementation of this resolution;
9. *Decides* to remain seized of the matter.

RESOLUTION 707 (1991)

Adopted by the Security Council at its 3004th meeting, on 15 August 1991

The Security Council,

Recalling its resolution 687 (1991), and its other resolutions on this matter,

Recalling the letter of 11 April 1991 from the President of the Security Council to the Permanent Representative of Iraq to the United

Nations (S/22485) noting that on the basis of Iraq's written agreement (S/22456) to implement fully resolution 687 (1991) the preconditions established in paragraph 33 of that resolution for a cease-fire had been met,

Noting with grave concern the letters dated 26 June 1991 (S/22739), 28 June 1991 (S/22743) and 4 July 1991 (S/22761) from the Secretary-General, conveying information obtained from the Executive Chairman of the Special Commission and the Director-General of the IAEA which establishes Iraq's failure to comply with its obligations under resolution 687 (1991),

Recalling further the statement issued by the President of the Security Council on 28 June 1991 (S/22746) requesting that a high-level mission consisting of the Chairman of the Special Commission, the Director-General of the IAEA, and the Under Secretary-General for Disarmament Affairs be dispatched to meet with officials at the highest levels of the Government of Iraq at the earliest opportunity to obtain written assurance that Iraq will fully and immediately cooperate in the inspection of the locations identified by the Special Commission and present for immediate inspection any of those items that may have been transported from those locations,

Dismayed by the report of the high-level mission to the Secretary-General (S/22761) on the results of its meetings with the highest levels of the Iraqi Government,

Gravely concerned by the information provided to the Council by the Special Commission and the IAEA on 15 July 1991 (S/22788) and 25 July 1991 (S/22837) regarding the actions of the Government of Iraq in flagrant violation of resolution 687 (1991),

Gravely concerned also by the evidence in the letter of 7 July 1991 from the Minister of Foreign Affairs of Iraq to the Secretary-General and in subsequent statements and findings that Iraq's notifications of 18 and 28 April were incomplete and that it had concealed activities, which both constituted material breaches of its obligations under resolution 687 (1991),

Noting also from the letters dated 26 June 1991 (S/22739), 28 June 1991 (S/22743) and 4 July 1991 (S/22761) from the Secretary-General that Iraq has not fully complied with all of its undertakings relating to the privileges, immunities and facilities to be accorded to the Special Commission and the IAEA inspection teams mandated under resolution 687 (1991),

Affirming that in order for the Special Commission to carry out its mandate under paragraph 9 (b) (i), (ii) and (iii) of resolution 687 (1991) to inspect Iraq's chemical and biological weapons and ballistic missile capabilities and to take possession of them for destruction, removal or rendering harmless, full disclosure on the part of Iraq as required in paragraph 9 (a) of resolution 687 (1991) is essential,

Affirming that in order for the IAEA, with the assistance and cooperation of the Special Commission, to determine what nuclear-weapons-usable material or any subsystems or components or any research, development, support or manufacturing facilities related to them need, in accordance with paragraph 13 of resolution 687 (1991), to be destroyed, removed or rendered harmless, Iraq is required to make a declaration of all its nuclear programs including any which it claims are for purposes not related to nuclear-weapons-usable material,

Affirming that the aforementioned failures of Iraq to act in strict conformity with its obligations under resolution 687 (1991) constitute a material breach of its acceptance of the relevant provisions of resolution 687 (1991) which established a cease-fire and provided the conditions essential to the restoration of peace and security in the region,

Affirming further that Iraq's failure to comply with its safeguards agreement with the International Atomic Energy Agency, concluded pursuant to the Treaty on the Non-Proliferation of Nuclear Weapons of 1 July 1968, as established by the resolution of the Board of Governors of the IAEA of 18 July 1991 (GOV/2532), constitutes a breach of its international obligations,

Determined to ensure full compliance with resolution 687 (1991) and in particular its section C,

Acting under Chapter VII of the Charter,

1. *Condemns* Iraq's serious violation of a number of its obligations under section C of resolution 687 (1991) and of its undertakings to cooperate with the Special Commission and the IAEA, which constitutes a material breach of the relevant provisions of resolution 687 which established a cease-fire and provided the conditions essential to the restoration of peace and security in the region;
2. *Further condemns* noncompliance by the Government of Iraq with its obligations under its safeguards agreement with the International Atomic Energy Agency, as established by the resolution of the Board of Governors of 18 July, which constitutes a violation of its commitments as a party to the Treaty on the Non-Proliferation of Nuclear Weapons of 1 July 1968;
3. *Demands* that Iraq:
   (a) provide full, final and complete disclosure, as required by resolution 687 (1991), of all aspects of its programs to develop weapons of mass destruction and ballistic missiles with a range greater than 150 km, and of all holdings of

such weapons, their components and production facilities and locations, as well as all other nuclear programs, including any which it claims are for purposes not related to nuclear-weapons-usable material, without further delay;

(b) allow the Special Commission, the IAEA and their Inspection Teams immediate, unconditional and unrestricted access to any and all areas, facilities, equipment, records and means of transportation which they wish to inspect;

(c) cease immediately any attempt to conceal, or any movement or destruction of any material or equipment relating to its nuclear, chemical or biological weapons or ballistic missile programs, or material or equipment relating to its other nuclear activities without notification to and prior consent of the Special Commission;

(d) make available immediately to the Special Commission, the IAEA and their Inspection Teams any items to which they were previously denied access;

(e) allow the Special Commission, the IAEA and their Inspection Teams to conduct both fixed wing and helicopter flights throughout Iraq for all relevant purposes including inspection, surveillance, aerial surveys, transportation and logistics without interference of any kind and upon such terms and conditions as may be determined by the Special Commission, and to make full use of their own aircraft and such airfields in Iraq as they may determine are most appropriate for the work of the Commission;

(f) halt all nuclear activities of any kind, except for use of isotopes for medical, agricultural or industrial purposes until the Security Council determines that Iraq is in full compliance with this resolution and paragraphs 12 and 13 of resolution 687 (1991), and the IAEA determines that Iraq is in full compliance with its safeguards agreement with that Agency;

(g) ensure the complete implementation of the privileges, immunities and facilities of the representatives of the Special Commission and the IAEA in accordance with its previous undertakings and their complete safety and freedom of movement;

(h) immediately provide or facilitate the provision of any transportation, medical or logistical support requested by the Special Commission, the IAEA and their Inspection Teams;

(i) respond fully, completely and promptly to any questions or requests from the Special Commission, the IAEA and their Inspection Teams;

4. *Determines* that Iraq retains no ownership interest in items to be destroyed, removed or rendered harmless pursuant to paragraph 12 of resolution 687 (1991);
5. *Requires* that the Government of Iraq forthwith comply fully and without delay with all its international obligations, including those set out in the present resolution, in resolution 687 (1991), in the Treaty on the Non-Proliferation of Nuclear Weapons of 1 July 1968 and its safeguards agreement with the IAEA;
6. *Decides* to remain seized of this matter.

NOTES ON THE CONTRIBUTORS

Fouad Ajami is the Majid Khadduri Professor and Director of Middle East Studies at the Paul Nitze School of Advanced International Studies of the Johns Hopkins University. An expert on the Middle East, Ajami is a contributing editor of *U.S. News & World Report,* and the author of *The Arab Predicament, The Vanished Iman,* and *Beirut: City of Regrets,* as well as numerous essays on Middle Eastern politics and culture. In 1982 he was awarded the five-year MacArthur Prize Fellowship for his work on the Middle East.

Abram Chayes is Felix Frankfurter Professor of Law, Harvard Law School. An expert on international law, he served as the State Department's Legal Advisor during the Kennedy and Johnson Administrations. He is the author of *The Cuban Missile Crisis: International Crisis and the Role of Law,* and *The International Legal Process,* as well as many other books and articles dealing with international law and politics. At present, Chayes is also Chairman of the Institute for Public Representation, Georgetown University Law Center and Vice-President of the Albert Einstein Peace Prize Foundation.

Antonia Handler Chayes is a Senior Consultant at Endispute, Inc. and an adjunct professor at the John F. Kennedy School of Government. An expert on dispute management, Chayes served as Under Secretary of the Air Force, Dean of the Jackson College at Tufts University, and was a partner in the Boston law firm of Casplar & Bok. She is the co-editor with Paul Doty of *Defending Deterrence: Managing the ABM Regime into the 21st Century* and has published widely on issues relating to nuclear strategy and arms control. In addition to her other activities, Chayes is a member of the Board of Directors of United Technologies Corporation and is on its Executive Committee.

Richard N. Cooper is the Maurits C. Boas Professor of International Economics at Harvard University. An economist, Cooper has served in the American government in a number of capacities, including Undersecretary for Economic Affairs, U.S. Department of State 1977–1981. Among his many other activities, Cooper serves as Chairman of the Federal Reserve Bank of Boston. He is the author of *The International Monetary System* and *Economic Policy in an Interdependent World,* as well as many other books and essays on international economics.

Richard N. Gardner is Professor of Law and International Organization at Columbia University's School of Law and Senior Counsel of the law firm of Coudert Brothers. A lawyer, Gardner served as Deputy Assistant Secretary of State for International Organization Affairs during the Kennedy and Johnson Administrations and later served as Ambassador to Italy from 1977–1981. He is the author of *Sterling Dollar Diplomacy* and *In Pursuit of World Order: U.S. Foreign Policy and International Organization.* Gardner is also the co-chairman of The Aspen Institute project on "The U.S. and the World Economy.

David R. Gergen serves as Editor-at-Large for *U.S. News & World Report;* in addition he is a weekly commentator for "The MacNeil/ Lehrer Newshour" on PBS as well as a frequent contributor to National Public Radio's program, "All Things Considered." An expert on American domestic politics, Gergen worked during the 1970s in the White House under Presidents Nixon and Ford, and from 1981–1984, he served as the White House director of communications. Prior to joining *U.S. News* he was a resident fellow at the American Enterprise Institute and at the John F. Kennedy School of Government, Harvard University.

Martin Indyk is the Executive Director of the Washington Institute for Near East Policy and is an adjunct professor in the Department of Middle East Studies at the Paul Nitze School for Advanced International Studies of the Johns Hopkins University. An expert on the Middle East, Indyk has served as Middle East Assessments officer and Deputy Director of Current Intelligence in the Australian Prime Minister's Office of National Assessments. He has published widely on American policy in the Middle East in such journals as *Foreign Affairs, Foreign Policy,* and *The National Interest.*

Bobby R. Inman is currently Chairman of the President's Foreign Intelligence Advisory Board. An expert on national security affairs, Inman's previous government service includes tours as Director of

Naval Intelligence, Vice-Director of the Defense Intelligence Agency, Director of the National Security Agency, and Deputy Director of Central Intelligence. Inman was the first Naval Intelligence Specialist to achieve the rank of full Admiral in the U.S. Navy. He is also co-chair of the Aspen Strategy Group.

Lawrence J. Korb is Director of the Center for Public Policy Education and Senior fellow in the Foreign Policy Studies program at the Brookings Institution. An expert on defense issue, Korb served from 1981–1985 as the Assistant Secretary of Defense for Manpower, Reserve Affairs, Installations and Logistics. Prior to joining Brookings, he served as the Dean of the Graduate School of Public and International Affairs at the University of Pittsburgh. He is the author of *The Joint Chiefs of Staff: The First Twenty-Five Years* and *The Fall and Rise of the Pentagon.*

Joseph S. Nye, Jr. is Associate Dean for International Affairs, Director of the Center for International Affairs, and Professor of International Affairs at Harvard University. A political scientist, Nye served from 1977–1979 as the Deputy to the Undersecretary of State for Security Assistance, Science and Technology, and chaired the National Security Council Group on Non-Proliferation of Nuclear Weapons. He is the author of *Bound to Lead: The Changing Nature of American Power* and *Nuclear Ethics,* as well as many other book and articles dealing with international relations. He also serves as the director of the Aspen Strategy Group.

William J. Perry is Chairman of Technology Strategies & Alliances, and a professor in the School of Engineering and co-director of the Center for International Security and Arms Control at Stanford University. A mathematician, Perry served as Undersecretary of Defense for Research and Engineering from 1977–1981. Prior to entering government service, he was President of ESL, Inc. In addition to his other activities, Perry serves on the President's Foreign Intelligence Advisory Board and is a co-chair of the Aspen Strategy Group.

Roger K. Smith is a research fellow on international security affairs at the Center for International Affairs, Harvard University, executive director of the Aspen Strategy Group, and an adjunct professor in the Department of Political Science, University of Massachusetts at Boston. A political scientist, Smith previously worked as a foreign policy analyst at the Congressional Research Service. He has published essays on international politics and arms control in such journals as the

Washington Quarterly, Journal of Strategic Studies, International Organization, and *Security Studies.*

Strobe Talbott is the Editor-at-Large and foreign affairs columnist of *Time Magazine.* An expert commentator on Soviet affairs, Talbott is the translator-editor of two volumes of Nikita Khrushchev's memoirs and the author of three books on nuclear arms control (*Endgame, Deadly Gambits,* and *Master of the Game*). He is currently at work with Michael R. Beschloss on a forthcoming book on U.S.-Soviet relations 1989–1991. Prior to becoming Editor-at-Large, Talbott was *Time's* diplomatic correspondent and Washington Bureau Chief.

Bernard E. Trainor is the Director of the National Security Program and Adjunct Lecturer in Public Policy at the John F. Kennedy School of Government, Harvard University. Before joining the Kennedy School, he was a military correspondent for the *New York Times* and a retired Lieutenant General in the U.S. Marine Corps. During his career as a Marine, Trainor served as Deputy Chief of Staff for Plans, Policies, and Operations and Marine Corps deputy to the Joint Chief of Staff.

INDEX

A

B

C

D

E

  events involving, chronologically, 297, 299, 300, 302, 304, 306, 308, 313, 315, 317, 318, 320, 323, 333, 335, 344

F

G

H

I

J

K

L

M

N

O

P

Q

R

S

T

U